Death on the Black Sea

also by Douglas Frantz *and* Catherine Collins:

Celebration, U.S.A.

Teacher Talking Out of School

Selling Out

Czernowitz

Jassy   Kishinev

Romania

Bucharest

Constanta

Dec. 12, 1941
'Struma' departs.

Bulgaria

Dec. 15, 1941
Turkish tug picks up 'Struma'.

Burgas

Feb. 23, 1942
Turkish tug sets
'Struma' adrift.

Istanbul

Sile

Turkey

Bosporus
Strait

Black Sea

Romania

Bulgaria

Black Sea

Turkey

Haifa,
Palestine →

→ Struma's Route

Death ON THE Black Sea

THE UNTOLD STORY OF THE *STRUMA* AND WORLD WAR II'S HOLOCAUST AT SEA

DOUGLAS FRANTZ AND CATHERINE COLLINS

ecco
An Imprint of HarperCollins*Publishers*

FIRST EDITION

Map on page iv by Jackie Aher

Designed by Fearn Cutler de Vicq

Printed on acid-free paper

Library of Congress Cataloging-in-Publication Data has been requested.

ISBN 0-06-621262-6

03 04 05 06 07   BVG/BVG   10 9 8 7 6 5 4 3 2 1

In honor of all refugees, past and present

Contents

Chronology

1919 to 1923	Thirty-five thousand Jews, mainly from Russia, immigrated to Palestine.
1923	Romania was the last European nation to grant Jews citizenship, although it did so only under duress.
1924 to 1932	Sixty thousand Jews, mainly from Poland, immigrated to Palestine.
1925	**July 18** Adolf Hitler's book, *Mein Kampf,* was published.
1927	The Legion of the Archangel Michael, also known as the Legionnaires, was founded by a young Romanian fanatic, Corneliu Codreanu. They were renamed the Iron Guard in 1929.
1933	**March 12** The first concentration camp opened at Oranienburg, outside Berlin.
1934	**August 19** Adolf Hitler became fuhrer of Germany.
1934 to 1938	One hundred sixty-five thousand Jews, mainly from Western and Central Europe, immigrated to Palestine.
1935	**September 15** German Jews were stripped of rights by Nuremberg Race Laws.
1938	**September 30** The British prime minister Neville Chamberlain appeased Hitler at Munich.

October 15   German troops occupied the Sudetenland; the Czech government resigned. |
| 1939 | **March 15 and 16**   The Nazis took over Czechoslovakia. Nineteen thousand and five Jewish immigrants arrived in Palestine. |

July 20   British Parliament adopted the white paper that severely restricted Jewish immigration to Palestine.

August 23   Germany and the Soviet Union signed a nonaggression pact, with a secret agreement that Bessarabia would be taken from Romania and put under Soviet control.

September 1   The Nazis invaded Poland.

September 3   Britain and France declared war on Germany.

September 5   The United States proclaimed neutrality.

September 27   Warsaw surrendered to the Nazis.

1940   As a result of the white paper and the British blockade, Jewish immigration to Palestine dropped to 8,398.

April 9   The Nazis invaded Denmark and Norway.

May 10   The Nazis invaded France, Belgium, Luxembourg, and the Netherlands; Winston Churchill became British prime minister.

May 15   Holland surrendered to the Nazis.

May 28   Belgium surrendered to the Nazis.

June 10   Norway surrendered to the Nazis.

June 22   France signed an armistice with the Nazis.

August   King Carol II approved law broadening the definition of a Jew in Romania. The new law was even broader than Germany's, categorizing Jews as a race rather than a religion.

September 7   The German blitz against England began.

General Ion Antonescu, prime minister of Romania, forced Carol II out and invited German troops into Bucharest.

The conflict over illegal immigration to Palestine reached a climax when the British heard that there were thousands of refugees preparing to leave the port city of Tulcea, Romania, on three ships—the *Atlantic,* the *Milos,* and the *Pacific.*

October 1   The *Pacific* and the *Milos* left Tulcea, Romania, with 1,061 and 702 passengers respectively. Both ships were intercepted off the coast of Palestine by the British several weeks later, and passengers were transferred to a larger ship, the *Patria,* to await deportation.

October 7   German troops entered Romania.

The *Atlantic* set sail from Tulcea, Romania, with 1,829 passengers, no lifeboats or life jackets, and an inadequate supply of fuel and food. The ship stopped in Cyprus and Istanbul for fresh supplies.

November 20   Hungary joined the Axis powers.

November 23   Romania joined the Axis powers.

November 24   After stopping in Cyprus and Istanbul for supplies, the *Atlantic* arrived in Haifa. Passengers were taken into custody by the British for immediate transfer to the waiting *Patria*.

November 25   Passengers on the newly loaded *Patria* devised a tragic plan to sabotage the ship and thwart their planned deportation.

December 12   The *Salvador,* carrying 333 Jews from Bulgaria and Central Europe, was wrecked in the Sea of Marmara, near Istanbul. More than 200 passengers, including 70 children, died.

1941   **January 21**   The fascist Iron Guard went on a rampage, slaughtering at least 120 Jews in the Bucharest pogrom.

February   Romania entered the war on the German side.

February 19   The *Darien II* left Constanta. It stopped in Istanbul to pick up 70 of the survivors from the *Salvador,* bringing its total number of refugees to 793.

March 19   The *Darien II,* the last major refugee ship to arrive in Palestinian waters, was intercepted by a British patrol boat and escorted to Haifa.

April 6   The Nazis invaded Greece and Yugoslavia.

April 17   Yugoslavia surrendered to the Nazis.

April 27   Greece surrendered to the Nazis.

May 20   Adolf Eichmann's office in Berlin prohibited all Jewish emigration from German-controlled territory.

June 22   In Operation Barbarossa, Germany declared war on the Soviet Union, and Romania moved to recover the lost provinces of Bessarabia and Bukovina. In coming months, at least one hundred thousand Jews were killed or died in camps and on death marches.

September 1   The Nazis ordered Jews to wear yellow stars in German-occupied territories.

September 3   The first experimental use of gas chambers at Auschwitz took place. The first newspaper advertisements appeared in Bucharest announcing the *Struma* would sail for Palestine.

Early November   The U.S. representative in Bucharest, Franklin Mott Gunther, wrote in a wire to Washington that the Romanian government's actions against its Jewish population "would seem deliberately calculated to serve a program of virtual extermination."

November 21   Twenty-one Jews from Bucharest boarded a train to Constanta and then a small pleasure yacht, the *Dor de Val,* that they hoped would take them to Palestine. The ship was wrecked near Istanbul, and the Turks rescued them in what they called a "one-time" act of mercy. Passengers were later sent on to Cyprus.

December 7   A special sealed train left Bucharest for the port of Constanta, carrying nearly eight hundred Jews bound for the *Struma*. Japan attacked Pearl Harbor.

December 11   Germany declared war on the United States.

December 12   The *Struma* set sail for Palestine. The engine failed a few miles out of port and was repaired.

December 15   After another engine failure, the *Struma* was picked up by a Turkish tug on the Black Sea outside the mouth of the Bosporus and towed to Istanbul harbor.

December 27   The British ambassador told the Turkish Foreign Ministry that no permission would be granted for the *Struma* to land in Palestine and the Turks should do everything in their power to stop the voyage and return the ship to the Black Sea.

1942   **January 20**   The Final Solution for the annihilation of Jews was formalized at the Wannsee Conference outside Berlin.

February 10   Turkish mechanics reported that the *Struma*'s engine operated for two hours during a test the day before.

February 15   Under pressure, the British government approved allowing children on the *Struma* between the ages of eleven and sixteen to go to Palestine.

February 19   The Turkish Foreign Ministry said Britain must provide a ship for the children because they could not land in Turkey.

February 23   A Turkish tug cut the *Struma*'s anchor, lashed a line to the ship, and towed it to the Black Sea, where it was set adrift, without a working engine.

February 24   A torpedo sank the *Struma* shortly before dawn.

February 25   The crew from a Turkish lighthouse in the seaside village of Sile rescued David Stoliar, the sole survivor.

February 27   Stoliar was transferred to Haydarpasa Numune Hospital in Istanbul.

March 6   Stoliar was arrested and imprisoned for being in Turkey illegally without a visa, and initially the British refused to grant him transit papers.

March 21   The British decided to admit Stoliar and one other *Struma* passenger, who had been in a hospital when the boat left the harbor, to Palestine based "on humanitarian grounds as an act of clemency," although they were slow to issue the actual papers.

April 22   Stoliar's transit papers in hand, Simon Brod went to the prison to take him to his own home.

April 23   Stoliar left for Palestine.

June   Mass murder of Jews by gassing began at Auschwitz.

August 19 and 20   The Soviet offensive in the Balkans began with an attack on Romania.

1943   Stoliar joined the British Army.

August 31   Soviet troops took Bucharest.

1944   **May 7**   German forces surrendered unconditionally to Allies.

Prologue

I̶t was around midnight when the young man climbed into the coffinlike berth. Three others were already sleeping on the wooden pallet, which was five feet wide and six feet long. David Stoliar was fully clothed as he lay unmoving and silent in the narrow space, staring at the underside of the bunks two feet above that housed the ship's human cargo. The bunks rose in layers both above the ship's deck and deep below. The stale air was filled with the sounds of troubled sleep from the hundreds of men, women, and children. From deep in the ship, he could hear quiet sobbing.

Sometime before the first thin light of day, the rhythm of the waves against the ship drifting on the Black Sea rocked the nineteen-year-old into unconsciousness, mercifully closing a day and night filled with haunting uncertainty.

The next thing Stoliar remembered was tumbling through the air, arms and legs flailing, as an unknown force tossed him from the ship. He landed with a sickening thud on the water and was driven several feet below its icy surface. Struggling up through the water and then gasping for air, he opened his eyes and spun around to shake the awful nightmare from his mind.

It was raining lightly, the *pock-pock* of drops on the sea drowned out by cries of panic and terror. The pandemonium was illuminated by the first hint of dawn touching the black horizon. The ship had disappeared. Even in his dazed state, Stoliar knew the force that tossed him into the air and splintered the ship must have been from an explosion.

Chunks of debris littered the water as far as the eye could see. The air smelled of the water's coldness, and the surface seemed to glow with a hard black light. Dozens of people were thrashing amidst the flotsam, fighting to grab anything that might keep them afloat. They were crying, screaming, calling out the names of children who had disappeared. They beseeched God for help. Stoliar could hear no children's voices. They had vanished without a sound. Somewhere in that maelstrom, Stoliar hoped to find his fiancée and her family. They had been in their berth in the deepest hold of the ship.

Sixty years later, Stoliar recalled those moments with clarity. The sea was calm enough to see his desperate fellow passengers. Not far from where he had landed in the icy water, he saw a handful of people clinging to something floating just below the surface. Still clad in his leather jacket, Stoliar swam stiffly toward them. They were holding on to a small section of the ship's wooden deck, with a bench and pieces of a metal railing sticking out on the edges. People clung desperately to those rails, four or five on each side. He grabbed one, too. Looking at the terrified faces around him, Stoliar recognized no one. He could hear voices in the distance, none that sounded familiar. He gripped his bar, and tried to survive. A few feet away, a corpse was tangled in cables trailing from the piece of decking that had moments before been part of the *Struma,* the ship on which Stoliar and nearly eight hundred others had fled Romania weeks earlier in a desperate attempt to reach Palestine.

The Coming Cataclysm

Chapter 1

When Greg Buxton walked up to the door, his manner was one of subdued excitement. Buxton was broad shouldered and just over six feet tall, with an easy smile and a pleasant, open face. He was twenty-one years old, a few months out of university in his native Britain. He glanced at the slip of paper in his hand, reading the address again, drawing a long breath as he did so.

He had come to Tel Aviv on a whim. Shy by nature, he was suddenly reluctant to follow through on what he had thought would be just a pleasant adventure. But he could not deny the excitement that now flooded over him as he raised his right hand to rap on the door.

Two weeks earlier Buxton had flown from London to Israel with a group of friends on holiday. They had taken a bus south to Egypt and crossed over to the Sinai Peninsula to scuba dive in the Red Sea, one of the most splendid undersea locations in the world. Buxton, an avid diver, had cut short his holiday and gone to Tel Aviv three days ahead of his mates. He hated to abandon the diving and drinking with his buddies, but a chance conversation with his father before he left Britain had changed Buxton's itinerary. He had no idea that it would alter his life, too.

Back in London, Buxton had been rummaging around in his closet at home for a bit of dive gear when his father walked into the room.

"What are you up to?" asked Michael Buxton.

"Getting ready for that dive trip to the Red Sea next month," his son replied.

Buxton told his father that he would be flying to Ben-Gurion International Airport outside Tel Aviv and then heading to the Sinai. The mention of Tel Aviv sparked the older man's memory.

"My parents bought a piece of property in Tel Aviv," the elder man said. "It was before the war. They never got there. I tried to find it once, but didn't have any luck."

Buxton knew the outline of what had happened to his paternal grandparents. In 1941, Grigore and Zlata Bucspan were living in Bucharest, Romania. They had sent their only son, Michael, to study engineering in Britain. Like many wealthy Jews, they had bought land in Palestine and dreamed of living there one day. As the Nazi persecution descended upon Romania, the Bucspans bought passage to Palestine on a ship called the *Struma* and set sail for the Promised Land. The ship never reached its destination. It exploded and sank on the Black Sea, not far from Istanbul, Turkey.

After the war, Michael changed his name to Buxton, married a Christian woman, and settled down in Britain. As the years went by, he came to think of himself as British and lost touch with his roots as a Romanian and a Jew. Yet he had thought occasionally about the land his parents had purchased. In the late 1940s and early 1950s, he had made halfhearted attempts to locate the property. He figured it might be worth some money.

Now, as he sat on the bed in his son's room, he described how he had written to lawyers in London and Tel Aviv. Eventually an Israeli lawyer located the property through old records dating to the period when the British still controlled what was then Palestine. The lawyer said it appeared to be a small parcel, not far from the Mediterranean coast north of Tel Aviv. The lawyer said the land was not worth much, so Buxton had pretty much forgotten about it.

"Wait a minute," the elder man said to his son. "I'll be right back."

He went to his own room and dug out the few papers he could find about the land. There was his correspondence with the London lawyers, but nothing from the lawyer in Tel Aviv. He must have tossed the papers when he decided the land was not worth the trouble. He could not even remember the lawyer's name.

As he ruffled through the documents, Michael Buxton found

something else. They were two postcards written to him by his father from the ship as it had sat in the Istanbul harbor. Both were written in February 1942, when the ship and its cargo of nearly eight hundred refugees were trapped in the harbor, caught up in a bitter, international diplomatic struggle.

"This is fascinating," Greg said as he read. He concentrated on the letters to and from the London lawyers, giving the postcards little more than a cursory glance. "Maybe I'll have a look at this property when I'm down there."

Greg's imagination was captured by the prospect of the possibly valuable land in Israel. He scarcely gave a thought to the grandparents he had never met and who had rarely been discussed in the Buxton household. As Greg set the postcards aside without reading them, he had no idea of the history that lay behind those final handwritten pleas.

The father had closed that chapter of his life. The son had never opened the book. Curious about the land after the discussion with his father, Greg wrote to the London lawyers who handled that end of the search, before leaving for the dive trip. The file had long since disappeared, he learned. They did, however, come up with the name and address of the lawyer in Tel Aviv who had handled the case: the last correspondence was in 1952.

Before leaving on the diving trip, Buxton had gone to the local library to look up the *Struma*. There was little information apart from what he found in a history of Britain and the Jews by Bernard Wasserstein, a British historian. There, he discovered that the ship's journey had been tragic from start to finish. Nearly eight hundred Jews fleeing Romania had been crowded onto a small vessel of dubious seaworthiness. The engine had failed and they had sat for weeks in the harbor at Istanbul. For some reason they had then been towed back to the Black Sea, where the ship had gone down after an explosion. The sole survivor was a man named David Stoliar, who had told police the ship had been sunk by a torpedo.

Tel Aviv was Israel's second-largest city after Jerusalem, and Buxton was astonished by the first all-Jewish city of modern times. Unlike the country's holy and contentious capital an hour's drive east, the coastal city was lively and sophisticated, a hub of commercial and cultural life. Its beaches and nightclubs were attractive to secular Israelis and magnets to the world's traveling army of sybaritic backpackers.

He checked into a youth hostel and met up with some rich American kids who were bumming their way around the region. After a day of partying and drinking, Buxton decided to get down to the business that had brought him there. He bought a map and found the address he wanted. Although Tel Aviv had been a small place in 1952, when the last letter was written by the lawyer, by the mid-1980s its population was almost three hundred thousand, and the streets were a tangled maze to a stranger who did not speak Hebrew. The lawyer's name was no longer listed with directory assistance. Buxton assumed he was dead, but he figured he would try to find the office as long as he was in the city. After wandering and asking directions several times, he found the address, a small building on a shady street. On the outside was a brass plate with the names of several lawyers, none of them the one he wanted. He knocked on the door and an officious woman quickly answered it.

"This is kind of weird," he said quickly, intimidated by her stern gaze. "About thirty years ago somebody used to work here who wrote letters to my dad."

The woman smiled slightly, invited him in, and asked him to wait. A few minutes later, an elderly lawyer appeared and introduced himself as Mr. Moser. The previous law firm had packed up many years before, he said. The man who had helped Buxton's father had gone on to become an important judge before he died.

Nonetheless, Moser took the file from Buxton's hands and began to go through the papers carefully, pausing occasionally. Moser was intrigued at the bit of history in his hands. After reviewing the file, he delivered his verdict. The information was contradictory. Some of the lot numbers indicated the land was inland on the northern edge of modern Tel Aviv; others seemed to show it was within one hundred yards of the coast north of the city. He said there was not enough information to resolve the differences or locate either piece of property with any specificity. There was no deed number, an absence that would make it difficult and expensive to track down the parcel. Buxton thanked the courtly man and left.

He was disappointed. He had hoped for an easy answer and, truth be told, maybe some easy money by claiming and then selling the land. With two possible locations and limited time before he had to return home, Buxton chose the more attractive possibility. He took a bus north along the coast. He had enough information to find the general area of coastline where his grandparents' property might be. He got off the bus and walked along the water, imagining for the first time not the money he could get selling the land, but the kind of house his grandparents might have built if their lives had taken a different turn.

"This is where they were coming," he thought. "This is about as close as I can get to a grave."

When he got back home to Brixton, in South London, Buxton described his search to his father and wrote about it to his sister, who lived in Paris. If they wanted to pursue finding the property, he said, they would have to hire a solicitor in Britain to start the process. Buxton had recently started his first job, as a production manager in a factory. He did not have the money to invest in a speculative venture. His sister was too busy with her job as a language teacher to do more than dream about it. His father was not interested. The idea languished.

The tentative search for a piece of land was not, Buxton would insist later, a revelation. But it sparked his first real interest in the life and death of his grandparents. For several years, the seed lay fallow until one night it returned, took root, and began to grow.

It was the early 1990s. Buxton's initial enchantment with scuba diving had deepened into a near-obsession. Unmarried and making a good salary as a computer programmer, he spent all of his extra money and holidays diving. Sometimes he got no farther than the English Channel, rich with wrecks. On other occasions he went to exotic spots in the Mediterranean. Always the diving was intoxicating.

This particular night Buxton had gone to a country pub outside

London to meet a friend for drinks. Geraint Ffoukes-Jones was a diving companion and close friend from their days as students at university. They had explored a number of shipwrecks along the British coast, going deeper and deeper as their skills improved. They were so focused on diving that when they were not reliving their most recent adventure, they were talking about their next one.

Over a couple of beers, Buxton started to tell the story of the *Struma,* resting somewhere on the bottom of the Black Sea, and his grandparents and the other victims. Even in the sketchy details by which Buxton knew it, the story was dramatic—a shipload of Jewish refugees refused haven in Turkey and sunk mysteriously in the sea. Divers are always on the lookout for unexplored wrecks, and one with such a history was particularly appealing.

Buxton had no way of knowing that the journey on which he was about to embark would immerse him in the intrigues of a romantic and glamorous city. He did not know that he would reexpose the diplomatic callousness that had doomed his grandparents and nearly eight hundred other people attempting to escape persecution by the Nazis.

Chapter 2

Romania was a bright and beautiful country when the early stages of World War II were just a distant rumble. Bucharest, the capital, was gracious and cosmopolitan, filled with elegant restaurants and first-class hotels. The famous Athenee Palace hotel stood on Calea Victoriei, not far from the popular Capsa restaurant, which overflowed with caviar, smoked salmon, all manner of meats, and canned asparagus, something the Romanians considered a delicacy. The city's public gardens were lush with flowers, and its streets were swept daily by an army of peasant women with stick brooms. There were wonderful parks, the most famous of which was Cismigiu Park, copied from New York's Central Park. The people of Romania seemed to think they would be spared the darkness and ugliness engulfing the world around them. They believed they could hold the war at bay by stringing party lights along the border. Before summer's end, the lights and the illusion would vanish.

Romania had been a province of the Roman Empire in the first and second centuries A.D., the period when Christianity was introduced. The Mongols conquered the country in the thirteenth century and were replaced by the Ottoman Empire two centuries later. Throughout those periods, its peasants worked on the vast estates of landowners and lived in abject poverty. Even after independence in 1878, the country remained the poorest in Europe, and its people lived semifeudal lives. Romania switched sides three times during World War I, joining the Allies just before the end of the conflict, which resulted in its being rewarded with lands taken from Austria, Bulgaria, Hungary, and Russia, almost doubling its territory.

The country had been declared a kingdom in 1881 and, in the summer of 1940, its ruler was King Carol II, the son of Romania's second king, Ferdinand. He was married to Queen Helena of Greece and had a son, Prince Michael. But Carol II was engaged in a highly public affair with his mistress, Madame Magda Lupescu, a slender redhead with creamy skin and green eyes who had supplanted other women to become the king's chief concubine and confidant. Interestingly, she was also Jewish.

Carol II was a corrupt man in a country renowned for corruption. One of the amusing anecdotes long circulating in the cafés and salons of Bucharest involved the arrival of King Carol I in Bucharest when he returned to claim the throne in 1866. At a banquet in his honor, the new monarch discovered that his wallet was missing. The festivities were halted, and it was announced that the candles would be extinguished for three minutes. During that time the missing wallet should be placed on a silver platter atop the main banquet table. When the candles were relit, the platter was gone, too.

Carol II and his mistress, Lupescu, had more sophisticated ways of stealing. For instance, in a country where men were fond of uniforms for every occasion, the couple had a monopoly on the manufacture of uniforms for the palace guard, the armed forces, and all manner of civil servants and officers. The prices were exorbitant, but no one could object.

The king was also well known for selling the national currency, the leu ("lei," plural), on the black market. A small portion of Romania's Jewish population was concerned enough about the potential consequences of the war that they were paying a premium to convert cumbersome stacks of lei into hundred-dollar bills. Should the need arise, the American money would be easier to smuggle out of the country and easier to spend. The king was aware of the purchases, and in an effort to improve his profit margin, he orchestrated the spread of a rumor that the market had been flooded with counterfeit hundreds. The price of the bills dropped sharply, and Carol II bought up huge amounts at the deep discount for resale later.

Romania had about three quarters of a million Jewish residents before World War II, one of the largest Jewish populations in Europe. By 1940, they had seen the storm of hatred unleashed across Europe, from Germany to Poland to Hungary, and they were well aware of the anti-Semitic streak that ran deep in their own country. Yet many of these people felt that their lovely country would somehow escape the horror engulfing the rest of Europe.

The roots of anti-Semitism in Romania, as in the rest of Europe, could be traced back several centuries. Romania had refused to grant citizenship to Jews until it was pressured to do so by Western governments in 1923. Soon after, when the worldwide economic crisis hit in 1929, mainstream and nascent fascist political parties began to exploit anti-Jewish feelings. But it was not until the start of World War II that that those twin hatreds, xenophobia and anti-Semitism, united to make Romania unbearable for Jews.

Even as the clouds gathered and the voices of the fascist elements in Romania became louder, the majority of the country's Jews were reluctant to flee. Life was too comfortable and the options for flight seemed too limited, despite the darkness threatening to eclipse the bright lights of Bucharest. Educated people from the upper class, like Grigore and Zlata Bucspan, were hanging on with the hope that the hatred would bypass them.

A year earlier, on September 1, 1939, German forces had crossed into Poland. The soldiers poured into Poland in railway cars painted with crude pictures of Jews with hooked noses and bearing the slogan: "We're off to Poland—to thrash the Jews." Two days after the invasion, Britain and France declared war on Germany, but they could not stop or slow the German progress across Poland. Everywhere they went, the German soldiers singled out Jews for abuse and massacre. In the first two months, five thousand Polish Jews were killed, and tens of thousands more, huddled in the Warsaw ghetto, were headed for starvation and worse.

The German invasion led to an irreversible change in the position of Europe's Jews. As many as three hundred thousand Polish Jews fled

east to the eastern part of the country, which was controlled by the Soviets. Eventually an estimated 1.8 million Jews sought safety in the
Soviet zone. A few thousand others fled to Hungary, Lithuania, Slova-
kia, and Romania. A whole population was suddenly in upheaval, desperate to find a safe haven.

In the early stages of the war, the Germans did not oppose Jewish
emigration. In fact, the Reich encouraged Jews to leave Germany and
the territories under its control. The problem was that there were few
places to go. Countries opposed to Germany's unfolding policies
and those that were simply attempting to remain neutral were reluctant to absorb a huge wave of refugees, particularly since the Nazis
stripped the emigrants of money and valuables on their way out of
their homelands.

The two countries most open to Jewish immigration at the outbreak of the war were Palestine and the United States, which was still
neutral. In 1939 and 1940, Jews represented fifty-two percent of all immigrants to the United States, but the actual numbers were small—
43,450 in 1939 and 36,945 in 1940. The number of legal immigrants
was far smaller for Palestine because of restrictions imposed by the
British, who controlled the country under a mandate from the League
of Nations.

One solution for desperate Jews was illegal immigration to Palestine. Adolf Eichmann, the head of the Nazi's Central Bureau for Jewish Emigration, was eager to take advantage of the illegal immigration
organized by Zionist organizations, which promoted creation of a
Jewish state in Palestine. Eichmann had no sympathy for Jews, but he
saw immigration as a way to rid Europe of them. Ehud Avriel, a representative of the Jewish Agency who applied for exit permits for
Jews, described the effect as being treated like preferred customers.

Still, the results were modest. Even with the necessary documents
in hand, Avriel and his colleagues faced the twin challenges of secur-
ing reliable transportation to get the Jews to Palestine and of avoiding
the formidable obstacles erected by the British to enforce their restrictions. Failure to overcome those challenges would cost untold thousands of lives.

From the outset, Romania was vital to the outcome of the war in the Balkans. It produced 54 million barrels of oil a year, enough to go a long way toward fueling the war machines of either the British or the Germans. Both sides were eager to get Carol II to join them. The British depended heavily on diplomacy and a traditional affection among elite Romanians for the culture of London and Paris. The Germans, on the other hand, had a potent ally in the existing anti-Semitic organizations like the Legion of the Archangel Michael, a fascist organization more commonly known as the Legionnaires, and later, as the Iron Guard.

After World War 1, the victorious Allied powers had awarded Romania three new provinces—Bessarabia from Russia, Bukovina from Austria, and Transylvania from Hungary. The additions doubled the size of Romania and swelled the country's Jewish population by several hundred thousand, and the Allies had insisted that they be granted Romanian citizenship.

The increase in the Jewish population added to the uneasy tension that had existed since the nineteenth century between Romanian nationalists and the country's Jews. Despite discrimination, Jews had played an important role in all aspects of Romania's economy, from trades and manufacturing in the urban areas to agriculture in the countryside. Yet as far back as 1866, the country's constitution had denied Romanian Jews the political rights accorded other Romanians. Other measures restricted their ability to compete with the rising Christian bourgeoisie and limited the land available to Jewish peasants.

The additions to the Jewish population and the Allied demands for their equal treatment ignited a new, more widespread bout of anti-Semitism. In the forefront was the fascist Christian National Defense League, created in 1923 by Alexandru Cuza, a professor who advocated revoking the citizenship of all Jews and whose organization used the swastika as its political symbol long before it was adopted by Adolf Hitler.

The Legion of the Archangel Michael was a radical offshoot of Cuza's group. Founded in 1927 by a young Romanian fanatic named Corneliu Codreanu, the Legionnaires, who were renamed the Iron Guard in 1929, regarded assassination and martyrdom as steps along the path to rid the country of corrupt politicians and Jews. Members wore green shirts and delivered an awkward greeting to each other, which involved touching their chest with their right hand, slapping their forehead lightly, and ending with the Nazi salute. Initiates had to suck blood from cuts on the arms of every other member of the "nest" and sign an oath to commit murder whenever ordered.

The Iron Guard specialized in terrorizing helpless Jews, burning their homes and looting synagogues throughout the country. They also attacked gypsies and other minorities. For a decade they operated with impunity. Eventually, however, Carol II came to regard the organization as a threat to his own authority. In January 1938, the king outlawed the Iron Guard and ordered Codreanu's arrest. In April, Codreanu was convicted of treason and imprisoned along with thirteen of his followers.

Later that year, Carol II was summoned to Berlin for a conference with Hitler. The German leader's demands for economic concessions by Romania so angered the king that when he returned to Bucharest, he secretly ordered Codreanu killed because of the Iron Guard leader's pandering to Hitler. On November 30, while the Iron Guard leader and his accomplices were being transferred between prisons, they were shot and killed, supposedly while trying to escape. The corpses were covered with lye to speed decomposition and buried in a ditch near the prison. Two tons of fresh concrete was poured over the ditch, and those involved swore an oath of secrecy.

Somehow word of the king's order leaked out to the remaining Iron Guard. A few months later, Carol II's police uncovered a plot to exact revenge on Armand Calinescu, who had been in charge of the police at the time of Codreanu's killing. Carol retaliated by ordering members of the Iron Guard rounded up and put to death without trial. The exact number executed was never known; estimates were as high as six thousand.

In response, nine young Iron Guard members ambushed

Calinescu, who by that time had become Romania's premier. One morning, while Calinescu was on his way to work, they pushed an ox-cart in front of his official car and fired twenty bullets into his body.

The assailants were caught shortly before midnight on the day of the attack. On Carol II's orders, they were taken to the spot where they had killed the premier. Huge floodlights from army trucks illuminated the area so that the assembled crowd could watch as the nine men were shot in the head with their own guns. The bodies were left under the lights for two days. Above them was a large banner reading: "Let This Be A Lesson To All Traitors To Our Country."

Soldiers and police were given a free hand to deal with any and all suspected members of the Iron Guard, and thousands of young men were shot, hanged from lampposts, or tortured to death. A few hundred escaped to Germany.

The bloodbath was unprecedented in Romanian history. As Robert St. John, who covered the country during World War II as a correspondent for the Associated Press, later wrote: "All this was background for what was yet to come." Romania had not seen the last of the fanatical Iron Guard.

The economic concessions granted by Carol II to Hitler in 1938 were followed by a far greater capitulation in the summer of 1940. As part of the nonaggression pact signed by Germany and the Soviet Union on August 23, 1939, Hitler and Joseph Stalin had reached a secret agreement to return Bessarabia to Soviet control. In June 1940, the Soviets issued an ultimatum to King Carol II—withdraw all Romanian troops from the territory within forty-eight hours. The Soviets added another provision—as a penalty for occupying its land—they demanded that Romania also cede northern Bukovina, which had never been Russian.

Both areas were rich in lumber, wheat, cattle, and minerals, so the economic price for losing the land to Russia was considerable. But the two hundred thousand Jews living in Bessarabia and northern Bukovina would pay a bigger price.

On Germany's advice, the Romanians retreated without firing a shot, except at the Jews, who were somehow blamed for the humiliation. The retaliation in Bessarabia marked the first massacres of Jews in Romania. One of the ugliest episodes occurred in the summer of 1940 in the Dorohoi district of Bukovina, where retreating Romanian soldiers abused women and beat and shot to death dozens of Jews.

In one episode documented in Romanian archives, ten Jewish Romanian soldiers were serving as an honor guard for a Jewish soldier who had been killed in an earlier clash. Shots were fired as the coffin was being lowered into the grave, and the Romanian officer in charge of the ceremony ordered the soldiers to leave the cemetery. As they got to the gate, the Jewish soldiers were disarmed and shot. The Romanian soldiers arranged the bodies to make it appear that the Jews had opened fire, and forty more Jews died in the resulting riot. Among the victims was a ninety-four-year-old man whose skull was crushed.

Estimates of the number of deaths in the Dorohoi pogrom vary from one hundred sixty to two hundred. Ambassador Miguel Rivera of Chile put the death toll at one hundred eighty in a cable to his government. Warning that the episode was merely a prelude of what was to come, he wrote: "It is hard to describe what Nazi bands and Romanian hooligans have done to the Jews of Romania. Human language is too poor to tell it in words. Jews in Romania have been robbed of their possessions, blackmailed, brutally attacked, and many of them massacred under most horrible circumstances. What my eyes have seen should not be passed over in silence."

The loss of Bessarabia and northern Bukovina pushed Carol II deeper into the German camp, though the event had been orchestrated secretly with German connivance. In July he appointed a new cabinet, laden with generals who had clear Nazi leanings. He also declared an amnesty for members of the Iron Guard and its commander, Horia Sima, who returned from exile in Germany to serve as minister of education and enlightenment in the new cabinet.

The regime quickly passed harsh anti-Semitic legislation.

In August of 1940, Carol II approved a law that defined who would be considered a Jew. The Romanian definition of a Jew became even broader than Germany's, categorizing Jews as a race rather than a religion. For instance, in addition to those practicing the "Mosaic" faith and born to parents practicing the Mosaic faith, Jews were defined as anyone who had converted to Christianity but was born of unconverted Jewish parents; anyone who had born to a Christian mother and a Jewish father and who had not been baptized, and anyone born illegitimately to a Jewish mother. Also included were Jews "by blood," even if they were atheists. Even if one wanted to, it was difficult to escape being identified as a Jew.

Jews were barred from adopting Romanian names, and they were forbidden to buy property. Jews were prohibited from marrying gentiles. They were dismissed from the army and civil service as well as from most positions in business and newspapers. Because they were not doing their share of military duty, because they were now forbidden to serve in the armed forces, young Jewish men were required to participate in forced labor.

There was a basic economic underpinning to this anti-Semitic legislation. Various Romanian officials defended the anti-Jewish laws, describing them as a process of "Romanization" of the country. In fact, Radu Ioanid, a Romanian-born scholar and associate director of the international programs at the United States Holocaust Memorial Museum, described it in an interview as "an economic expression of anti-Semitism."

Under the guise of law enforcement, some Jewish businesses were openly expropriated by plunder. Other businesses, such as forestry companies, mills, and distilleries, were seized by nationalization. Yet another law required all businesses to remove all professional Jews. Only those Jews and businesses deemed "essential" by the Council of Ministers were given exemptions. Also in the fall of 1940, professional organizations from the bar association to the Society of Architects expelled Jewish members. To enroll in medical school one had to be of Romanian, Aryan, Magyar, or Turkish ethnicity and practice either a Christian or Muslim religion. Jews could no longer work as engineers, doctors, lawyers, teachers, or businessmen.

The repression was not enough to calm Romanian nationalists, nor would it prove sufficient to save King Carol II's government and his throne. Street demonstrators demanded that the king abdicate because he had given up Bessarabia and northern Bukovina. Any hopes that the protests would end quietly were dashed within days when the weakened king was forced by German pressure to return Transylvania to Hungary.

Someone had to go. The prime minister appointed by King Carol II in July 1940 resigned that August. To replace him, Carol II picked General Ion Antonescu, although just a few weeks earlier, when Antonescu had publicly argued that Romania should have fought to keep Bessarabia and Bukovina, the king had ordered him confined to a convent.

Antonescu was not a member of the Iron Guard, but its ranks respected him. The king hoped that his appointment would silence the demands for his own ouster. The diminutive former defense minister's coloring and temper had earned him the nickname of Red Dog. As the price for his support, Antonescu demanded that Carol II grant him full authority over the government. The king hesitated, so Antonescu sent word to Horia Sima to apply pressure to Carol II. Suddenly the street in front of the royal palace was filled with a frenzied mob. Gunshots were fired. The king got the message and acquiesced to Red Dog's demands.

This was not enough to satisfy the Iron Guard. They demanded that Carol II abdicate and leave the country. The Iron Guard's Sima also warned Antonescu that he would not be secure until the king was out of the way. So Antonescu told Carol II to abdicate and leave the country, but the king hesitated once more. Robert St. John, the AP reporter, watched through binoculars what happened next outside the palace and described it later in his book *Foreign Correspondent:*

> In the distance we could hear the dull sound of marching feet and the semihysterical voices of the legionnaires, faintly at first, then stronger and stronger.
>
> Soldiers and police were throwing up barricades in the streets leading to the Royal Palace as rapidly as they could. Double squads of guards stood before the palace gates.

Now the voices of the marching men were loud enough so we could make out the words. "Down with the king." "Carol must go."

King Carol II and his mistress, Lupescu, boarded a train to Spain, taking with them $2.5 million worth of her jewelry and a cache of gold. A contingent of Iron Guardists tried to ambush the train along the way, and the king and his concubine hid in the bathtub of their private car as the nine-car train raced across the border to safety in Hungary.

Antonescu installed King Carol II's eighteen-year-old son, Michael, on the throne in September of 1940 and declared himself *con-ducator*—the Romanian equivalent of *fuhrer*. He put on the green shirt of the Iron Guard for the inauguration of his "National Legionary State," and he appointed prominent fascists to key positions in the new government. Sima, former Iron Guard commander, was made vice premier.

What was even more troubling to Allied diplomats in Romania was that Antonescu then allowed the Germans to send more officers and troops into Romania. Two motorized divisions of thirty thousand German soldiers occupied the oil wells around Ploesti in the heart of the Romanian oil region in early October, and a German military mission, headed by two generals, arrived in Bucharest.

Most of Bucharest's elite, including its prominent Jews, seemed to remain unfazed as a foreign power expanded its presence. Meanwhile, the worst of the atrocities were being inflicted on the Jews from Bessarabia, Bukovina, and other areas outside the cosmopolitan capital.

Chapter 3

The new fascist government in Bucharest embarked on a systematic program to cleanse the economy of Jewish interests. Within a short time, most professions and businesses had been purged of Jews. Jewish businessmen were prohibited from selling products that were part of the state monopoly, such as salt and tobacco. Jewish-owned shops were ordered to shut their doors on Sundays so they would not take business away from Christian stores, which were closed in observation of their Sabbath. Jews were expelled from the Romanian countryside, and their property was expropriated. Jewish-owned boats and barges were confiscated, too. Some Jews were able to hold on to their businesses by transferring them to Christian associates. Others resorted to bribery.

The henchmen of the Iron Guard enforced these orders, threatening and beating any Jews who resisted selling their businesses or property to Christians for paltry sums, or giving them away for nothing at all. In November 1940, a fifteen-year-old Jewish boy, Lucien Rosen, was charged with posting Communist handbills. He was dragged to the police station by the Iron Guard, savagely beaten, thrown from a sixth-floor window, and finally, on the street below, shot in the head. That same month, Iron Guard police arrested a merchant, Solomon Klein, confiscated the money he was carrying, and returned his battered corpse to his family the following day with the explanation that he had thrown himself out a window at the police station.

Not all of the victims of the frenzy of persecution were Jews. In late November 1940, some sixty-three Romanian politicians, military officers, and policemen accused of complicity in the death of Corneliu Codreanu were executed by the Iron Guard in the Jilava prison near Bucharest.

In a bizarre spectacle, the Iron Guard dug up the bodies of their fallen leader and his thirteen colleagues and carried them in a procession through the streets of Bucharest. An estimated one hundred fifty thousand people turned out to watch the macabre parade, a chilling indication of the solid support for the fascists.

Some of Romania's Jews could no longer watch in silence as conditions deteriorated. The Union of Jewish Communities of Romania submitted a twenty-six-page appeal to Antonescu in December 1940. It summarized the arrests, abuses, expropriations, and murders that had been carried out in thirty-nine communities in the preceding months.

Antonescu promised an investigation by the minister of interior, a longtime Iron Guard member, and Antonescu's reply to the Jewish organization indicated the leader's growing impatience with the Iron Guard, as well as the Jewish community, "I will not be able to tolerate indefinitely the disorder which shakes the entire country," he wrote. "I do protect Jews who are primarily guilty of the misfortunes afflicting our nation. At the same time, as head of the government, I cannot tolerate acts that compromise the effort to achieve recovery by means of law and order, an effort impeded daily by the thoughtless actions of people unconscious of the evil they are causing to the nation and to the Legionnaire movement."

His concerns were ignored, and the atrocities continued on a regular basis. A month later, Wilhelm Filderman, the head of the Union of Romanian Jews and an outspoken defender of his people, sent a sharply worded letter to Antonescu demanding an end to the abuses. There was no reply.

Antonescu continued to worry about the excesses of the Iron Guard. His concerns may have focused more on the impact of the confiscation of businesses on the nation's economy than the anti-Semitic abuses, but he decided that the zealots had to be reined in. Antonescu's attempt to exert control sparked a revolt in which Horia Sima tried to

gain control of the government. The Iron Guard leader expected support from Germany, but Hitler was not inclined to see an important
potential ally turned into a bastion for fascists who were even more
brutal than his own troops. When Germany refused to support Sima
and the Iron Guard, the attempted coup was over. The violence, however, was not. It degenerated into a brutal pogrom as the Romanian
thugs lashed out in anger and frustration at the Jews.

There are numerous accounts of the wild rampage and slaughter on
January 21 and 22 of 1941 as the Guard's anger turned on the Jews of
Bucharest. Without so many different sources, it would be difficult to
accept the level of brutality and inhumanity. As a newspaperman, St.
John was trained to be dispassionate and aloof. His professional tone
in *Foreign Correspondent* was all the more shocking:

> Accounts of the atrocities by the Legionnaires during the
> 36-hour pogrom might never have been believed by anyone,
> except that we saw some of it happen, we counted the corpses,
> we noted the mutilations, we inspected what little was left of
> the seven once-beautiful synagogues, we saw the whole quarter
> in ruins, we took careful notes on exactly how the Jews of
> Bucharest were killed that afternoon, that night, and the
> next day.
>
> During the night members of the Legion of the Archangel
> Michael, after praying and drinking some of each other's blood,
> went to the homes of some of Bucharest's most distinguished
> Jews and loaded nearly 200 men and women into trucks. The
> victims were taken to the abattoir on the edge of the city. There
> they were stripped naked, forced to get down on all fours, and
> were driven up the ramp of the slaughterhouse. Then in a
> mockery of a kosher preparation of meat they were put
> through all the stages of animals at slaughter until finally the
> beheaded bodies, spurting blood, were hung on iron hooks
> along the wall. As a last sadistic touch the Legionnaires took

rubber stamps and branded the carcasses with the Romanian equivalent of: Fit for Human Consumption.

An unnamed correspondent for Reuters, the British news service, filed an equally chilling and more personal account of what he had seen:

> I am forced to admit that atrocities can and do occur and that those which occurred in Bucharest far exceeded in bestiality anything that might ever be imagined. Dozens of Jews—women and children as well as men—were literally burned alive. I am not speaking of those who were burned to death in hundreds of buildings to which the Guardists set fire, after shooting and beating the inhabitants and looting the contents of their homes. I am speaking only of Jews who were beaten senseless on the streets, robbed, then doused with gasoline and set afire.
>
> In the Bucharest morgue yesterday a military surgeon showed me the charred bodies of nine persons, burned beyond recognition. All of them, he assured me, had been picked up in the streets of the Jewish quarter following the most frenzied stage of the pogrom, last Wednesday.
>
> Trusted friends have told me, and officials have confirmed, numerous cases of Jewish women whose breasts were cut off, not to mention sadistic mutilations like gouged-out eyes, brandings, and bone breakings.

The correspondent also recounted descriptions of the horrors of the Bucharest slaughterhouse and bands of forty or more Iron Guard members beheading people with axes and knives.

An English-language radio station picked up by news outlets across Europe broadcast an interview with a chemistry professor from Bucharest, whose identity was kept anonymous to protect him. In the monotone he might have used in a classroom lecture, he delivered the following account of what he had witnessed:

"One of my dear friends, Rabbi Hersh Guttman, and his two brilliant young sons, Jancu and Josef, aged 25 and 27, were among the hundreds of Jewish leaders and scholars who were taken in wagons to the forest of Jilava, thrown out, and machine-gunned in groups of 5 or 10. As it happened, Rabbi Guttman was one of the few who was not killed. He lay in the snow, bleeding. He held the wrist of each of his sons, counting the pulse beat. When his sons died, Rabbi Guttman, a great and good and compassionate man, my friend Rabbi Guttman crawled through the forest, leaving a trail of blood behind him. Somehow he got back to the city.

"Another group of Jews, businessmen, bankers, were herded together in the confiscated home of Oscar Kaufmann, director-general of the Banque de Credit Roumain. All the older persons in the group were driven in trucks to Jilava at one end of the city and murdered. The rest were taken in the opposite direction to Baneasa Woods. They were beaten and then released. A few hours later another group of Jews were stripped naked, whipped, then mutilated and murdered in the Baneasa Woods.

"A student of mine, Moise Silberstein, was made into a human torch, burned to death on the Jewish street called Vacaresti. Another dear friend—I omit his name out of deference to the way he died—was flogged in a public square while a crowd watched and jeered. His genital organ was exposed to ascertain that he was, indeed, a Jew. It was then cut off. My friend was locked into a pillory. The Iron Guard invited school children to throw snowballs at him. Which they did. Eventually he froze to death.

"A friend of my mother's, Ernestine Riegler, was in the synagogue in Calea Mosilor, praying. The synagogue was burned down and all the Jews who had assembled for prayer were murdered.

"There were more Jews killed in the slaughterhouse. Beheaded with mechanical instruments used for killing cattle. Many of the corpses were then hung on meat hooks."

The final toll remained uncertain, but it appears that hundreds of Jews were killed in the rebellion by the Iron Guard. Several hundred others were tortured and abused. Synagogues in Bucharest were vandalized and looted, two destroyed by fire. Certainly higher numbers of Jews were being killed across Europe at the time. Few people, however, had suffered such rabid savagery.

Within the terror, the survival of Rabbi Hersh Guttman had transformed him into a heroic figure in Bucharest. He became an almost mystical holy man who symbolized the will to live. His story was described in detail at the time in a cable by Miguel Rivera, the Chilean ambassador. It was not finished until many years later by his grandson, Rabbi Elhanan Guttman, as he sat in a synagogue in Tel Aviv dedicated to the victims of the Holocaust in Romania: "It was light when he woke up and started to walk home," the grandson said. "The Iron Guard found him again. Angry that he was still alive, they shot him a second time. He fell to the ground again and stayed there for a long time. Eventually he woke up and again began to walk home. When the Iron Guards found him a third time, they were very angry. They shot him. And again he awoke and walked home to us. This is the reason so many people would come and ask for his blessing."

The months that followed were relatively safe for Romania's Jews. Romania had entered the war on the German side in February 1941, and most of the government's efforts were focused on raising a million-man army to fight alongside the Nazis. The confiscation of Jewish property and the dismissal of Jews from their jobs went on. Long lists of Jews fired from governmental and semi-official positions were published in newspapers. Urban property was expropriated under a new law, and authorities required Jews to carry their passports and have them stamped with their Jewish origin. Jews were forbidden to change their religion, and they were prohibited from participating in the plebiscite on Antonescu's handling of the government in March 1941. But worse was still to come.

Chapter 4

At five-thirty on the morning of June 22, 1941, Germany's ambassador to Moscow announced that the nonaggression pact between the countries was over, and Germany declared war on the Soviet Union. While the Russians had been tipped off to expect an invasion, the scale and timing came as a surprise. In a huge gamble, Hitler threw 183 divisions into the assault, code-named Operation Barbarossa.

In Bucharest, Antonescu was eager to recover the lost provinces of Bessarabia and Bukovina. The army he had mobilized was ready to join the Germans in the epic battle on the eastern front. The alliance also opened a new chapter in Romanian anti-Semitism as Romanian citizens and soldiers joined their Nazi compatriots in the murder of tens of thousands of Jews.

In the initial fighting, Romanian and German troops moved through eastern Romania and Bessarabia to clear out the Soviets, who had occupied the region since the previous summer. The Soviets retaliated with devastating air raids that killed hundreds of Romanian soldiers. The deaths of the Romanian soldiers kindled the fires of anti-Semitism, and Romanian mobs unleashed a brutal and barbaric assault on the region's Jews under the guise that they were Soviet agents and saboteurs.

The focal point of the pogrom was Jassy, an old Romanian city of one hundred thousand people, about half of whom were Jewish. The killing started in a small way on June 26. Three men were arrested on charges of signaling Soviet planes about the location of a building housing Romanian troops. One was murdered, and the two others escaped after being seriously wounded. That evening, police conducted house-to-house searches in the Jewish neighborhoods, arresting 317 people on spying charges and detaining another 207 who owned flashlights or possessed red clothing. The following day saw more arrests and killings.

On June 29, Romanian police and soldiers, under the watchful eye of Nazi SS troops, went on a rampage. At least two hundred sixty Jews were killed in their homes, and hundreds more were lined up and shot or forced to lie in ditches, where they were beaten and killed. Others were killed indiscriminately. When a crowd of Jews corralled by police near a movie theater panicked and ran, they were hunted down and murdered one by one by the soldiers.

By sunset, five thousand people had been arrested and marched through the streets under a gauntlet of beatings from Romanian police and German soldiers. Those who fell were shot on the spot, and those who made it to the railway station were forced to lie on the ground while their rings, money, and other valuables were confiscated. They were then loaded onto thirty-nine sealed cattle cars, as many as one hundred people to a car, and shipped southward. Several thousand men and boys in the cars were without any water or food.

One of the survivors later recalled the trip in an account contained in the papers of the British Foreign Office: "The heat and stench inside were fearful. Before our eyes our children fell, our parents and our friends. They might possibly have been saved if only we had had a few drops of water. There were some who drank their own urine or that of their friends. A little water was afterwards poured into the car through its holes when the death train was halted at different stations. Meantime the heat in the truck became fearful, it was literally an inferno."

At various points during the eight-day journey, the train was stopped and dead bodies were tossed along the tracks. At one place, more than 600 corpses were removed. At the next stop, 172 bodies were discarded. The train stopped in a town called Roman, and the survivors were ordered out and made to strip naked so they could be sprayed with disinfectant. They were then forced to spend the night naked on the ground. By the time the train reached its destination, a camp at Kalarash, the toll had risen to 1,300.

A second death train had left Jassy the following day with nearly 2,000 people in the eighteen cars. Its last car contained 80 corpses of people who had been shot and disemboweled with bayonets at the train station. At one stop, a man slipped through a hole in the planks to get some water for his father and son. A German soldier shot him. Another passenger paid his last money for a glass of water and gulped it down, too late to realize it had been laced with lye, which caused a horrible death. An eighteen-year-old boy, desperate for water, reached between the floorboards of a car at one stop to run a cup through a puddle. His hands were shot off. When the train arrived at Podul Iloaei, a small city, 1,194 people had died and only 708 had survived.

The total number of victims of the Jassy pogrom has never been determined. Government reports put the death toll at 500 and claimed the victims were Jewish Communists who had fired at Romanian and German troops. The actual toll was far higher. A report prepared a few months later by the World Jewish Congress said 7,900 Jews were "mowed down by machine-gun fire on the fields of Jassy."

Radu Ioanid, the Romanian scholar at the United States Holocaust Memorial Museum, quoted figures in his book, *The Holocaust in Romania,* ranging from 3,200 to more than 13,000. The most compelling data he discovered was from lists of the dead prepared by the synagogues of Jassy—that figure was 13,266, including 40 women and 180 children.

Jassy was not an isolated incident. Throughout late June and July, thousands more Jews across Romania were victims of popular violence, often carried out by police and the mobs they instigated. Organized death squads assigned to liquidate all Jews and Communists also accompanied the German and Romanian troops that moved through the area. The German killing units were called the Einsatzgruppen, and their Romanian counterparts were the Special Echelon.

On July 17, Romanian and German troops entered Kishinev, the historic capital of Bessarabia, and the mobile death squads slaughtered Jews in the city and surrounding area. Tragically, the population of Jews in Kishinev had grown sharply in recent months because the city and surrounding area had been returned to the Soviet Union and refugees from Romania had sought safety there. An estimated ten thousand people were killed, and the remaining seventy-five thousand to eighty thousand people were herded into camps in preparation for being taken out of the region in what authorities termed "the purification of Romanian land." By the end of the killings and deportations, fewer than 100 Jews remained in Kishinev.

In one incident described by survivors, 440 people were taken out of the camp at Kishinev one day and the next day 40 returned, most of them women and older men. They said the other 400 had been shot as punishment for supposedly signaling Soviet aircraft and for the shooting of four German soldiers in the area. The people in the camp were warned that in the future 200 Jews would be killed for every German or Romania soldier who died.

Estimates of the death toll at the time exceeded twenty thousand in Bessarabia and three thousand in Bukovina, though figures compiled from official reports and other records later placed the number higher.

The goal was to rid the region of Jews. In August 1941, the German and Romanian military commanders signed an agreement to deport the Jews from Bessarabia and Bukovina to a camp in Transnistria, German-held territory between the Bug and Dniester Rivers in western Ukraine. Beginning in October, the first one hundred thousand Jews from the region were shipped to the camp. The Jews from Bukovina arrived mostly by train and those from Bessarabia on foot, with thousands perishing on the death marches. Throughout the remainder of 1941 and 1942, an estimated eighty thousand Romanian Jews would die in the camps along with more than one hundred thousand Jews from Odessa and the surrounding territory, where the slaughters were equally devastating. In the city of Odessa itself, Romanian soldiers were responsible for the massacre of sixty thousand people.

The time of bright lights and illusion had ended for the Jews of

Romania. The turning point was recorded in a memorandum to the American secretary of state, Cordell Hull, written on August 19, 1941, by Franklin Mott Gunther, the American ambassador in Bucharest. Earlier in the year, Gunther had warned Romanian officials that the country faced international condemnation for its harsh treatment of Jews. As the situation deteriorated to what Gunther called "butchery and brutal deprivation of human rights," the Romanian officials expressed regret and claimed Germans were provoking and staging the attacks, an explanation that Gunther found dubious. "But the fact remains that there has been no popular uprising or movement against all these cruelties," wrote Gunther. "It may well be that the ethical sense of the Romanian people has been somewhat dulled by recent miseries and disasters. . . . Whatever the cause, 1941 has thus far proved to be a black year for the Jews in Romania."

For those who had survived the violence of Bucharest and Jassy and escaped being shipped to the death camp in Transnistria, the hope of avoiding the fate of Jews in France, Germany, and Poland had been erased, swept away on the flood of gruesome murders and abuses as horrible as anything that occurred in the rest of Europe. Survivors with the money and the means were determined to escape.

One of the victims of the Bucharest pogrom was Ami Atir's grandfather, Menasche Reichman. The Iron Guard murdered him on January 21, 1941, the first day of the rebellion of the Legionnaires, not long after he had visited the site where *Struma* was being renovated for a voyage to Palestine. His body was discovered several days later, with the bodies of twenty other Jews, in the local slaughterhouse. Their bodies had been stripped naked, mutilated, and hung on meat hooks. Some were stamped "kosher." In telling his family's story in his own plain words during an interview, Atir wrenched this account out of the history books and made it personal.

Reichman's family had had doubts about the *Struma,* but the increasing violence on Bucharest streets convinced them that they should leave Romania as soon as possible.

Half of the family already had emigrated to Palestine in the 1930s. Reichman's son, among the first members of his family to go to Palestine, later told his own son, Ami Atir, that as he said good-bye to his mother, Aneta, she wept. A superstitious woman, she had been vehemently opposed to her children's plans to emigrate because a gypsy had once warned her, "Beware of great waters."

As many of Romania's Jews realized that the time had come to abandon their country, they would also discover that the Nazis were not their only enemy. The British were determined to restrict immigration to Palestine regardless of the consequences to Europe's Jews, who were facing what the Nazis had begun to call the Final Solution.

Within a few weeks of ordering the extermination of Europe's Jews in January 1942, Hitler began to worry that Germany was in danger of being outdone by Romania in terms of implementing the Final Solution and that the whole situation there might deteriorate into bloody chaos.

Later that year, when Antonescu proposed sending 110,000 more Jews to concentration camps that were regarded as horrible even by the Germans, Eichmann asked the Foreign Office in Berlin to order a halt to the Romanian efforts to "get rid of the Jews" at this point. He said the Romanians should be informed that "the evacuation of German Jews, which is already in full swing," had priority. The Romanians, it seemed, would have to wait their turn.

In assessing the actions of Antonescu and Romania in general toward the country's Jewish population, historian Raul Hilberg would one day conclude that "no country, besides Germany, was involved in massacres of Jews on such a scale."

Chapter 5

For five centuries, the blood of conquerors and conquered alike stained the earth in the city of Czernowitz, the capital of Bukovina. The city on the banks of the Prut River in the foothills of the Carpathian Mountains had been ransacked by the Tartars and captured by the Ottomans in the seventeenth century. In the nineteenth and early twentieth centuries it served as a western outpost of the Austro-Hungarian Empire and became the focal point for Ukrainian nationalism. In 1918, the region was integrated into greater Romania, and in 1940 it was annexed by the Soviet Union in the nonaggression pact with Germany.

Despite the turnovers and violence, the city remained a beautiful and cultured place, hospitable for the many prominent Jewish intellectuals and artists who were members of its elite. Residents liked to refer to Czernowitz as "little Vienna" because of its architecture and tree-lined boulevards, and because of the dominance of the German language. The five-story Jewish community center shared pride of place with a thirteenth-century fortified castle and a nineteenth-century Eastern Orthodox cathedral.

When the Romanians pulled out and the Red Army rolled into town in June 1940, unfurling their red banners extolling the glory of Communism, the atmosphere was more curious and festive than ominous. To many in the Jewish community, who comprised half of the population of one hundred thousand, the Soviets were a welcome alternative to the Romanians in view of the rising anti-Semitism of King Carol II's regime in Bucharest.

"The grinning, good-natured, singing soldiers impressed me," Ruth Glasberg Gold, then ten years old, later wrote in her memoir, *Ruth's Journey*. "It was a reassuring feeling after a year of anxiety."

The drawbacks of Soviet occupation soon overtook the euphoria. Private enterprise vanished, replaced by unemployment and a grim economic outlook. Intellectuals were lucky to find work as manual laborers, and bureaucrats arrived from throughout the Soviet Union to impose the rigid rules of Communism. The prayers with which Christians and Jews alike began each school day were banned. The new rules were only a short-lived prelude to the events of the following year, when the German and Romanian armies would drive out the Soviets and turn their guns on the Jews of Czernowitz.

David Frenk was eighteen years old when Bukovina was annexed by the Soviet Union in 1940. His father, a wealthy businessman and a Zionist, had taken his mother to see Palestine the previous year. He wasn't ready then to forsake everything and leave Romania, but as a Zionist, he was curious.

"My brother and I, we told him, 'Go, go like a tourist. What will you lose? Put down a stone there.' " Frenk said during an interview in his home, in Tel Aviv, decades later. "So he did. He bought a house in Tel Aviv and he bought a business. He was not ready yet to say good-bye to Romania, so he returned during the summer. My brother and I were in the mountains, and while we were away, the Russians arrived. Walking into the city, we noticed immediately the change in decoration. My father and mother, being wealthy people, had been able to escape to Bucharest and then quickly to Palestine." Before leaving, their parents had left word that money and travel documents had been given to their sister in Bucharest so that they, too, could go Palestine.

The Frenk brothers did not realize the seriousness of their situation. Israel Frenk found work in a factory; David got a job as a clerk. "Another two or three months, we thought we would be Romanians again," he said. But time passed and the Russians occupied their buildings and life became more and more uncertain. Eventually, they decided to relocate.

When Germany declared war on the Soviet Union in the summer of 1941 and German and Romanian troops first crossed into Bukovina to retake the region, David Frenk was working as a bookkeeper for a Russian who was married to a Jew. His employer and other Soviet subjects were warned to get out ahead of the advancing troops. The man told David Frenk that he and his wife were leaving immediately, and he urged his young bookkeeper to accompany them. Frenk agreed, and he hurriedly packed a bag and bid farewell to his brother.

The railway station was filled with panic-stricken people struggling to board the train destined for the safety of the Ukraine. When Frenk tried to board with the Russians, a policeman stopped him.

"Where were you born?" demanded the policeman.

"Balti, Romania," said the young man.

"You cannot get on," said the policeman. "This is only for Russian people."

The policeman would not relent, despite the pleas of Frenk and his employer. The Russian businessman emptied his pockets and his wallet, handing his money to his young bookkeeper. "I cannot help you," the Russian said as he and his wife disappeared into one of the cars.

The German and Romanian soldiers came to Czernowitz on July 5. Helped by local residents and informers, the troops rounded up and killed two thousand Jews. Most were buried in mass graves, two of them at the Jewish cemetery. Four days later, four hundred people were executed by German troops, who also set fire to the main synagogue.

Houses and apartments in the Jewish quarter were transformed overnight into a ghetto. Soldiers rounded up the city's remaining fifty thousand Jews and confined them there under guard. They were allowed to bring a single bag, and Frenk filled his with family photos and letters from his parents. In early September, an order was issued requiring everyone to wear a yellow badge denoting that they were Jewish. Failure to do so was punishable by execution.

Crammed fifty and sixty to a room, sweltering in the heat, they waited. Rumors spread like wildfire—they would be deported to a concentration camp outside of Romania; they would be sent to Germany; they would be killed by death squads moving through the ghetto and the rest of the town street by street, their bodies dumped in the Prut River.

For some, there was salvation, at least for the moment. Many of the city's doctors, engineers, and other professionals were Jews. They received special permits to return to their homes and continue to work in the city. Even in such hard times, the city had to operate. Israel Frenk's wife, Tivia, was a doctor, so the two of them were released from the ghetto. David was desperate to escape the ghetto, join his brother and sister-in-law, and find a way to get out of Czernowitz before the deportations began.

"The police who were in charge of the ghetto were Romanian," he said later. "With Romanians, you can give them some money and they will find a way. I found a policeman and I gave him money and he agreed to help me. So I escaped from the ghetto and went to my brother's house."

His brother and sister-in-law would face death if they were discovered hiding a fugitive. After the way their Christian neighbors had turned on them earlier, the family trusted no one. Some bricks were removed from behind the furnace in the house, and any knock at the door sent David into hiding in the cavity there. All three knew the game could not go on forever, and they suspected that the need for Jewish doctors and other specialists that had spared a few would not last either. They had to escape, though they were not sure how or where to go.

Late one night near the end of August, there was a knock on the door. No one had the courage to answer. The knock was persistent, and the people outside called for them to open the door. "Izia," they called. "Open up, Izia." It was Israel Frenk's childhood nickname, and when he peered out the window, he recognized the two men on the doorstep. They were friends from his youth. He opened the door quickly and ushered them in. The men said they had urgent business. Tivia was called to the room, and the younger brother emerged from his hiding place.

"A committee has been formed in Bucharest to organize emigration to Israel," the men said. "The Romanian government has agreed that a ship can leave, and one has already been rented from a Greek named Pandelis. It is called *Struma*."

The men were members of Betar, a Zionist youth movement formed to promote immigration to Palestine. The group had chapters in cities across Romania. When the British had clamped down on immigration to Palestine, Betar had assumed a key role in organizing ships for the illegal immigration of Romanian Jews. The *Struma* was one of several ships that the group was trying to fill with refugees for a journey to Palestine.

This night, the men from Betar urged the Frenks to gather a dozen or so other trusted friends to escape Czernowitz and head for Bucharest. From there, they explained, transportation was being arranged to Constanta, the port on the Black Sea from which the ship would depart. There was no time to waste. The plan was for the *Struma* to sail in late September and the ship was filling fast.

All three of the Frenks were eager to join. The question was how to get to Bucharest, nearly three hundred miles away, on roads lined with military checkpoints and monitored by German and Romanian patrols.

"It seemed impossible to us," David Frenk said. "We had no idea how to do it."

Had the Frenks realized that getting to Bucharest would be the easiest part of their odyssey, they might have remained hunkered down in the small house in Czernowitz, awaiting their fate with thousands of others. But they did choose to leave, and they set out to find people willing to accompany them on a perilous journey to Bucharest.

PART II

Holocaust at Sea

Chapter 6

September, 1998

The Black Sea is a kidney-shaped body of water about seven hundred miles long and two hundred fifty miles wide. Many millennia ago, it was a freshwater lake about two thirds of its present size. During the last Ice Age, glacier melt gradually raised the water level enough that it breached the Bosporus Valley, creating the straits that linked the Black Sea with the Sea of Marmara and, beyond, the Mediterranean.

Somewhere in that vast sea, in the predawn hours of February 24, 1942, the *Struma* had sunk, carrying to the bottom Greg Buxton's grandparents and nearly eight hundred other people. In the years that followed his trip to Tel Aviv to search for the land his grandparents had bought and as his experience as a diver grew, Buxton had given occasional thought to organizing a diving expedition to search for the ship's remains. But when he did some research, he discovered how difficult the project would be. The Black Sea, he learned, was a deep body of water, seven thousand feet deep in some areas and hundreds of feet deep even close to most shore locations. From the little solid information that Buxton could find in old newspaper articles about the *Struma,* he knew the ship had not sunk near the shore, which meant it was probably in deep water.

Experienced recreational scuba divers usually restrict themselves to depths of eighty to one hundred feet. Going deeper requires not only practice and technical skill, but expensive special equipment to protect a diver from the cold and other dangers. For depths of two hundred feet or more, divers use special gas mixtures whose percentages of oxygen and nitrogen differ from what is found in air and that include helium, to improve their breathing ability and avoid narcosis and a potentially life-threatening condition known as decompression sickness.

The deeper the dive and the longer the time on the bottom, the greater the threat when resurfacing of getting decompression sickness, also known as the bends. The problem is that the pressure at great depths forces nitrogen into the body in increasing amounts. During ascent the pressure is reduced and the greater concentration of nitrogen in blood and tissues can turn into bubbles, causing the bends. The analogy divers often use is a bottle of soda. Carbon dioxide is dissolved in the soda under pressure, and it remains in solution until the pressure is suddenly reduced by opening the bottle. The rapid drop in pressure causes the carbon dioxide to bubble, and the drink foams. Essentially the same thing happens with the nitrogen accumulated inside a diver's body unless the person ascends slowly to allow the pressure to equalize gradually. In extreme cases, the bubbles actually appear under the diver's skin. As the bubbles circulate in the blood and tissues, they can impair circulation and lead to extreme fatigue, joint pain, and, in severe cases, paralysis and unconsciousness. It is a diver's worst nightmare, and the likelihood of this and other problems happening increases geometrically with the depth of a dive.

"Deep diving is like climbing K2," Buxton said as he described the effect of his hobby on his outlook on life. "You are doing something that no one else has ever done. It's right at the edge of what's technically possible and physically possible for you. And you are doing it with friends who support you every step of the way."

Just as mountain climbing carries risks, deep diving is a dangerous sport. Divers who go beyond one hundred feet carry two of everything, so that if the device that regulates the flow of air to them or any other vital piece of equipment fails, they have another. Diving at those depths, they could be dead before they reached the surface if something key malfunctioned.

In 1993, when Buxton was teaching diving and running one of the diving clubs at London University, he had some lucky encounters that would help him in the years to come. There he met a veteran diver named Nick Hope, who was finishing up his training for ultra-deep dives in preparation for joining a team that was planning the first amateur dive of the *Lusitania,* a British ship torpedoed by the Germans during World War I.

For divers, the *Lusitania* had unique appeal. It was a grand ship from the golden era of Atlantic passenger crossings. The Cunard Line had launched the ship at the River Clyde in 1906, and it was the largest liner afloat at the time—785 feet in length and 31,550 gross tons. The *Lusitania* had been financed with loans from the British government, which meant it could be summoned for duty in time of war. When World War I broke out, the British navy officially requisitioned the *Lusitania* and two sister ships, the *Mauretania* and the *Aquitania*. The other two were given orders and put into navy service, but the *Lusitania* continued its regular transatlantic trips.

On May 1, 1915, the ship had left New York with 1,200 passengers and crew. Among the passengers were 123 Americans, including the wealthy tycoon Alfred Vanderbilt and theater producer Charles Frohman. On May 7, off the coast of Ireland, a German U-boat torpedoed the ship, and it sank in eighteen minutes, taking with it 1,195 people, including Vanderbilt and Frohman. Although the United States did not declare war on Germany for nearly two more years, the sinking of the *Lusitania* helped to turn the tide of American public opinion against Germany.

The ship lay in about three hundred feet of icy cold water, a depth and temperature that had kept away all but the best-protected commercial divers. In 1994 and 1995, Polly Tapson led a group that conducted three successful excursions to the *Lusitania*. The expeditions, in which Hope took part, proved that deep wrecks, previously thought unreachable without commercial saturation diving techniques, could be visited safely by amateur scuba divers, using the right techniques and safety disciplines. The success of these trips transformed the global image of mixed-gas diving and proved to be the most important factor in the rapid development of technical diving in the years that followed.

Fascinated by the tales of the dives that Hope told upon his return, Buxton began planning to test the limits of his own diving abilities. In 1996, however, he had a diving accident that nearly killed him. For a time, it appeared that his days as a diver were over.

He and Geraint Ffoukes-Jones, a dive buddy, were exploring a wreck off the coast of South Wales. Somewhere in those murky depths, Buxton developed a bubble that got into his arteries and lodged in his brain stem. He managed to struggle to the surface and get out of the water, and was rushed by helicopter to a treatment center. Buxton could not walk for nearly two weeks, and the doctors said he was lucky that he had not suffered permanent damage. As he lay in the hospital, he kept going back over the dive. He could not figure out what error had created the bubbles that nearly killed him. His ascent had been slow and methodical, and he had not exceeded the precalculated bottom time. It turned out that he had not made a mistake. Doctors found a small hole in his heart, something that occurs at birth in a large fraction of the population. In Buxton's case, the tiny hole had allowed a bubble to pass into his arteries and lodge in his brain stem. The doctors told him he would be risking his life if he ever dove again.

Diving entails risk every time someone drops beneath the surface. A careless diver can get crippling bends from depths of twenty feet or less. For Buxton, the odds had gone up sharply, but he decided the risk of diving was worth it because it had become such a vital part of his life—and because, like all deep-water divers, he reveled in the danger.

His comeback was slow. He was nervous even on shallow dives, and he began to wonder if he would ever make the deep ones that were so tantalizing. In the meantime, Ffoukes-Jones had been spending time with Hope and his new group of amateur divers, Starfish Enterprises. They were planning another historic dive in early 1998, this time on the *Britannic* in the Aegean Sea. Ffoukes-Jones was going as one of the principal divers, and he invited his old friend to join the support team. Buxton still had not returned to deep diving on his own, but he agreed immediately. He would not be one of the primary divers, but he would have to be ready to fill in or help out in an emergency, so he began to train rigorously.

RMS *Britannic* was a sister ship of the *Titanic,* the most famous sunken ship in history. At 852 feet in length, the *Britannic* was a few feet longer than the *Titanic,* and the White Star Line, which owned both ships, had planned to call it the *Gigantic.* The company decided to tone down the name after the *Titanic* hit an iceberg in the Atlantic Ocean in 1912 and went down, taking 1,700 people with it.

The *Britannic* was launched two years later. Recruited by the British navy, it was outfitted as a hospital ship when World War I started. On November 21, 1916, off the coast of Greece, an explosion shook the ship. In fifty-five minutes the biggest steamship in the world was on the bottom of the Aegean Sea. All but thirty of the eleven hundred people on board escaped in lifeboats. The reason for the sinking is a mystery. Some claimed the ship struck a mine; others said it was torpedoed. There also were unproven allegations that, under cover of being a hospital ship, the *Britannic* was running military supplies and went down after an onboard explosion.

This shipwreck, the world's largest known, had been discovered and first explored in 1976 by an expedition led by Jacques Cousteau, the famous underwater adventurer. The mechanical device sent down for a look found the ship lying on its side at a depth of three hundred fifty feet. Except for a huge break near the bow, possibly caused by the explosion, the ship was remarkably intact. In those days, the wreckage was deemed too deep for scuba diving.

In the fall of 1997, the first team of scuba divers had managed to reach the *Britannic* and film the remains. The Starfish team planned to duplicate the feat in September 1998. The amount of preparation and planning was enormous, giving Buxton his first taste of what would be required for an assault on the *Struma.*

The logistics were demanding. The Greek government provided permission for a legal dive, essential to any expedition. A base hotel was established on an island near the wreck site, and a ship to serve as the dive platform was hired. Hundreds of pounds of equipment, from air tanks and compressors to extremely expensive underwater cameras, were loaded into a huge truck. Two of the divers started off a week ahead of the remainder of the crew and drove the truck down the length of Europe to Greece, where it was loaded onto a ferry and taken to the small Aegean island of Kea, near the wreck site.

The gear for the divers alone weighed several tons. Each diver would carry at least four large cylinders, with different mixtures of helium, oxygen, and nitrogen: the helium was to improve breathing at depth, and the oxygen was vital for decompression. Two additional cylinders for each diver would be waiting at the decompression station in shallower water, because the divers had to spend at least four hours underwater decompressing from the dive. One diver would also wear a rebreather, which is a self-contained device used to recirculate and regulate breathing gases to extend diving times. For protection from the long exposure in the icy water, they would wear specially designed neoprene dry suits and carry propulsion vehicles to overcome the strong wind-induced currents of the Aegean. In all, the divers would carry up to three hundred pounds of equipment, though it became essentially weightless in the water.

In the months of preparation for the expedition, Buxton took numerous technical courses so he would be as qualified as the primary divers. Eventually he was certified for the required depth and equipment. But he was still anxious.

The divers were amateurs, drawn from all sorts of professions—computer programmers, firemen, engineers, laborers—who shared a fascination with big wrecks. Everyone paid his own way; one diver sold his car to buy a special camera that could operate at the depth of the wreck.

The expedition lasted two weeks and encompassed dozens of dives and hundreds of hours of videotape of the wreck. For Buxton, it was the most grueling and satisfying experience of his life, though he managed only one dive on the wreck. He had overcome the fears created by the bubble episode and had worked alongside some of the world's leading deep-water scuba divers. More important in the long run, the idea of diving the *Struma* had gone from a dream to the drawing board.

"As we packed up on the last day and got on the ferry boat from the island where we were staying, I said to Geraint and some of the other guys, 'I've seen what happens. I know what a big expedition is about. I'm pretty sure I can put this *Struma* expedition together.' "

Buxton had learned that diving a deep wreck presented more challenges than just keeping the cold and the bends at bay at three hundred fifty feet. As he planned his own expedition, however, he would discover that even the best logistics are not always enough to overcome the hurdles when it comes to revisiting a time and an incident that influential people would rather not see resurrected. Along the way, the once-shy young man who preferred blending in would confront challenges that would redefine his purpose.

Chapter 7

The British were determined to block illegal immigration to Palestine. Everything in the diplomatic arsenal was arrayed to stop Jews from reaching the country. The British government would prove itself willing and able to go beyond passive cables and raised voices. Active steps were taken against the illegal immigration, from trying to prevent the acquisition of ships for refugees to deploying naval craft that otherwise could have been used in the war effort to patrol the coast of Palestine. Even proposals to sink shiploads of refugees would be discussed, and unfounded accusations that refugee boats were infiltrated by Nazi spies would be used repeatedly to justify the blockade.

The motives were coldly strategic. The British did not want to devote even more military resources to keeping a lid on hostilities between Arabs and Jews in Palestine, and more important, they did not want to antagonize the Arabs of the Middle East, who controlled huge reserves of oil that were deemed essential to the Allied war effort. The region had risen dramatically in its strategic importance.

Since the turn of the century, the British government had found itself inextricably involved in the question of a Jewish homeland. In 1902 and 1903 the British had proposed Jewish settlement in the Sinai Peninsula or in part of East Africa, though the plans came to nothing. During World War I, the British proposed large-scale Jewish settlement in Palestine. After the British took control of Palestine from the Ottoman Empire at the end of the war, the concept was formalized with the Balfour Declaration. The document undertook to establish a

Jewish homeland in Palestine, with the provision that nothing be done to damage the civil and religious rights of the Arabs already living there. As the world knows well today, this would prove to be one of the century's most impossible provisos.

In 1922, the League of Nations entrusted Britain with authority over the area, still embracing the notion of establishing a Jewish state in coexistence with the Arabs. The Jews, however, were restricted to the one quarter of the territory west of the Jordan River; the remainder eventually became the Kingdom of Jordan.

There had always been small numbers of Jews living in the Holy Land. Two English missionaries estimated that there were eight thousand to ten thousand Jews there in 1839, and the first Jewish agricultural settlement, Tiqva, was founded in 1878. Arabs far outnumbered Jews, however, until successive waves of immigrants began to arrive between 1919 and the late 1930s. The first major influx was about thirty-five thousand people, mainly from Russia, who arrived between 1919 and 1923. They influenced the character and organization of the growing Jewish community for decades to come, developing agriculture and establishing communal rural settlements, known as *kibbutz* and *moshav*. The next influx of some sixty thousand people arrived between 1924 and 1932, and they were primarily from Poland. These immigrants settled mainly in Tel Aviv, Haifa, and Jerusalem, where they were instrumental in developing urban life. The last major wave of immigration before World War II followed Hitler's rise to power in Germany. This contingent of about one hundred sixty-five thousand people was the first large-scale immigration from western and central Europe, and it brought many professionals and academics to the new land.

While the Jewish people did not have a right to self-government, the mandate that gave Britain control over Palestine set forth a mechanism for establishing a Jewish agency to represent the interests of the Jewish people and serve as a quasi-government. The World Zionist Organization filled this role initially. In 1929 the Jewish Agency was established to carry out the day-to-day relations with the British and the international community. The Haganah, founded in 1920, existed alongside the Jewish Agency as a defense militia to safeguard Jews from increasing attacks by their Arab neighbors. Beginning in the mid-1930s, Haganah also retaliated against Arabs and responded to British restrictions on Jewish immigration with mass demonstrations and sabotage of railways, ships used by the British to take illegal immigrants out of Palestine, and British military installations. Other underground groups would follow, some with more extreme agendas.

Each wave of Jewish immigration was greeted by a corresponding wave of hostility from Arab nationalists. They feared the displacement of tens of thousands of Arabs who had been living in Palestine for generations. The violence was intense at times, but as long as the British retained dominance over the Middle East and Jewish immigration was moderate, the situation remained tolerable, at least in London.

The growing threat of war, and Hitler's ascendancy, changed the diplomatic dynamic. More Jews were pressing to escape to the new Jewish state, which led to further outbreaks of violence from the imperiled Arab population. The British tried to ease the tensions in 1937 by proposing a partition into separate Jewish and Arab states, an idea that the Jews accepted and the Arabs rejected.

Fed up with the violence and fearing a convulsive escalation on the eve of war in Europe, the British government proposed a drastic solution—they would restrict Jewish immigration at the very time the Jews needed an escape route most. The solution was set forth in a "white paper," which was published in May 1939 and would remain the operating document for British policy in the region throughout the war. The details of paper are instructive because they quickly reversed two decades of British policy.

The first section of the paper renounced the British guarantee under the Balfour Declaration and said "unequivocally that it is not part of their policy that Palestine should become a Jewish State." Partition was abandoned in favor of creating a single state shared equally by Jews and Arabs. Land transfers to Jews were restricted to protect the Arab population. But it was the second regulation that caused the most outrage, and ultimately the biggest catastrophe.

The white paper said that Jewish immigration would be restricted to seventy-five thousand people over the next five years. Under the formula, ten thousand immigrants would be allowed each year, if the economy permitted their absorption. In addition, another twenty-five thousand refugees would be admitted if the British high commissioner felt there were adequate provisions for them. Within this category, special consideration would be given to children and dependents of people already in Palestine.

The white paper was a terrible setback for Jews. They felt betrayed, particularly because there had never been a greater need for large numbers of people to escape persecution. "It is in the darkest hour of Jewish history that the British government proposes to deprive the Jews of their last hope and to close the road back to their homeland," the Jewish Agency said in a public statement. "It is a cruel blow, doubly cruel because it comes from the government of a great nation which has extended a helping hand to the Jews, and whose position must now rest on foundations of moral authority and international good faith. This blow will not subdue the Jewish people. The historic bond between the people and the land of Israel cannot be broken. The Jews will never accept the closing to them of the gates of Palestine nor let their national home be converted into a ghetto."

The Jews sought to mobilize international opinion, and they found allies in the British government, too. Among them was Winston Churchill, the future prime minister, who was then part of the war cabinet and who had long been sympathetic to the Zionist cause. In a debate in the House of Commons on July 20, 1939, some members, most notably Churchill himself, spoke out vehemently against the policy, pointing out the dangers of trying to placate the Arabs. They spoke with sympathy about the illegal immigration, which was the only road left open. But their voices were not loud enough, and the hard-liners won the day. The white paper was approved, and its impact was evident in the sharp drop in legal immigrants at a time when Jews were most desperate to escape Europe. There were 19,005 legal Jewish immigrants to Palestine in 1939; more than half immigrated before the white paper went into effect. In 1940, the number was cut to 8,398.

The British decision had been spurred by more than Arab-Jewish violence alone. Another factor, one of incalculable significance, was the discovery of huge reserves of oil throughout the Persian Gulf in the 1930s. The discoveries had set off fevered efforts by foreign governments and companies to win concessions to control the oil. By 1940, the production still did not amount to much. Only about five percent of the world's oil was being produced across the entire Arabian Peninsula, while the United States produced sixty-three percent. America had a fading dominion, and most oil companies, as well as their countries' governments, recognized that the Arabs were sitting on oil that could tip the balance of world power in the future. And this created a motive to resist efforts by Jews to increase migration.

"If H.M.G. [Her Majesty's Government] were to yield to this pressure, the result would be a renewal of the Palestine rebellion, and probably anti-British uprisings in neighboring Arab countries, which would jeopardize our whole position in the Middle East," Thomas M. Snow, head of the Foreign Office Refugee Section and a former ambassador to Finland, wrote in a January 1941 memorandum. "And we must remember that our position in the Middle East is of the highest importance to us, in view of the world position in regard to oil, and also in regard to our imperial communications."

Snow's attitude reflected beliefs widely held in the Foreign Office and the Colonial Office, which together were responsible for the administration of Britain's colonies and other territories under its control, like Palestine. The policy could be interpreted most generously as representing the tough reality of geopolitics, the painful insistence of placing the good of the many over the good of the few. What his memo actually embodied was a view held by many senior government officials that the Jews simply were not important enough to merit consideration when weighed against the advantages of keeping the Arabs happy and the oil flowing.

The clearest evidence was in the next paragraph of Snow's memo, which said: "It therefore seems to the Eastern Department desirable that we should have some alternative scheme in hand for disposing of these surplus Jews who, having escaped from persecution in Europe, are going to be kept in detention camps in British Colonies. . . . And yet we must have some alternative in mind, other than the wreckage of our Middle Eastern policy."

The outbreak of the war had redefined the importance of the Middle East. Not only was the region a potentially key battleground, but also both sides were desperate for its oil to fuel their war machines. The British were pitted against the Germans, Italians, and the Japanese in a battle to influence the region's governments through diplomacy and financial assistance. Palestine was a critical piece on this strategic chessboard, and the British were playing to win.

Even as the position of Europe's Jews deteriorated throughout 1940 and into the following year, the British government maintained its insistence that the restrictions would not be lifted to admit more homeless Jews to Palestine. British patrol boats, though desperately needed for the war effort, constantly patrolled the coast of Palestine to intercept ships carrying illegal immigrants.

The British government also used every available diplomatic and legal means to keep the Jewish refugees at bay. The Foreign Office tried to persuade the governments of southeastern and central Europe to cooperate. The Bulgarians were warned as early as 1939 that any illegal immigrants caught aboard Bulgarian-flagged ships would be returned to Bulgaria. The Yugoslav government, under pressure from London, promised to exercise strict control over any Jews embarking ships sailing under its flag and to stop transit by Jews without valid visas. And in early 1940 the Romanians pledged to prevent ships carrying Jewish refugees from passing down the Danube River.

The Montreux Convention of 1936, on the other hand, forbade Turkey from stopping ships on the Bosporus, which the treaty declared an open international waterway. As a result, British efforts failed to close the critical passageway leading from the Black Sea to the Sea of Marmara and Mediterranean.

In Palestine, the British government imposed a law that enabled ships carrying illegal immigrants to be seized and their captains and crews imprisoned. When the groups tried to evade the law by sending immigrants ashore in dinghies, the British authorized naval vessels to intercept and confiscate ships on the high seas. The government knew that these seizures were illegal and amounted to piracy. The policy was pursued because no foreign government protested.

The measures had an effect. The rampant sea traffic of 1939 dwindled to a trickle by early 1940. But in the fall of 1940, as more Jews fled from German-occupied territory and the land and rail routes through Bulgaria to Turkey were closed by the war, the ships began to set sail again. The British effort, however, had produced one evident effect: it drove ticket prices to astronomical levels and sent the refugees to sea in unsafe ships that would not be missed if they were seized by the British.

In early September 1940, about three thousand refugees from Danzig, Prague, and Vienna sailed down the Danube on a convoy of four ships. When they reached the Romanian port of Tulcea, they were moved to three Greek cargo ships—the *Atlantic, Milos,* and *Pacific*—for the voyage to Palestine. They flew under the Panamanian flag, since Panama had effectively ignored British pressure to restrict its vessels.

The ships were overcrowded and conditions were terrible. The *Atlantic,* which carried 1,875 passengers, was in the worst shape, with women, children, and the elderly pressed into quarters so tight they could not stretch their limbs. "The boat was supplied with a little fuel and food which may be stretched to last a fortnight with utmost thrift," three passengers said in a later deposition. "The crew were apparently 'pirates.' In front of the lavatories, the number of which was by no means sufficient, there were long lines of people waiting. These conditions became almost unbearable when due to the bad food and the spoiled water, the majority of the passengers suffered from diarrhea."

When the *Atlantic* stopped in Istanbul, the local Jewish community provided a small measure of supplies before the ship left on October

16. It limped as far as Cyprus off the southern coast of Turkey, where it was intercepted by a British military craft and towed into port on November 12. The British governor refused to allow the passengers to disembark, though in a written report he lamented the conditions on the ship and said the passengers faced "an epidemic death toll" from illness and starvation.

The *Milos* and the *Pacific* made faster progress, arriving in the waters off Palestine at the beginning of November. The ships were intercepted by British naval vessels and escorted under guard to the port of Haifa. The passengers were transferred to a larger vessel, the *Patria*. The *Atlantic* arrived under escort from Cyprus a few days later, and it was anchored near the *Patria*.

The Colonial Office had been following the progress of the ships with alarm, and it issued dire warnings that the ships could carry enemy agents and young Jews who would threaten the security of Palestine. As an alternative, the British government decided to send the refugees to Mauritius, a volcanic island five hundred miles east of Madagascar in the Indian Ocean. The British had captured the island in 1810, and it was inhabited primarily by Indians imported to work in the sugar cane fields. The island's British governor agreed to accept up to four thousand refugees, so long as they brought their own bedding and were accompanied by guards and doctors.

The activities in Haifa increased dissension in London and among Zionists. Demonstrations and a one-day general strike were held in Palestine to protest the planned deportations. Chaim Weizmann, president of the World Zionist Organization, was a moderate on the issue of illegal immigration. He preferred to work with the British and he accepted their argument that the passengers may have included spies planted by the Nazis. In a meeting of Jewish advocates, Weizmann argued that Zionists should have nothing to do with the incident because the three thousand people "might later turn out to be a millstone round their neck." Berl Locker, another Zionist leader, objected to Weizmann's remarks and reminded the committee members that "among these refugees were many of their own people—*halutzim*, Zionists, and persons having near relatives in Palestine."

The dispute reflected the essential ambivalence that would mark official Zionist policy toward the illegal immigration throughout the war years. David Ben-Gurion, the president of the Jewish Agency, came to doubt the wisdom of jeopardizing cooperation with the British by openly supporting the illegal immigration. Rather than fighting for greater illegal immigration, he viewed the Jewish Agency's role as helping to gain residency for those illegal immigrants who had already arrived and avoiding activities that would weaken Britain's position in the war. He did not go so far as to accept that the agency should take no role in the illegal immigration, but he was ambivalent about it.

The second-most influential person on the issue of illegal immigration was Moshe Shertok, the head of the political department of the Jewish Agency. His views were similar to those of Ben-Gurion: he believed that the way for the Jewish people to win concessions from the British on legal immigration and other issues was to cooperate and negotiate. His priority was supporting the British effort against Hitler, so he rejected calls from less moderate officials that the agency make illegal immigration a major campaign. Still, like Ben-Gurion, Shertok rejected the idea of abandoning illegal immigrants.

Ambivalence also marked the attitude of Sir Winston Churchill during the war years. Though he was clearly sympathetic to the plight of the Jewish people and Zionism in general, perhaps the most sympathetic of the senior British officials, Churchill also had to weigh the opinions of his military commanders and the hard-liners in the Colonial Office, who argued that allowing too many Jews into Palestine threatened to anger the Arabs and disrupt the flow of oil.

By the time the *Milos, Pacific,* and *Atlantic* arrived in Haifa harbor, Churchill had become prime minister and his sympathies carried substantial weight. On November 13 the Colonial Office sent him a memorandum outlining plans to deport the passengers to Mauritius. "Provided these refugees are not sent back to the torments from which they have escaped and are decently treated in Mauritius, I agree," replied Churchill. The prime minister was alarmed a few days later, however, when he learned that the refugees would be held in a concentration camp on the island. The day he heard the news, Churchill wrote: "I had never contemplated the Jewish refugees being interned in Mauritius in a camp surrounded by barbed wire and guards. It is very unlikely that these refugees would include enemy agents, and I should expect that the Jewish authorities themselves, as Weizmann can assure you, would be most efficient and vigilant purgers in this respect."

Churchill said the passengers should be interrogated and allowed to remain in Palestine. A telegram was sent to the high commissioner for Palestine, telling him to delay announcing the deportations. It arrived too late. The plans had been announced already. Faced with the public disclosure, Churchill relented, saying that the deportations should proceed, since the policy had been announced.

Then, a tragic event intervened.

On November 25, 1940, passengers were being transferred from the *Atlantic* to the *Patria* to begin the voyage south to Mauritius. The people from the *Milos* and *Pacific* were already on board. As the *Atlantic* transfer started, an explosion tore through the *Patria,* killing 267 people. One of the victims was a baby born on the ship the previous day. Suspicion fell correctly on militant Zionists determined to block the departure. Saboteurs from Haganah, the underground Jewish army, had set off the explosion to prevent the ship's departure. They had miscalculated and used too much explosive. A political act had turned into a tragedy.

The survivors were transferred to an internment camp at Athlit in Palestine. Despite the deaths, the British government refused to stop the deportation. The passengers would be sent to Mauritius on the next available ship and forbidden to set foot in Palestine. The military backed the deportation, arguing that failure to do so would harm relations with the Arabs.

Churchill found the deportation of survivors from such a tragedy to be so callous that it was dishonorable. "Personally I hold it would be an act of inhumanity unworthy of the British name to force them to re-embark," he wrote to General Archibald Wavell, the British military commander in chief in the Middle East. "I wonder whether the effect on the Arab world will be as bad as you suggest. If their attachment to our cause is so slender as to be determined by a mere act of charity of this kind it is clear that our policy of conciliating them has not borne much fruit so far. What I think would influence them much more would be any kind of British military success."

Wavell, however, continued to oppose allowing the survivors to remain. He warned: "From a military point of view it is disastrous. It will be spread all over the Arab world that the Jews have again successfully challenged a decision of the British government.... It will again be spread abroad that only violence pays in dealing with the British."

The deaths on the *Patria* led to a public outcry among Jews in Palestine and elsewhere and demands that the British prove the allegation that there had been Nazi infiltrators among the refugees, something the government was never able to do. The prospect of deporting the survivors also outraged the Zionist community. Shertok got into a fierce argument with Sir Harold MacMichael, the British high commissioner for Palestine and the person with overall responsibility for dealing with immigration in the country. When Shertok begged that the deportation orders be lifted for the survivors to avoid potential violence by others, MacMichael callously replied, "Well, governments have sometimes to face unpleasant situations."

The two central figures in crafting the anti-immigration policy were MacMichael and Walter E. Guinness, an aristocratic landowner who was secretary of state for the colonies and leader of the House of Lords. Guinness had been elevated and became Lord Moyne in 1932 and later served as minister of agriculture. When he took over the Colonial Office in 1941, his opposition to Jewish immigration to Palestine became hard policy. Both men saw the immigration in strictly military and political terms, without regard for its humanitarian aspects. Moyne's comments sometimes betrayed the anti-Semitism that lurked among some of London's aristocrats, and he would later challenge Churchill himself, saying that the prime minister's "extreme Zionism" clashed with the hard facts of the Palestine situation.

There were hard-liners on immigration in both the Colonial Office and the Foreign Office, though the Foreign Office authorities tended to take a slightly more tolerant view. In the wake of the *Patria* disaster, the Foreign Office cautioned against indiscriminate use of the claim that German spies were infiltrating the ranks of refugee groups. Rather, the office said, the argument should be used only in cases where there was absolute proof that Nazi agents had been found among refugees.

"I cannot help feeling that we have been sailing a little close to the wind," complained Thomas Snow of the Foreign Office. "If it is really the case that neither the authorities in Palestine or here know definitely that a single agent has arrived in this way, we would suggest that there is reason for caution in including this argument in our propaganda."

Although the 267 deaths were caused directly by the Jewish underground, the horror had the effect of momentarily softening attitudes in the British government toward the survivors enough that the cabinet accepted Churchill's position and reversed MacMichael's decision. The survivors were allowed to remain in Palestine, though they were placed in the internment camp. This was, however, an exception, and the overall British policy was unaffected.

In fact, the fifteen hundred passengers who were still on the *Atlantic* when the explosion occurred were deemed not to be covered by the new decision, and they were ordered to return to the *Atlantic* to proceed to Mauritius. MacMichael insisted on carrying out their deportation immediately. Many resisted when the police came to the internment camp, stripping off their clothes and refusing to move or pick up their luggage. Eyewitnesses accused the British authorities of brutality as they forced the people, many of them hurt and naked, onto the ship. The British rejected the allegations of brutality. What was irrefutable, however, was the outbreak of typhoid that occurred on the journey, killing twenty-two people. Another nineteen died from other causes on the trip.

Chapter 8

On December 12, three days after the *Atlantic* resumed its journey to Mauritius, the *Salvador,* a wooden boat with a small auxiliary engine, left the Bulgarian port of Varna with 333 Jews from Bulgaria and other central European countries.

The British government sent cables urging the Turkish government not to allow the ship to pass the Dardanelles and go on to the Aegean Sea and ultimately the Mediterranean and Palestine. The cables turned out to be unnecessary. The ship would not get that far.

The *Salvador*'s engine quit on the Black Sea, and it was towed into Istanbul by a passing motorboat just ahead of a massive winter storm. The ship was given permission to wait out the storm in the harbor, though no one was allowed off because the passengers lacked landing papers or visas. The storm relented slightly by evening, and after receiving some fuel and food, the ship weighed anchor and headed into the Sea of Marmara.

The weather was still bitter, with strong winds and sleet pelting the small ship. Not far outside the harbor, the *Salvador* hit submerged rocks near the coast. It started to break apart, the aged wood splintering and sending its passengers into the icy water.

Simon Brod, who worked for the Jewish Agency in Istanbul, had spent the day arranging provisions for the *Salvador*. He was a short, energetic man who had abandoned his family textile business to devote himself to helping refugees fleeing Nazi persecution. Over the years, he would prove himself a savior to thousands of Jews who passed through Istanbul, by land and by sea.

A friend within the police force telephoned Brod's home that night with word that the *Salvador* was sinking. He jumped into his black car and raced to the Park Hotel, a spot popular with diplomats and spies, and directly across the street from the huge German consulate. He went to a room and knocked on the door. The door was opened by a bleary-eyed young woman, Ruth Kluger.

Kluger was an agent of the Mossad, the secret arm of the Jewish Agency in Palestine and predecessor of Israel's intelligence service. In the early days of World War II, the Mossad was orchestrating the illegal immigration of Jews, and Kluger was one of its only women operatives. She later recounted her days of helping Jews escape in a book, *The Last Escape,* written with Peggy Mann.

A Romanian Jew who had emigrated to Palestine in the 1930s, she posed as a real estate agent selling land to Jews in her homeland, but her real job was organizing ships bound for Palestine. She had come to Istanbul to make final arrangements for a shipload of Jews who would be leaving Romania in the coming weeks. Brod had been assisting in that effort, which was proving extremely difficult, and seemed suddenly unimportant in light of his startling news.

"What is it?" she asked as she opened the door and saw Brod.

"A ship of illegals is sinking in the Sea of Marmara," he said. "We must get there at once. My car is downstairs. Hurry, for God's sake."

A strong slashing snow pelted the car as it careened down the narrow streets to the Galata Bridge over the Golden Horn. Sirens cut through the darkness.

"Now they come to help," Brod said, sobbing softly. "They commit the murder. Then they come to pull in the bodies."

"What was the name of the ship?" asked Kluger.

"*Salvador*. In Spanish it means savior."

As they rounded a curve beyond the domes of Topkapi Palace, they encountered a frenzied scene. Rescue workers were standing waist deep in the water, reaching for swimmers trying to reach the shore. A few hundred yards out, they could see the tilted mast and the hulk of the sinking ship.

This was the nightmare that Kluger and the Mossad had feared. They had been loath to put refugees aboard the unseaworthy ships that were being offered by scoundrels as illegal transportation to Palestine. But their greater fear was leaving those same people behind to face the ravages of the Nazis. In the end, the Mossad decided it was better to face the risks of a calamity at sea than the prospect of death at the hands of the Reich.

Kluger had no time to indulge in sorrow or second-guesses. She stifled her emotions and waded out into the water in search of survivors. The waves knocked her over as she reached for someone's hand, and the person disappeared beneath the surface. Nearby she saw a child's limp body slip under the water and reached down desperately, grabbing the child's hair and pulling her up. She struggled to get her to some rocks near the beach.

She carried the child to Brod's car and went back for other victims. Other rescuers had come with blankets, horses, and donkeys. When the black limousine was filled with victims, Kluger later wrote that a stranger drove her and the others to the hospital. On the way the driver spoke to her in German. "I tried to save my wife," he said. "But I couldn't. I saw her drown. We have a little girl named Gretchen. Three years old. She doesn't know how to swim. I looked and looked for her in the water. But I couldn't see her. She doesn't know how to swim."

Two hundred refugees drowned that night. Seventy of them were children. The 133 survivors were permitted to remain in Istanbul, pending a decision on their fate. News of the deaths rippled through the Jewish community in Europe and Palestine.

The British blamed the tragedy on the Bulgarians for allowing the rickety vessel to leave Varna. They also saw to it that the sinking and deaths were publicized widely in a callous attempt to exploit the event to slow the traffic of illegal immigrants.

Five days after the sinking, a British official wrote to a colleague: "If anything can deter these poor devils from setting out for Zion, that story should." The colleague, Thomas Snow, the hard-liner in the Foreign Office, replied that he could not imagine a more opportune disaster to frighten potential refugees into suspending the illegal ferrying.

Other British officials recognized that even disasters like the *Salvador* and the *Patria* would not outweigh the horrors occurring under the Nazis. "We broadcast to Central Europe accounts of these sufferings and risks," said Richard T. E. Latham of the Foreign Office in a December 28, 1940, report. "But there is no ground for hope that, so long as Hitler is in power, there will be any lack of candidates for the adventure. The risks are known in Central Europe, and there is every reason for thinking that Jews who embark on these voyages do so with their eyes open to them. The hazards of the journey are therefore no more likely to stop the traffic than are the penalties we inflict."

Near the end of his long report, Latham raised the prospect of sinking ships carrying illegal Jewish refugees. "This is the only way in which the traffic can with certainty be stopped," he wrote. "It is, however, a step which, for obvious reasons, His Majesty's Government would hardly be prepared in any circumstances to authorise."

Even as the *Salvador* was sinking, arrangements were continuing to prepare for more illegal refugees to sail on the *Darien II,* a four-hundred-ton ship that the Mossad had purchased. In fact, Kluger had gone to Istanbul to try to resolve a crisis that threatened to stop that vessel.

The issue of illegal immigration, or *aliyah bet,* as it was called in Hebrew, had divided the Jewish community since the British white paper. On one side were the so-called Legalists. They contended that breaking the law would only anger the British and lead to more restrictions. Indeed, the British threatened to freeze all legal immigration if the illegal actions did not stop. The restrictions could be lifted, insisted the Legalists, only through cooperation and persuasion. The Legalists dominated the Jewish Agency and its militia, Haganah. Opposing them were the agents of the Mossad, Betar, and other semisecret organizations of the *aliyah bet.* They argued that the Holocaust left no room for moderation. They had no patience with talk of lawful and unlawful immigration when thousands of Jews were dying.

The dispute over the *Darien* exemplified the divisions. Haganah was working with British intelligence in the Balkans in sabotage missions against the Germans. One of the most important missions was finding a way to stop Romanian oil from flowing to the German forces. Haganah and MI-6, the British intelligence service, hatched a secret scheme to sink the *Darien* in the middle of the Danube River to block the oil transports.

Backed by the Jewish Agency in Palestine, Haganah officials ordered that the *Darien* be turned over to the British, who would sail it up the Danube and blow it up. Some within Haganah and the Mossad objected, and a dispute broke out, with Kluger and her associates refusing to turn over the ship that they had purchased for transporting illegal refugees. On January 3, 1941, Chaim Weizmann entered the controversy, ordering that the ship be turned over to the British and warning that failure to do so could disrupt relations with British intelligence.

There were divisions and heated arguments within Mossad, when Kluger and other agents met in Istanbul. In the end, the agents in Istanbul controlled the ship's fate, and they refused to follow orders. Nothing was more important than saving Jewish lives, they argued. To buy time, they told their superiors that the ship would be turned over to British intelligence when repairs and refurbishing in Greece were completed.

The ship, however, was ready and was dispatched to Constanta on the Black Sea, where several hundred Jews had been assembled from across Romania. On February 19, 1941, less than a month after the Iron Guard pogrom, the *Darien* was loaded with its initial cargo of refugees. It then stopped at Varna to pick up Bulgarian refugees before continuing to Istanbul.

The British government did not want the *Darien* to reach Palestine. They tried to persuade the Turkish government to block its passage and force all of the passengers to be returned to their countries of origin. Ankara refused, explaining that it had no legal authority to stop a vessel on the Bosporus and no reason to do so on the Sea of Marmara.

In Istanbul, the ship picked up seventy survivors from the *Salvador*.

Turkish authorities already had deported sixty-three of the survivors back to Bulgaria. The others had managed to remain in the city until the arrival of the *Darien* and they were permitted to leave on it.

The *Darien* arrived in Palestinian waters on March 19 with 793 passengers. The ship was intercepted by a British patrol boat and escorted to Haifa. The passengers were interned at the Athlit camp. The British were angered by the ship's arrival, fearing that it spelled the beginning of wholesale illegal immigration by sea. So they became more determined to crack down on illegal ships, promising to use the navy and every other means at their disposal to halt them. Indeed, the *Darien* would prove to be the last major refugee vessel to make it to Palestine.

But other ships would try to follow the *Darien*. On January 4, 1941, before the *Darien* sailed, the British vice counsel in Bucharest, F. P. Baker, sent a memo under the title "M/V *Struma*" to London. An aging vessel called the *Struma* had been sold to a group of Bulgarian businessmen and was being converted to carry refugees to Palestine. "Bunks have been installed to accommodate a great number of passengers—to allow overcrowding, in fact," he said. "The vessel is now ready to put out on a contraband voyage," said Baker.

Chapter 9

Late September, 1941

Darkness was approaching quickly. One by one faint lights appeared in windows. The small group of people felt exposed in the empty streets of the once friendly city that now seemed like a trap.

David Frenk felt closely watched. The slightest noise echoed like a rifle shot as he and his brother, Israel, guided their friends through the streets of Czernowitz to the midnight rendezvous with a German major. This was the group's second escape attempt. If they did not make it this time, they feared the *Struma* would sail without them.

A few weeks earlier, the brothers had arranged for an Italian air force officer stationed nearby to help them and a dozen friends get to Bucharest, three hundred miles to the south. There they intended to meet up with others planning the journey by sea to Palestine. A friend had put them in touch with the Italian. He promised to drive the whole group for one million lei, or about twenty-five hundred dollars, all of the money they could gather.

When the time came, the group went to a spot in a forest outside the city at the designated time, two o'clock in the morning. They shivered with excitement and fear, and they waited. Night passed and dawn arrived, with no sign of the Italian. Finally, as the disheartened people were about to give up, he walked into the clearing. He was pale and frightened.

"We're not going," the Italian said, staring at the ground.

Everyone was stunned. Hearts sank, and finally Israel Frenk spoke up. "Why not?" he demanded. "We've waited all night for you."

"When I left the air base, they wrote down the number of my car," said the Italian, with fear showing on his face. "They never did that before."

They begged him to change his mind. They tried to convince him that it was a small matter. The Italian officer refused. Before leaving the clearing in the forest, he returned the money he had been given in advance, and the would-be escapees slipped back into their hiding places.

At the apartment, disappointment turned to anxiety. The news on the street was that the Germans and Romanians were going to start deporting Jews to a permanent internment camp in Transnistria any day. Nearly fifty thousand people had been jammed into the city's ghetto for weeks. They were growing weak from hunger, and many would probably not survive the deportation. The Frenks and their friends were among the lucky few who had found refuge outside the ghetto. They feared their days were numbered.

"We knew this was our last chance to get out of hell," Israel Frenk remembers. "We thought we would go crazy. Suddenly we had a crazy idea. Let's go straight to the lion and tempt it to save us."

One of the young men in the group agreed to contact a German soldier stationed in the city. He had known him before the war. It was an enormous risk, but the group agreed they had no alternative. The soldier agreed to ask around quietly for someone willing to help them escape, for a large sum of money.

Days passed, with the clock ticking down. Then one evening the young man brought news. A major in the German air force said he would drive them to Bucharest if the price was right.

They met with him the following night. The major demanded an exorbitant amount, more than they had. The Frenks promised to get him the rest of the money at their sister's house in Bucharest. The German agreed.

"I want you to know that even though I'm taking you, to me you are still damn Jews," he snarled. "And the Reich does not mind if they kill you here or in Bucharest."

The Frenks and their friends did not react. They simply wanted the ride. They agreed to meet at midnight in the forest the next day. The German arrived with another soldier, a sergeant. They were driving a large truck with a covered bed. He looked at the Frenk brothers, Israel's wife, Tivia, and the twenty other people, men, women, and a handful of children, gathered in the forest. When he saw that one family had brought a baby, he hesitated.

"What do we do if that baby starts crying at a checkpoint?" he demanded.

They were not willing to leave the infant behind. It was the German, eager for his money, who came up with a solution. The sergeant went to a nearby farm and stole a small pig. If the baby cried, they were to poke and pinch the pig so that its squeals drowned out the infant.

Two families were late. The German said he had wasted enough time getting the pig. He refused to wait any longer, and he ordered them into the rear of the truck, pulled the tarp over the back, and headed toward Bucharest. The truck's papers read: "Attention! Ammunition!" Perhaps it would be enough to scare away prying eyes.

They passed through several checkpoints without a problem. About fifty miles from Bucharest, as the sun was rising, the major stopped the truck. He walked to the back, threw up the tarp, and ordered everyone out. He said there were too many checkpoints into the city, and it was getting too light. They would have to make it the rest of the way on their own.

"We're not getting out now," the group said. "Kill us now if you want."

They had heard stories of people who promised to smuggle Jews out of harm's way and killed them instead. They figured they stood a better chance if they remained in the truck.

The major was uncertain of what to do. He did not want to attract attention by stopping in the road with a truckload of Jews. He called the sergeant over, and they spoke in hushed tones. Then he walked back to the truck.

"Get out you scum," he shouted. "They will catch you and slaughter you like pigs at the next roadblock."

"We are not getting off," the young men said. "You can kill us right here."

The major was infuriated, but he was afraid to kill twenty people in the back of his truck. The mess would be hard to explain. "Get down," he said at last. "You stink. At the next checkpoint they will find you and kill you like pigs." Then he walked back to the cab and headed down the road passing checkpoints and moving fast toward Bucharest.

At the final checkpoint outside the city, the search promised to be more thorough. The people could hear the soldiers demanding to see the papers and telling the major and his assistant to get out of the truck. Sensing the tension, the baby started to cry. Someone poked the pig hard. It squealed and squealed.

They could hear the boots of the soldiers scraping across the road as they headed toward the rear of the truck to investigate the noise. Suddenly the phone rang in the guard post. A subordinate called out to the officer in charge of the inspection, and he went inside to get a phone call from a woman. As he walked away, he gestured at the truck and said, "Okay, you can go on." Later, David Frenk said, "That girl saved our lives. And when I am looking back now, I do not have anything against that man. Somebody else would have taken our money and then murdered us. At least he brought us to Bucharest."

Inside the city, the major followed the directions to the house of Frenk's sister. He knocked on the door. When a woman opened it, he said, "I've brought your brothers. Give me the rest of my money."

The sister fainted. Her husband paid the German as the escapees from Czernowitz piled out of the truck and into the house.

Chapter 10

A few days later in Bucharest, the Frenks learned about the horrors they had escaped as word arrived of the initial deportations to Transnistria. In early October 1941, the first fifteen hundred people were forced out of the ghetto in Kishinev, Bessarabia, the majority forced to make the eight-day journey to the internment camp on foot, with little food or protection against the plunging temperatures.

In a protest to General Antonescu, Wilhelm Filderman, the Jewish leader in Bucharest, begged for a halt to the deportations. "Only the sick, the aged, and children left in carts," he said. "This is death, death, death of innocent people with no other guilt than that of being Jews. I implore you again . . . not to permit such a staggering tragedy to take place."

In his reply, the Romanian leader justified the harsh treatment of the Jews of Bessarabia and Bukovina, arguing that they had sided with the Soviets. He accused them of committing atrocities against Romanian citizens and soldiers, of mutilating wounded troops and conspiring with the Communists. And he chided Filderman sharply for daring to enter a plea on their behalf. "Did you ask yourself why did Jews in Bessarabia burn their homes before fleeing?" Antonescu said. "Can you explain why we found 14- and 15-year-old Jewish children with their pockets full of hand grenades when we returned? Did you ask yourself how many of my people were treacherously killed by Jews? How many were interred alive? If you want proof, you shall have proof."

Filderman and Antonescu had been schoolmates, and the Jewish leader was able to keep his lines of communication open only through the use of the most diplomatic language. A month earlier he had persuaded the leader to rescind an order that Bucharest's Jews wear the dread yellow badge identifying them as Jews, which Hitler had ordered them to wear on September 1. The order had already been imposed in the provinces, and it would have been another devastating blow to the community in Bucharest. People wearing it would have been forbidden to ride public transportation or enter government offices, and they would have become easy targets for attacks. Filderman appealed to Antonescu's nationalism, arguing that the badge was only for German-occupied countries. Romania, he said, was not occupied by Germany.

Faced with Antonescu's attack on Jews in Bessarabia and Bukovina, Filderman conceded that some Russian Jews had attacked Romanian troops. He said he deplored their actions and pledged the loyalty of Romanian Jews, and he still asked for an end to the deportations. There was no evidence of widespread atrocities committed by Jews, and the isolated acts of resistance did not justify the wholesale slaughter and mass deportation of the region's Jewish population.

Antonescu's reply this time was even more vitriolic. Separating the Jews who had lived historically in Romania from those of Bessarabia and Bukovina, Antonescu declared that any Jew who had arrived in Romania after 1914 would be deported. "Only Jews from the old kingdom who came here before 1914 will be allowed to stay, if they abide by the laws of the land, except those who are Communists, spread subversive propaganda, who associate themselves with the enemies of our nation, and who attempt sabotage, one way or another," he railed. "We now have to defend our Romanian rights in our own country because our tolerance and hospitality have tempted others, mostly Jews, to take advantage of us."

After the Romanian occupation, conditions in Kishinev had deteriorated. Fires started by the Red Army as they retreated in the face of the German-Romanian advance in July 1941 had consumed large sections of the city. Armed bands of thugs and out-of-control soldiers roamed the streets, stealing and murdering almost at will.

Samuel Aroni was fourteen years old when he and his family

sought refuge with his paternal grandfather after they were driven from their home in Kishinev on the morning of July 24. Within hours, two Romanian soldiers arrived to rob and threaten everyone in the house. The whole family was lined up against the wall, with guns aimed at them.

"I clearly remember my thoughts, at the age of fourteen, when I believed I was going to die," Aroni later wrote in a personal report on the persecution in Bessarabia. "My six-year-old brother was put on a table with his hands held high in surrender. I remember realizing for the first time that my parents could not protect me."

The soldiers left after robbing them of all their valuables. That evening the family fled to the ghetto in the lower part of the city. The grandfather, Aaron-Iosef Cervinschi, refused to leave his home. Later that night, the soldiers returned and dragged the old man from the house by his white beard and deposited him in the ghetto.

The survivors of the early killings, nearly fifteen thousand people, had been herded into the neighborhood and surrounded by fencing and guards. They were allowed to take few of their belongings, and the ghetto was chronically short of water and food.

After a few months, during which hundreds more people were executed, Antonescu decided to deport all of the surviving Jews from Bessarabia and Bukovina to the camps of Transnistria, the renamed part of the Ukraine that the Germans had given Romania as a bounty for joining the war. The Kishinev ghetto was being liquidated, and the starved people, who lacked strength and health, were terrified of the long march and the expectation of new brutality and deprivation.

On the morning of October 15, a Wednesday, the Aroni family slipped through the fence surrounding the ghetto and made their way to the railway station. They were helped by three Romanian policemen who had been paid and sent by Monia Apotecher, an uncle from Bucharest. Sam and his younger brother, Shraga, were accompanied by their parents, an aunt and uncle, and the aunt's sister. Sam's maternal grandmother had left the previous day on the same journey, driven to Bucharest by a Romanian army major who was a family friend.

The policemen provided the family with papers identifying them as police prisoners who were under arrest and being transported to Bucharest. Aaron Cervinschi, an orthodox Jew, refused to shave his beard for the journey, so he would have been identified immediately as a Jew. He also insisted that he would not leave his spiritual leader, the Skvere Rebbe. Cervinschi chose to stay behind, and he would later perish on the death march or in the camps of Transnistria. After the war, the family changed its name to Aroni in his honor.

With false travel papers provided by the Romanians, the rest of the family boarded a train for Bucharest. The train was filled with soldiers returning from the front, many of whom had been injured. Frequently the family heard soldiers say, "There are *jidani* on the train," using a derogatory term for Jews. At each stop, the family moved to another car in the hope that they would not attract attention for too long a time. Shraga was suffering from scarlet fever, and in his sleep he often talked aloud in Russian. The family struggled to keep him silent so that the Russian would not draw unwanted attention.

The train arrived in Bucharest about five o'clock on the morning of October 16, after a nineteen-hour terror-filled journey. The Romanian agents took them to the apartment of Monia Apotecher, who had hired police. The family lived in hiding in an apartment arranged by Monia and made plans to reach their ultimate destination, Palestine.

Jews who lived in Bucharest had more freedom of movement than those who were imprisoned in the ghettos of Bessarabia and Bukovina, although the vise was tightening in the capital, too. On October 20, Romanian newspapers published a decree requiring all Jews to contribute to the authorities exorbitant quantities of clothing and other articles in proportion to their income. For example, a person with an income of twenty dollars a month was required to provide twelve each of shirts, undershirts, underwear, towels, and pairs of socks, and four each of suits, overcoats, hats, pairs of shoes, blankets, and bedsheets. The goods were to be provided to needy Christians. Those Jews who failed to comply with the decree faced prison.

"Naturally, these unconscionable demands have panicked anew the Jewish population, shocked all sober observers, and even drawn the sharp and ashamed criticism of thinking and intelligent Romanians," Franklin Mott Gunther, the American ambassador in Bucharest, said at the time.

The rose-colored glasses were gone. The decree and the continuing flow of news about the fate of Jews in the provinces created a near panic in Bucharest. "There is not one Jew in Bucharest who does not want to emigrate," concluded a report by the World Jewish Congress. The problem was how to get out of the country.

Chapter 11

An immensely bloated mountain of a man, Jean D. Pandelis was a shipping agent of last resort for the illegal immigration movement. With offices in Bucharest and Constanta and a network of contacts from the Balkans to Greece, he used cajolery, bribery, and lies to scrounge ships for refugees. Far from altruistic, the Greek-born businessman was earning a fortune arranging the illicit transportation.

"My price is a firm one," he told Mossad representatives in the summer of 1939, as the illegal immigration struggle was getting under way on the eve of the war. "If your people prefer to pay the standard cruise fare, let them go on *legal* ships."

That was an unlikely option. Because of the war effort, few legal ships remained, so the Mossad and others organizing the immigration had little choice except to deal with Pandelis and meet his extortionate prices. Most decent ships had been requisitioned by the military, and owners of most of the remaining vessels feared confiscation by the British if they carried illegal immigrants. The result was a marked deterioration in the quality of available ships. The shortage contributed to the higher prices, and so did the bribes paid to port and customs officials, the cost of material to transform aging ships into passenger vessels, and the pervasive greed up and down the line.

Under the code name "Shamen," or "Fat One," Pandelis helped the Mossad transport 1,400 refugees from Bulgaria, Czechoslovakia, Poland, and Romania to Palestine aboard the *Tiger Hill*. The voyage ended when a British patrol boat fired on the ship and killed two passengers. The others had landed safely in September 1939. In the months that followed, Pandelis helped with other ships, like the *Hilda,* which carried 726 refugees to Palestine, and the *Darien,* with its nearly 800 passengers.

By the fall of 1941, the supply of seaworthy vessels had dwindled even further and ticket prices had risen even higher. The deaths on the *Patria* and the *Salvador* and the internment of those who had made it to Palestine had sapped the resolve of some of the supporters of the *aliyah bet.* In the aftermath of the *Darien* episode, the Mossad had pulled its agents out of Romania and Istanbul. Yet even the risks of internment or sinking seemed more appealing to many than the consequences of staying in Romania.

A year earlier, Pandelis had tried to interest the Mossad agents in the *Struma* as a candidate for a voyage. The ship was old and in terrible condition. It was first registered in 1830 as the *Macedonia* and at the time it was a two-masted sailing vessel. It weighed one hundred thirty tons and it was one hundred fifty feet long, with a maximum width of slightly less than eighteen feet. Over the years, a small auxiliary engine had been added and its weak wooden sides buttressed with metal plates. Before World War II, its Bulgarian owners had used the ship as a cattle barge on the Danube, but by the time war broke out it was deemed so unfit for sea travel that the German military had not bothered to requisition it.

The Mossad had intended to lash the *Struma* to a larger and more powerful ship, the *Darien,* to enable another two hundred or so additional passengers to escape earlier in 1941. But the German occupation of Bulgaria had stranded the smaller ship there, and the *Darien* had eventually sailed alone.

Later Pandelis had made arrangements to get the *Struma* towed to Constanta. Refitted and sailing under a Panamanian flag, he planned to use it in the refugee trade. He had contacted the New Zionist Organization, a right-wing group also known as the Revisionists, and proposed that they organize refugees for a voyage. The Revisionists agreed, and in turn enlisted the militant young Zionists in the Betar to find passengers. Pandelis set about preparing the ship.

The plans were not a secret. Word of the ship traveled quickly through the Jewish community, with help from the two groups. Bickering broke out between the Revisionists and the Betar over the advisability of the voyage. Support for the illegal immigration had waned in many quarters, and many Zionists in Romania were having doubts because of the dangerous condition of the ships and the British blockade of Palestine. The two groups also argued over how many of the young Zionists would be allowed to go on the ship. Few of them had the money for a ticket, and nearly one hundred were insisting on going without charge. They argued that their costs should be spread among the paying passengers, since they were organizing the voyage. In the end, the Revisionists withdrew from the organizing effort and the Betar took over.

In September and October, the Romanian press carried regular advertisements for passage on the *Struma,* which had been placed by two Jews affiliated with the Revisionists who had set up a company, Turismul Mondial, near Capsa's restaurant on Calea Victoriei in Bucharest. The initial ticket price was thirty thousand lei, or about one hundred dollars: children under twelve years old were half that amount. Everyone needed to get his or her own exit visa from Romania, and the organizers promised that entry permits for Palestine would be ready and waiting in Istanbul. Initially the sailing date was September 30, 1941, but the departure date was pushed back to October 8, then to the end of the month as repairs to the ship dragged on.

Demand increased as time passed. Crowds gathered daily in the courtyard near the company's office, begging for a ticket on the ship. To make matters worse, refugees from the countryside were pouring into Bucharest. They slept in hallways around the office and in the courtyard, stacking their meager belongings beside them and waiting for an opportunity to escape.

Pandelis took advantage of the delays and the rising terror by insisting on more money. On top of that, the number of nonpaying Betar members on the ship kept going up, which meant passing on more costs to paying passengers. As the first sailing date came and went without departure, the organizers canceled the tickets that had been sold. People were told that they had to buy a new ticket at a higher fare to cover rising costs of ship preparation. By the time the ship sailed, the price of a ticket would increase dramatically.

Despite the prices, no one expected a luxury cruise, but the wreck of the *Salvador* and the loss of some smaller craft had caused anxiety. To reassure skittish passengers, the Betar put together flowery instructions and descriptions of the ship that would turn out to be fiction.

Prospective passengers were offered photographs of what was described as the ship's new 240-horsepower diesel engine and cabins with six beds. Details were spelled out in a written prospectus that read like a summer camp brochure. Passengers were allowed to bring twenty kilograms of luggage, which was to include three sets of garments, an overcoat, six sets of underwear, toiletries, a watch, a wedding ring, a fountain pen, three sets of bedding, and a blanket. Passengers were instructed to bring their own plates and cutlery, along with a thermos and a flashlight. There would be tea in the morning and full meals for everyone at lunch and dinner. There also would be medical facilities.

The prospectus also carried the stamp of Zionist idealism, tempered with a dose of reality. Passengers would be organized into groups of twenty, with a leader assigned to each one to supervise food distribution, access to the washing facilities, and sharing of chores.

"The instant you step on board the *Struma* you start a trip toward a new life, and all differences of rank and class must disappear," said the instructions, recognizing that the high price of the tickets meant that most of the passengers would be wealthy professionals and their families.

"You are Jews on your way to your own country and a new kind of life," it read.

"Bon Voyage.

"Welcome to Palestine!

"On reading this document you are advised to get used to the idea that this is not a pleasure trip. It involves living with 600 people in a cramped space bereft of comfort, on a sea that is often turbulent, and far from the comfort you were accustomed to in your home, and you must adapt to this new situation.

"Consider yourselves equals, Jews, brothers, and help one another as good brothers do."

In conclusion, passengers were cautioned to bring medication for seasickness and, if they became ill and needed fresh air, to avoid crowding the small deck so the balance of the ship would not be disrupted.

Horia Lobel was a young neurologist in Bucharest. When the government imposed its restrictions on Jews in the military, he had lost his position as an army captain. Like most Jewish professionals, his job prospects were nonexistent in Romania. Eager to escape with his wife, he heard about the *Struma* and went to the office on Calea Victoriei. Lobel did not have enough money for two tickets, so he offered his services as ship's doctor. The organizers accepted and guaranteed passage for him and his wife, Rosalie, who was pregnant.

Jews were forbidden to travel outside their own communities in Romania, but Lobel insisted on personally inspecting the ship before the voyage. Pandelis arranged for him to go to Constanta. He was horrified by what he saw. The ship was old and tiny, far too small for the hundreds of passengers expected to go. The tiny engine was not new and it did not look big enough to power the ship out of the harbor, let alone through the Black Sea and the Mediterranean to Palestine. The promised hospital was not there and neither were other necessities required for a safe trip, including storage tanks for fresh water and bathrooms.

His complaints were met with promises. Repairs were being made. The engine was more than adequate for the voyage. He and his wife would have better conditions than other passengers. He was assured that the ship would be supplied with the proper medicines and medical facilities.

Alarmed and disheartened, Lobel returned to Bucharest. On the train he agonized over his dilemma. Bound by the Hippocratic oath he had taken when he became a doctor and by the discipline and sense of duty he had learned in the Romanian army, Lobel was determined to keep his word and accompany the ship as its doctor. Could he risk the life of his wife and unborn child on an unsafe vessel? How could he weigh the dangers of the *Struma* against the peril faced by his wife if she remained in Romania? By the time he arrived home, he had made up his mind.

He described the condition of the ship to his wife, told her of the promises made by the owner that everything would be in order by the time it sailed. He also talked about his responsibilities as a physician and his responsibilities as a husband and prospective father. Rosalie objected to staying behind, and she objected to her husband's risking his life, especially with their first child on the way.

"You must stay here," he insisted. "I will go to Palestine and make a home for us. You wait for a better ship."

Dismal accounts of the ship's condition began to appear in the Romanian press. A rumor circulated that the government had approved the voyage so that hundreds of Jews would drown on the way to Palestine. Because of the travel restrictions on Jews, no one except the physician was allowed to see the *Struma,* and he kept his deep reservations to himself, presumably trusting that the promised improvements would be made.

Others were less sanguine. In September, one concerned family hired a Romanian naval engineer to inspect the ship. His report was as bleak as Lobel's had been to his wife. The family turned in its tickets.

Concerned about losing his passengers, and his profit, Pandelis hired two senior officers at the port, Lieutenant Commander D. Niculescu and the harbor captain, George Ribicescu. There is no record of how much he paid them. From the results it must have been a substantial sum. The report they prepared on October 13 to calm anxious passengers was riddled with lies.

The *Struma,* they said in a written report, was equipped with an eight-bed hospital, ten toilets, a kitchen, a washing facility, two drinking water tanks with a capacity of twenty tons, four lifeboats, and an adequate supply of life preservers. For good measure, they added: "The ship was meant to carry 748 passengers, but this was reduced to 650 because of the limitations of facilities installed."

As further proof, Pandelis circulated an inspection report dated

January 1, 1941, which said the ship was in good condition and had a new 250-horsepower engine. "The inspection having been concluded satisfactorily, and the ship having been found to be currently in good shape and fit for navigation, my findings were so reported in a classification document," wrote Constantin Zerkovsky, an engineer from Varna, Bulgaria. Zerkovsky did not specify what cargo the ship was suitable to transport. At the time the document was prepared, the *Struma* had been ferrying cattle, not human beings, up and down the Danube. It was also dated New Year's Day, a day when most offices are closed, putting its authenticity in even greater doubt.

Any potential problems in filling the passenger list vanished behind the curtain of half-truths, outright lies, and desperate dreams. Perhaps the truth would not have made a difference to many of those who had signed up for the voyage. Perhaps none would have made the decision of Horia Lobel to leave his pregnant wife behind.

Chapter 12

On May 20, 1941, Adolf Eichmann's office of emigration in Berlin had sent a memorandum to all German consulates, informing them that Field Marshal Hermann Goering had prohibited all emigration by Jews from German-occupied territories in expectation of the "doubtless imminent final solution." Two years before, Hitler had made a public statement that he had a vision that he would bring about the end of the Jews of Europe. "We are going to destroy the Jews," he said. The memo was the first written reference to the eradication.

In July, Goering sent an order to General Reinhard Heydrich, chief of security police for the Reich. Heydrich was ordered to "carry out preparations as regards organizational, financial, and material matters for a total solution of the Jewish question in all the territories of Europe under German occupation. I charge you further to submit to me as soon as possible a general plan of the administrative material and financial measures necessary for carrying out the desired final solution of the Jewish question."

On the military front, the Germans seemed invincible. One after another, nations had fallen to the Nazis. Britain was suffering an unprecedented air attack. In May 1941 Hitler's deputy, Rudolf Hess, had flown to England in an attempt to negotiate peace between Britain and Germany, which would have effectively ended the war. Hitler denounced his deputy as a lunatic, and Britain remained at war. The United States was neutral, and the Soviet Union had not been drawn into the conflict until the surprise of Operation Barbarossa in June, which had opened an eastern front, where the Nazis were winning victory after victory and slaughtering Jews along the way.

With the Russians fighting a losing battle against the Germans and Britain on the defensive, no one in Europe had the power to stop the German butchering of Europe's Jews. In London, Winston Churchill knew more than any other leader about the extent of the suffering. The British had broken the German code and were secretly monitoring thousands of military and government messages, including reports of entire Jewish villages being wiped out.

On August 24, 1941, Churchill went on radio to spur the flagging morale of his countrymen and to alert the world to the barbarism of the German troops. He picked his words carefully to avoid tipping off the Germans that their code had been cracked, so he did not mention Jews directly, but his message demonstrated the early British knowledge of the Holocaust. Despite their grim discovery, the British did not change the white paper's restrictive immigration policy.

"Scores of thousands—literally scores of thousands—of executions in cold blood are being perpetrated by the German police-troops upon the Russian patriots who defend their native soil," Churchill said. "Since the Mongol invasions of Europe in the sixteenth century, there has never been methodical, merciless butchery on such a scale, or approaching such a scale."

Describing the German atrocities as "the most frightful cruelties," Churchill added, "We are in the presence of a crime without a name."

Romanians were active participants in the butchery taking place in their country. The Jews of Romania, even those living in the safer large cities, could see that the end was near. Doctors, dentists, and lawyers were not allowed to work. Young men were shipped off to labor camps. The Jewish community had followed each phase of the war outside their borders. They knew the list of countries that had fallen, and they saw the net closing as one avenue of escape after another was closed off. Antonescu had joined the Axis powers in February, and his million-man army was fighting alongside the Germans on the eastern front. Romania remained an independent country, with its own emigration policy, and Antonescu was reluctant to acquiesce to German demands that he toe their line and cut off all emigration of Jews. No one could be sure how long Antonescu would hold out against Hitler, so the *Struma* was a nearly irresistible magnet for those desperate to escape.

The spirits of those who wanted to leave were also buoyed by news that three small motorboats had successfully crossed the Black Sea. The first, the *Hainarul,* had reached the Mediterranean Sea before sinking in a storm. Its nineteen passengers were rescued, and after a brief detention, they reached Palestine. Another ship, the *Cari Nou,* had made it to Cyprus with twelve passengers. A third and final boat, the *Dor de Val,* was captured in Turkish waters, and its twenty-one passengers were being held in Istanbul. Other small boats had been purchased by various groups and had not yet managed to leave Romania. The determination to survive was unabated.

Aron Rintzler and his wife, Fani, had visited Palestine in 1935. He fell in love with the country and the dream it embodied, but he had few financial prospects in the raw new land, where younger people and agricultural skills were in demand. The Rintzlers returned to Bucharest, where he ran an automotive parts company. Rintzler was determined that his dream would be fulfilled someday by sending their only child, Ogen, to Palestine. When the war broke out, Rintzler decided that the time had come, though his son was only fifteen years old.

A limited number of special certificates for entry to Palestine were available for children under the provisions of the British white paper, and Rintzler secured one. In early 1941, he made arrangements for Ogen to travel by a small ship to Istanbul and by train to Haifa in northern Palestine.

"It was hard to leave, but my father was very obstinate in this," Ogen Rintzler said during an interview. "He was very keen that I should get started on his dream."

At the port in Constanta, Rintzler gave his son some American dollars that he had smuggled past the customs officers, who took anything of value from the departing Jews. He told his son to find a job in agriculture because that was what the new land needed most. Rintzler's final words to his son were that he and his wife would follow as soon as possible.

The journey to Istanbul was uneventful, except for one incident. As young Rintzler prepared to disembark for the train, a rumor spread that the authorities would detain anyone discovered with dollars. A fellow Romanian offered to smuggle dollars through customs, and Rintzler and several others entrusted the man with their money. When the train left Haydarpasa Station on the Asian side of the Bosporus, the man with the money was nowhere to be found. Apparently he had remained in Istanbul, with the money.

Despite the setback, Rintzler arrived safely in Palestine. He was sent to a kibbutz, where he moved in with a man who was born in Palestine and his Polish wife. Ogen learned to speak Hebrew and work on the land, and he waited for his parents.

Nearly sixty years later in a hotel lobby in Tel Aviv, Rintzler told what he knew about his parents' attempt to escape. But everything he knew, he knew only thirdhand because he never saw or heard from his parents again. "Everything I am telling you now is from hearing it from my relatives," he said, explaining how he had filled the void with scraps of memories from others. "I never received letters. I never spoke with them again. Everything I know of them after that is from hearsay."

A few months after his arrival in Palestine, word came that Ogen's parents had gotten berths aboard a boat bound for Palestine. Aron Rintzler's family opposed the trip. Visas for Palestine had run out months earlier, and they knew the fate of the illegal immigrants—even those who made it faced deportation or an internment camp. A local rabbi sent by the family urged him not to go, not to risk his life and that of his wife. Even Fani Rintzler did not want to go and begged her husband to postpone the trip. But Rintzler was an obstinate man. He and his wife were going on the *Struma*.

Fani Rintzler had struggled for years to have a second child. In the fall of 1941, when she was thirty-eight years old, she became pregnant. Her husband was determined that this second child would be born in the new land. He was also determined to see Ogen again.

Those who got a ticket felt lucky. Those who did not would prove to be the fortunate ones.

Tudor Chefner turned out to be one of the lucky ones. He had graduated from high school in Bucharest in 1938 and gone to London to attend engineering school with his brother, Michael, and two close friends, Michael Bucspan and Norbert Storfer. They left Bucharest before the avenues of departure had closed. But in 1940, the Chefners and Storfer were told by their parents to return to Bucharest. They apparently feared being cut off from their sons. Bucspan chose to remain in London to finish school, and he later joined the British army.

By late 1940, the Chefner brothers' parents had realized their mistake, and they wanted to get their sons out of Romania. The family was wealthy, so they bought tickets on two ships—the *Darien* and the *Struma,* though the second was only in the earliest planning stages.

"My father said we should go on whichever ship left first, so when it came time for the *Darien* to sail, we decided to leave," Chefner said in an interview. "I tried to convince Bubbi—that was Norbert's nickname—to come along, but I couldn't convince him. He decided to wait for the *Struma*."

While Michael Bucspan stayed behind in Britain, his parents decided the time had come for them to leave Romania, too. Grigore Bucspan, fifty-four, and his wife, Zlata, fifty-five, were among the oldest passengers who signed up for the journey. It would mark the second time they had been forced to leave their homeland. In 1917, they had fled Russia after the Bolshevik revolution.

Before the revolution, Grigore Bucspan had been a respected economist in Russia who, like other Jews in Russia, had been ordered to fight on the front line in World War I. He had performed with skill and bravery, and his fellow soldiers had chosen him to represent them in the provisional government of Alexander Kerensky after the abdication of the Czar during the Russian Revolution in February 1917. When the Bolsheviks drove out Kerensky's short-lived government in November 1917, Bucspan fled on a Russian military ship. His wife, a physician, stayed behind with their six-month-old son, Michael.

The Turks captured the Russian ship on the Black Sea and imprisoned its passengers, including Bucspan, for several months. After the end of the war, he was freed by a British ship and made his way to his father's house in rural Romania. After he arrived, he sent for his wife and infant son. Together they moved to Bucharest, where Bucspan grew wealthy in the shipping business and his wife practiced medicine. But the Bucspans were ardent Zionists, and they had bought a small parcel of land near Tel Aviv in the late 1930s when the Jewish Agency and other groups were trying to raise money and attract settlers. This was the same parcel of land that would beckon to Grigore's grandson and namesake nearly fifty years later.

Unlike the Bucspans, many of those who signed up for the trip were adventurous young men from Betar, the Zionist youth movement. They wanted not only to escape persecution, but to fight for a new life in a new land. Shmuel Guttenmacher, twenty-one years old, was the leader of the Betar chapter in the small Romanian town of Barlad, so he got a free spot on the ship. Two years earlier, his older brother, Nadiv, had gone to Palestine with a group of young pioneers, and Shmuel was eager to join him.

Yitzhak Tercatin had trained to go to Palestine for years. Like many Betar members, he exercised and studied agriculture and other trades that would be useful in the new country. In 1938, he had taken his ten-year-old brother, Baruch, to the Trianon Theater in their hometown of Jassy to listen to a Zionist leader's speech extolling the virtues of emigrating. Later he helped to organize passengers for the *Darien,* though he remained behind with his family in Jassy to arrange for more immigrants.

After the pogrom in the summer of 1941, Tercatin fled first to

Bucharest. The rest of his family followed later. Tercatin, who was twenty-six years old, was reluctant to leave them there, but his determination to emigrate grew stronger as events darkened in the capital. "My brother, who was at the time the head of the local Betar chapter in Jassy, was very active in preparing and organizing emigrants for Aliya. I remember that when emigrants of the vessel *Darien* were not allowed to disembark in Haifa, a respectable Zionist gentleman yelled in anger at my mother over the fact that it had been my brother, Yitzhak, who had convinced his only daughter to participate in that journey," Baruch Tercatin said years later in Tel Aviv.

"I remember once walking down the street with him," Baruch said. "A member of the Legionnaires suddenly apprehended him and sent him to unload cement bags from a vehicle. My brother was later taken to a labor camp and was released."

When the chance of a spot on the *Struma* came up later that year, there was no hesitation on the part of Yitzhak Tercatin. He did not even give the fitness of the ship a second thought. The pull of Palestine and the push of Romania outweighed the risks.

Also among the Betar who would be going was Yaakov Bercovici from Dorohoi, the district in northern Romania where retreating Romanian troops had killed Jews in 1940, when the region was turned over to the Soviets, and then slaughtered and interned thousands more when they returned in the summer of 1941. Bercovici and many of his militant colleagues had escaped to Bucharest and were among those organizing the passengers for the *Struma*.

Two other refugees from the northern part of the country were intent on being on the ship. When David and Israel Frenk had arrived at their sister's house from Czernowitz, they discovered that their mother had paid a huge sum for three certificates for their passage to Palestine—one for each of the brothers and one for Tivia, Israel's wife. The bad news was that the visas stamped into their passports had expired. But they were assured that new visas would be supplied in Istanbul, so all three booked passage.

The Aroni family, who had been smuggled out of the ghetto in Kishinev in October, were offered tickets on the ship. Four of them were to have made the trip, including the two boys, Sam and Shraga, but fortune would intervene.

On November 24, the police arrived at the apartment of their uncle, Monia Apotecher. The three Romanian policemen who had helped the Aronis escape Kishinev had been caught assisting another Jewish family and had led the police to the uncle. Indicating that they were willing to accept a bribe of their own, the police persuaded Apotecher to take them to his relatives.

"Initially the atmosphere was relaxed, since the policemen made my uncle believe that they were ready to be paid off," Sam Aroni said. "When he produced the money, they also arrested him for bribery. My parents, uncle, and grandmother were all arrested and taken away. My father told me to take my brother and run away through the rear door."

The two young boys escaped and made their way to the home of friends. They would remain in hiding there until they were rescued by other relatives in January 1942, a month after the *Struma* had sailed away. Another two years would pass before the family was reunited for their journey to Palestine, but other would-be passengers—the Frenks, the Bucspans, Norbert Storfer, and the young idealists of the Betar movement—were making final preparations.

Chapter 13

In the summer of 1941, David Stoliar was a strapping eighteen-year-old digging trenches in the countryside outside Bucharest. Jews were forbidden to serve in the Romanian armed forces, so able young Jewish men had been ordered to spend their days in forced labor. The trenches Stoliar and the others dug were used for training by Nazi soldiers. They worked until dark, went home, and returned at dawn the next morning.

Stoliar, who had been born in Kishinev, had traveled widely before the war. He wound up back in Bucharest through a piece of bad luck and worse timing. His father, Jacob, was a Russian Jew, one of five brothers who fled Moscow during the Bolshevik revolution. Some of the brothers went to France, but Jacob settled in Kishinev. He stayed long enough to marry a local woman and have a son, David, before moving the family to Nice, France, where he joined one of his brothers in the hotel business.

Dissatisfied with being a hotelier, he moved the family to Bucharest in 1927 and joined another brother in running a textile factory. The business prospered and the family lived in a luxurious apartment near the center of the city. If they were too peripatetic to consider themselves Romanians, they certainly did not consider themselves practicing Jews.

These were the pre-fascist years, and Bucharest was known fondly as "the little Paris," a charming and modern city with beautiful boulevards lined with private palaces and first-class hotels. The Stoliars were part of the upper-class, dressing in western fashions and moving comfortably about Europe.

In 1932, when David Stoliar was ten, his parents divorced and his mother moved to Paris. David was sent to a private school a few miles south of the French city. Four years later, in 1936, his father sent for David, and he returned to Bucharest and enrolled in school there.

In France and those first years back in Romania, Stoliar did not experience anything that prepared him for the events that came with the war. He didn't detect elements of anti-Semitism and did not think of himself as an observant Jew. He was a handsome, athletic young man who enjoyed sports and girls. He spoke Russian, French, and Romanian and visited his mother in Paris frequently on weekends. But gradually life changed. The trips to Paris ended when the Germans invaded France in May 1940, and it became increasingly difficult to stay in touch with his mother. The war also was making its impact in Bucharest.

"Slowly we were discriminated against," he said. "There were fights and insults. The teachers discriminated against us, too. The Jews were put on one side and the non-Jews on the other side in class. In my German class, the teacher was German and she flunked every Jew in the class, so I had to go to summer school to graduate in 1941. For a time we had to wear yellow badges, so we couldn't ride the streetcars unless there was a second wagon for Jews."

Stoliar had planned to become an engineer, but Jews were not allowed to attend university. He was uncertain what the future held. His father had remarried. Stoliar sensed that his stepmother resented any time his father spent with him, probably because Jacob Stoliar also spent so many hours at work struggling to keep his textile factory operating. Many Jews had lost their businesses. David's father and uncle were allowed to keep their factory operating only because it had been converted to the war effort. The Stoliars manufactured uniforms for the Romanian army, and the brothers were needed to keep production at optimum levels.

For David, the one bright spot during that summer occurred when he met a young woman, Ilse Lothringer. She came from a prominent family and they began to date and even talked of marriage. Their families came from the same social stratum and accepted the courtship happily, even as the clouds over Romania darkened.

As the discrimination against Jews heightened and the situation became increasingly dangerous, Jacob Stoliar wanted to get his son out.

Most doors were closed to Jewish immigrants, and Palestine seemed to be the only possible destination. About the time of his son's nineteenth birthday, on October 31, Jacob Stoliar heard of a refugee ship that was being organized by the Betar. One night after his son returned exhausted from the labor camp, he took him aside.

"I'm going to get you out," he said. "There is a ship going to Palestine, and I will manage to get you on it."

His father explained that the Betar was organizing the voyage and the first places had gone to members of the youth movement. He explained, however, that Betar needed money to finance the operation, so they were selling tickets to other Jews. He would get one, no matter what the cost. And the cost—as high as one thousand dollars—would prove to be well beyond the reach of middle-class Romanians at the time.

David embraced the plan. He tried to persuade his father to come, too, but Jacob rejected the idea because his wife refused to leave. She was from a large and prominent family and hoped that their connections would be strong enough to keep them from danger. "I won't get pushed around much," his father told him. "My life is not in danger yet. But they are targeting the young people and you must go."

His mother was already lost behind Nazi lines in France. Shortly after Paris fell to the Germans, she had boarded a train headed for the part of France held by the Vichy government of the Free French. At the last station before entering the safety zone, German soldiers had boarded and ordered all the Jews off the train and onto one headed back to Paris. She had come so close to escape and had not been heard from since her return to the city. Now, facing the prospect of leaving his father, too, David balked and asked him to please come along. His father was adamant. The young man's outlook improved slightly a day later when Ilse told him that her parents already had tickets for the same ship, the *Struma*.

Jacob Stoliar spent thousands of dollars to finance his son's escape. He had to buy a passport, a difficult item for a Jew to obtain in wartime Romania. Two weeks before the departure date, he was forced to pay the full one thousand dollars for a ticket. Additional bribes were paid to obtain an exit visa and to get his son out of the labor camp so that he could get on the train to Constanta. What he could not buy, no matter how much he offered, was an entry certificate to Palestine. By the time the bribes were tallied, Stoliar was broke. He felt confident, however, that his son was headed for freedom, even if he had no visa for Palestine.

Before David left, Jacob Stoliar wanted something that money could not buy. In early December, he took the young man to the apartment of Rabbi Hersh Guttman, who lived in the center of the Jewish quarter. Since miraculously surviving the pogrom that killed his two sons, the rabbi had been revered in the Jewish community as a holy man whose blessing and protection were sought by many. Jacob Stoliar wanted a benediction for young David, too.

"I remember distinctly going to the rabbi's apartment," the son said. "It made an impression on me because my father did not take me to synagogue regularly, but only during the major Jewish holidays and here I was receiving a blessing from this distinguished rabbi. He asked God to protect me and blessed my voyage. There were tears in his eyes."

Stoliar soon realized how badly he, Ilse Lothringer, and their fellow passengers needed a blessing.

Another pair of young lovers left Bucharest on that same ship. Their journey began not with a blessing, but with a curse. Some people believe words cannot harm and a prayer is as empty as a swear. Medeea Salamowitz was not one of them.

Medeea was born in Bucharest in 1919. Her father was a poor cloth dealer from a nearby town and his wife was a homemaker. She was a good student who mastered English, French, and German in high school. After her graduation in 1937, she went to work as a clerk in an architect's office in Bucharest and quickly rose to become the head secretary.

In 1940, she fell in love. She was twenty-one and still poor. The young man with whom she was in love, Saimon Salamowitz, was two years older and the son of a wealthy textile trader. The difference in their social positions did not matter to Saimon. He knew only that he wanted to marry this beautiful and independent woman. His mother objected, claiming Medeea was not good enough for her son. In the face of pleadings from Saimon and his father, she would not withdraw her objection. When Saimon decided to go ahead with the wedding, with the blessing of his father and his sister, his mother refused to attend the ceremony.

Saimon's father thought his mother would come around in time. He bought the young couple an apartment in Bucharest, and Medeea quit her job to stay at home. Saimon worked in his father's business. In the fall of 1941, Medeea became pregnant. Even the news that a grandchild was on the way did not soften the mother-in-law's position. She refused to have her son and his wife in her home.

The breach seemed impossible to heal, so Saimon's father decided to give the young couple a fresh start. He bought them tickets on the *Struma* and wished them well in the new land. The day before the train left Bucharest for Constanta, Saimon and Medeea stopped at his family home in a final effort to make peace with his mother and say good-bye. The maid who answered the door told the young couple they had to wait in the foyer while she informed the mistress of the house of their arrival. A few minutes later, the maid returned with a solemn face. Saimon's mother refused to see them, she explained. She had given the maid a message to deliver to the couple on their way to start a new life. It was this: "May you suffer cold, thirst for water, and starve for bread."

As the *Struma*'s future passengers bid farewell to loved ones and headed for Constanta, the war was entering a pivotal phase. Throughout 1940 and well into 1941, the Germans had seemed invincible. They rolled over Poland, France, and other countries with their blitzkrieg and pounded Britain mercilessly from the air. As 1941 drew to a close, the British refused to give up or give ground. The Russians, after suffering loss after loss to the Germans, had turned away the assault on Moscow and launched a counteroffensive. Still, the Germans controlled most of Europe, and the first gas chambers had begun to operate at Auschwitz. No longer was a German victory assured. An event half a world away was about to make those odds even longer.

On a Sunday morning, December 7, six Japanese aircraft carriers sent 423 planes to attack Pearl Harbor, the American naval base in Hawaii. The surprise attack was devastating, killing 2,335 American servicemen and destroying six ships. News of the "sneak attack" was broadcast to the American public via radio bulletins, interrupting many popular Sunday afternoon entertainment programs.

The news sent a shock wave across the nation and resulted in a tremendous influx of young volunteers into the armed forces. The attack also united the nation behind President Franklin D. Roosevelt and effectively ended isolationist sentiments in the country. The next day, the United States and Britain would declare war on Japan with President Roosevelt calling December 7 "a date which will live in infamy." Four days later, Germany and Italy would follow suit and declare war on the United States. Thus the European and Southeast Asian wars would become a global conflict, with the Axis powers, led by Japan, Germany, and Italy, united against America, Britain, France, and their allies.

Chapter 14

December 7 was an important date for David Stoliar, too. That evening a special overnight train was being loaded to leave Bucharest for the port of Constanta, where the *Struma* was waiting, its refurbishment finally completed. The platform of the railway station was jammed with passengers and their loved ones who had come to say good-bye as well as Romanian police and railway agents.

As he was struggling to squeeze aboard the train, Stoliar noticed a group of men watching from across the platform. They leaned on shovels and picks, their breath condensing in the icy evening air. These were Jews doing forced labor, to which Stoliar had been condemned not long ago. He thought their eyes showed envy as they watched the passengers crammed aboard the train bound for freedom. As the train pulled out, he thought he heard someone bark at them, "Back to work."

The Romanian government had approved the emigration of passengers holding tickets for the *Struma* after a debate at the highest levels. The main issue had been whether the country's Jews would be more trouble at home or abroad. On November 25, 1941, at a meeting of the Council of Internal Affairs, Antonescu himself demanded an update on the status of the *Struma*.

"Where exactly is the ship now?" the prime minister asked, according to minutes of the meeting.

He was told that it was in Constanta, in the final stages of preparation for departure. Eugen Cristescu, the head of the secret service, tried to mollify Antonescu by assuring him that the ship would not reach its destination, though he offered no reason for the prediction.

When one of his ministers suggested stopping the ship so that its passengers could not criticize Romania once outside their borders, Antonescu said, "What interests me is that these Jews should leave the country. You were against it lest they agitate against us abroad. But don't they agitate anyway?"

The decision was made to allow the ship to proceed, though the secret police were ordered to make sure no one left with any gold or jewelry. Later, in the face of German anger at the escape of nearly eight hundred Jews, Romanian officials would rewrite the administration's attitude toward the departure of the *Struma*.

Certainly the Romanian government was determined to make it as difficult as possible for the passengers to leave. Once they were packed into the cars of the special train on December 7, the train was sealed, and nearly eight hundred men, women, and children were locked inside, carrying their personal belongings weighing no more than the designated limit of twenty kilograms. They had packed and repacked their belongings, leaving treasured heirlooms and valuable items with relatives and friends.

The train arrived in Constanta at about eight o'clock on the morning of the eighth, and it sat for more than three days, as passengers were processed through customs in groups of twenty-five. Constanta resembled a refugee camp; thousands of Jews formed lines in front of travel offices set up by shipping companies that had nothing to sell but the false promise of freedom. Romanian Jews mixed with refugees from Poland, Germany, and Austria who had fled months before and were still searching for a way out.

Alexander Segal, a young *Struma* passenger who at the age of fourteen had yet to feel the sting of anti-Semitism, described waking that first morning: "The first time that I saw an armed soldier was from the train that we took from Bucharest to Constanta. We had the blinds pulled during the first night in Constanta, but in the morning, when we lifted the shades, there he stood. A soldier, carrying a gun. He was actually standing guard over us. It was, for me, a frightening scene."

Inside the customs building at the railway station, each group had to get off the train and carry their luggage to an inspection station. They emptied their bags and watched helplessly as the inspectors took jewelry, money, anything that appeared to have value. Then each person's bag was weighed. They had been told the allowance was twenty kilograms or forty-four pounds. At customs the amount was suddenly reduced to ten kilograms. More goods selected so carefully the previous day were discarded, left in sad piles beside the scales for the guards to pick through later. Many people emptied the contents of their bags into their bedsheets, wrapped them tight, and proceeded like hoboes toward the ship.

The process was painfully slow. The guards harassed the passengers mercilessly. No one wanted to part with the little they had brought, so they would pull out a few items and put their suitcase back on the scale, pull out a few more and repeat the process. At one point an elderly man nearly collapsed, and a Romanian soldier brought him a cup of water. An officer rebuked him loudly, shouting, "You are a soldier in the Romanian army, not a servant of Jews."

When his turn came, Stoliar kept his thick leather jacket on to avoid having it weighed. He had fifteen kilos the first time. Casting aside clothing and other items, he managed to whittle his essentials down to the required weight. Beneath the jacket and his sweater was a money belt with the last of his father's cash. A customs agent felt the thickness of the money belt and demanded the contents.

Even after what he had been through in the ghetto of Czernowitz and his harrowing escape to Bucharest, Israel Frenk was shocked by the procedure that he and his wife and brother underwent. "Before getting on board, the Romanian customs personnel and Gestapo agents taught us what humiliation meant," he said. "They robbed us of all the clothes and jewelry we had. They even took our food."

Those who dared protest the thefts or having to leave so much behind were mocked by the guards. "You won't need it," they said. "You are going to live like a rat on the ship."

Martin Segal, Alexander's father and an oil company executive in Bucharest, was becoming more and more impatient with the treatment and the waiting. Alexander remembered what happened when the soldiers took the only thing of value the family had brought. "We didn't take anything we weren't supposed to take," he said. "My mother didn't have furs or jewels. But the soldiers took something from my parents; it may have been an old watch. The soldier was obviously impressed by it. But when my father objected, he said, 'Where you are going, you will not need this.' I know today that there are two ways to interpret that. Either that you are going to the land of milk and honey, or that you are going to the bottom of the sea. But I didn't know then what to think of his strange comment."

No one fully understood the meaning of these remarks until they were herded onto the dock, after nearly four days of customs checks, and glimpsed the *Struma* for the first time. Romanian officials had forbidden the passengers to see the vessel that would supposedly carry them to salvation. On December 12, following days of humiliation, the passengers got their biggest shock yet.

If anything, the Romanian press had been too kind about the condition of the ship. The *Struma* was about half the length of a football field, with rusting steel sides clamped onto rotten wood. It seemed impossible for so many people to fit onto such a small space, let alone travel a thousand nautical miles. Perched in an ungainly manner on the deck was a crude wooden superstructure about twelve feet high, which had been constructed as quarters for the captain and additional passengers who had purchased the extra tickets the greedy Pandelis had not been able to resist selling. There was not a lifeboat in sight, nor were any life preservers visible.

"Seeing *Struma* was so discouraging that we covered our eyes," said Frenk. "It was simply a wreck. We had never seen anything like it."

Stoliar's recollections were similar. "The view exceeded our worst fears," he said. "We couldn't believe that such a miserable contraption of rusted metal and rotten wood could be called a ship, let alone be capable of transporting hundreds of people over open sea. We were stupefied. For a while, we hoped that this boat was supposed to take us to the real ship. When the truth hit home, we were disconsolate. In that mood we climbed the narrow plank linking the quay to the ship, depressed with worry and gloom."

The ship was so narrow that only one hundred or so people could be on deck at any one time, for fear of tipping the whole structure. So as it filled, the crew hurried passengers to the quarters below deck. There was the grimmest discovery yet. As the stunned passengers filed on board, they underwent yet another inspection, this time by agents who demanded their tickets and again weighed their belongings. Finally they were directed down a set of stairs near the middle of the ship.

The stairs descended three flights to the dank bottom. Instead of cabins with cots, as promised in the photos, each deck had been divided into wooden warehouses for sleeping. The ship was not deep, maybe eighteen feet at most, so the sleeping quarters were barely three feet high. It was not room enough to sit. Five people were expected to jam into each berth, where they would sleep on the wooden pallet that formed its floor. Men, women, and families were segregated on separate levels, with single men assigned the space directly below the deck because it was the tightest. As everyone squeezed into the berths, they discovered that even the densely packed cubicles would not hold all of the passengers. Those left without a spot set up in the narrow aisles.

Eight toilets, little more than holes to the water below, lined the back end of the ship. A small area was set aside to store food and water, but Romanian customs agents had boarded the ship before departure and demanded half of the meager food supplies. The Romanians had also taken the copper pots from the single makeshift kitchen, leaving behind only a few iron skillets. There was no sign of a medical area, let alone an eight-bed hospital. In fact, though there would turn out to be nearly thirty doctors among the passengers, the ship carried not so much as a bottle of aspirin. Two aged lifeboats were added later, strapped to the sides of the ship, not nearly enough for even the women and children in an emergency.

The sight of the ship caused a near panic among some passengers. A few stopped on the stairs below deck, too afraid to go deeper into the bowels of the vessel. There were pleas to leave and tears, particularly among the children. In the end, no one was willing to give up his place on the ramshackle converted cattle carrier. The final measure of their desperation to escape was that fathers and mothers would bring their children onto that decrepit and overcrowded construction that resembled a coffin more than a boat.

What the passengers could not see, but many might have surmised were they not so numbed by their surroundings, was that the engine was not what had been promised either. The ship had originally been a two-masted sailing vessel and a small auxiliary engine had been added later. The ship no longer even carried sails, and Pandelis had promised to install a new 250-horsepower diesel engine for the journey to Palestine. Such an engine would have been expensive, even if it could have been found in wartime, and Pandelis had cut yet another corner. The *Struma* was powered by an eight-cylinder engine salvaged from a tug that had been resting on the bottom of the Danube since it had sunk four years earlier.

For three days before departure, two mechanics who were part of the ten-man crew had struggled to get the engine to turn over. They finally succeeded in coaxing most of the cylinders to fire; the others were cracked too badly to repair. The captain, Grigori T. Garabatenko, a Bulgarian like most of his crew, had been under pressure to sail for fear that the Romanian government would change its mind and keep the ship in port. That would have meant sending the passengers back to Bucharest and possibly returning their money. So Garabatenko deemed the engine good enough and had issued the orders to proceed with the boarding.

It was mid-afternoon by the time Stoliar tucked his small suitcase into a sleeping cage in the superstructure added to ship's deck and crawled in. The roof of the superstructure was inches above his face. Lying there, young Stoliar thought of the familiar faces he had seen while boarding. In addition to Ilse and her parents, who were settling in somewhere among the five layers below, he saw his dentist and several businessmen and lawyers he had seen his father talking to at one time or another. Most of the people, however, were strangers.

The young men from the Betar moved with assuredness among the passengers, trying not to betray their shock at the conditions. They organized everyone into groups of thirty to forty, each with a Betar leader who would assign chores and a schedule for eating and getting some air on deck. The bustle and plans took the edge off people's emotions until the passengers felt a solid pull on the boat. A tug had tied a line to the ship and had begun towing it out of the harbor toward the open sea.

Late that afternoon, after the pale winter sun had started to disappear and the air had grown colder, passengers jammed the deck and lined the narrow stairs, trying to get a final view of Romania. Someone's voice rose in song, and others soon joined. From the dank and crowded bowels of the ship to the deck, hundreds of people joined in singing the anthem of the new homeland, *Hatikva*.

> *So long as still within our breasts*
> *The Jewish heart beats true,*
> *So long as still toward the East,*
> *To Zion, looks the Jew,*
> *So long our hopes are not yet lost*
> *Two thousand years we cherished them*
> *To live in freedom in the land*
> *Of Zion and Jerusalem.*

Chapter 15

An hour after dusk, when the last light disappeared into the sea, the first disaster arrived in silence. Families were still settling in and adjusting to the cramped quarters as the ship moved slowly out of Romanian waters. Gradually, the passengers were overcoming their initial shock at the ship's condition, and spirits were buoyed by the fact that they were finally under way to Palestine. They found comfort even in the wheezing, sputtering engine, which they expected to carry them the few hours south to the Bosporus and Istanbul, the first destination. And then, quiet. Instantly, the small sense of comfort was replaced by yet another wave of anxiety when the engine coughed to a stop and the ship began to drift, rocked ever harder by the waves. In the crowded compartments below deck, people stopped and listened, hoping for the engine to come back to life.

Captain Garabatenko must have felt the loss of power immediately. He left the chief mate, Lazar Dikof, on the bridge and hustled below to determine the problem. The Bulgarian captain had encountered as many obstacles assembling a crew as he had trying to make the ship seaworthy. Almost every able Romanian seaman was in the armed forces or working on one of the cargo ships ferrying war supplies up and down the Danube. The few qualified sailors still looking for work in Constanta had refused to sail on a ship as ill-equipped for its voyage as the *Struma*. Garabatenko had scrounged among the port's remaining sailors—Bulgarians, Hungarians, and Romanians—to fill the crew. Now, as he squeezed into the tiny engine room, the two mechanics stood staring helplessly at the engine salvaged weeks earlier from the bottom of the Danube.

As the exasperated captain berated them, the mechanics managed to start the engine again. After a few minutes it stopped. Again and again, the small engine turned over briefly, the boat started to move forward, and then it would fail. Rumors spread through the ship—the engine was hopeless; they were drifting back into Romanian waters and would be forced to return to Constanta; the ship would hit rocks and sink. The captain tried to calm the passengers, relaying a message to them through the ship's team leaders that the repairs would be finished momentarily.

There were other problems. Without power, the ship was rocked by the waves and throughout the night passengers were seasick. The tight quarters meant few people could reach fresh air, and the smell of vomit began to pervade the area below deck. If they were marooned at sea for any length of time, the ship was likely to run out of food and fresh water. Pandelis had provided only enough food for a few days, and the Romanian soldiers had stolen half of that.

The ship also was taking on small amounts of water and it was beginning to accumulate in the engine room. It was not enough to cause widespread alarm, but too much to be ignored. A water brigade was formed to fill buckets in the engine room and carry them to the deck, where the water could be dumped into the sea.

Aron Rintzler slipped past the men of the water brigade and into the engine room. He had operated an automotive parts factory in Bucharest and he knew about engines. It did not take long for him to determine that this engine would carry the *Struma* no farther. It would be impossible to repair, given the fact that there were none of the usual spare parts and no skilled mechanics on the ship. Others among the crew with some knowledge of engines looked at the situation and came to the same conclusion.

The verdict left the captain with two choices—allow the ship to drift until it ran aground somewhere along the coast of Romania, or signal for help and risk being towed back to Constanta. For the captain, returning to port would probably mean canceling the voyage and forfeiting the bonus he had been promised to get the ship to Palestine. For the passengers, returning held more dire consequences, including being returned to Bucharest or worse. Drifting had its perils, too. If the ship hit rocks and foundered, few, if any, would survive.

The captain weighed his options and decided to send a distress signal. It was better than risking a wreck. The order was relayed to the radioman, who managed to send a weak signal before the radio, too, stopped working.

Uncertain what to do next, Garabatenko called a meeting of the ship's leaders and told them about the problem. He said the engine could not be repaired with the equipment on board and the attempt to send a distress signal had apparently failed. Yaakov Bercovici, the young Betar leader, suggested that one of the two lifeboats be manned and sent for help. The shore was not visible, but they knew it could not be far.

The boat was lowered into the sea and two young passengers who had volunteered to go climbed in and began to row toward the invisible shore. After several hours, the boat returned and the young men described what had happened. Near shore. they said, they had seen a coast guard station. When they approached, the soldiers there began to fire at them with rifles. They quickly turned the boat around and headed back out to sea. A short time later, they encountered a commercial fishing boat and its crew promised to find a larger ship to try to rescue the *Struma* when they returned to port.

As it grew dark on December 13 a surprising savior appeared. The tugboat *Istria,* which had towed the *Struma* out of Constanta the previous day, pulled alongside, and its captain came aboard. The initial distress signal had gone through after all, and the tug had been sent back out. The tugboat captain inspected the stricken engine and said that he would bring his mechanics on board to try to fix it. The price was three million lei, about seventy-five hundred dollars.

Garabatenko relayed word to the passengers through the Betar leaders. It was an exorbitant sum, especially since the Romanian customs and the German agents already had taken almost everything of value. An alternative offer was put to the tug captain: Would he accept the wedding rings, other jewelry and valuables, and whatever cash had been hidden from the customs agents? The captain agreed to consider the offer, depending on how much of value was left. Women prized off the gold bands on their fingers and dropped them into small cloth bags along with watches and cash as the Betar representatives made their way solemnly among the passengers. Many women turned away as they handed over their rings, embarrassed by their tears. The last items of value from the passengers of the *Struma* did not approach seventy-five hundred dollars, but it was enough to satisfy the tug's captain.

The tugboat's mechanics boarded the ship, toolboxes at their sides. They spent three hours working on the engine before it finally started again. It was far from a purr, but it seemed to be smoother than before. The *Istria* chugged powerfully off, headed back to Constanta with the last of the passengers' valuables. The tugboat left behind a measure of hope that the ship could make it to Istanbul, where the engine would be repaired or even replaced and visas would be waiting to get them into Palestine.

The engine ran sporadically and the ship moved slowly down the coast. On Sunday afternoon, December 14, the sputtering engine quit for good. By this time, the *Struma* had nearly reached the Bosporus, gateway to Istanbul. The passengers saw birds flying around the ship, a sign that land was near. The captain pulled out his binoculars and confirmed that he could see the coast of Turkey in the distance. The Panamanian flag was hauled down, replaced with the star and crescent of the Republic of Turkey as a sign of friendship.

The entrance to the famed strait had been mined by Germans to prevent ships from carrying supplies for the Red Army to Russian ports on the Black Sea. The Turks had strung nets outside the minefields, with bells attached to warn ships away. Without an engine, the *Struma* was powerless to avoid the mines. Their lives depended on the sputtering engine, the current, and the speed at which a rescue ship could be summoned by the faltering radio.

Two lookouts were posted atop the unused mast to keep an eye out for nets or the mines as the ship drifted inexorably toward the

Bosporus. At the same time, the radioman tried to persuade his device to send one last signal that would bring a pilot to navigate the ship through the minefield. Suddenly one of the lookouts shouted, "Mines ahead. Mines ahead." He had seen the chain of mines stretched across the water, about fifty yards away. The captain ordered the engine slowed, and it responded by stopping altogether. The engine refused to start again, and the ship slowly drifted toward the mines as the radioman frantically signaled for help.

As the ship drifted closer, the passengers began to panic. They were shouting and crying. There was no place to go. Alexander Segal raced to find his mother waiting in her berth. "The stairs were wide enough for just one person, suddenly they were rushing up two abreast," he said. "I pushed and shoved and even used my fists to get down to her. They were like human animals. When I did and I told her what was happening, she said only, 'Yes, we will wait.' "

With only two lifeboats and no life preservers, abandoning ship seemed to mean certain death for many of the passengers, particularly the children. Nonetheless, Captain Garabatenko decided quickly that he had no choice. It was either plunge into the icy Black Sea and swim for shore or wait until the ship hit a mine and exploded. He rang the ship's bell to signal "abandon ship."

At the last minute, as mothers and their children were getting ready to be lowered into the only two lifeboats, a Turkish navy tugboat appeared on the horizon, steaming toward the *Struma*. Surely, thought Stoliar as the tugboat secured a line to the ship and began to tow it south, this was a good omen.

It was December 15. The sun was pale and gray that winter morning, turning the waters of the narrow Bosporus deep green as the tugboat pulled the ship down the eighteen-mile stretch toward Istanbul harbor. The ship had stopped briefly at a navy checkpoint just inside the strait. Inspectors had boarded the vessel, talked briefly with the captain, and about an hour later sent the ship and its tug on their way.

The weather did not shroud the mood of the passengers as they passed the tall, slender minarets of Istanbul's domed mosques and the gracious Ottoman-era wooden houses and elegant winter palaces along the waterway and climbing the forested hills stretching back from the water. The shores of the Bosporus were lined with villages famous for their fish restaurants, and steam-powered ferries moving between the Asian and European shores vied for space in the narrow waterway with brightly colored fishing boats.

Europe was on the right side as the *Struma* headed south down the straits. Those lucky enough to have a view could see Rumeli Hisari, the thick-walled castle erected in just four months in the fifteenth century in preparation for the conquest of Constantinople by the Ottoman sultan Mehmet II. Opposite the castle on the Asian side stood the ruins of Anadolu Hisari, a smaller fortress built in 1390. The two fortresses stood at the narrowest point on the Bosporus, a width of about seven hundred yards. After capturing or torching the farmlands that supplied Constantinople with food, the ingenious Turks had stretched a massive chain between the fortresses to block any effort to resupply the city from the Black Sea.

"I remember my first sight of Istanbul," Alexander Segal said sixty years later. "The city we had left—Bucharest—was dark. There were shortages and rules that no light could show at night. It was a black city in the midst of a black country. But Istanbul, it was lit up like a Christmas ornament. From the boat in the harbor, it looked like an enormous decorated tree. It was magical."

The tug took the *Struma* to the southern mouth of the Bosporus, about three hundred yards from shore, and the captain was ordered to drop anchor and wait for a police boarding party. He also was told to raise the yellow flag that signaled a quarantine. It was not a warm welcome. No one on the ship understood what was happening as they sat in the harbor of the city that, in an earlier time, had given the world a new word to describe the sort of intrigue-ridden political complexities about to engulf the *Struma*. The word was "Byzantine."

PART III

Istanbul Intrigues

Chapter 16

Turkey's history has been both rewritten and forgotten at times, sometimes conveniently. New generations of Turks, although able to list their country's military triumphs, sometimes seem unaware of some of its darkest hours. One such episode is the massacre of hundreds of thousands of Armenians between 1915 and 1922, which has been scrubbed from the history books in Turkish schools.

Mustafa Kemal Ataturk imposed this break with the past when he ousted the last sultan and rode a revolutionary upsurge in nationalism to create the Turkish state in 1923. In a highly symbolic move, he moved the capital from the storied city of Constantinople to Ankara, then a sleepy village, and was determined to remake his nation in the image of the nationalist-states of Europe.

Islam was scoured from the precincts of government. Constantinople, the traditional seat of the Ottomans, was renamed Istanbul. One example of Ataturk's fealty to secularism was the fate of Hagia Sophia, one of the city's most magnificent buildings. The Byzantine-era church had been transformed into a mosque after the Ottoman conquest of Constantinople in 1453, and for five centuries it functioned as one of the city's central religious points for Muslims. Ataturk converted it into a museum in 1935. This was not an easy, open regime, and criticizing Ataturk and any of the generals who ran the country was against the law. Archives recounting centuries of triumph and defeat were closed. And so were the government's internal records of more recent episodes.

Within this atmosphere of universal denial that persists today, it had been easy to forget the *Struma*. And, as Greg Buxton was discovering, finding the ship and resurrecting its memory involved more than planning and executing the perfect dive, though that was part of the challenge, too.

By the summer of 2000, Buxton was finally ready to make the expedition to find the *Struma*. He had assembled a team of fourteen divers, an underwater archeologist, and raised sixty-three thousand dollars to finance the search. The United States Holocaust Memorial Museum made the first contribution to the project, but Buxton found he had to sell his apartment in Birmingham, England, to come up with most of the remainder. Along the way, a project that had started out as an adventure had turned into a more personal and emotional journey.

The actual diving was not expected to be the most difficult part of the expedition. After the *Britannic,* Buxton and his colleagues were confident they could deal with the cold and the depths; the biggest obstacle was the Black Sea's reputation for low visibility. Far tougher, Buxton knew, would be locating the wreck itself. He had already spent months researching the ship's sinking.

One of the most intriguing things he had come across was the conclusion, reached first by a German researcher and later by an Israeli scholar and diplomat, that the *Struma* had been sunk by a Soviet submarine. It seemed to be an astonishing claim, but compelling evidence had been discovered in Soviet naval archives from World War II.

Buxton obtained copies of the archives, and he pored over them and other accounts of the ship's sinking that appeared on the Internet until his eyes blurred. He also read sections about the ship in the half dozen or so books that mentioned the *Struma*. Through the Internet, he had initiated correspondences with relatives of many of those who died on the *Struma*. They provided him with information from letters they had received from people onboard the ship. More important, their memories of loved ones who had died imbued the project with a human dimension that had been missing. Buxton began to recognize that he was involved in something larger than another diving adventure.

In late 1998, Buxton had contacted the sole survivor of the *Struma*'s sinking, David Stoliar, by e-mail and outlined his project. Stoliar, who by then was living in Bend, Oregon, was intrigued and agreed to help as much as he could in finding the ship. In the months that followed, the two men exchanged voluminous e-mail correspondence about Stoliar's memories of the ship's structure, the departure from Istanbul, and most important, the hours he spent in the water after the explosion. Geraint Ffoukes-Jones, who had taken on the job as the dive's technical director, also participated in the exchanges.

In the press and other publications details surrounding the ship were often conflicting, or confusing, or both. Only broad facts were recorded: The *Struma* and its passengers sat in Istanbul harbor for ten weeks before the ship was towed back to the Black Sea and set adrift. A mysterious explosion had sunk the vessel, leaving one survivor.

Buxton and Ffoukes-Jones needed as much accurate firsthand information as possible: When did the Turkish navy tugboat start to pull the ship up the Bosporus? How long was the haul from the mouth of the Bosporus into the Black Sea? How long did the ship drift before the explosion? They also pressed Stoliar about the details of his survival. How long was he in the water? How fast did the piece of decking seem to move? How far out to sea was he when he finally caught sight of land? How badly damaged was the boat before it sank?

Buxton knew the current in that part of the Black Sea flowed from west to east. The current's speed could be estimated with a good degree of accuracy, since Stoliar said the sea was calm at the time. Other elements of the calculation—how far a tug could have pulled a ship of the size and weight of the *Struma*, which direction they would logically have gone, how accurate were the coordinates from the Soviet submarine—were more open to mistakes. A small miscalculation in a sea the size of this one could mean they would never find the ship. The point was to establish the coordinates as accurately as possible in order to conduct a search in the most efficient manner possible.

Another uncertainty was Stoliar's memory. Fifty-eight years after a traumatic event, there were questions about how precise he could be in recounting events that occurred when he was in shock, freezing cold, contemplating his own death. Psychologists also know that over time actual memories become intermingled with learned memories in a way that makes it almost impossible to distinguish between the two. Still, Stoliar was an intelligent and articulate man, and most important, he seemed to recall the experience with detailed and consistent clarity.

In January 1999, Buxton went to Washington, D.C., to meet with Radu Ioanid, the Romanian-born scholar and specialist in the Romanian Holocaust at the United States Holocaust Memorial Museum. Though the museum itself had no public display related to the *Struma,* Ioanid was able to offer a wealth of information from the museum's archives about the ship, its passengers, and the events leading up to its departure. Among the files was a videotaped interview that Stoliar had given to the museum in 1997. Ioanid also provided financial help—the museum agreed to donate ten thousand dollars to the expedition.

At Buxton's invitation, Stoliar went to Washington and participated in the meetings with the museum officials. He also accompanied Buxton and three officials from the museum to the Turkish embassy, where they met with one of the embassy counselors.

Two officials from the museum, Wesley Fisher and Henry Mayer, had already approached the Turkish government to persuade them to open their World War II archives. An estimated twenty thousand Jewish refugees had passed safely through the country during the war, and the museum wanted to gather as much information as possible about their experiences, along with those of passengers on the *Struma, Salvador,* and other refugee ships. The Turks never said no to the request, but they never said yes either. Initially, when the Turkish government said its archives were still too disorganized for scholarly research, the museum offered to pay for sorting and cataloguing them. Again, the Turks stalled, never saying no and never saying yes.

At the imposing Turkish embassy on Massachusetts Avenue in Washington, Buxton found the answer was much the same when it came to diving such a politically sensitive site. From its treatment of the Armenians at the turn of the century to its dealings with its own Kurdish minority today, the Turkish government has been notoriously thin-skinned. The attitude has been to ignore the dark moments of the country's history rather than admit past mistakes. The *Struma* episode carried additional baggage: Turkey is Israel's closest ally in the Middle East, and the government did not want to upset the relationship.

The Turkish counselor did not reject the idea of granting permission. In Turkey's unfailingly polite culture, an outright "no" is a rarity; the tendency instead is to delay and deflect. So rather than saying no, the counselor suggested that, as a British citizen, Buxton would have to apply through the Turkish embassy in London.

For Buxton, meeting Stoliar was a moving experience. Though Stoliar had not known Buxton's grandparents, his recollections made the entire ship and their last days come alive. Here, Buxton realized, was someone who had spent weeks on the ship, endured the same deprivations, and managed to survive and go on to lead a rich and full life. This new perspective, coupled with his tour of the Holocaust museum, drew Buxton deeper than ever into the plight of his grandparents and other Jews during the war. Slowly the purpose of his dive was changing. Finding the wreck remained the priority. The chance for him and other relatives of victims to bid a proper farewell to those who had died was becoming outright crucial.

Over the course of his research and planning for the expedition, he had become more sensitive to his Jewish roots. He wanted to retrieve items from the *Struma* in the hope that they would be used in an exhibit at the United States Holocaust Memorial Museum in Washington and at Yad Vashem, the extensive Holocaust museum and research facility in Jerusalem. He wanted to do so only if he could comply with the ethical and religious constraints involved in diving on a gravesite. So he paid a visit to Rabbi Barry Marcus at London's Central Synagogue, the largest in the city.

"From a Jewish point of view," Marcus told him, "there is an obligation to honor someone in life and in death. That means that the body, the vehicle that houses the soul, demands an honorable burial.

From dust you come, to dust you go. Jews always try to bury their people in a gravesite and mark that place. Diving for the boat is in no way contrary to Jewish practice."

He described an Israeli submarine that had sunk in the 1960s. The Israeli armed forces went to enormous lengths to find the ship, not because they cared so much about the vessel, but because they wanted to retrieve the bodies of the sailors for proper burial. In the same way, the Israeli defense forces and its political leaders devote enormous resources to recovering bodies of soldiers killed in action. When a suicide bomber kills Jews in Israel, special squads of religious volunteers comb the bomb site to recover even the smallest bits of flesh and bone.

Marcus found nobility in Buxton's quest. If the *Struma* and its victims were properly honored, he said, perhaps the passengers would, in the end, receive the honor they had long been denied. "This is why *Struma* is important," he explained. "It begins to address this imbalance. The most devastating condition on earth is indifference."

During their meeting at the museum, Stoliar asked Buxton if he was certain he could locate the wreck. Yes, he said confidently, they would find the wreck. And when they found it and completed their diving, he said, he would hold a memorial service. Buxton asked if Stoliar would come to the service. Stoliar agreed, but Buxton detected a hesitation. It was only natural, he assumed, that the prospect would resurrect old ghosts and unpleasant memories.

Buxton knew he needed local expertise to make the dive go smoothly. Locals could help get the government permits for the dive, arrange boats to take the divers to the site, and help get compressors and other equipment, which would cost less than transporting everything from Britain.

Most diving in Turkey takes place far from Istanbul on its Aegean and Mediterranean coasts, where the water is warmer, visibility is better, and there are plenty of wrecks and Greek and Roman ruins to explore. Images of elegant yachts and ancient sites now underwater litter the pages of travel brochures to entice divers, from rank amateurs to expert explorers, to those pleasant spots. Few tour guides beckon visitors to take a peek into the murky depths of the Black Sea. There, most marine life has been wiped out by decades of pollution, and unpredictable currents can turn deadly in a moment.

The result was a scarcity of dive shops in Istanbul with the technical expertise and equipment that Buxton needed. However, through his Internet searches, he discovered a small shop on a side street in the busy Taksim area of the city. He also had turned up a group of experienced amateur divers, the Turkish Underwater Research Society. When he contacted the divers by e-mail, they seemed willing to provide that local expertise.

In his initial discussions with anyone outside the expedition team, however, Buxton took extra precautions not to identify the wreck he intended to dive. He did not want other divers to get a jump on his mission.

Buxton flew to Istanbul for two days in November 1999 to meet with the dive shop owner, Sadi Tanman, and a couple of representatives of the Turkish diving group. The divers told him that he would need a government permit for any diving in Turkish waters, and to get it, he would need Turkish citizens as part of his dive team. This meant providing the detail that Buxton had withheld—that he was looking for the *Struma*. The Turkish divers agreed to help in applying for the permits, and Buxton experienced only a tingle of concern that he had disclosed his mission too early in the game. Later, he would say, "Maybe I was naïve or too open. I sure didn't see what was coming until it was too late."

During the trip, Tanman told a story that disturbed Buxton. He said that twelve years earlier he had conducted an expedition to find the wreckage of the *Struma*. They had used a homemade submarine and planned to take artifacts from the site and sell them at what they thought would be a huge profit to Jewish museums and other institutions around the world. Tanman also said he had heard rumors the ship carried a hoard of gold.

Jeff Hakko, a Turkish Jew whose family owned the country's most upscale department stores and who was an avid amateur diver with a huge personal collection of old-fashioned deep-diving suits, told Buxton that he was eager to help make arrangements but would not do so publicly.

Buxton also met Ishak Alaton, a vibrant man in his mid-seventies, one of the few Jews in Turkey to wield influence in political affairs. Alaton had fled Turkey for Sweden after World War II when his family lost its business. After he returned in 1954 at his father's request, Alaton and a partner had built one of the country's largest and most profitable conglomerates, Alarko. Because of his wealth and government contacts, he was influential in circles that would prove useful to Buxton. Most important, Alaton's personal recollections of the *Struma* made him an instant and ardent backer of the expedition.

For weeks, Buxton worked with the Turkish divers by e-mail and telephone to prepare applications for permission to dive for the *Struma*. The documents had to be filled out with care, and there were constant hassles over translations and delays on the Turkish end. In exasperation, Buxton and one of his closest diving buddies, Jonathon Lewis, went to Istanbul to try to straighten out the mess with the Turks.

Early in the summer of 2000, the dates for the dive were being fixed and the Turkish government had agreed verbally to allow the dive because Turkish citizens were involved in the expedition. Then Buxton had a falling-out with the Turkish divers that threatened to cancel the expedition.

Buxton had grown wary of the Turks because of what he interpreted as anti-Semitic references to the wreck as "the Jew ship" and because of Tanman's stories about his search for the *Struma* in order to find treasure. The idea that someone might plunder the ship made Buxton's skin crawl. He also believed the Turkish divers saw him as a source of endless funding to finance their subsequent dives for the *Struma*. In late 1999, the Turkish dive group had given Buxton a proposed budget of one hundred thousand dollars for the expedition, excluding airfares and lodging for his divers. It was twice the amount Buxton had expected to spend.

The Turks did feel a proprietary interest in the wreck, since it was in Turkish waters. Buxton knew about Tanman's strange submarine expedition. He did not know that they had been planning not only a *Struma* dive but a possible movie deal before they met him. The latter would prove to be decisive because of Buxton's own movie deal.

Early in March of 2000, Buxton's research had come to the attention of Simcha Jacobovici, an independent documentary film producer from Toronto, through the Romanian community in Israel. The project seemed made to order to Jacobovici: He was the Israel-born son of Romanian refugees who had fled during the war, and the *Struma* was part of the lore of the Holocaust in his family. "I was sucked into the story," Jacobovici, an intense man, said later. He already had produced and directed a number of award-winning films, such as *The Selling of Innocents,* about child prostitution in India, and *The Plague Monkeys,* about Ebola virus outbreaks.

Jacobovici flew Buxton to Toronto and convinced him to give the exclusive film rights to the expedition to Jacobovici in exchange for a ten-thousand-dollar contribution toward the cost of the dive. Buxton also had been talking with a producer from Public Broadcasting System in the United States. But it was Jacobovici's passion for the story that won him the deal. The filmmaker quickly sold the rights to Home Box Office in the United States and Channel Four in Britain for a substantial sum.

The Turkish divers also had written a rough script for a movie they hoped to sell. When they learned of Buxton's movie deal, they argued with him about who controlled the dive and the movie rights to the expedition. They wanted him to finance the search, but to allow them to keep the rights to their own movie. The Turkish dive team had almost no money, and Buxton's funds were limited. He insisted on spending his money as he saw fit, which meant searching the sites he had located through his research and diving the locations that he thought were most promising.

"I can only pay for what I've got money for," he told the Turkish team. "If we run out of money, I decide what we're going to pay for."

They suggested that he turn the entire sum over to Jeff Hakko, who could serve as a neutral paymaster. Again, Buxton refused. He tried to explain that, to him, the dive had become not just a search for another wreck. It was a personal mission that he intended to conclude with a memorial service to the victims. He promised the Turks equal billing when it came to diving and said he didn't care what they did with their own movie, but Buxton insisted on financial control over the expedition and total control over the memorial service. They could attend the remembrance service, of course, but they would not be part of it because they had not lost anyone on the ship.

"Why does this have to be a Jewish thing?" asked one of the Turks.

"Well, the Holocaust was kind of a Jewish thing," Buxton shot back.

"The boat is in Turkish waters," insisted the Turk.

"Well, only because you bloody put it there," said Buxton.

Chapter 17

December 15, 1941

The *Struma* was towed into the main port of a country caught between a gloried past and an uncertain future. For a thousand years before the Ottoman conquest in 1453, Constantinople had been the most renowned capital of Christendom and capital of the Byzantine and Roman empires. After Sultan Mehmet II conquered the city, it was transformed into the center of the Ottoman Empire and the Islamic world. When the Turkish republic rose from the ashes of the Ottomans in 1923, Constantinople was renamed Istanbul and it became Turkey's largest and most modern city.

The first census of the modern republic took place in 1924, and it showed Istanbul with a population of 1.1 million. Sixty-one percent were Muslim Turks, but there were sizable numbers of Greeks and Armenians as well. Jews, who had long been welcomed by the Ottomans, made up six percent of Istanbul's population. These groups maintained their own neighborhoods, customs, and languages, giving Istanbul a reputation as a tolerant metropolis, despite the brutalities of Turkey's recent war of independence.

By the time the *Struma* arrived that gray morning in December 1941, attitudes were hardening. Because of Turkey's determined neutrality in the war, the city was a magnet for desperate refugees from Bulgaria, Greece, Hungary, Yugoslavia, and Romania. These refugees had swollen the city's population by one hundred thousand, adding a new burden to a country where many were already suffering from hunger and poverty.

Neutrality meant the city had attracted another type of resident, too. Countless foreign agents and spies operated in the consulates, restaurants, and hotels, testament to Istanbul's strategic importance. By one count, seventeen foreign intelligence services were operating in Turkey during the war, transforming the country into a covert battleground where elegant manners and polite language concealed baser motives.

World War I had been disastrous for Turkey. In the words of Mustafa Kemal Ataturk, the general who had founded the republic after the war, "Millions of men were sacrificed for no purpose." With those memories still sharp, the country's leaders were determined to avoid being dragged into another conflict.

Other considerations underlined the folly of joining the war. Turkey's state-run economy was in disarray, and though its soldiers were regarded as among the world's best, its military equipment was obsolete and insufficient to defend the country or embark on a major offensive.

Turkey was a prize that could not be ignored, however. The Germans wanted the country as a foothold against the Soviets and a base from which to launch attacks on the Middle East. The Allied forces wanted their own bases in Turkey to start a campaign to dislodge the Germans from the Balkans.

No one lusted after the country more than Russia, though, Turkey's enemy for the past century. For Moscow, the country offered control over the Black Sea and access to the Mediterranean. Indeed, the Turks were most concerned that the Russians might use the pretense of any supposed Turkish partisanship toward the Germans as an excuse to attack, in the guise of saving the country for the Allies.

Ismet Inonu, who had become president after the death of Ataturk in 1938, had tried to guarantee Turkey's neutrality by signing nonaggression pacts with all sides. In 1939 he had initialed an agreement with Britain and France pledging assistance in the event of war in the Mediterranean area. To appease Moscow, he added a clause specifying that Turkey could not be compelled to help if Britain and France took up arms against Russia. Two years later, Inonu balanced the diplomatic scales by signing a friendship pact with Germany. Throughout the war years, Turkish diplomats would be careful to offset the appearance of concessions to one side with equal favors for the other.

Neutrality brought perils, too. Turkey's leaders recognized the need to stay on good terms with all sides in anticipation of the inevitable geographic reshuffling once the war ended. While the Germans were constantly threatening to bomb Istanbul and Ankara, the capital, Turkey's biggest fear was that an Allied victory would lead the British and Americans to give Russia control of the Bosporus.

For the passengers on the *Struma,* Turkey's determination not to offend either side and the resulting political intrigue and gamesmanship would spell disaster, though no one knew it on the day they were towed into Istanbul harbor. The passengers fully expected that the engine would be repaired, they would receive the promised visas, and they would be on their way to Palestine. They did not count on the British.

From the moment it arrived in Istanbul, the *Struma* presented a dilemma for the British government. While many British officials, including Winston Churchill, were personally sympathetic to the plight of Europe's Jews, certain elements of the government were so adamant about their opposition that in late 1940 they had considered a strategy of actually sinking ships carrying illegal immigrants. "This is the only way in which the traffic can with certainty be stopped," said a chilling and at-one-time secret Foreign Office memo. "It is, however, a step which, for obvious reasons, His Majesty's Government would hardly be prepared in any circumstances to authorize."

Cooler heads had prevailed, and the British were relying on a combination of diplomacy and bullying, with mixed results. The illegal traffic had been slowed by bringing pressure on friendly governments to prohibit their ships from carrying refugees and by seizing vessels that did make it to Palestine, deporting or interning the refugees and jailing the crews.

But the British government had been unable to convince the Turks to prevent the passage of ships navigating down the Bosporus, through the Sea of Marmara and the Dardanelles to the Mediterranean. The simple fact was Turkey did not have the legal right to do so, and no amount of persuasion by the British could change those facts.

Turkey had lost control over the Bosporus and its sister strait, the Dardanelles, after World War I. It had been a terrible blow to the country's prestige, and it had taken Ataturk nearly two decades to regain a small measure of sovereignty over the vital waterways. In 1936, Turkey and the other countries that used the straits had signed the Montreux Convention in the Swiss city of Montreux. The convention returned a degree of control over the straits to Turkey, with the restriction that commercial vessels be permitted to transit without interference, in times of peace and war.

The Russians wanted control of the Bosporus in order to keep their supply routes open from the south. This made the issue of Turkish sovereignty over the waterway even more vital to the Turks during World War II. So its leaders followed the Montreux Convention to the letter, which meant steadfastly refusing to block the passage of boats carrying refugees, whether legal or illegal. The British had disputed the Turkish interpretation in 1940 when it unsuccessfully tried to persuade Turkey to stop the *Salvador*, and the matter had arisen again even before the *Struma* left port.

To the British, the *Struma* represented the first of an armada of refugee ships poised to descend on Palestine. They were so eager to stop it that they had jumped the gun and gotten the departure date wrong twice. Part of the reason for the mistakes was that Britain had broken off relations with Romania in early 1941, so British intelligence information from the country was spotty. There were reports in September 1941 and again in October 1941 that the *Struma* had sailed from Constanta. The second erroneous report had sparked an exchange of cables that reflected once more the lengths to which the British government was prepared to go to stop the immigration.

Sir Harold MacMichael, the British high commissioner for Palestine, notified the Colonial Office in London in October that the ship had left Romania loaded with refugees and asked that action be taken to stop its reaching Palestine. The Montreux treaty allowed Turkey to stop vessels for a health inspection, and MacMichael proposed trying to persuade the Turks to use this exception to order the ship back to Romania. If that failed and the ship managed to get past Istanbul, he suggested using British naval vessels to force the ship to the nearest Turkish port.

"The admiralty will try to intercept the *Struma* before she gets to Palestine, but they want to know whether they may tell [the naval commander] that in case of necessity he may enter Turkish territorial waters for the purpose," said a Colonial Office cable sent after receipt of MacMichael's message. "It will be remembered that during the Syrian campaign we attacked the *St. Didier,* a Vichy supply ship, in those waters, but this case is of course not parallel."

The reaction of Britain's ambassador in Ankara was a bit of a surprise. Hughe Knatchbull-Hugessen, the ambassador to Turkey, was a product of Eton and Oxford, the grandson of a prominent Conservative politician and son of a cabinet minister. Beyond his pedigree, he looked like central casting's idea of a British diplomat with a hyphenated name: He was slender, prim, and dressed impeccably, and he was chauffeured about Ankara and Istanbul in a long limousine by a uniformed driver and footman.

He might have been expected to represent the official view, whatever his own feelings. But in this case, he warned that violating Turkish waters, as proposed by MacMichael, would bring unpleasant consequences and no good results. The ship, he said, would simply be sent back out to sea by the Turks if its captain told them he had been ordered to port by the British military.

The objection was grounded in a diplomat's regard for not upsetting the country of his posting. It was also a small signal that Knatchbull-Hugessen was a man willing to follow his own best judgment. In the coming weeks, he proved to be one of the few British diplomats with any sense of compassion for the *Struma*'s passengers, though he would not be able to withstand the power of the Colonial Office in London and MacMichael in Palestine.

Once the *Struma* really did anchor in Istanbul harbor, the captain sent a message to the port authorities that he had engine trouble and requested assistance. The first Turks to board the ship were police, who were suspicious that the captain had faked the engine trouble in an attempt to disembark passengers from the overcrowded ship. On Tuesday, December 16, a team of Turkish marine engineers was brought to the ship and their inspection confirmed the captain's story. The Turks estimated that the work would cost about five thousand dollars and take a week.

Neither the captain nor any passengers would be allowed off the ship while efforts were made to find the money to make the repairs. Food and fresh water were running perilously short, but the Turkish authorities refused to allow any assistance until they decided what to do about the unwanted ship and its unwanted passengers. As food and water dropped to dangerously low levels and its passengers grew more frightened and weaker by the day, the *Struma* was forced to remain isolated in the harbor, surrounded and watched by Turkish authorities.

Chapter 18

On December 20, 1942, five days after the ship arrived, the British ambassador met with the assistant secretary of Turkey's Ministry of Foreign Affairs in Ankara. The Turkish official told Knatchbull-Hugessen that the *Struma* was entitled by law to sail through the straits and the Turkish government could do nothing to stop it.

The official, however, confided that he was inclined to have the ship sent back to the Black Sea. His biggest fear, he said, was that it might founder in the Sea of Marmara and leave any survivors in Turkey, as the *Salvador* had done. It was a callous attitude, and the Turkish official was quick to say that the British could grant a kinder fate to these unfortunate refugees, if they chose.

"If on the other hand His Majesty's Government would let these immigrants enter Palestine, I will let the ship proceed on its voyage and even assist it," the Turkish official told the ambassador.

"His Majesty's Government does not want these people in Palestine and they have no permission to go there," replied Knatchbull-Hugessen, following the official London line before veering off course. "But from a humanitarian point of view, I do not like the proposal to send the ship back into the Black Sea. If the Turkish government must interfere with the ship on the ground that you cannot keep the distressed Jews in Turkey, let her rather go toward the Dardanelles. It might be that if they reached Palestine they might, despite their illegality, receive humane treatment."

Knatchbull-Hugessen recounted the conversation in a cable to the Foreign Office that was received in London at 7:55 on the morning of December 21. The replies were swift and stinging enough that, were it not for his pedigree, the ambassador might have found himself out of work. Britain's Colonial Office, which had authority over Palestine and other extensions of the empire, had always taken a much harder line on immigration than the Foreign Office, and the responses to Knatchbull-Hugessen's humanitarian suggestion were sharpest from those quarters.

From Palestine, MacMichael fired off a response that same day warning that the policy was still to prevent illegal immigration. He bemoaned the fact that the ambassador had missed a golden opportunity to urge the Turkish government to follow the official's inclination and return the ship to the Black Sea.

Edmund Boyd, an official in the Colonial Office in London, followed the same logic in a memorandum for the Foreign Office. "As you will remember, we have on several occasions in the past repeated to the Turkish Government the great importance, both on political and military grounds, of taking all possible steps to stop the traffic in illegal immigrants to Palestine, but the Turkish Government have hitherto not felt able to give much assistance in the matter," he said. "It is therefore a matter for considerable satisfaction that they should have adopted a helpful attitude in the present case, and it would be very unfortunate if they were to be given any impression that His Majesty's Government had modified their policy or that, if the illegal immigrants were allowed to proceed, there would be any prospect of their being allowed to remain in Palestine."

Lord Moyne, an opponent of Jewish immigration, was the head of the Colonial Office at the time. In response to Knatchbull-Hugessen's remarks, he wrote to Richard Law, the parliamentary undersecretary of the Foreign Office, demanding that steps be taken to reverse the position and that further steps be taken to convince the Turks to stop the ship from going to Palestine, where the British were still having trouble deporting recent refugees.

"The landing of seven hundred more immigrants will not only be a formidable addition to the difficulties of the High Commissioner who already is unable to get shipping to take the last party on to Mauritius, but it will have a deplorable effect throughout the Balkans in encouraging further Jews to embark on a traffic which has now been condoned by His Majesty's ambassador," said Lord Moyne. "I find it difficult to write with moderation about this occurrence which is in flat contradiction of established Government policy and I should be very glad if you could perhaps even now do something to retrieve the position and to urge that Turkish authorities should be asked to send the ship back to the Black Sea, as they originally proposed."

On December 27, the chastened Knatchbull-Hugessen met again with the Foreign Ministry official in Ankara. This time he followed the London line to the letter, explaining that Britain had no intention of permitting the *Struma*'s passengers to land in Palestine. He said the British government wanted the Turks to do everything in their power to stop its voyage and send the ship back to the Black Sea. "He replied that he realized this and that I had not given him any other impression," the ambassador told London in a cable the next day. "I said that His Majesty's Government saw no reason why the Turkish Government should not send the *Struma* back into the Black Sea if they wished."

The message could not have been clearer—the British did not want these Jews, and Turkey did not want them either. Getting rid of the unwanted ship and its passengers, however, would prove to be a difficult task.

As the political machinations began, conditions on the ship deteriorated. Food was running low, and the passengers were isolated, told nothing of the discussions concerning their fate. Hopes rose and fell with the waves as they sat in the harbor. Many still expected to continue on to Palestine, and they viewed this as a temporary delay, even a victory, since they were in neutral waters. A minority, however, feared that every day they spent in the harbor was a day closer to being sent back to Romania.

The ship spent ten miserable days in the harbor before the passengers saw the first sign of help. Simon Brod, the indefatigable representative of the Jewish Agency in Istanbul, had finally persuaded the authorities to allow him to ferry food, water, medicine, and some old French newspapers to the ship. His small boat was stopped thirty yards from the ship, and the goods were transferred to a police launch, which took them the final distance. As passengers on deck pleaded for help, Brod shouted encouragement and promised to return with the most precious commodity—word about their fate. The goods Brod brought were sufficient to keep people alive. It was not nearly enough to feed all of the hungry or heal the increasing numbers who were growing ill.

Word of the deteriorating conditions and continued deprivations leaked out. Eleven days after the ship's arrival, Samuel W. Honaker, the American consul general in Istanbul, wrote a lengthy cable to the State Department in Washington. "Conditions aboard are described as deplorable," said Honaker. "As a matter of fact, reports from all sources depict dreadful conditions prevailing on the S.S. *Struma* and are chiefly attributable to overcrowding and lack of proper and sufficient foodstuff. It is even said that there are no means of cooking because of the lack of fuel or of proper utensils."

Honaker was not entirely sympathetic, however. The ship, he wrote, "has various enemy characteristics and is actually transporting enemy subjects." This was a reference to the fact that Romania had sided with Germany. The canard that the desperate men, women, and children posed a threat to the Allies would be used again and again in the campaign to stop the ship from leaving Istanbul.

Lord Moyne had raised the same supposed security risk in his sharp response to Knatchbull-Hugessen, though he had cast it in darker terms. British intelligence suspected that the Nazis had infiltrated such ships. "We have good reason to believe that this traffic is favoured by the Gestapo and the security services attach the greatest importance to preventing the influx of Nazi agents under the cloak of refugees," he wrote.

It was a ridiculous accusation for which no evidence would ever be found, either for the *Struma* or any other ship of immigrants. It was part of the arsenal that the British government was prepared to unleash to stop the flow of desperate Jews in search of a haven from the Holocaust. It was also part of a subtle attempt by isolationists and anti-Semites in Britain and America to avoid dealing directly with the Jews desperate to flee Europe.

The Saturday Evening Post was known as "America's magazine," and its covers, particularly those done by Norman Rockwell, reflected both the best of American patriotism and the best, or worst, of its propaganda machine. On March 29, 1941, the magazine published a lengthy article claiming the Nazis had infiltrated spies into the ranks of Jewish refugees to undermine the Allied effort. The article asserted that Nazi spies had been sent on refugee ships to Palestine to help sow discord in an attempt to swing the Arabs to the German side. It also quoted an unidentified "unofficial report" saying that the Germans had set up a special school in Prague to train Nazis to act as Jews. "They learn to speak Yiddish, to read Hebrew, to pray," said the article. "They are supposed to submit to circumcision."

In *Are We Our Brothers' Keepers?* a 1985 book analyzing international response to the plight of Jews in World War II, Haskel Lookstein wrote that in the United States there was a "veritable security psychosis, a fear that Nazis would plant agents and spies among refugees." In January of 1945, The National Opinion Research Poll reported that forty-six percent of all Americans opposed admitting Jewish refugees to the United States. The good news was that the figure was down from a high of seventy-seven percent opposing in 1938. As a reflection of his own concern about public opinion, Lookstein wrote, President Roosevelt avoided referring to the "Jewish plight" and called the victims of Nazi persecution by "the bland term of 'political refugees.' "

By late 1941, the issue of Nazi spies hidden among the refugees had been used for at least a year by the British to justify restrictions on immigration to Palestine. In numerous cables, the office of the high commissioner in Palestine and his counterparts in the Colonial Office in London speculated about Nazi infiltrators and fifth columnists. It, like the *Post* article, was speculation, with absolutely no proof.

Indeed, these accusations in one of America's most influential magazines were part of a long-running propaganda campaign aimed at justifying the ill treatment of refugees seeking haven from history's worst nightmare. The campaign allowed officials in the United States, Britain, and other countries to turn their backs on ships like the *St. Louis,* an ocean liner that carried 1,128 German Jews to the United States and Cuba in the summer of 1939 on a futile voyage that ended when all but twenty-two of them were returned to Europe. At the time, the United States State Department and particularly Breckinridge Long, an assistant secretary of state, were most unsympathetic to Jewish refugees and insisted on enforcing legal requirements to the letter in immigration cases, arguing in part that the refugees might be German agents. The same ill-founded sentiment would play a role in the fate of the *Struma,* too.

Chapter 19

In the winter of 1941, Izak Abudaram was ten years old, and every day after school he went to his grandmother's bread shop in Istanbul to give her a hand. One day he arrived to find her standing on the step outside and engaged in an intense discussion with three men he had never seen before. Izak could not hear what was being said. He was too shy to move closer. From his grandmother's face and gestures, he decided that something important was happening, and he watched closely.

After a few minutes, the men walked to a nearby truck. They pulled out twenty to twenty-five large, empty sacks, took them into the store, and handed them to Izak's grandmother. She began to fill them with loaves of bread from the shelves. Then she went next door to another shop and filled more of the bags with sugar and cheese. The men carried the sacks to the truck and tossed them into the back.

"Can I go along?" asked the boy, enticed by the mystery.

No one responded, so he climbed into the back of the truck with the bread, sugar, and cheese. The truck followed the narrow streets down to Kadikoy, one of the harbors on the Asian side of the Bosporus. It pulled up to the dock alongside one of the paddle-wheel ferries that plied the strait, carrying commuters back and forth across the Bosporus. Izak heard the men talking to the ferry captain. After a few minutes, the captain motioned toward the truck and nodded. The men walked back and began carrying the sacks to the ferry. Still, no one told the boy to go home, so he got on the ferry and rode with them across the water.

At the bustling Eminonu dock on the European side, the evening commuters were beginning their trek home. The sights and smells of this most-crowded part of the city were overwhelming for a ten-year-old, and Izak stayed close to the men, helping as they carried the sacks off the ferry and loaded them into a waiting truck. From there they drove to another dock, called Sarayburnu, in the shadow of Topkapi Palace, where two customs officials inspected the sacks. They pulled open the tops and poked among the loaves of bread, ran their hands through the sugar, and sniffed at the cheese.

When the inspection ended, the goods were loaded onto another boat and they headed out a few hundred yards into the harbor toward a slightly larger ship at anchor. They pulled alongside, and ropes were lowered, tied to the tops of the sacks, and then given a yank so they could be hauled aboard the larger ship.

What had started as an adventurous game for the boy turned into something grim the moment he looked up at the deck of the larger ship, which was not far above the supply boat where he stood.

There, above him hanging over the railing of the *Struma,* in the dim light of the early winter evening, were what appeared to be the haunted faces of the damned.

By now many of the refugees had fevers, especially the children. They slept in the dank bowels of the ship, moving as little as possible, but trying to keep warm. There had been no hint of illness when they left Romania. Now sickness was spreading through the ship. One child had almost died from the high fevers before they got medicine to save him. They slept embracing each other to keep warm. They talked about Palestine. They dreamed about it. When this boat arrived with its meager supplies, it was simultaneously an event in itself and a symbol that they had not been forgotten.

"I would never forget children's shining eyes against the gas lamps," Abudaram said, overcome by tears almost sixty years later. "They looked as if they were on top of each other. Children, with their hands outstretched, calling out to me in a language I could not understand. Women, their hair dirty and wild in the wind. Gaunt men. It was so frightening to me. I was so close to them."

It was past ten and dark by the time the boy got to his home on the

Asian side of the straits. His mother was worried sick, and she beat him for his transgression, demanding repeatedly, "How could you have done this to me?"

He was unchastened. The second time the men came to his grandmother's shop, he made the same disturbing trip again. But there wasn't a third time. He was not sure why the men stopped coming as abruptly as they had appeared. He decided later that his grandmother had given as much as she could to those poor passengers. There was a war going on. Everyone in Istanbul was suffering from shortages. The city's Jewish community, dwindling in size and facing an undercurrent of anti-Semitism in the predominantly Muslim country, was reluctant to extend too visible a hand.

"We kept away from them, including keeping a distance from the *Struma*," Abudaram said. "We went to work. We went to school. The help came from a few people in each Jewish neighborhood who organized what they could. Mostly we kept our distance."

For six hundred years, the Ottoman Empire had risen and declined, as had the fortunes of the religious minorities in the lands they ruled. The Turks advanced from the barren foothills of Anatolia to rule from the Danube to the Nile, spreading a civilization that was at once militaristic and tolerant. The Ottomans admired all forms of self-government, often folding newfound concepts into their own organizations. "They pay great respect to the customs of foreign nations, even to the detriment of their own religious scruples," noted Ogier Ghiselin de Busbecq, a Flemish nobleman who wrote extensively about the Ottomans while serving as ambassador in Constantinople from 1554 to 1562.

As long as they did not come into conflict with Islamic society, Christians and Jews who were conquered by the Ottomans were permitted to maintain their own laws and religious practices. After Sultan Mehmet II drove the Christians out of Constantinople in 1453, he gave the Greek patriarch wide religious and secular powers and issued a decree inviting the Jews to stay and maintain their own communities.

When the Jews were expelled from Spain in 1492, they found a haven among the Ottomans. "They say Ferdinand is a wise monarch,"

Sultan Beyazit II said of the Spanish king. "How could he be, he who impoverishes his country to enrich mine!" The Spanish Jews settled in the Balkans, then under Ottoman control, in what is now western Turkey. They were exiled bankers, physicians, teachers, and craftsmen who found that they and their religion were treated on a par with the Christian minority in their new home, which was how it remained for centuries to come.

The Republic of Turkey, which replaced the Ottoman Empire in 1923, recognized Jews and Christians as minorities and Turks and accorded them the freedoms they enjoyed under the sultans. During the early 1930s, Turkey took in several hundred of the first refugees from Nazi persecution. The circumstances of their arrival were unusual.

Ataturk had set an ambitious course for modernizing his country along European lines. He had banned the traditional fez, ordering his countrymen to wear fedoras instead. He had changed to a Latin alphabet, introduced modern dancing and European music, and moved the capital to Ankara.

As it happened, Ataturk had considerable problems with his teeth, and his dentist was Sami Gunzberg. During their many lengthy sessions, Gunzberg had spoken with Ataturk about the plight of Germany's Jews under Hitler. Turkey's leader had an idea: He could offer asylum to some of the most gifted Jews, and they would help him transform his country into a modern state.

Among those who accepted Ataturk's offer were a number of leading German professors, who were appointed to posts at Istanbul University, which was a major focus of the efforts to modernize the country. There also were top-rank scientists and doctors, as well as archeologists, artists, and musicians. Most had fled Germany because they were Jewish, though some were non-Jews who had left because they opposed the Nazi regime.

"The authorities at Ankara have attempted to give the German professors every possible facility for carrying out their work," the American embassy reported to the secretary of state in 1936. "Enormous sums have been spent on equipment for laboratories and hospitals. One now sees in Turkey hospitals equal in equipment to any in the world. In addition, more or less adequate appropriations have been made for operating these physical plants. It is understood that strong advocates and protectors of the professors exist in high circles in Ankara, and that any complaints which are made against them fall on deaf ears in the Capitol."

Many Turkish professors and scientists resented the Germans. The newcomers were paid more than their Turkish counterparts, received the latest equipment, and had been allowed to bring their own assistants. The Germans did little to mitigate the situation. Most taught their classes in German, with translators at their side, and they lived together in Bebek, the Bosporus village that was Istanbul's most exclusive suburb. The German medical professors were prohibited from engaging directly in private practice, but Turks flocked to the clinics they operated to receive treatment that was better than that provided by most Turkish doctors and free, too. The natural result was a widespread dislike of the Germans in Istanbul's medical community.

Had Turkish resentment gone no further than the privileged German professors, it would have had little effect on the country as a whole. However, fueled by Nazi propaganda and fanned by Nazi sympathizers, anti-Semitism gained momentum in certain circles. In 1934, Jews were forced to flee riots in western Turkey after rumors circulated that they were plotting to overthrow the republic with the help of the worldwide Zionist movement. To his credit, Ismet Inonu, prime minister at the time, responded to the incident by defending the Jews in a speech to a special session of the Parliament. "Anti-Semitism is neither a Turkish product nor part of the Turkish mind." he said.

But anti-Semitism persisted, as evidenced in various publications and organizations. There were vicious cartoons published at the time showing penurious Jews with large noses. One pictured a refugee boat, perhaps even the *Struma,* the crowded passengers looking over the sides at two fish. One fish is saying to the other, "Why are there no scraps near this ship?" "Because those are Jews on that boat," replies the other. On the other hand, Abraham Galante, the only Jewish member of the Turkish Parliament, wrote extensively to defend his country's treatment of Jews, placing full blame for the troubles of the Jews at the feet of the British.

Throughout the 1930s there were also attempts to pass laws

prohibiting the immigration of Jews to Turkey. In June 1938, the government adopted a measure that forbade transit through Turkey to people without proper visas or enough cash, a law clearly aimed at the Jews fleeing Europe.

Chaim Weizmann, the president of the Jewish Agency in Palestine, paid a secret visit to Ankara in November 1938 to try to persuade the country to reverse its policy. The trip was arranged by Gunzberg, who, after his successful role in bringing German Jews to Turkey, had offered to help again.

Weizmann's goal was audacious. He wanted to buy access to Turkey for two hundred thousand European Jews trying to escape Hitler. While he did not meet with Ataturk, who was gravely ill and died that same month, Weizmann made his case to a number of senior ministers, including Inonu. He offered to transfer half a million pounds sterling in gold to Turkey per year for an indefinite period in exchange for providing refuge to Jewish refugees. While Turkey's finances were in terrible shape, leaving the country unable to rebuild its military despite the German threat, the ministers rejected the proposal. They told Weizmann that settling so many Jews in the country would disrupt the social structure and trigger more active anti-Semitism against Jews already in Turkey.

In early 1939, the police in Istanbul began deportation proceedings against German and Italian Jews because their own governments had revoked their citizenship, leaving them technically stateless and unable to remain legally in Turkey. The policy was reversed after complaints from Jewish leaders that the deportees faced persecution and they remained in Turkey.

The government went on record saying it would not accept foreign Jews. Refik Saydam, who had become prime minister when Inonu took over as president upon Ataturk's death, made policy clear in a speech before Parliament. "As to foreign Jews, we are not going to accept any Jews facing oppression elsewhere into our country either in groups or on an individual basis," he said. "However, there are Jews among experts that we have brought in for our national and administrative needs. If they happen to have sisters or families or close relatives in other countries who would wish to come to our country, we would welcome them to enable the experts to work with comfortable minds, only provided that they would not ask for employment."

The outbreak of war increased the pressure on Turkey from all sides. Its location made the country a natural haven for Jews trying to evade Nazi persecution as central Europe and the Balkans fell to the German army. The Germans demanded that neutral Turkey not permit the immigration of Jews, and the Turks did not want to do anything that would risk a Nazi invasion. Simultaneously, the British renewed their demands that Turkey halt the flow of Jews to Palestine.

In February 1941, as the wave of refugees was building across Europe, Turkey's Parliament finally passed a law imposing new restrictions on Jewish immigration. The first clause of the law said, "The entry into Turkey of Jewish individuals—whatever their religion is today—who are subjected to restrictions in regard to living and travel by the countries of which they are citizens, is forbidden." The clause applied to virtually every potential Jewish refugee, since their own countries refused to allow them to travel. The only exceptions to the stringent policy would be professionals whose skills were deemed necessary in Turkey.

The law not only closed off Jewish immigration to Turkey, it took a far more serious step: It restricted the passage of most Jewish refugees through the country. Only Jews who held valid visas for another country were to be allowed to pass through Turkey. The limitation applied to the vast majority of refugees, since most of the world also had closed its doors to Jewish immigrants and the British were restricting visas for Palestine.

At the same time, the government authorized hard currency for the Jewish Agency to help pay for its efforts to feed and clothe the handful of refugees who did have visas on their journey through Turkey. The money, and the implicit authorization to operate, was essential to the agency's ability to help hundreds of Jews escaping through Turkey.

This policy covered only a fraction of those desperate to escape the

Nazis. The practical result of the transit law was that the Turkish government admitted and assisted Jewish refugees only when it was certain they would continue on to Palestine or another country. The most desperate refugees, who had fled without visas for Palestine or appropriate permission from their own governments, were condemned.

Even as the Turkish government made it harder for Jews to pass through the country, some of its diplomats were risking their lives to help Jews. Thousands of Jews had left Turkey in the early part of the twentieth century. Some fled during the country's bloody war of independence in the 1920s, and others left in the face of economic uncertainty in the 1930s. Under Turkey's constitution, however, they could retain their citizenship by registering with local consulates in their new countries.

Few expatriate Jews had bothered to undertake the formalities of registration, but when they faced persecution by the Nazis in countries like France and Greece, many Turkish Jews sought help from their former country's diplomats. In Paris, for instance, a young vice consul named Namik Kemal Yolga issued visas and passports to several hundred Turkish Jews to help them avoid anti-Jewish laws in occupied France and, in some cases, leave the country. On the Greek island of Rhodes, Consul General Selahattin Ulkumen's assistance to Turkish Jews led to Nazi sympathizers bombing the consulate, an incident in which his pregnant wife was injured.

Another young Turkish diplomat in Marseilles, France, Necdet Kent, threw himself into the line of fire when a young consulate worker alerted him that German soldiers were loading Turkish Jews onto a train destined for Germany. When Kent arrived at the Saint Charles train station, he found cattle cars filled with Jews by following the sounds of sobs and shouts.

"The one single memory of that evening, which will never be erased from my mind," Kent said, "was the inscription which I saw on one of the wagons: 'This wagon may be loaded with twenty heads of cattle and five hundred kilograms of grass.' Inside, the wagons held about eighty people, packed on top of each other."

One of the cars on the train was filled with Turkish Jews. A

German officer approached Kent and demanded angrily that he leave. When Kent refused, saying that he could not leave his fellow Turkish citizens, he was told that they were not Turks, just Jews. Realizing that he would not win the argument there on the platform, Kent stepped past the officer into the cattle car, swearing that he would go, too, and upping the ante in what the Germans feared would become an international incident.

The train pulled out, with the young diplomat in the car. At the next station, several German officers entered the car and said that there must have been a misunderstanding, that the train had left the station before Kent had the opportunity to leave. They offered him a ride back to Marseilles in a waiting Mercedes.

Still, Kent held his ground. He said that there had been no mistake, that eighty Turkish citizens had been loaded onto the cattle car because they were Jews. He told the Germans that he was a representative of a government that denounced such treatment. Defeated, the German officers let all the Turkish Jews off the train, and they returned with Kent to Marseilles.

"The inner peace I felt when I reached my bed toward morning that day is one that I have not savored much since," Kent said. "What I have done is what I should have done."

Later the Turks would hail the two diplomats as heroes, and certainly they behaved heroically, but they were the exception to the general rule in Turkey and elsewhere. Turkey was not the haven for wartime Jewish refugees that the Turks would one day claim, and the Turkish government's contention that 100,000 Jews passed safely through their country in the war is regarded by most historians as a gross exaggeration. Though exact figures are difficult to find, the authoritative *Encyclopedia of the Holocaust* said that a total of 16,474 documented and undocumented Jews passed through Turkey during the course of the war.

And when it came to the *Struma,* there were few such acts of heroism. Perhaps this was inevitable in a country struggling to remain neutral, besieged by its own domestic problems and deprivations. But even within the small Jewish community, there was a reluctance to speak out, much less help out, too openly.

Chapter 20

In many ways, Turkey's response to the potential flood of Jewish refugees was no different from that of numerous other countries. Many nations used quotas and legal technicalities to turn away Jewish refugees. Turkey's circumstances were special, which made its behavior both understandable and tragic. The constant possibility of German invasion created a threatening atmosphere in Turkey that did not exist in places like the United States, which also limited Jewish immigration. Turkey's location, however, made it a critical transit point for European Jews; shutting its doors condemned unknown thousands to concentration camps, suffering, and death.

As in any tragedy of such monumental proportions, the Holocaust left a legacy of heroes. The efforts of some are memorialized by history. The actions of men such as Oskar Schindler and Raoul Wallenberg illuminate the best of humanity in its darkest hours and stand as symbols of good against evil. Many other people performed their deeds in near anonymity, though their efforts were no less important and their sacrifices no less harsh. One of those little-known heroes was Simon Brod, the fifty-year-old Turkish Jew who, since before the wreck of the *Salvador* in 1940, had devoted himself to helping as many Jewish refugees as possible make it safely through Turkey and on to Palestine.

When others were silent and fearful, Brod worked obsessively on behalf of those fleeing the Nazis. He sacrificed his business, his family, and his health on behalf of the thousands of Jews on the run. In a city with a population of sixty thousand to seventy thousand Jews, Brod was one of the few who refused to be cowed by the anti-Semitism that ran just below the surface.

Some sixty years later, Ishak Alaton remembered what it was like to be a Jew in the winter of 1941 in Istanbul. "There was a total fear of speaking out," he said. "There is a saying in Turkish. It's actually a mixture of Turkish and Ladino, the Spanish spoken by the Sephardic Jews who came from Spain. It says, 'I do not mix myself with matters of the government.' This had become a motto. The help given to the *Struma* was not done ostentatiously."

The only official help for Jewish refugees in Turkey came through the Jewish Agency. It was a small operation, headed by Chaim Barlas, who had been sent from Palestine to run the office. This office became increasingly important as European countries fell to the Nazis and the agency's other offices closed in country after country.

Barlas was supposed to deal only with legal immigrants. His ability to operate in Turkey, where refugees tried to enter from the Balkans, was hobbled further by the refusal of the Turks to grant the agency full legal status, for fear of offending the Germans. As a result, Barlas concentrated on legal immigrants and left the illegal refugees primarily to Brod, who knew the way the clandestine game was played and had an extensive list of useful contacts from his many years as a businessman in Istanbul.

The son of Polish Jews who had emigrated to Turkey in the late nineteenth century, Brod was a short, balding, red-faced man given to explosive displays of temper and tireless in the cajoling of Turkish police and customs authorities. A colleague described his eyes as being "like the heads of steel-blue pins that darted around to take in every new situation; they could be angelic one moment and scornful the next."

After turning over the operation of the family's prosperous textile business to a brother in the early 1940s, he spent all of his time and most of his money on refugee issues. He was the first to learn of a brewing crisis, the first to come up with the bribe that Turks called *baksheesh,* and the last to give up. He could often be seen walking briskly between the various consulates and government offices in

Istanbul's busy Taksim neighborhood, head down, muttering to himself, and scribbling furiously on his cigarette packages.

"He was a chain smoker, and he used to write down everything he spent on those cigarette packs, but he was always throwing them away and he couldn't tell the exact amount he spent helping people," said his daughter, Marta, who left Turkey after the war and now lives in Spain. "He spent from his own pocket."

Some of the information on the cigarettes packages was transferred to logs, which were filed with the Jewish Agency for reimbursement. They offer a glimpse of the tireless efforts and varied tasks that Brod undertook. In a two-week span in June 1940, he bought eggs and bread for one family, vegetables for another; he paid twenty-five Turkish lira for wood and coal to heat the apartment where another family was staying and fifty lira for an atlas to help guide a group of refugees out of the country. He bought butter, eggs, bread, and fish for a large group of people and three beds for a family. With all that he was responsible for, it is testimony to his sensitivity that he also bought hundreds of postcards and stamps in early 1942 to be given to the people on board the *Struma,* so that they could write to those they left behind. Brod's contribution to David Stoliar is also recorded in those notes—one watch, one valise, a pair of shoes, and photographs.

The kitchen of the family's villa on the Asian side of the Bosporus in Istanbul was always filled with refugees who needed money or a place to stay or a ticket out of Turkey. Marta and her mother were constantly preparing food for the visitors, helping them rebuild strength for the next leg of their journey.

Sometimes Brod would get a telephone call in the middle of the night. Someone needed food or papers. He would rouse his wife, and she would begin cooking while he telephoned other people in the small circle willing to take the risk of helping the refugees, demanding that they come to his house immediately.

"I would receive a phone call from him at two in the morning, and he would call me to an immediate meeting," recalled Hayim Eliezer Kohen, then a young university student who worked with Brod in the early 1940s. "Mrs. Brod would be there making soup, and she would help us with the packages all night long. There were six to ten people in these meetings. I never knew where the food for those packages came from, but I knew Brod was spending his own money."

In one of the kitchen cupboards, Brod stashed blank passports supplied by an Englishman who worked at the British consulate and other friendly diplomats. When someone needed papers, he would get their photo taken and paste it into the passport. Because of a shortage of passports, he often combined strangers—a man, woman, and child—into an instant family, providing them with a single passport containing all three photos.

Often he sent his wife and daughter out of the kitchen so that he could concentrate on his forgeries. Then he would storm out of the house, headed for the next place he felt he was needed. For a while he had a black Nash and a driver. He later abandoned both and relied on the ferries and taxis because they were more efficient. Besides, he could no longer afford the car.

An Istanbul police officer, Ahmet Demir, lived near Brod's home and often stopped or telephoned to provide information when a group of refugees had been arrested or when a ship had docked. He had notified Brod in December 1940 when the *Salvador* foundered and sank in the Sea of Marmara, and he telephoned the morning the *Struma* was towed into port, initiating one of Brod's most desperate and unsuccessful missions.

Hayim Kohen joined Brod at the Sarayburnu dock that day. All they could do initially was look at the decrepit ship anchored about three hundred yards offshore. "It looks terrible," Kohen said to Brod. "It hardly looks like a boat it's in such horrible condition."

Over the next few days, Brod held urgent meetings with anyone in the government who would see him, demanding that he be allowed to take supplies to the stranded ship. Only after he agreed that the effort would be coordinated through the Turkish Red Crescent, an official aid organization, was he allowed to approach the *Struma*.

Ten days had passed since the ship's arrival, and the passengers were on the edge of starvation. Even then, Brod was prohibited from getting closer than thirty yards, and the supplies had to be transferred to a police boat for the final leg.

Eventually the Turkish authorities relaxed the prohibitions, their strictness eased by bribes from Brod. The weekly supply boat was allowed to pull up alongside the *Struma* and pass the food and medicine directly up to the passengers. Occasionally the aid workers were allowed on board to distribute the food, along with newspapers and, once, a stack of blank postcards. The amount of food delivered to the ship with help from the Red Crescent grew—dozens of kilos of bread, cheese, dried fish, potatoes, and nuts. It was never enough, but it kept starvation at bay.

Kohen and his colleagues were told to speak as little as possible to the passengers. He and the others feared angering the Turkish authorities and possibly being banned from returning to the ship. Despite the desperation in the eyes of the passengers, they were orderly and well behaved when the aid workers came on board. These were professionals, intellectuals, and other people with too much dignity to crack in front of outsiders. Instead, they thanked the workers profusely and maintained an aura of calm and organization as they collected the goods for later distribution among the other passengers. What Kohen did not see were the real conditions on the ship—the squalor below deck, the rising tensions, the lengths to which some were willing to go to stay alive.

Chapter 21

Standing on the polished deck of a British Royal Navy cruiser in January 1942, Olivia Manning experienced a moment of utter confusion. She and her husband, a British journalist, had joined a party of diplomats and officials for an evening's pleasure cruise along the Bosporus and around Istanbul harbor. The city lights sparkled in the chill air, and the ship's forward searchlight played across the night water. The guests danced and sipped martinis and gin and tonics. The festivities stopped abruptly when the searchlight paused on what appeared to be a derelict ship, illuminating rows of faces, white and unsmiling, as they stared back at the partygoers.

"Who are they?" asked one of the shocked guests.

"What are they doing there?" asked another.

Someone suggested it was a prison ship.

"The light shifted and the party forgot its grim audience hidden in the dark," Manning, a novelist who had lived in Romania briefly before the war, later wrote in a newspaper article. "The ship was the *Struma*."

The images of gaunt, ghostlike men and women from the Nazi death camps were not yet stamped on the world's consciousness: The hair-raising atrocities were proceeding largely behind closed gates at the end of 1941. In the harbor of one of the world's largest cities, though, a place teeming with diplomats and journalists, the panorama of Jewish suffering was visible to anyone who cared or dared to look.

A routine, like the dull ache of a rotten tooth, had fallen over the passengers during Istanbul's harshest winter in twenty-five years. Temperatures dropped below freezing at night and rarely rose above thirty-five degrees Fahrenheit. Sometimes a sharp pain jolted everyone from the torpor; a fight over food or an illness could quickly escalate into something that seemed almost cataclysmic. People slept much of the day and all night, huddled together for warmth, numbed physically and psychologically. The acrid smell of urine and feces was everywhere. When the sun went down, the ship was blanketed in a darkness interrupted only by the flicker of the occasional candle that left people on the edge of the weak light, mothlike. Buffeted by winter storms and icy winds, and by the gyrations of their own hope and despair, they no longer called the ship by its hated name. Instead, it was the "floating cage" or the "rat trap."

Moments of relief occasionally disrupted the ache, times when the passengers believed they would resume their journey or at least be taken from the ship to quarters on land. Rumors swept through the ship in minutes—the British were going to give them visas, the Turks would let them off, the children were going to be allowed to proceed, everyone would be transferred to a better ship, and the journey would resume. People wanted to keep hope alive, fanning each small ember with care and patience. No one was willing to let the dream of Palestine grow cold and expire.

"Slowly we began to realize that, although we had reached neutral territory, salvation would not be quick," David Stoliar recalled. "We tried to cope with the misery on board—lack of food, lack of space, lack of soap, with the cold and the dirt and the insects sticking to our unwashed shirts. Baths or showers were impossible, and we suffered stoically cold and dirt and hunger pangs. The only daily routine was the meals, once a day, and as meager as they were, they constituted our sole rhythm of life. The rest of the day was an exercise in hollow hope."

Food became an obsession. Not just eating, but remembering. "These were very intellectual people, but the daily discussions were not about books or important subjects," David Frenk remembered. "They were about food." Passengers would gather in small groups and recount in great detail the vast buffets at wedding receptions, the caviar and smoked salmon at Capsa's in Bucharest, their favorite recipes. Like condemned prisoners ordering their last meal, the passengers imagined feasts from better days.

This obsession manifested itself other ways, too. Istanbul's Jewish community continued to bring supplies to the ship, but the deliveries were meager and irregular. Despite the Turkish government's initial approval, Brod and his colleagues had to bribe the police guarding the ship to bring food onboard each week. One particular police commander oversaw the collection of bribes. When he was off for a day or in a bad mood, the supply boat would be turned back without unloading its precious cargo. There was so little food to go around that a loaf of bread was sliced into twenty-five pieces to feed twenty-five people. There was never more than one meager meal a day.

The Betar leaders had been replaced with a new committee elected by the passengers. Some members of the youth group remained in authority, but the new leadership comprised older men with real-life experience running business or law firms. The new leader was Moritz Ignat Merlaub, a thirty-seven-year-old lawyer from Bucharest. The new team organized crews to distribute the food each evening. Sometimes the distribution team had to be tough to keep people from grabbing the bread and cheese as it was hauled aboard. Guards were posted outside the storage area.

With a diet of bread, cheese, and salted dried herring, the occasional arrival of fresh oranges was cause for celebration. One day a passenger, a prominent engineer from Bucharest, crouched on deck, watching carefully as a hefty sack of oranges was pulled up the side of the ship. He followed the men with the oranges until their backs were turned and he quickly snatched one. Someone saw and raised a cry. The engineer was caught clutching the treasured orange, and he was punished.

When another man was caught stealing an orange from a sleeping child, there were irrational shouts that he should be hanged. The leadership committee held a trial, and the verdict was that the offender would not get another orange until the ship reached Palestine.

Alexander Segal kept one warm memory from that time on the ship, and it involved an orange and his first love, a young girl named

Valerie. "What I do remember is a paradox," he said. "In the midst of all that unpleasantness, oranges arrived. Hundreds of them. An orange was such a luxury in those days. Elsewhere in the world, an entire family would share an orange at the holidays. But on board the *Struma,* we got an orange to ourselves. What a luxury it was to eat an orange, to share it with a special friend."

Once, a short-lived mutiny against the leadership erupted. The ship's leadership committee was in a difficult position. It was the only available target of passenger hostility and frustration as well as the gatekeeper for the irregular shipments of food. Someone claimed he had seen a committee member eating a whole herring when everyone else had only a half. Angry passengers called for a revolt. When confronted, however, the witness admitted that he had not really seen anything, and the furor dissolved.

David Frenk, who had proven his ability to survive during his passage from Czernowitz to Bucharest, managed to get one of the coveted jobs hauling food aboard. Each time someone from the supply ship handed him a sack full of loaves of bread, he went through the same covert ritual. Frenk would break off a small piece of bread and hide it inside his shirt. By the end of the day, he and the other guards would have enough bread to ensure their survival for another week.

Efforts were made to construct a normal existence, or as close to one as possible under the circumstances. Two brothers, Jacob and Solomon Leibovici, provided a welcome and entertaining distraction by singing songs that were popular when they left Romania. Small plays and readings were performed, often involving the children. There were classes in Hebrew and Jewish history as well as religious services, though many of the passengers were not particularly observant. People gathered in small groups above and below decks, to reminisce about the lives they'd left behind, and to dream about the new lives they hoped to undertake.

As the clock counted down to the end of 1941, the captain and the second mate decided to throw a New Year's Eve party for the passengers. A table was set up in the middle of the largest sleeping quarters and it was decorated with colorful pieces of fabric. In the middle stood a single bottle of wine, reserved for the captain and second mate. The mechanics even coaxed the generator to work for a few hours, providing lights as midnight approached.

When the sirens of the ships in the harbor began to sound at midnight, Horia Lobel, the ship's doctor, rose and proposed a minute of silence in memory of the Jews who were being slaughtered by the Nazis and their sympathizers across Europe. Standing in the halo of faint light, he talked about the tragic history of the Jews and the necessity of making certain it never happened again. Once the *Struma* arrived in Palestine, he said forcefully, the young men among the passengers must take up arms and join the fight against fascism to ensure the future for generations of Jews.

If Lobel was thinking about the wife and unborn child he had left behind in Bucharest, he did not say so. Though only thirty years old, he spoke with a power and emotion that was deeply moving to young and old alike. There was a profound recognition of the barbarism and discrimination faced by Jews over the centuries, and a somber reminder that their own arduous journey was not only a quest for their freedom, but part of the larger struggle on behalf of the generations that would come after them.

There were no pops of champagne corks, no bands striking up a tune to welcome 1942. There were only the doctor's words, heavy and serious, bearing a message of hope that the coming year might offer an avenue out of despair and into the new land. People hugged their loved ones. Husbands and wives kissed each other. The Liebovici brothers sang a medley of Romanian songs, and others joined in a hopeful chorus to welcome the New Year onboard.

Even the gruff captain, so exasperated with his plight and his passengers, was moved by what he saw. When Garabatenko rose from his table, wobbly from the wine and touched by Lobel's speech, the ship fell silent. The captain sang a traditional Bulgarian ballad. Then, his voice choked with emotion, he vowed that he would never abandon his ship or his passengers. "I will not consider my job done until I have led all of you to Haifa," he proclaimed to cheers.

Not long into the New Year, a joint wedding ceremony offered a joyful diversion. Three young couples married simultaneously, with wedding papers drawn up in French and Hebrew, with the captain as the chief civil authority on the ship, officiating over the civil portion of the ceremony. As he was concluding the ceremony, he pronounced the couples "united until death." Under his breath he muttered in Bulgarian, "Perhaps it would be more appropriate to say 'united after death.' "

A few people heard and understood what he had said, and they told other passengers. The remark lit a fire of anxiety that swept through the vessel. Always fearing the worst, people interpreted it to mean that Garabatenko intended to scuttle the ship. After all, he could return to Bulgaria or, at worst, remain a prisoner in Turkey. The leaders of the ship's committee met in secret to discuss the captain's loose lips. They decided to keep him under constant observation in case he decided to carry out what they believed was a threat. Though the captain had not been held in particularly high regard, this last potential source of safety and trust was now demolished.

Worse, the climate of distrust spread among the passengers. People began to suspect that others were stealing food and that the leaders were hoarding provisions or receiving more than their share. Some were sure that the doctors and lawyers and rich businessmen were getting better treatment—more time on deck, more food, bigger sleeping quarters. For the most part, these suspicions were unfounded, a symptom of the fraying nerves and exhausted patience. Still, they tore at the bonds formed by their common plight and added to the tension.

Within this atmosphere of deprivation and sometimes desperation, many behaved magnificently, with conduct that proved to be a source of inspiration.

One of these quiet heroes was Horia Lobel, who had boarded the *Struma* despite its dire condition, of which he had been aware long before. He supervised the many doctors and several nurses among the passengers. Organized into small teams, they worked around the clock tending to the sick as best they could with the limited rations of rudimentary medicines that the Turks allowed aboard.

Lobel constantly feared that the isolated cases of dysentery would spawn an outbreak that would sweep the ship, threatening the lives of the smallest children and the elderly. Another persistent problem was people fainting as a result of poor nutrition and insufficient food. Despite the shortages and handicaps, the doctors and nurses kept most serious illnesses at bay.

The ship's leaders never gave up hope that they would reach Palestine. They spent hours and hours plotting various routes to their destination, going so far as to debate amongst themselves over a plan to shorten the sea voyage by stopping in another port and continuing by train.

Wilder schemes were floated, too. There was constant talk of people swimming to shore. Sometimes the goal would be to alert the world to their plight; others just wanted to escape. Each time, the idea was rejected. The water was frigid and the ship was well guarded, even at night.

Other vessels were moored in the harbor, trapped by the war or awaiting cargo. *Struma* passengers tried to communicate with them, seeking any kind of help they might provide. One ship replied that they could rescue the passengers if they started a fire on the ship and everyone jumped into the water. The idea was actually debated by the leadership committee, and abandoned after someone pointed out that there were no life preservers and many of the passengers were children who could not swim.

Through December and early January, the Turks refused to allow Turkish mechanics to work on the ship's engine, and the efforts of the passengers and crew were fruitless. What everyone eventually learned through the ship's grapevine was that, even with a working engine, prospects for reaching Palestine were dim. On January 10, Captain Garabatenko sent a letter to the Istanbul port authorities refusing to proceed south toward the Dardanelles. Because Bulgaria had joined the Germans, he said, he feared arrest by the British as an enemy alien. Instead, he asked to be taken from the ship and repatriated to Bulgaria with the rest of his crew.

In his letter to the Turkish authorities, however, Garabatenko said that the *Struma* was unfit to continue its journey or return to Romania, regardless of whether the engine could be repaired. "As I reported to you, the defective structure of the ship, a fact that was unknown to me before our sailing, does not allow me the possibility of continuing the journey without endangering the lives of my passengers," he wrote.

The accuracy of the captain's assessment was evident to anyone who boarded as well as to the passengers. The wooden sides were rotten, held in place by metal plates welded like a skin around the vessel. The engine compartment continued to leak, and a water brigade was constantly carrying water buckets from the hold to be dumped over the side. Under the pressure of a voyage, the leaks would undoubtedly grow. There were two lifeboats and no life preservers. The radio transmitter did not work, and the generator worked sporadically.

The passengers also feared that, if the ship did get under way, Garabatenko would land in German-occupied Greece, where he would turn them over to the Nazis to spare himself from being captured by the British. They passed messages to the Turkish authorities asking for the appointment of a Turkish captain to command the ship, once it was under way.

According to a Turkish government document from 1942, Turkish port authorities weighed the possibility of finding a Turkish captain and crew to take over for the Bulgarians because of their refusal to proceed. The officials went so far as to contact a captain who had taken an earlier ship of refugees to Palestine. He said the British had imprisoned him for several months when he was caught on his first journey and he refused to make another voyage, the document said.

One of the most difficult parts of life in the harbor was watching the daily traffic of ferries and cars and the hustle and bustle of people on the not-so-distant shore. Yet the *Struma* was cut off from the rest of the world. Except for the occasional old newspapers that Brod brought aboard and snatched conversations with the Turkish guards, there was no news of the war and no word on their precarious fate.

Convinced that the world would come to their aid if it only knew of their plight, some people tried to bribe the police to deliver messages or send telegrams to journalists, foreign consulates, and relatives. They had no money to pay the police. Instead they gave them cigarettes, precious food, and even pieces of clothing. One man gave a policeman his raincoat and begged him to send a telegram to Palestine. The police later brought him a receipt for the telegram. The receipt was three years old.

Occasionally someone would call out to one of the police boats stationed around the ship, asking if there was progress. The reply was always the same: The British won't let you pass to Palestine.

The British remained implacable. The *Struma* would not be allowed into Palestine, and they kept up the diplomatic pressure on Turkey to turn the ship around and send it back to Romania. The Jewish Agency and other Jewish organizations had been slow to respond to the plight of the *Struma*. The ship was first discussed formally by the Jewish Agency in Palestine at a meeting on December 14, 1941, the day before its arrival in Istanbul. Its cause was not taken up in earnest by the agency's political department for more than a month. During that period, precious time was lost in which they might have worked out a deal with the British and mobilized public opinion on behalf of the stranded passengers.

One reason for the delay was the split within the Jewish community in Palestine and London. Many senior people wanted to avoid a major confrontation with the British, fearing a backlash if they pushed the case of the illegal immigrants. In fact, the British had threatened several times to freeze legal immigration if the illegal effort did not stop. Others argued that the agency had to do whatever was necessary to save as many Jews as possible from the Nazis and their collaborators.

The world's press paid little attention to the ship's plight. Even if Turkish newspapers had wanted to publicize the story of the decrepit ship sitting in full view of Istanbul, they were operating on the censor's tight leash and gave it scant attention. On January 6, 1942, the mainstream newspaper *Tasvir-i Efkar* ran a one-paragraph story, the first official notice of the ship's presence. Beneath the headline, "Jews in the Harbor Have Fallen Sick of Cold," the article said: "It has been understood that Jews coming from Romania with a Panama flagged boat *Struma* have been suffering severe cold found in the country lately. There is a very low temperature on board due to the mechanical repairs to the engine. Therefore, some Jews have fallen sick and extra medication has been requested. They are not anxious about medical assistance because there are many doctors on board."

Five days later, the newspaper published a second brief article on the subject. "The trade administration has ordered the supplements for 750 Jews that arrived from Romania to our harbor with a Panama flagged boat named *Struma,*" said the one-paragraph story. "According to this order, Red Crescent has been assigned to provide food supplies in equivalence to how much the Jews would need regularly on a daily basis."

A few other Turkish newspapers ran similar accounts, all equally brief. Nothing appeared in the international press. Although many of the world's major newspapers had correspondents in Istanbul, the people marooned in the harbor were virtually ignored.

Chapter 22

It would take an unusual effort by two powerful men to attract attention to the plight of the *Struma*. One was acting out of passion and an abiding opposition to fascism and Germany. The other was motivated by his own financial interests.

Archibald Walker was the fifty-nine-year-old country manager in Turkey for Socony-Vacuum Oil, the product of a merger between Standard Oil of New York and Vacuum Oil Company, another big American corporation. Vacuum Oil had done a considerable amount of business in Germany in the 1930s, and its Vienna office had employed Adolf Eichmann as a traveling salesman. When war broke out, some company funds had been frozen by the American government.

Walker had served Standard Oil throughout the Balkans for three decades, and he was an outspoken opponent of Nazi Germany. People who visited the German embassy or consulate were forbidden to enter his house, which was one of Istanbul's most beautiful homes and the scene of many popular parties.

He was as generous to Nazi victims as he was unforgiving of Nazi supporters. "No sooner is some country invaded than he rushes up to [its ambassador] and offers him his home, his car, his purse," Betty Carp, an Istanbul-born secretary at the American embassy who helped organize Washington's espionage corps in Turkey, wrote about Walker.

Soon after the *Struma* arrived in Istanbul, Walker had learned that among its passengers were Socony-Vacuum's Romanian manager,

Martin Segal, his wife, and their young son, Alexander. He had become determined to rescue them, even if it seemed impossible to save the other refugees.

Walker had already proven himself adept at diplomatic intrigue. In 1939, as Poland faced defeat by Germany, the Polish government was desperate to save its gold reserves for future resistance efforts. As a result of Walker's work, ten million dollars in Polish bullion was shipped by train from Warsaw to Constanta, where it was loaded onto a British tanker and taken to Istanbul. Michael Sokolnicki, the Polish ambassador, then took control of the gold and was under orders to forward it to London, where a government-in-exile had been established.

A French ship was standing by to take the shipment, but the Turkish Foreign Ministry refused to allow the gold to be transferred because they did not want to risk offending the Germans. The Turks told the Polish ambassador he could turn the gold over to the Turkish government, which would consider it a loan and then reimburse the Poles. The other option was to ship it by train to Syria, which was controlled by the French.

Sokolnicki chose to ship it by train. The Turks then tossed another complication at him. They demanded fifty thousand dollars cash in advance as insurance, a requirement of Turkish law that they said could not be breached. Sokolnicki rejected the suggestion that he sell enough gold to make the payment, and he approached Walker with his problem. The oil manager agreed to help and returned a few hours later with fifty thousand dollars in cash to get the gold on its way.

Walker was even more determined to help the Segals. Through his own connections and the influence of Standard Oil, he persuaded the British to grant emergency visas to allow the family off the boat to continue their journey to Palestine. The next step, and the most difficult, was persuading the Turkish government to allow the Segals off the ship. For help he turned to Vehbi Koc, one of Turkey's most influential businessmen.

Koc had close alliances with the top levels of Turkey's government. He was also well on his way to building what would become one of the country's richest business empires, with stakes in everything from insurance and banks to food production and auto manufacturing. Part of his business involved selling chromium to the Germans, which they used to keep their war machine operating.

Chromium is a relatively rare mineral that is used to harden steel, which made it essential for manufacturing military equipment. Throughout the war, Turkey was almost the sole supplier of chromium to the Nazis, and Koc was Turkey's biggest chromium exporter. Though Turkey was neutral, Koc's sale of the essential mineral to the Germans had gotten him into trouble with the British government, which had put his firm on a blacklist that prohibited it from doing any business with British companies.

The contribution Turkey's chromium supplies made to the German war effort cannot be overestimated. Albert Speer, who was the armaments minister for Hitler, wrote in his memoirs that in 1943 he told Hitler that "should supplies from Turkey be cut off, the stockpile of chromium is sufficient for only five to six months. The manufacture of planes, tanks, motor vehicles, tank shells, U-boats, almost the entire gamut of artillery, would have to cease from one to three months after this deadline, since by then the reserves and distribution channels would be used up."

The importance of these shipments was not lost on the Allies. In October 1941, the Soviet leader, Joseph Stalin, was so alarmed that he took the extraordinary step of issuing a secret order to his submarine corps: They were to sink any neutral ships that emerged from the Bosporus into the Black Sea. For the passengers on the *Struma,* this secret order amounted to a death sentence, though no one knew it at the time.

Another bitter irony would be attested to in 1998, when the United States government determined that chromium from Turkey had been critical to Nazi Germany's war effort and it had been purchased with gold looted from victims of the Holocaust and deposited in Swiss banks.

When Archibald Walker came into Vehbi Koc's office in Ankara and asked for help, Koc saw an opportunity to do some good for both the Segals and himself.

"We have received permission from the British," the American said to Koc. "The family will leave the country the same night by the Taurus Express for Haifa."

Koc replied that he would try to persuade the authorities to allow the family off the ship, but he cautioned that he might not have that much influence. After Walker left, Koc went directly to the government's security headquarters and met with a friend and high-ranking official, Ihsan Sabri Caglayangil. He explained the situation to Caglayangil, who would later become foreign minister.

"There are so many requests, such great sums are offered, but no one dares to touch the matter," the official said. "Only the minister is competent to decide. Go and speak to Fayik Oztrak, the minister of interior. The family can only be allowed to land on his orders. There is no alternative."

The following morning, a religious holiday, Koc visited Oztrak at his home in Ankara. He joined a parade of visitors paying their respects to one of the most powerful men in the Turkish government. Others came and left. Koc remained sitting in the house. Finally the businessman asked permission to speak privately to the minister, and he was escorted into the next room. There, Koc asked for his favor.

"He understood that the family would leave Turkey that same evening, and he had faith in me," Koc recounted later in his autobiography. "And not least, the man's time to die had not yet come. The minister gave orders to let the passengers land."

Koc telephoned Walker with the good news. In return, he asked a small favor. "After this I knew that Mr. Walker would comply with any request I was to make," Koc wrote. "I was unhappy at being included on the British blacklist because of my trade with Germany, and I told Mr. Walker of the circumstances. He was a resourceful man; he applied to the British and the Americans, took a great deal of trouble, and finally succeeded in putting our firm in the clear: and we resumed our regular transactions."

Walker managed to get Koc off the blacklist, but he did not stop with helping the Segals. The costs of providing food to the *Struma* were mounting, and the resources of the Jewish Agency in Istanbul were limited. Walker petitioned the American government to lift the freeze on some of Socony-Vacuum's money so that it could be transferred to the agency for the *Struma*.

By the time Walker got the approval to use the funds, the Segals were gone. A police boat had pulled up alongside the *Struma* the night of Koc's visit to the interior minister. A small group of policemen went onboard and got the Segals. The family had no idea what was happening. The policemen explained only that they were going to leave the ship but not that their ordeal was over and that they were free to continue their journey to Palestine.

As the Segals had packed their meager belongings in stunned silence, their fellow passengers had gathered round, assuming that they would be allowed to continue the journey to Palestine. They begged the Segals to tell their story to anyone who would listen when they got to Palestine. They pleaded for help so that they, too, could make the journey soon. Word spread and the line grew.

Aron Rintzler sought out Martin Segal and made him promise to find his son in Palestine and tell him that his parents were fine and that they would join him soon. David and Israel Frenk came together to explain that their passports contained the expired visas for Palestine that their parents had obtained for them, as did the passport for Israel's wife, Tivia. They asked Segal to let the proper authorities know about their situation so they, too, might escape the ship. Overhearing the conversation, another passenger said that he had an expired Palestinian visa in his passport.

With those pleas echoing in their ears, the first people to leave the *Struma* boarded the police boat and headed for shore on January 15, a month to the day after the ship's arrival in Istanbul. It was too late to catch the train that night. They spent the night in luxury at the Pera Palace Hotel. The following evening they were put on the express to Haifa, new visas in hand and a mission to carry out.

Alexander, too young at the time to remember the mission, did recall the contrast from one day to the next. "The first thing we did was take a bath," he said, sitting in his Paris living room sixty years later. "Then we ordered tea. I remember my mother getting angry. Then she laughed. 'Two hours ago,' she said, 'we were six people to a berth and now I am getting angry because my tea water is not hot? This is a good thing. It shows you how quickly the human being recovers. An hour ago, I would have been happy to wash my hands.' "

The family ate dinner that night with Walker in a restaurant with a view, and young Alexander was struck all over again by the city lights "like a Christmas tree" that had greeted him on his arrival a month earlier. Alexander remembered his father buying him four pounds of oranges for the journey. "They were like sunshine," he said.

Chapter 23

Immediately upon their arrival in Palestine, the weary, elated Segals insisted on telling officials at the Jewish Agency about conditions on the *Struma* and demanding help for those left behind. They recounted the wretched journey from Constanta to Istanbul and described the deplorable conditions in which the passengers lived—the lack of food, fresh water, and medicine; the inhumanly cramped quarters; the cold; the vacillation between hope and despair.

The couple provided a vivid and moving description, verbally and in formal statements. These statements were distributed to British officials and possibly the local press in an attempt to change the *Struma* from an abstraction to real life, to remove its passengers from the status of faceless names to actual people in need of salvation.

Moshe Shertok, the head of the political department of the agency and de facto second-in-command after David Ben-Gurion, was the most important person to listen to their story. A handsome man with dark wavy hair and a neatly trimmed mustache, Shertok was born in the Ukraine and grew up in a Zionist atmosphere. His family emigrated to Palestine in 1906, where he finished high school, and later he studied law in Istanbul, which was still known as Constantinople at the time. Stranded there during World War I, Shertok had served as an interpreter for the German army in Turkey. When he returned to Palestine, he joined the Jewish Agency's political department, becoming its head in 1933.

During World War II, his primary job was maintaining day-to-day contact with the authorities of the British government in Palestine, chiefly the high commissioner's office. Most often, those contacts involved alternating between pleading and demanding that the white paper restrictions be lifted. Though usually a soft-spoken and poised man, he often erupted in anger at the inflexibility of the British officials in the high commissioner's office. The deaths resulting from the *Patria* explosion had seared his soul, and the ongoing internment of the *Darien* passengers angered and frustrated him further.

As he listened to the Segals' story, he realized that he had not paid enough attention to the *Struma*. The fate of almost eight hundred hung in the balance, and he was determined to do all he could to make sure they arrived safely in Palestine. The challenge was to devise a strategy that would force the British to focus on the *Struma* as a special case. If he couldn't do this, Shertok knew he had little chance of saving these people.

The passenger count that the Segals were able to provide gave him some hope. While it was only a partial census and there hadn't been enough time to gather full statistics in the sudden rush to leave the ship, the couple estimated that were sixty-nine children on the *Struma*. (A complete count listed 101 children under 18.) Could the presence of children penetrate the wall of British indifference? Could it, in fact, serve as a strategy to save everyone?

On January 19, 1942, two days after the meeting with the Segals, Shertok started his campaign by going to the offices of the British government in Palestine to meet with John Macpherson, the director general for the territory. Shertok wanted to avoid a confrontation with Macpherson and the British government over the larger issue of illegal immigration, so instead of addressing it directly, he raised the subject of the ship in the context of previous discussions about providing unused visas provided by the white paper to children from the Balkans. Why not, he asked Macpherson, allow the *Struma* passengers, and especially its children, into Palestine with some of those certificates?

Macpherson did not reject the request immediately and even promised to look into the possibility of using surplus certificates for entry. Encouraged, Shertok sent another lengthy memo to Macpherson, noting that the admission of the Segal family proved there was no "hard and fast rule" prohibiting special cases from entering Palestine. He asked that the official consider a wider category of special cases that would include most or all of the *Struma* passengers, including the children.

On February 8, Macpherson replied that children from Balkan countries would be allowed entry, but no one from the *Struma* would get a visa, including the children. The arguments against creating an exception were not new—that the ship was part of the wave of illegal immigration that the British were determined to stop, and that it was suspected of carrying Nazi infiltrators, particularly since it had departed from an enemy country.

Shertok's tactic had failed, and some Jewish leaders began to advocate direct unilateral action to save the passengers aboard the *Struma*. Desperate to find a better way, Shertok sent Macpherson a detailed description of the *Struma*'s ordeal and pleaded for mercy. Citing the plaintive story told by the Segals, he recounted the flight of the Romanians from certain persecution and possible death, described the awful conditions on the ship, and tried to knock down the notion that there were Nazi spies among the bedraggled people aboard a broken-down ship in Istanbul harbor.

"Under these circumstances it appears utterly unreal to assume that the *Struma* should have been used by the Nazis in order to smuggle agents into any country under British or Allied control," he wrote on February 13. "All one could be more or less certain of when the boat left Romania was that it would get to Turkey, and the Nazis have plenty of opportunities of introducing their agents into Turkey without having to resort to such desperate means."

Since the outbreak of the war, he went on, thousands of refugees from countries overrun by the Nazis had made their way to Palestine. Not a single case pointed to a concrete possibility of Nazi infiltration. The Jewish Agency, he said, was willing to perform the required security checks to ensure there were no infiltrators.

The following day Shertok met again with Macpherson, who told him that there was no way that the government was going to change its policy on illegal immigration or its position on the *Struma*. No one who began their trip to Palestine illegally would get to the Promised Land, not even children.

Time was running out for the passengers of the *Struma*. The Turkish government, in its conversations and communications with British diplomats, was constantly threatening to send the ship back. There were no illusions about what would happen if the passengers were returned to Romania. Early in 1942, the Germans had decided to implement the Final Solution.

The Final Solution had been formalized on January 20, 1942, when Reinhard Heydrich, the second in command of the Nazi SS, convened a conference in the Berlin suburb of Wannsee. At the meeting, the top bureaucrats and SS commanders, men Adolf Eichmann later called "the Popes of the Third Reich," gathered to coordinate efforts to exterminate the eleven million Jews of Europe and the Soviet Union.

"Instead of emigration, there is now a further possible solution to which the Fuhrer has already signified his consent—namely deportation to the east," Heydrich said. "Although this should be regarded merely as an interim measure, it will provide us with practical experience which will be especially valuable in connection with the future final solution."

Europe would be combed from west to east, with Jews conscripted and shipped to labor camps and the gas chambers at Auschwitz and similar killing complexes under construction at Belzec, Sobibor, and Treblinka. Those who were not eliminated by what he termed natural causes, which meant starvation or being worked to death, would be executed by Nazi firing squads or sent to gas chambers.

At his war crimes trial in Jerusalem in 1961, Eichmann described, with chilling banality, what became known as the Wannsee Conference. He said that he stopped taking minutes while butlers served liquor and the officials stood "in small groups to discuss the ins and outs of the agenda . . . they spoke about methods for killing, about liquidation, about extermination."

But in February 1942, the details of the conference were not widely known. Nevertheless, the implementation of its tactics were already evident throughout the occupied territories. The fate of the *Struma*'s human cargo if it were to return to Romanian soil was clear. In the Warsaw ghetto, deaths from starvation in 1941 approached fifty thousand. In the Minsk ghetto, the Germans shot dozens of Jewish leaders. Behind the lines on the Russian front, a German private identified only as Christian wrote in his diary: "Since we have been in this town we have already shot more than thirteen thousand Jews. We are south of Kiev."

In October 1941, the Germans had taken the city after a two-month siege. The day of the conquest they had forced nineteen thousand Jews into a square near the port, sprayed them with gasoline, and burned them alive. The next day, sixteen thousand Jews were led out of the city in long columns to a spot near the village of Dalnik. There, they were thrown in groups of forty and fifty into a ditch and shot to death. When that method proved too slow, they were herded into four huge warehouses and machine-gunned to death.

In January 1942, the thirty thousand survivors in Odessa were deported to camps in the Golta district. Nearly ten thousand died along the way, most of their bodies covered with gasoline and burned, and over the eighteen months that followed, all but a few of the survivors died—some from starvation and untreated diseases, others by firing squads.

If diplomacy could not spare the people on the *Struma* from a similar fate, perhaps direct action could. Direct action meant finding a way to spirit the passengers off the *Struma* and onto a vessel that would complete their journey. It would be a daring venture, which would have to be carried out under the noses of the Turkish police who guarded the ship twenty-four hours a day. Senior officials with the Jewish Agency and its branches were well aware of what would happen to the passengers if they returned to Romania, and the only organizations that could help them were Haganah and the Mossad.

Haganah would not stage such an escape, fearing that the action would disrupt its covert alliances with British intelligence and touch off a backlash against all immigration. The Mossad could have helped. By coincidence, the organization had bought a small yacht from the Danish ambassador in Turkey in November 1941. The boat, renamed *Lilly-Ayala,* was sitting in Istanbul harbor at the same time as the *Struma,* though the Mossad was having a hard time finding a country that would register it for use.

Zeev Shind, the Mossad's primary agent in Istanbul at the time, defended the decision not to use the *Lilly-Ayala* to help the *Struma.* He said the Mossad knew the larger ship was not seaworthy and that its engine could not be fixed. The primary effort, he said, was to persuade the Turks to allow the passengers off the ship so that they could proceed to Palestine by train.

"We had the *Lilly,* but it was useless," he later explained in testimony contained in the Haganah archives in Tel Aviv. "It no longer flew the Danish flag, and there seemed to be no country in the world willing to place the boat under its protection. In Palestine people could not understand why we did not transfer at least part of the *Struma* passengers to the *Lilly.* From far away, without on-the-scene knowledge of the particulars, this seemed a legitimate complaint. In actual fact, though, it was impossible. We simply did not have the means to accomplish it. Given the condition of the *Struma,* there was only one power that might have helped—the power of the Allies and of the English in particular."

The decision by the Jewish Agency not to order the Mossad to try to save as many passengers as possible raises larger questions about how energetic the agency was on behalf of the ship. In *Escaping the Holocaust,* a scholarly book that recounts and analyzes the illegal immigration effort between 1939 and 1944, historian Dalia Ofer concluded that the mistake was not the failure to set loose the Mossad in February, but rather the inattention to the *Struma* by the Jewish Agency and Mossad in the first weeks that it sat in Istanbul harbor.

"Did they seek help from British intelligence (with whom they were in contact), with Turkish harbor authorities, or with shipping agents like Pandelis, with whom they had worked, in order to find a flag of registry for the Lilly?" wrote Ofer. "Did they step up their activities significantly in early February, when Shertok realized that his political tactics had failed?"

The answers were negative. No effort was made in those critical first weeks. By the time the *Struma*'s passengers got the attention that might have saved them, it was too late. The *Lilly-Ayala* sat idly by not far from where the doomed ship was anchored, and Shind and his colleagues did not have enough time to do anything but watch the tragedy unfold.

Another group of Jews was monitoring the fate of the *Struma* in Istanbul. Their journey had been eerily similar to that of the *Struma*, and they were facing the prospect of sharing the same fate as their fellow refugees.

On November 21, 1941, twenty-one Jews from Bucharest had quietly boarded a train to Constanta. The number was small, so they did not attract the kind of attention that passengers of the *Struma* would later on. In Constanta, they were hurried through customs, thanks to the significant bribes paid for permission to leave the country. The bribes, however, did not protect them from being stripped of their valuables by the inspectors. In the harbor the *Dor de Val,* a pleasure yacht with a small auxiliary motor, waited for them.

Two men were responsible for buying the boat and assembling a small group of friends also desperate to escape. The costs were divided equally among the passengers, and three sailors were hired to guide the ship. No one was certain how far they would get, but the goal was to get out of Romania.

Not long after leaving Constanta, the yacht encountered a storm. The craft was not designed for weathering heavy seas, and it was tossed about mercilessly. "It was very cold, and the sails froze to a point where they were no [longer] manageable," Albert Finkelstein, one of the passengers, later recounted. "The motor failed and so did the steering wheel. Our yacht had not been intended for high and stormy seas."

The craft was adrift, at the mercy of the storm. At one point, it came within shouting distance of the Bulgarian coast. Efforts by two crew members to swim ashore for parts to repair the engine were met with threats of gunshots from the coast guard.

Winds and currents pushed the ship for four days, until it finally capsized in a huge gust. Fortunately the ship was close to shore, and the passengers swam to safety, with the assistance of the crew. They were saved, but trapped in a cove with sheer cliffs on three sides and the Black Sea on the fourth.

On the second day, the people huddled on the rocky beach spotted a man with a rifle at the top of the cliff. He was not a soldier, but appeared to be a hunter. He could not hear them yelling, and he soon disappeared. The next day, a group of soldiers arrived at the cliff and tossed down ropes. The men had seen them. The *Dor de Val*'s passengers and crew members were hauled to safety, and into the waiting arms of the Turkish army.

"We walked to a small farm where we spent the night on the floor," Finkelstein said. "Then the next day we walked to a village where we stayed a few days, waiting for authorities to get in touch with their chiefs in Istanbul."

Eventually a bus arrived, and the refugees were taken to a quarantine site outside Istanbul. A few days later, they were moved to a hotel and given rooms. They were told not to leave. The quarters were far better than what they had experienced during the previous ten days. The man who arranged the hotel for them was Simon Brod.

The group languished for weeks in the hotel. The Jewish Agency could not convince the British to grant them exit visas. At one point the Turkish authorities told the *Dor de Val* group that they would be moved to the *Struma* and accompany its passengers back to their country of origin. Brod argued passionately with the authorities not to move the passengers. There was no room on the ship, he told them. He would pay for the upkeep of these people for as long as necessary. He begged for this group, which included a two-year-old boy and several people over sixty, not to be moved to what he was beginning to feel certain was a doomed ship. For the time being, he succeeded, and the Turks agreed to delay a final decision on the move.

Much of Brod's work was conducted in secret. Paying bribes was never a public activity, of course. In this case, he wanted to avoid alerting not only Turkish authorities, but a Greek named Litopolous, the Istanbul shipping agent for Jean Pandelis, the owner of the *Struma*. Brod was convinced that Litopolous and Pandelis did not want the *Struma* to continue on to Palestine, since the British at some point along the journey would no doubt seize it. He believed they wanted it returned to Constanta, where it could be outfitted for some other journey and bring in another sizable profit for its owner.

Others also came to believe that Pandelis had never intended for the ship to reach Palestine because he did not want to risk its confiscation by the British. So he had equipped it with an engine that he knew would not make the journey. The theory was supported by the fact that the promised visas for Palestine were not waiting in Istanbul. Clearly the Greek ship owner was motivated by greed. In the weeks before the *Struma* left Romania, he had taken delight in every canceled ticket because it meant he could sell it to some other desperate person for a higher price.

The ship was going nowhere without a working engine. After the Turks' initial inspection of the engine the day after the ship arrived, they did not return to start the repairs. Moritz Merlaub, the leader of the ship's committee, had passed several messages to Brod asking for help in persuading the Turks to work on the engine. Finally around January 10, mechanics from the Istanbul Port Authority had come back and started work. On January 21, Merlaub sent a note to Brod, which said, "The information is that work on the repair of the engine will last until the end of January."

With the return of the Turkish mechanics, the mood improved sharply on the ship. Most of the passengers believed that they would continue on to Palestine once the engine was repaired.

Chapter 24

Since leaving the *Struma,* Martin Segal had been considering the work needed to be done on the engine. Before the Turkish mechanics arrived, he had often seen Aron Rintzler, the Bucharest auto parts dealer, laboring over the old engine in the standing water that seeped in constantly. So after his debriefing at the Jewish Agency and other formalities, Segal had asked to be driven north to the kibbutz where Aron's son, Ogen, had lived and worked since his arrival in early 1941 on the last of the legal children's immigration ships.

When he tracked down the seventeen-year-old, who was living with a local family on the kibbutz, Segal explained that he and his family had been passengers on the *Struma,* too. They had been allowed off the ship and given visas through the intervention of an influential American. He assured the young man that his parents would be along soon. The ship's engine was not working, and they had no visas yet, he explained, but they expected permission to travel any day. Once the visas came, he said, it was only a matter of fixing the engine or being transferred to another ship to finish their trip. Pressed for details, the older man avoided describing the conditions on the ship. Instead he offered words of encouragement.

"Your parents are fine," Segal said. "The last time I saw your father, he was working on the ship's engine. I'm sure they will get it fixed. Don't worry."

They shook hands and wished each other well. Rintzler had been consumed by guilt and worry since arriving in Palestine, often feeling that he should have stayed behind to help his parents. With Segal's arrival, however, he had a surge of hope. His father would fulfill his dream of coming to Palestine, and it would not be long.

Segal probably knew that he had been overly optimistic, but the boy had needed to hear some good news. What Segal did not know, but guessed, was that conditions had not improved and that the *Struma* was unlikely to resume its journey anytime soon.

The relief that Segal brought to young Rintzler paled in comparison with the good he and his wife did for the tiny group of *Struma* passengers with expired visas for Palestine. Before leaving Istanbul, the Segals had urged Walker to try to help this group, and in Jerusalem the couple insisted that the Jewish Agency demand their freedom. Telegrams were sent to the British passport control office in Ankara, and eventually the British officials agreed to examine the documents and consider honoring the visas, if they were authentic.

On February 1, a Turkish customs agent boarded the ship and asked for the passports of the people who claimed to have expired visas for Palestine. David and Israel Frenk and Israel's wife, Tivia, handed over their passports and so did two other men, Emanuel Geffner and Theodor Bretschneider.

The customs agent inspected the passports. The Frenks and Geffner possessed valid visas, though expired. Bretschneider, a former officer in the Polish army, carried a passport from a South American country, and he had forged a visa that passed the first inspection. His attempt to affix his fiancée's photo to his passport as a family member, however, raised the inspector's suspicion. He said she had no chance of leaving the ship, then he pocketed the passports and left.

For four agonizing days, the group waited, uncertain about whether they would get permission to leave. Finally the port police returned and told all five they had to leave the ship immediately. Bretschneider begged for his fiancée to be allowed to go, too, but the authorities refused. Reluctantly he left her behind.

As they got into the police boat, they could hear the cries from the ship. "Tell the world what is happening to us," the passengers pleaded. "Don't let them forget us." When the boat started to pull away, those left behind sang a mournful rendition of *Hatikva,* the anthem that had started them on the journey what seemed like a lifetime ago. The trip that had started with the Frenks' escape from the ghetto of Czernowitz in the back of a German military truck was going to end in Palestine, though there was a stop in Istanbul first.

Israel Frenk's legs were wobbly when he touched land for the first time in nearly two months. "When we arrived ashore, we were dirty, hungry, and very tired," he recalled. "We could hardly stand."

Brod was waiting for the bedraggled party at the dock. Before the police could take them away to a hotel, where they would be kept under guard until they left the country, he whispered to all of them, "You will eat nothing of what they give you. No food, no water, nothing. My wife and I will bring you food every day. Every morning and every night until you are established."

Brod's fear was the Turks would poison them to silence these witnesses to the horrors of the *Struma*. He and his wife faithfully took food and water to all five people. After weeks of deprivation, they could not get enough to eat, and the Brods always provided.

A few days later, Brod handed them their passports, stamped with new visas for Palestine, and travel permits to get through Syria. He also gave each of them twenty pounds sterling and paid a policeman to drive them to the train bound for Aleppo, Syria. From there they went by train across Syria, through Lebanon, and finally arrived in Haifa, Palestine. Throughout the trip, they were always the first into the dining car when it opened in the morning and the last to leave at night.

"We started with the chocolate and then meat and then sandwiches," David said. "And then we started again with the chocolate. When we left the restaurant car, we always took bread, just to be sure. Even when we came to Palestine, when I went to sleep, I put a piece of bread under the pillow at night. I was always thinking of food."

Despite the lack of medicine and proper facilities on the ship, the doctors and nurses had managed to keep anyone from dying. A few people had become mentally unstable, driven to fits of anger and despair by the seeming hopelessness and the confined quarters. Occasionally some poor soul would become hysterical, screaming and striking out. In mid-February the lack of equipment nearly cost the life of a young woman who was already living under the curse of an unforgiving mother-in-law.

From the beginning, the journey to Palestine held more heartbreak and hardship for Medeea and Saimon Salamowitz than for most of the other passengers. The newlyweds had married and were expecting their first child under the shadow of her mother-in-law's curse.

Medeea's difficult pregnancy had forced her to spend many days in her bunk, unable to muster the strength to rise. Despite her husband's efforts and the kindness of other passengers in sharing the little they had, she never seemed well.

After two months on the ship, she suffered a miscarriage. The doctors treated her as best they could and pleaded with the police guards to take her to a hospital for emergency care. The police agreed, and she was gently transferred to a police boat. The police, however, steadfastly refused to allow her husband to accompany her, and he watched the boat head for the port without knowing whether his wife would live or die.

She was taken to Or-Ahayim Jewish Hospital in Istanbul, where doctors stabilized her condition. They said it would be several days before she was well enough to return to the ship, despite the demands of the authorities who wanted to get her back on the *Struma* immediately.

While recuperating, she wrote a letter to her cousin Erna describing the hardships, the heartbreak of leaving her husband behind, and the haunting words uttered by her mother-in-law on the day of their departure from Bucharest, when they had tried one last time to win her blessing. She asked Erna to send a message to her mother-in-law: "Tell her that every word uttered in her curse has been realized."

Chapter 25

The Turkish government was eager to get rid of the problem sitting in Istanbul harbor, one way or another. Several times in early February, mechanics from the port authority managed to get the engine running, though never for long. In a letter given to Brod when the supply ship arrived alongside the *Struma* on February 4, Merlaub described the progress on the engine and the hopes of the passengers. "Before finishing this letter," he wrote, "we want to inform you that the technical representative of the Port Authority visited us, and after examining the engine and the anchor, assured us that before our departure, all will be in order."

In his letter the following week, Merlaub reported that more tests had been run on the engine by the Turkish authorities. He said the fuel mixture was still causing problems. "The commission which visited us the day before yesterday apparently gave us a favorable report on the test, telling [us] that the continuation of the trip will take place in a few days," he wrote. "We draw your attention that the needed consumption of benzene and oil was not established by the commission which visited us, and this is very important. All our reserve fuel is made up of a mixture of 75 percent benzene and 25 percent gas, and this mixture was not tested to see if the repaired engine supports it. The test was done with light benzene, since the commission hesitated to perform an additional test with the present fuel in order to check its efficiency."

This was no small matter. The Turkish mechanics had coaxed the

This is the only photograph of the Struma *known to exist, and there is some dispute as to whether it is, in fact, the correct ship. Haganah Archives, Tel Aviv, Israel.*

A notice for the ill-fated Struma. *Yad Vashem Archives, Jerusalem, Israel.*

David Stoliar's ticket for the Struma, *which, like him, survived the sinking and his ordeals afterward. Yad Vashem Archives, Jerusalem, Israel.*

Ilse Lothringer, David Stoliar's fiancée, before leaving Romania in 1941. Yad Vashem Archives, Jerusalem, Israel.

David Stoliar with Simon Brod, who worked tirelessly, first for the people on the Struma, and later to arrange for Stoliar's safe release from jail and transport to Palestine. Central Zionist Archives, Jerusalem, Israel.

LEFT: *Simon Brod, looking out at the Bosporus. Courtesy of Marta Brod.*

BELOW: *Simon Brod's gravestone in Istanbul, Turkey. Courtesy of Marta Brod.*

Postcards written from the *Struma* by Grigore Bucspan to his son, Michael.
Courtesy of Greg Buxton.

Zlata Bucspan.
Courtesy of Greg Buxton.

Grigore Bucspan.
Courtesy of Greg Buxton.

The Reichman and Rosenzweig families at a wedding before World War II. Eleven of the nineteen people pictured died when the Struma sank. Courtesy of Ami Atir and Esthi David.

Aron, Fani, and Ogen Rintzler, in a family photo taken before young Ogen was sent on to Palestine in advance of his parents, who waited to go on the Struma. Courtesy of Ogen Rintzler.

In 1942, the Jewish underground accused Sir Harold MacMichael, the British high commissioner for Palestine, of murdering the Struma passengers by refusing to grant them entry visas and posted thousands of Wanted for Murder posters of him throughout Palestine. Courtesy of Simon Wiesenthal Center Library and Archives, Los Angeles, CA.

MURDER!
SIR HAROLD MAC MICHAEL
Known as High Commissioner for Palestine
WANTED for MURDER
OF 800 REFUGEES DROWNED IN THE
BLACK SEA ON THE BOAT „STRUMA

Nine hundred Jews have arrived on their way to Palestine:
The first refugee says to the second, "Palestine is going to be our homeland, for us alone."
The second refugee replies, "But how is that possible? Are we going to cheat each other?"
Akbaba, *an Istanbul magazine, January 1944.*

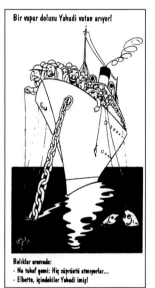

A boat filled with Jewish refugees headed to Palestine:
One fish says to another, "What a strange boat! They are not throwing any food scraps."
"Of course," says the second. "The passengers are Jews."
Akbaba, *December 1934.*

A boat filled with Jewish refugees has passed through the Izmir Harbor.
One refugee calls out, "We're hungry and without any money. For God's sake, let us land for five minutes so that we can become rich and leave."
Akbaba, *August 1939.*

David and Marda Stoliar visited Istanbul in the spring of 2001. It was the first time he had returned to Turkey since he had been pulled from the Black Sea fifty-nine years earlier.
Catherine Collins.

Ismail Aslan (right) was a teenager in the winter of 1942. He stood on the shore of Sile, a small fishing village on the Black Sea, and watched David Stoliar (left) being carried ashore. The men had not seen each other since the winter of 1942, and even then, they had not spoken. But fifty-nine years later, each remembered with clarity the moment their paths crossed, when Stoliar half walked and was half carried up the shore, and Sile villagers watched, impressed by his will to survive. Catherine Collins.

The Sile lighthouse, which David Stoliar could see from the wreckage of the Struma.
Catherine Collins.

The Sile watch-tower boathouse, where Stoliar stayed for several days, sleeping, eating plain, hearty food, and beginning the recovery from his twenty-four hours on the Black Sea.
Catherine Collins.

The Buxton family at the wedding of Candida Buxton to Joël Le Pénuizic. From left to right: Greg Buxton, Joël Le Pénuizic, Candida Buxton, Michael Buxton, and Patricia Buxton.
© 1993 Philippe Montaut.

Greg Buxton's diving team, standing left to right: Dave Wilkins, Atil Gelgor, Jeannette Plant, Greg Buxton, "Hungry Harry," Gary Fones, John Oldham, Louise Trewavas, Nick Hope, Julie Neal, Neil Dobson, Geraint Ffoukes-Jones, John Chatterton. Kneeling from left to right: Greg Mossfeldt, Alex Vassallo, Jonathon Lewis, Carla Madrigal. Team members not photographed: Jamie Powell, Mark Brill (photographer). ©2000 Mark Brill.

Dozens of relatives and guests who had traveled to Istanbul, gathered at the bow of the ship on which they held a ceremony to commemorate the victims of the Struma. INSET: *Before the ceremony, candles and flowers were placed in the water off Sarayburnu, where the* Struma *had been moored during her long stay in Istanbul harbor. Both ©2000 Mark Brill.*

engine to operate on a mixture of light benzene and oil. They had not tested the fuel onboard the *Struma* to see if the engine would also run, even sporadically, on the different mixture.

The Turkish mechanics were far more positive in their report to the port authority. In a February 10 report, Sefik Civa, the mechanical engineer, and Nuri Gokser, another engineer, said the ship's engine had operated for two hours on the afternoon of February 9. The report listed many engine parts that had been replaced or repaired and said: "During two hours of the test run after the repairs, we witnessed no major problems as the machine left the buoy in the harbor, reached the islands, and returned to the same buoy. As a result of this major and general repair, like every new machine, adaptation took some time, and although it did not work in perfect state at the start, this clearly improved towards the end of the test run. Therefore, it has been concluded that the repairs were proven to be correct and that the ship is technically fit to continue its trip."

Much in the report does not ring true. The islands mentioned in the report were presumably the Princes' Islands, about twenty kilometers southeast of Istanbul in the Sea of Marmara. The report does not say whether the engine was on the *Struma* during the test or had been removed from the ship and tested in another boat. All the evidence, however, indicates that the engine must have been tested in another boat. The repairs listed in the Turks' report were extensive, and they could most easily have been done by pulling the engine and taking it to a proper facility onshore. Had the ship itself taken a trip to the islands, Merlaub would surely have mentioned such a momentous event in his letter to Brod on February 11, just two days after the test. Finally, David Stoliar was certain that the *Struma* never moved from Istanbul harbor under its own power.

The report that the engine was operating was enough for the prime minister's office in Ankara to decide the time had come to send the ship back to the Black Sea. The British government was notified that the *Struma* would be towed out of Istanbul on February 16. After towing the boat far from shore, the Interior Ministry was instructed to post patrol boats to make sure it did not return. The British government was informed of the deadline, and word was passed to the Zionist organizations.

As the days counted down to February 16, the Jewish Agency and other organizations pleaded with the British to relent and allow passage to Palestine. The American Jewish Joint Distribution Committee offered to contribute six thousand British pounds toward the absorption of the refugees in Palestine and promised to pay all travel costs. L. B. Namier, a senior staff member with the Jewish Agency in London, argued that the three thousand visas for Palestine issued in the last six months under the white paper were more than sufficient to cover the *Struma*'s passengers.

A glimmer of hope came out of a lunch in London between Chaim Weizmann and Oliver Harvey, the principal private secretary of Sir Anthony Eden, the secretary of state for foreign affairs. Weizmann said it would be impossible to stop Jewish immigration from eastern Europe, so the British may as well facilitate and control it. The *Struma* offered an opportunity to start a new policy.

Harvey was already sympathetic to the refugees' situation, and the plea made an impression on him. The next day, February 11, he wrote a telegram to Ankara about the Turkish plan to send the ship back to Romania, asking: "Can nothing be done for these unfortunate refugees? Must H.M.G. take such an inhuman decision? If they go back they will all be killed."

Harvey was in the minority at the Foreign Office, where the prevailing view was expressed in a response a day later from Charles W. Baxter, who countered that "if we were to accept these people, there would, of course, be more and more shiploads of unwanted Jews later! Personally I feel strongly that it would be unwise for us to intervene, and that our intervention would only mean more shiploads later and more suffering." In a second memo, Baxter used the old and unproven excuse, "These are illegal immigrants who may include Nazis."

Nonetheless, there was a group within the Foreign Office who remained sympathetic to the passengers, and Jewish refugees in general. Typical of them was Alec W. G. Randall, a counselor in the Foreign Office, who proposed diverting the ship to Cyprus, the British-controlled island off the southern coast of Turkey in the Mediterranean. It was a short distance from Istanbul, and the refugees might be kept there temporarily pending transfer to Mauritius, he reasoned. Randall suggested in a memo that the idea be raised with Eden.

Anthony Eden, however, was no friend of Jewish refugees. He had long argued that enforcing the restrictions of the white paper was vital to maintaining Britain's position in the Middle East. Harvey once described his boss's attitude by writing: "Unfortunately A. E. is immovable on the subject of Palestine. He loves Arabs and hates Jews." Eden himself expressed the same notion in a private note to Harvey in September 1941: "If we must have preferences, let me murmur in your ear that I prefer Arabs to Jews."

Following Randall's recommendation, Harvey prepared a report for Eden arguing in favor of dispatching the *Struma* to Cyprus. "I am inclined to think that we should press the Colonial Office very strongly to admit them to Cyprus *pro tem*," he said. "After all, these unfortunate people are on our side. The exodus could hardly assume very great proportions, and it should be possible to sort out the enemy agents." Though Eden still did not support using Cyprus, he sent Harvey to raise the possibility with Lord Moyne's private secretary at the Colonial Office. Harvey did not find much reason for hope. Moyne's secretary agreed to raise the diversion to Cyprus with Moyne, though the secretary added that it had been decided well before that all illegal immigrants would be denied admission to any British territories.

Once again, the Colonial Office stood its ground. As justification for another refusal, Moyne went directly to Eden and told him he had learned from secret sources that the *Struma* was the first of several ships being chartered to carry illegal immigrants to Palestine. Moyne also argued that it was impossible to send the ship to Cyprus because the island was on a war footing, and no accommodations were available for refugees. No change in policy was desirable or permissible, Moyne argued. The government, he said, must remain committed to carrying out the cabinet's last instruction on the matter, a November 1940 decision that declared, "Illegal immigrants attempting to enter Palestine should be diverted to Mauritius or elsewhere."

Moyne's assessment left the door ajar. It would have been possible, under the 1940 decision, to permit the *Struma* to continue its journey and then divert the ship to a destination other than Palestine. The tactic would have allowed the British to spare the passengers and remain true to the cabinet's 1940 decision. However, the only proposed alternative destination, Cyprus, had been vetoed, and the idea of letting the ship proceed was never broached with the Turks. Indeed, no one seemed to grasp the possibility, leaving Eden to agree with Moyne that the ship would have to be returned to the Black Sea by the Turks. "I feel, too, that there is, alas, no other choice," he wrote in a memo to the prime minister on February 13.

Churchill, however, was not yet satisfied that enough had been done to save the passengers. He was among the most consistent supporters of finding ways to rescue Jewish refugees, though he did not always do enough to control what he himself described as "the usual anti-Zionist and anti-Semitic channel which it is customary for British [officials] to follow." This time, he sent round a notice to the various agencies involved that he intended to raise the issue with the cabinet on February 16, the deadline day.

The prime minister's refusal to close the matter created a dilemma at the Colonial Office. Moyne and his hard-line colleagues feared Churchill's sympathetic attitude could lead to a decision to let the ship proceed to Palestine, opening the dread floodgate of vessels filled with illegal immigrants. The entire policy of restricting Jewish immigration, they reasoned, could come undone at a time when more and more Jews were trying to escape Europe. Moyne faced a deadline within the deadline: He had three days before the cabinet meeting in which to come up with a compromise to mollify the prime minister and protect the blockade.

In Jerusalem, Shertok had not given up on rescuing everyone on the *Struma*. As the Turkish deadline approached, however, he concentrated on winning freedom for the children. Certainly, he argued to the high commissioner's office, none of them could be regarded as enemy agents, which defeated one of Britain's primary arguments for blocking the ship's passage to Palestine. In addition, the number of children was small enough to avoid the precedent that the Colonial Office seemed to fear would open the way for the imagined armada of refugee-crammed ships.

The agency wanted to be able to respond to any objections that the British might raise and soften public opinion, so a campaign was started. Arrangements were made in Palestine to house and care for the children. Relatives of some were located, and other families agreed to take in the remaining children. Public meetings were organized to persuade people to appeal to the high commissioner's office. Efforts to stir publicity for the plight of the children in the press, however, were blocked by the British censor.

In the end, it was not the pleadings and preparations of the agency that swayed the British. From the start, those opposed to the free flow of Jews into Palestine had been coldly pragmatic, and they proved as immune to the idea of sparing children as they had been to sparing anyone else who did not fit within the tight parameters of the white-paper formula. So it was Moyne's desire to placate Churchill with a small victory and thereby avoid a potentially larger defeat that carried the day and led the high commissioner to relent on the fate of the children.

On February 15, in a cable to the Colonial Office, High Commissioner Harold MacMichael wrote: "It has been decided to admit to Palestine children from the *Struma* between the ages of eleven and sixteen years. No repeat no adults can be accepted."

The decision apparently mollified Churchill, for he did not make a fuss about the *Struma* when the cabinet met on February 16. The prime minister also was no doubt distracted by the surrender of Singapore to the Japanese the previous day, a military disaster of enormous proportion. Whatever the reason, the *Struma* was mentioned only in the context of other illegal immigrants from the *Darien,* who were interned in Palestine. When Churchill argued for the release of the people from the *Darien,* it was Moyne who raised the *Struma* to underscore his position that "any weakening of our attitude in this matter would afford encouragement to the very undesirable trade in illegal immigration to Palestine." The matter of the *Struma* was tabled while a report was to be prepared on the internees from the *Darien*. The Colonial Office had won—the overall policy was unchanged, though some children had been granted a reprieve.

If the Turks had followed through on their threat to return the ship to the Black Sea on February 16, there would not have been time to get the children off. The deadline passed, however, and the ship remained in the harbor. The Turkish government did not convey an explicit message to the British about why the deadline was not enforced; the ship simply did not go anywhere that day. However, the British decision the day before to spare the children had come as a surprise to the Turks, and it may have caused the postponement. Regardless of the reason, a window had opened through which the children might be pulled to safety. No one knew when it would slam shut.

The events that would determine their ultimate fate were taking place without the knowledge of the ship's leaders and the passengers. They were unaware of the deadline, and they were unaware that the determination had been made to send them back to Romania, not on to Palestine. Many of them still harbored the hope that they were going on to Palestine.

The needs of his refugees so occupied Brod that he was rarely found outside the offices that Barlas had established for the Jewish Agency. The offices were at the Continental Hotel, a slightly downscale establishment away from Taksim and Beyoglu, the neighborhoods where the fancier hotels and most of the foreign consulates were located.

Word that the British would release the children was the first welcome news in weeks for Barlas and his small group of volunteers. The agency's headquarters in Jerusalem had sent a telegram to the Continental Hotel late on February 15. In the terse language of the medium, it read: "Government agreed admission Palestine *Struma* children aged eleven–sixteen others refused stop embassy Ankara and BPCO Istanbul informed accordingly stop please act immediately cable arrangements and number children benefiting from above permission."

The telegram touched off frantic efforts to make the necessary arrangements to rescue the children. The agency workers in Istanbul did not know how many children between eleven and sixteen years of age were on the ship, let alone how many of them had their own passports, since families often traveled on a single document. At least as difficult, and potentially far more wrenching emotionally, would be the task of separating the children from their parents, of rescuing a boy or girl of eleven and leaving behind others who were only ten years old.

It had taken four days to get the Frenks off the ship, and each of them had a passport and expired visa. This time nobody knew how long it might take, or how long they had.

Joseph Goldin, a volunteer from the Jewish Agency, contacted the British passport office immediately on Monday, February 16, to start the process. He was told that he would need a list of the children on the ship and the names and addresses of the people in Palestine who had agreed to care for each of them. The agency officials had no direct contact with the passengers, so Goldin asked the Turkish customs authority to send a policeman to the ship to obtain an exact count of the children and retrieve the passports of each. The customs officials balked, saying they would have to refer the case to Ankara before making contact with the ship.

Precious days passed, and the urgent pleas and outraged threats from Goldin, Barlas, and others only seemed to ensure that the bureaucrats moved more slowly. The Turks were taking their own sweet time with this most serious of issues, and the great fear was that they would send the ship back to the Black Sea with the children onboard.

What Barlas and the others did not know was that the Turkish government objected to allowing the children to travel by land across Turkey to Syria and on to Palestine. On February 19, the Turkish Ministry of Foreign Affairs told the British ambassador that the children would be allowed to proceed only if the British sent a separate ship to transport them by sea.

The British government was unwilling to spare a ship, and its officials thought the Turkish refusal to allow the children to go by land was unreasonable. The Foreign Office and Colonial Office agreed to pressure the Turks to change their minds, but the discussion of the matter was decidedly pessimistic. The opportunity was about to be squandered because of bureaucratic intransigence on the part of the Turks and the refusal of the British to even consider providing a boat to save the lives of dozens of children.

"I see no way of ending the deadlock except by either the Turks sending the ship back, or sending the ship on for action as may be authorized against it, or finally, our pressing the Turks to reconsider their decision against letting the children travel overland," Alec Randall, who had earlier advocated sending the passengers to Cyprus, wrote on February 19. "Even if we get the Turks to agree I should imagine that the process of selecting the children and taking them from their parents off the *Struma* would be an extremely distressing one. Who do you propose should undertake it, and has the possibility of the adults refusing to let the children go been considered?"

Indeed, the matter had not been raised among the passengers because the entire proceeding was taking place without their knowledge. Held incommunicado for weeks, they knew nothing of any plans to save the children. They were also unaware that one deadline for their departure had expired and their stay in Istanbul was continuing on a day-to-day basis.

By the end of the second month at anchor in Istanbul, the *Struma*'s passengers were entering a phase of utter gloom. By the middle of February, some passengers spent most of their waking hours crying quietly. Others broke into loud sobs. Some passengers coped with the horror by praying constantly. Many would wrap themselves in their fraying prayer shawls to beseech God. Others could not bring themselves to address a god who had allowed them to suffer so much. Even the work on the engine contributed to the depression. The passengers could hear it running smoothly for a few minutes during a test, then hear it stop with a clunk that reverberated along the metal sides of the ship.

The suffering seemed most threatening to the older passengers.

More than forty people onboard were past the age of fifty; several were in their late sixties; and one, Liza Glicman, was seventy. They went through the same deprivations as everyone else, but many had less in reserve than their younger shipmates, and their health seemed most in jeopardy.

Grigore Bucspan's worst moments were occasioned by fits of coughing. The fifty-four-year-old had contracted bronchitis not long into the journey, and at his age, it was a debilitating scourge that seemed impossible to shake. His wife, Zlata, fifty-five, one of the doctors on the ship, could do nothing to help because there was no medicine. So he coughed until his chest ached.

He sent a postcard to his son, Michael, during this time, which reached him at an army base in England. The message, in cramped writing, sounded like the abbreviated will of someone who realized time was running out: "We are still here and do not know when we will [go] further towards Palestine," he wrote on February 17. "We have now been 70 days onboard ship. We are in a cabin in terrible conditions. Health, I suffer from bronchitis, which I cannot shake off. We hope to continue our journey in 5–10 days, perhaps longer. . . . We have no contact whatsoever with the shore."

He and his wife had bought land in Tel Aviv and opened an account at Barclays Bank there. With an economist's precision, he detailed the luggage that had been shipped ahead to start their new life: two large trunks, a suitcase, a container with three Persian carpets, another container with bedding, cushions, and blankets, and yet a third filled with cut crystal. Unwritten was the implicit notion that it might be the son who would one day claim these items.

The card also listed substantial bank deposits in other locations to help family members and friends trying to finance their own escapes. "Without that, I do not know how to save them," he wrote. "It must be understood that this involves considerable expenses." He lamented the unknown fate of family members who had been deported from Odessa in rags and barefoot.

By the end of the short note, his despair was evident. "My dear son, hope for a speedy solution for we are all suffering," he wrote. "Your mother and I kiss you. . . . Let us hear from you. We embrace and kiss you our son."

Almost sixty years later, this card would touch the imagination of his grandson, when he first thought of going in search of the remains of the *Struma*.

Bucspan's postcard was taken off the ship by the weekly supply boat on February 18. In Jerusalem the same day, Moshe Shertok received a telegram that confirmed his worst fears. The telegram said there was an unconfirmed report that the Turks had given in to British pressure and taken the *Struma* out of Istanbul, presumably to begin its journey back to Romania. His first concern was for the children, and he demanded that the British act immediately to fulfill their promise to get them off.

"Should the report be true, there would be no way of taking the children off and bringing them to Palestine as approved by the government unless some immediate action is taken," he said in an urgent, hand-delivered notice to John Macpherson in Jerusalem. "I would accordingly ask that a cable be immediately sent to His Majesty's representative at Istanbul to inquire whether the boat has actually left; instructing them that, if the boat has not left yet, urgent representations be made to the Turkish authorities for its departure to be stayed pending the removal of the children; if it has left, the boat to be stopped at the nearest Turkish port with the same object in view."

Shertok used the plea as an opportunity to renew his request that the reprieve be expanded to everyone. "Even if the children can thus be saved," he wrote, "the fate of the whole transport will remain a matter of grave anxiety. There are two dangers threatening them: a sea disaster or their falling into the hands of the Axis. To prevent either calamity, the Jewish Agency would most earnestly plead, on humanitarian grounds, that steps should be taken to secure the cooperation of the Royal Navy in intercepting the boat as soon as possible."

The report to which Shertok was responding proved to be a false alarm; it may have been an overreaction to someone on shore hearing the ship's engine start up, or it may have been manufactured by the Jewish Agency to provide a dramatic opportunity to plead their case once more. When Shertok received no reply from Macpherson beyond confirmation that the *Struma* was still in port and the British did not know what the Turkish schedule was, he followed up with another letter.

Adopting yet another tactic, he raised the prospect that the British were discriminating against the refugees because they were Jewish. The Jewish Agency had tried before to argue that Jewish refugees should be accorded the same rights to enter Palestine granted to non-Jewish refugees from other countries who had fled the Nazis, even countries now collaborating with Germany. Hundreds of Arabs as well as Christians from countries like Poland, Yugoslavia, and Greece had been allowed into Palestine.

"We cannot conceive that Jews who have fled from such horrors as has been the lot of Romanian Jewry to endure should be left to perish and denied their only chance of salvation, particularly after the gates of this country had rightly been opened to give shelter to considerable numbers of non-Jewish fugitives from enemy territories," Shertok said. "The Jewish Agency begs to address a most urgent appeal to government for the reconsideration of the whole case of the *Struma* transport in the light of the present submissions."

By February 22, a week after the British had agreed to take the children in Palestine, there had been no word from the Turks regarding getting them off the ship. A list had been gathered, identifying thirty-one children between the golden ages of eleven and sixteen, and the British passport control office in Ankara was working on assembling the proper papers. The Turkish government in Ankara still refused to grant permission for them to land and travel by train. On that Monday morning, Goldin persuaded the port authorities in Istanbul to send another telegram to Ankara urging the government to allow them to take the children off the ship. There was no reply.

Curiously, none of the advocates for the *Struma* raised the most obvious legal objection to Turkey's insistence that the ship could not proceed to Palestine. As signatories to the 1936 Montreux Convention,

Turkey had promised not to intervene with commercial traffic on either the Bosporus or the Dardanelles. The language was straightforward: "In time of war, Turkey not being belligerent, merchant vessels, under any flag or with any kind of cargo, shall enjoy freedom of transit and navigation in the Straits subject to the provisions of Articles 2 and 3."

Article 2 was not relevant. It stated: "In times of peace vessels shall enjoy complete freedom of transit and navigation by day and night under any flag and with any cargo." Article 3 provided that, except for stops to carry out health inspections, vessels could not be required to make any stops along the way. In other words, Turkey had no authority to stop the *Struma* under the treaty.

Both the British and the Turks were aware of the treaty's requirements. MacMichael had argued to Turkey that it should use the health inspection clause to stop both the *Salvador* and the *Struma:* in both cases Turkey had refused. Germany was also a signatory and, therefore, could not object legally to allowing ships carrying refugees to pass. Yet, apparently, none of the *Struma*'s advocates were aware that international maritime law was on their side.

Chapter 26

The Bosporus is steeped in history. The name itself comes from the myth of a young beauty who was once Zeus's object of desire. According to the legend, Zeus disguised the girl as a cow to protect her from Hera, his jealous wife. Hera discovered the trick and dispatched a fly to chase the cow until she fled by plunging into the water and swimming across the strait, which was known ever after as the Bosporus—"Ford of the Cow." Legend also says Jason and his Argonauts traveled along the Bosporus in search of the Golden Fleece, barely escaping the narrows at one point near its northern entrance.

In the centuries since those legends arose, the Bosporus had become a busy commercial waterway. Ferries, cargo ships, and fishing boats plied its waters daily, and docks and houses lined much of its eighteen-mile length. The waterway was never so wide that onlookers could not see the other side clearly: at its narrowest point, where the two ancient fortresses of Rumeli Hisari and Anadolu Hisari flanked each other on opposite shores, the strait was less than seven hundred yards wide, and ships sometimes passed close enough that it seemed possible to reach out and touch them.

After long weeks of arduous waiting on one of the world's busiest waterways, the final verdict for the *Struma* arrived around noon on February 23. A massive Turkish military tugboat approached the ship. Its arrival drew passengers to the deck and sent alarm shivering through all of them. The passengers were still not sure if the *Struma*'s engine was working, and no one thought any good would come from the muscular red-and-white boat circling like a vulture eyeing its half-dead prey.

One of the small boats always on guard near the *Struma* pulled alongside, and two policemen climbed aboard. The military tugboat, called the *Alemdar,* moved closer and passengers could see the tug's crew preparing to toss a line to the policemen. Someone among the passengers shouted in anger, more voices called out, and suddenly several men grabbed the policemen. The action had been so quick, and so unexpected from the docile passengers, that the police barely struggled as they were hoisted over the edge and thrown into the sea.

The reprieve was short-lived. The police were fished from the water by their colleagues, and soon more police boats began to arrive. A growing number of boats idled ominously near the *Struma,* waiting until their numbers were large enough for a stronger assault. About mid-afternoon, nearly one hundred policemen, many of them armed, swarmed onto the ship, too many for the passengers to resist as the tiny boat shifted dangerously in the water.

"The police started pushing everybody inside the ship," David Stoliar later recalled. "There were some fights between police and ourselves, but they succeeded in pushing us inside, and then they tied a rope to the boat from the tugboat and cut our anchor. They didn't pull the anchor. They just cut it and started towing us out of the harbor."

Had the police pulled the anchor, it might have indicated that the ship was being taken to a new resting spot. Cutting it ensured that the vessel could not stop anywhere other than a dock. Without a working engine, there was no chance for the *Struma* to reach a dock without assistance from the tugboat, and few people on the ship believed the tugboat meant to take them anywhere near a dock. The action had been too brutal and abrupt to allow room for hope.

The tugboat drew the line taut and swung round, aiming up the Bosporus toward the Black Sea. It was the moment so many people had dreaded. Desperate passengers gathered shirts and sheets, strung them together, and painted huge letters on them—"Save Us," "SOS," and "Jewish Immigrants." They draped them from the sides of the ship and cried out to the shore as they proceeded slowly up the strait.

No one reached out to intervene that February day, though thousands of people must have seen the desperate procession and the tattered pleas draped from the sides of the *Struma*. Just as they had sat isolated for weeks in the harbor, the passengers proceeded up the Bosporus in isolation, their last calls for help unanswered. In one of the small inlets they passed, the Mossad's *Lilly-Ayala* still lay at anchor. In one of the city's hotels, the refugees from the *Dor de Val* idled away another day, unaware they had escaped joining the *Struma*'s lost cargo.

There are twelve distinct turns to navigate on the winding Bosporus, and the tugboat would have had to keep its speed slow to avoid swinging the *Struma* too far to one side or another as it proceeded up the waterway. The journey took four to five hours, continuing beyond the wide mouth where the Bosporus meets the Black Sea. It ended outside the three-mile limit of Turkey's international waters, and well past the point where the passengers could make out land in the fading light. The tug's captain had been given orders to take the ship far enough out that it would not return to Istanbul, and the coast guard was on alert in the event the ship drifted back toward the straits.

Ten or twelve miles into the sea—nobody would ever learn for sure how far it was—the *Alemdar* crew cut the rope to the *Struma*. With a snap, the ship was set adrift on the calm waters. As the Turkish boat pulled away, the passengers could hear its crew shouting. The words were indistinct. They sounded like "Go to Burgas," the name of a Bulgarian port about one hundred miles northwest.

Was it possible the Turks on the tugboat were unaware the *Struma*'s engine did not work? Certainly Captain Garabatenko and the crew would have been happy to steam up the coast to their native Bulgaria if the ship had had a working engine. The prospect would have terrified the Jews, since Bulgaria was by then under Nazi control. Regardless, it was not a real choice for them. The *Struma* had no working engine, and the fate of its passengers and crew was exactly where it had been for more than two months—completely out of their hands.

Two days earlier, there was still hope among the ship's leaders that they would be going to Palestine. Moritz Merlaub had written to Brod that the leaders were considering various alternatives to continuing on the unsafe ship. "Debarkation and travel by land [is] the ideal solution . . . but with few chances," he wrote. "The continuation of the travel with the *Struma:* Probably the most realizable alternative, but for its execution, certain difficulties will need to be remedied."

The engine remained the primary difficulty. "The present repair will be finished in a short time, then it will be tested," Merlaub wrote. "We hope that it was done in optimal conditions, and the ship will bring us to our destination." Merlaub also said the generator and radio transmitter did not work, food provisions were low, and serious doubts remained about the willingness of the captain and the crew to go to Palestine.

Even if the engine worked for a short period, as the Turkish mechanics reported on February 10, the authorities were well aware that the *Struma* was not a seaworthy vessel. Merlaub's report of February 21 indicated that work was continuing that day on the engine, clear evidence that new problems had cropped up in the intervening days. There was no further written correspondence from the ship regarding whether the engine was working, and it is clear the *Struma* did not leave the harbor under its own power. Further, Stoliar was adamant that the engine had not worked from the time the ship had first been towed into Istanbul the previous December until it was towed up the Bosporus.

Equally as shocking as their having set an unseaworthy ship adrift without a working engine was the fact that the Turks acted in secret without advising the British of their final decision, despite the continuing negotiations to remove the children. Had the engine been working and the captain and his crew managed to get the ship to Bulgaria or back to Romania, the passengers, including the children, would certainly have been interned by the Nazis and most likely murdered. The Romanian government had made plain to Turkey that it would not accept the return of the passengers.

The British government learned of the Turkish decision only a few hours before the ship's departure, and then it was by chance. A British passport officer in Ankara working on travel papers for the children was told by a Turkish official late on the morning of February 23 that the government was preparing to tow the *Struma* from the harbor. The passport officer conveyed the news to Knatchbull-Hugessen, the ambassador, and at 12:55 PM he sent an urgent message to the Foreign Office in London, warning, "Preparations are being made to tow the S.S. *Struma* toward the Black Sea where she would doubtless be cast adrift outside Turkish territorial waters."

The Foreign Office responded with a telegram urging the embassy in Ankara to seek a delay. "Please represent urgently to the Turkish Government that they should at least postpone action reported while question of admission of children to Palestine is being considered," said the telegram. "You should also take opportunity of pressing for re-consideration of Turkish decision regarding transit of children."

The response had been sent at 7:40 PM, February 24. By that time, the children were at the bottom of the Black Sea.

Chapter 27

After it was set adrift by the Turkish tug, the *Struma* sat silent and forlorn. The sea was calm and the ship drifted with the current, its engine lifeless. The passengers grew increasingly frantic, yet there was nothing they could do. Like everything that had beset them since leaving Romania more than two months before, the next and, unbeknownst to them, final chapter in this disastrous voyage was out of their control.

The two lifeboats were rickety and offered no real salvation, even for the few who might be crammed into them. There was no place to go, no way to flee.

Below deck, the crew struggled to bring the engine to life. The Turkish mechanics had managed to get it running several times in recent days, but it had never worked for long and had never actually been used to propel the *Struma*. The captain listened to progress reports from the bridge and watched the sea, wondering what would happen next on this terrible journey. He was a tough man brought to his knees by forces outside his command.

The end came as dawn approached on February 24. The weather was cloudy and there was a light rain, with a gentle wind out of the northeast and waves less than three feet high. The blast tore through the ship as if it were made of kindling. In an instant, the metal plates girding the rotten planks on the sides of the ship fell away and the wood splintered. Passengers below deck in their sleeping cages in the ship's midsection, closest to the point of explosion, would have died immediately from the explosion. Hundreds of others would have been trapped and drowned quickly as the broken vessel plunged beneath the surface. Many others were hurled into the frigid sea by the force of the blast. Their deaths would come on slower.

David Stoliar had been sleeping in his cage with four other men. The deck above them disintegrated instantly. Stoliar and the others were tossed into the air like rag dolls. When he landed, Stoliar was driven below the surface of the sea. Fighting his way back up, gasping for air and already shivering, Stoliar saw the horror around him. Almost all of the ship had already disappeared. People struggled to stay afloat and called out for missing loved ones or for help. But none came. The two lifeboats had been destroyed. Whatever had sunk the ship in the early morning hours of February 24 had come without warning, without a moment's notice to allow people to prepare.

Not far from where he fought to stay afloat, Stoliar saw people clinging to something just below the waves. A strapping young man despite the weeks with little food, he swam toward them and found they were holding on to a large, partly submerged piece of wood. It turned out to be a chunk of decking, the largest remaining piece of the *Struma*. A bench was attached to the wood, which made it visible to the survivors bobbing in the water. The wood was too deep in the water for anyone to haul themselves on top, so the dozen or more people held on to keep their heads above water as their bodies grew colder from the sea. Around them, they could still hear splashing and wails for help, but as the minutes passed, the sounds diminished.

As hours passed, the water grew silent, and the growing hypothermia and exhaustion made it harder to hold on to the piece of debris. A man next to Stoliar disappeared noiselessly beneath the surface. Sometime later, the man on the other side of Stoliar lost his grip. He grabbed Stoliar from behind as he went under, acting on the natural instinct of a drowning person. The man's grip was like iron on the collar of Stoliar's stiffened leather jacket. Stoliar's own frozen fingers slipped from the decking, and both men plunged beneath the surface of the sea.

Stoliar broke free and grabbed the decking again and clung to it desperately once more. One by one, over the hours, the others slipped beneath the Black Sea's waves. Eventually, with less weight dragging it down, the wood rose far enough out of the water that Stoliar was able to drag himself onto it. He collapsed on the bench, which by then was clear of the water. The only other person he saw was a corpse tangled in cables attached to the decking. Almost every other bit of the ship and all of its passengers had been swallowed by the sea.

After hours of silence, Stoliar heard splashing. Freezing and hallucinating from exhaustion, he thought his mind was playing a sad trick on him. Shaking the frost from his head, he looked around and saw a man miraculously paddling toward him. Carefully he pulled the man onto the decking, trying to avoid capsizing, and propped him on the bench.

"I am the chief mate," the man said through chattering teeth in Russian. "My name is Lazar Dikof."

"I am David Stoliar," his rescuer replied in halting Russian.

Dikof's story of how these two strangers came to be there, together, was as chilling and bitter as the sea. He said he had been on duty at dawn, standing near the bow of the ship, when he saw the telltale trail of a torpedo coming toward the ship. The shore was visible in the distance, and Dikof was certain the torpedo was coming from that direction. He raced to the captain's cabin on the bridge to sound the alarm.

"As I pulled the knob to open the cabin, the ship exploded," he told Stoliar. "I was thrown into the air, still holding on to the door. I landed in the water with that door, and I used it to float until I saw you."

Stoliar's mind was too numb with cold and fear to process the information. A torpedo? From the direction of shore? Who or what had fired it? Surely not the Turks. Was it only the hallucination of a half-frozen sailor?

At that moment, what seemed more important than how they got in the water were the chief mate's instructions on how they might survive. They were to sit with their backs together to help them stay upright and to generate whatever warmth they could. They had to keep talking, shouting if necessary, and prodding each other to stay awake and stay alive.

"If you fall asleep," Dikof said, "you won't wake up."

The men talked through the night about how to survive and anything else that came to their minds. Their voices grew hoarse with shouting and cold. When one dozed off, the other prodded and shook him.

Shortly before dawn on February 25, after nearly twenty-four hours on the sea in below-freezing temperatures, the chief mate stopped responding to Stoliar's shouts and prods. Stoliar could no longer feel his companion's weight against his back. Stiffly, he turned to look and saw that Dikof had fallen into the shallow water lapping over the decking. Stoliar bent down and shook him. The chief mate did not move. He had frozen to death. In the beginnings of daylight Stoliar could see the other body, still tangled in the cables protruding from the deck. Nowhere could he see any sign of life.

Stoliar feared that he, too, would soon succumb to the cold. The sun was starting to come up, and for the first time he could see the shore, though he had no real idea how far it was. He knew that if he stayed on the bench, he would end up like the chief mate, facedown in the water. His mind locked on the task of staying alive, focusing on nothing else—not the others who died, not the dead chief mate, or his lost fiancée. He decided to swim for land. Loosening his numbed limbs, Stoliar held his breath, jumped into the water, and struggled to swim. He got only a few yards. Land slurred into the distance, salt water stung his eyes. He knew that he would never make it.

"When you are above the surface of the water, the shore is clearly visible," he said. "It seems possible. But when you are in the water, with your head barely above its surface, the shore seems much farther away. I got scared that the shore was just too far away. So after swimming a little, I turned around and went back. I was afraid to be away from that piece of wood. I swam back and I went back to that bench."

Perched again on the edge of his fractured world, Stoliar could not bear to wait for the inevitable. Bleakness and grief enveloped him along with the chilled salt air, and all he could think about was collapsing into the water, choking and gagging as seawater filled his lungs.

With immense effort, he pulled a small pocketknife from a pocket of his jacket. He would slit his wrists, he thought, a better way to end his life than in that black water. His numb fingers refused to cooperate. They were useless. He could not open the knife. Unable to kill himself, unwilling to plunge again into the frigid water, he waited for death.

Thwarted by the barbarous cold and his own weariness, Stoliar was ready to join the others when a large ship passed within two hundred yards of him. He yelled hoarsely and waved his arms, desperate to attract attention. Miraculously, he saw three or four people gesture frantically toward him. They were shouting, but he could not make out what they were saying. They pointed toward the shore, and at first he thought they were telling him to swim. Then he noticed another person on the ship, waving small flags toward the land. He looked again in the direction they were pointing. A rowboat was coming across the water. The ship had signaled the shore. Help was coming.

As it grew closer, Stoliar could see his salvation. Eight men, maybe ten, made powerful strokes in unison, the boat surging as the oars propelled it forward, struggling to reach Stoliar before it was too late. He rose to his feet to greet them, to make certain they knew he was alive. His legs buckled and he fell back onto the bench. The next thing he knew, two men were lifting him gently into the boat.

"I remember them setting me down in the boat and picking up two dead men, one who was caught in the wire and the chief mate, and they turned around and they went back to shore to a boathouse," Stoliar said. "They carried me into the boathouse because I could not walk. They gave me some food, and they covered me with a blanket and laid me down on a cot."

After more than twenty-four hours in the icy sea that had claimed 768 of his countrymen, including 101 children, as well as the captain and nine Bulgarian crew members, one man had been saved. The rescuers had come from the government watchtower at Sile, a sleepy, out-of-the-way fishing village on the Asian shore, nearly thirty miles east of the point at which the Bosporus meets the Black Sea, a long way from where their countrymen had set the helpless ship adrift.

Chapter 28

Sile sits on a spit of headland where waves splash against spires of rock around the tiny port. Above the port stand the ruins of a small Genoese fortress from the fourteenth century. The people in Sile had grown accustomed to bodies occasionally washing ashore because the prevailing current on the Black Sea moved from west to east. Soviet submarines were active in the sea, sinking ships suspected of ferrying supplies to German forces. Sometimes boats simply bumped into a mine and sank. Survivors were rare, particularly in winter.

"We became used to the bodies that washed up on our shores," Ismail Aslan, who was a young man during World War II, recalled years later as he sat on a small stool, mending his fishing nets, in his cottage near the center of Sile. "Often the little boats would come across dead bodies. They would catch them with their hooks, strip their clothes, and check for valuables."

This episode was different, and it would remain fresh in the lore of the village for decades. A handful of people in Sile had contributed to a food drive for the unfortunate people on that ship in Istanbul harbor. Although the Muslims of Sile had little in common with the Jews aboard the *Struma*, something about the plight of these refugees had touched them. So the village residents listened with heavy hearts to the radio reports when the *Struma* departed Istanbul harbor on February 23. They heard about how the passengers had hung banners from the sides of the ship begging for help. They did not learn where the ship had gone until Turkish maritime officials sent out an alert to every watchtower along the Black Sea coast. The *Struma*, the alert said, had gone down after an explosion. Everyone should be on the lookout for survivors.

As his hands stilled in his nets, Aslan told the story, as he knew it. "The *Struma* and its Jewish passengers came to the straits from Romania," he said. "They were headed toward Palestine, you know. They were running from the Romanians. I was just a kid then, so I didn't understand the politics. After the boat sank, there were three people floating. Two were dead. One was alive. The watchtower crew brought him in. I went down to the shore, but I couldn't see him well because there were so many people. No one knows why that boat sank. Some say it was torpedoed. Some say it hit a sea mine. There was a lot of speculation. But no one is really sure. At least here."

When asked why no one went out immediately to look for survivors, Aslan shrugged. "We had only our little boats," he said. "They didn't have motors. Only rowing power. What could we do? We did not have the courage to interfere when we knew that everything or anything on the Black Sea could be a target for the Russian submarines."

Shortly after dawn on February 25, a man on duty in the Sile watchtower got word that the *Struma* remains were approaching their area, about five miles from shore. The watchtower crews were usually responsible for an area closer to shore because their boats lacked engines. The Sile crew left the warmth of their long, low command center and headed out to sea in their long rowboat about dawn. The wreckage was not visible from land, even though Stoliar could see the shore. The rescue boat was guided by the flag signals from the ship that passed the wreckage, until the rescuers discovered the little that was left of the *Struma*.

The Sile watchtower was the eighth in a long series of watchtowers guarding Turkey's coast that the *Struma* had passed in its slow journey along the coast before it was sunk by the explosion. Whether or not the blast could be seen from the shore is difficult to determine today because the Turkish government has sealed the official logs kept by the watchtower crews. But if the disaster was observed from land, and no one responded until the brave men of Sile undertook the rescue, it is understandable that the government would not want to open those files.

One of the rugged men pulling at the oars that morning was Mehmet Ay, whose young son, Izmit, was watching from the balcony of the family's apartment above the port. "The boat sank at the entrance to the Bosporus, too far from Sile for us to see," said Izmit Ay, who later became one of Turkey's most famous actors. "My father said that the ship had been sunk by a torpedo and that they thought all the people had died. All the watchtower men were called out for duty after the explosion, waiting for the next thing to happen. The fishermen could not go out because they did not have motors for their boats. Only the watchtower boat, which was manned by ten men, was fast and powerful enough to go out."

Ay, then a seventeen-year-old student home for a holiday, watched the rowboat head out to sea. It was a clear, cold day, and the sun was growing bright in the sky. The youngster was still on the balcony when he saw the rowboat coming back to port. He could see three extra men onboard. He rushed to the pier, where the rest of the village was waiting, hopeful that three survivors had been rescued.

"As they got closer we could see that two bodies were draped over the gunwale and they were dead," Ay said. "It was so sad. The crowd watching from the shore became silent. Only one man still lived. He sat upright. His arms were crossed over his chest because they were frozen."

Ahmet Akarsu was also seventeen that winter. He remembered the arrival of the rescue boat and the survivor. Akarsu described a young foreigner, about his own age, taller, but much thinner. He could remember that he spoke a language that he did not recognize.

"I saw him walk from the shore, but he was having trouble. I remember his leather jacket and his boots," said Akarsu, who knew firsthand the threatening nature of the nearby Black Sea. "He must have worn a wool sweater, too, to survive that long in the Black Sea in winter. Some people can survive twenty hours on the sea. Some die immediately."

Stoliar recuperated those two days on a cot in the watchtower's boathouse. Long afterward, Stoliar would recall it all in great detail. The black olives and hot bean soup the village women brought him. The herringbone pattern of the ceiling far above his head. The muffled voices in Turkish, a language that he could not understand.

When he walked into the fresh air outside the boathouse, three days after the explosion and two days after his rescue, he saw the landscape as something altered, no longer so familiar. He would never think of himself as a hero; the term was too grandiose, too idealized. He was a survivor, the only one. Maybe he lived because his leather jacket had shielded him. Perhaps it was the blessing of Rabbi Guttman, as many would believe as the story grew into another legend of the Bosporus. Perhaps it was his own courage, or fate itself. Whatever the reason, Stoliar's survival was a blessing and a burden, and he would carry each for the rest of his life. As two soldiers escorted him to a waiting bus, a handful of villagers watched in silence.

Later, after the stranger had gone, Mehmet Ay told his son about the rescue. He described rowing into a field of debris and the miracle of discovering one man alive. He told of dragging him into the boat along with two other bodies. No other bodies were found that day. Most of them sank, Ay surmised, though a few would wash ashore in the days that followed and be buried anonymously in the village cemetery.

The elder Ay was a tough man who made his living on the sea. He had seen death before and he would see it again. As he described that awful day, his son could not help noticing his father's hands shaking.

"How could they have done this to people?" Ay asked his son over and over, covering his eyes with his forearm. "How could they have done this?"

Stoliar had boarded a commercial bus. His escorts had cleared the front seat for him in the aged vehicle, filled with curious Turkish peasants and assorted farm animals. They bounced from village to village on the journey back toward Istanbul.

PART IV

After the Sinking

Chapter 29

Though news of its sinking would echo for weeks to come, the fate of the *Struma* was recorded officially by the British government in two short installments called minutes in the Foreign Office file in London. Both were handwritten by Alec Randall, a counselor in the Foreign Office.

The first, dated February 24, read: "The Black Sea is rough at this time of year and the *Struma* may well founder. I do not at all like the idea that we may be acting as accessories in bringing about the death of these miserable people."

The second, written on February 25, said: "The ship is today reported as having sunk with all on board. The message is from Reuters' correspondent and probably correct. The Turks must have acted before receiving our urgent pleas for postponement, but of course the ship could have run on a mine in whichever direction it traveled. We shall no doubt hear a good deal more about this most deplorable affair."

Like the British government, the Jewish Agency in Istanbul had had no advance word that the ship was going to be towed. Late in the afternoon on the twenty-third, someone saw the *Struma* leaving the harbor and notified the office at the Continental Hotel. The people at the agency were shocked that the ship had left with the children still onboard and were desperate for news of its fate. A preliminary count from a ship's manifest showed thirty-one children between the ages of eleven and sixteen and thus qualified to enter Palestine under the February 15 decision.

News that the *Struma* had met a worse fate arrived on February 25. Initial reports were sketchy, but grim. There had been an explosion and the ship had sunk. There was no word on whether anyone had survived. Confusion over the number of survivors would continue for many days: In the case of the cause of the explosion, it would be years before proof emerged.

The exchange of telegrams between the agency's office in Istanbul and headquarters in Jerusalem testified to the frenzy and the fear:

"*Struma* wrecked Black Sea four miles from Bosporus missing details disaster and number survivors stop fearing great number victims," Goldin telegraphed on February 25.

"Cable immediately full details *Struma* disaster circumstances survivors if any," Shertok fired back.

"Continuing ours yesterday fearing greatest part drowned or killed stop very few survivors stop no official statement re number victims yet published stop shall wire further details," replied Goldin on the twenty-sixth.

The next day he still had only the barest details, and some were wrong: "*Struma* exploded and sunk on 24/2 about 10 am 5 miles off cape jeun unclear whether torpedoed or mine lifeboats hurried place disaster stop presumably only four survivors of whom three died later about 759 victims stop awaiting official confirmation re number victims."

Official word was slow in coming, partly because there were no witnesses except for the sole survivor who was still recuperating in Sile, partly because neither the Turks nor the British had any reason to fuel the publicity with more information.

The seeds of misinformation, however, were planted early as the Turks sought to evade responsibility for the disaster. In its first dispatch on the sinking, the Anatolia Agency, the official government-run news operation, accused the passengers of having arrived in Istanbul on the pretext of repairing damaged engines and trying to prolong their stay by sabotaging the engines. The report, dated February 24, said other countries had rejected the passengers and Romania had refused to permit their return, saying they had left illegally.

Although the dispatch claimed repairs to the ship were completed, it said Jews refused to continue their trip. In the most benign language, the official government news agency said the ship had been returned to the Black Sea, where it had sunk after an explosion of undetermined origin.

The Anatolia Agency was not just state owned. Because a curtain of censorship hung over the rest of the Turkish press, the agency's dispatches set the agenda for the entire Turkish press, defining the acceptable political and policy lines to follow. As a result, the idea that the Jews were responsible for their own fate gained widespread currency within Turkey's press and public.

In a desperate search for absolution, the Turks would later claim in a handful of government documents generated after the sinking that the *Struma*'s engine was working when the ship was towed to sea. All the other evidence is stacked against that self-serving idea. Along with the compelling and detailed account of the only survivor, there are numerous logical rejoinders to the notion that the ship could have gotten anywhere under its own power.

Most compelling is the fact that the captain did not head for Bulgaria, the nearest country and the one where Garabatenko and his crew knew they would be granted a safe haven because of their nationality. Even if the captain had for some reason decided to bypass the safety of his homeland and proceed to Romania, the ship would have traveled far beyond reach from the shore at Sile before it sank. Indeed, if the *Struma* had been able to move under its own power, no matter which direction the captain had chosen, the vessel would have been far from the location of its demise.

The post-sinking Turkish claims defy logic on another front, too. The government documents that claimed the engine had been repaired offered a proof—they declared that the ship had been taken on a test sail well out of the Istanbul harbor during the time it was under quarantine. Had this occurred, Brod and others from the Jewish community who were keeping a daily eye on the *Struma* would certainly have noticed and reported the momentous event. Plus, passengers would surely have included optimistic messages about it in their

postcards and reports. The complete absence of such information un-
dercuts the Turkish assertion that the *Struma* had a working engine.

To be sure, Turkish mechanics tried to repair the engine. They
were under great pressure from their government, which wanted to
be rid of the passengers and the political dynamite that they represented. There is no credible evidence, however, that the mechanics
were able to do anything more than repair the engine enough that it
ran in place for a few minutes on a handful of occasions.

Two days after the sinking, it was still uncertain whether there were
survivors. "One thing is clear," Joseph Goldin wrote to the agency's
main office in Jerusalem, "the disaster is enormous and nearly all passengers have drowned or [been] killed. It is rumored that only five
persons have been saved, of whom three died later of their wounds.
No official confirmation to that rumor has been given. We are still
awaiting more official details concerning the number of victims and
the circumstances in which the ship wrecked."

Goldin added a postscript: Medeea Salamowitz was still in the hospital recuperating from her miscarriage. "This is the only sure survivor of the ship," he said.

Shortly before five o'clock on the afternoon of the twenty-fifth, the
Jewish Agency in Jerusalem issued a press statement announcing that
the *Struma* had sunk. It described the conditions on the ship before
the disaster and the efforts to persuade the British government to allow the refugees to proceed, in light of the existence of three thousand
unused visas for entry to Palestine. "If treatment of Jews trying to enter their national home [had] been the same as treatment of non-
Jewish war refugees seeking shelter [in] Palestine, Jewry already
stricken would not mourn today another thousand martyrs," it concluded.

The American government played no active role in deciding the
fate of the *Struma,* though it could be argued that its inaction constituted a passive acceptance. The United States had only been in the war
for a few weeks by the time the ship was towed from Istanbul.

Samuel W. Honaker, the American consul general in Istanbul, had alerted the State Department to the deplorable conditions shortly after the ship's arrival back in December. Its existence had barely registered since then. Honaker did not alert the State Department to the sinking until February 27, when he sent a telegram that contained a few errors, but captured the essence. "According to unimpeachable sources," he wrote in a telegram, "the Turkish police boarded the *Struma* at 5 p.m. February 23, caused the ropes to be cut and the vessel to be taken out of port by a Turkish salvage tug. The vessel was towed up the Bosphorus leaving the entrance at 10 p.m. and when approximately twenty-three miles into the Black Sea was cast adrift and abandoned without water, food and fuel."

The New York Times had carried an item on February 25 about the sinking of the ship. The length and placement of the article in the country's leading newspaper was a measure of American concern: A four-paragraph article on page seven summarized the sinking and the presumed death toll.

Simon Brod was mourning the dead when he learned from a friend in the police that someone had survived the sinking of the *Struma*. It seemed extraordinary, and Brod worried that it would be even more extraordinary if whoever it was managed to live through the custody of the Turkish military.

The soldiers escorting Stoliar had taken him from Sile to Haydarpasa Numune Hospital at Kadikoy, on the Asian side of the Bosporus. There, he encountered a gaggle of reporters. Word had leaked that someone had survived the sinking of the *Struma,* and the reporters were eager for details. They started to ask questions in English, French, Russian, and Turkish.

"Where are you coming from?" they asked. "What is your name?"

The police tried to hustle him through the crowd. Stoliar could not move fast on his damaged feet. A Swiss reporter managed to get close enough to speak to him in French, asking his name and what happened.

"My name is David Stoliar," he replied in a rush. "I was on the *Struma*. It was blown up. I think I am the only survivor."

The police hurried Stoliar into the hospital. The reporter had enough for a story. That night he filed a dispatch for Reuters, the British-based news agency, confirming that the *Struma* had been blown up and that a man named David Stoliar had survived. It was a small item, and it would prove to be more important than its subject could know at the time.

At the hospital, doctors wrapped Stoliar's frost-bitten hands and feet in bandages soaked in camphor. It was impossible to tell how deep the damage had gone into the tissue or whether he would lose any of his limbs. He was alert, but there was no one to talk to because he was kept in isolation, with a police guard outside the door. He had no visitors, no contact with Turkish authorities or anyone from the Jewish Agency.

After about a week, when the doctors determined that he was out of danger, he was moved to a prison on the other side of the straits. Loaded onto a police boat and taken across the Bosporus, he passed within a few hundred yards of the spot where the *Struma* had been marooned for ten weeks.

Astonishingly, Stoliar was jailed for being in Turkey illegally, since he had no visa and no permission to land. He was interrogated for hours by policemen who demanded to know what had happened to the ship, how it had gone down, if he knew what caused the explosion. He answered their questions as best he could, but Stoliar had little more information than the police. He did, however, recount what the chief mate had told him about seeing a torpedo headed for the ship before it exploded.

His fellow inmates were an intriguing lot, reflecting the political stew of Istanbul at the height of the war. There was a Bulgarian spy who had worked for the Allies, a German caught spying for the Nazis, an Englishman, and assorted Turks charged with political crimes. During the day, the prisoners shared a small stove, making Turkish coffee and chatting.

The rations were meager and of poor quality for everyone except

Stoliar. At each mealtime, his food was delivered in three metal containers from a nearby restaurant. He shared his bounty of mysterious origin with the other inmates. Throughout the six weeks he was imprisoned, he never knew who was providing his meals.

As his health improved, Stoliar became more insistent about demanding his freedom. He could not believe the Turks would stick with the absurdity of keeping him in prison as an illegal alien. Repeatedly he demanded to know why he was being held. There was never a response. He began to wonder whether his fate would be the same as that of the other passengers. If the Turks had towed a disabled ship full of passengers into the Black Sea, what would it matter if another Jew died?

"If they had the intention of eliminating me at the beginning, what could prevent them from eliminating me at the end?" he asked later. "Because I was the only witness to their inhumanity, really, from the beginning to the end."

Chapter 30

The wave of publicity that might have spared the passengers of the *Struma* washed over them in death. The tragedy became a rallying point for Jews around the world, sparking protests, death threats against British officials in Palestine, and memorial services in Britain and the United States.

The manner in which the British government now responded to the boatload of people lying at the bottom of the Black Sea was another dark chapter in the troubling story of the *Struma*. It further exposed the callousness and anti-Semitism that had been hidden in the exchanges of cables and intergovernmental memoranda.

News of the tragedy was slow to spread, and the British government used the lull to shape opinion at home and contain the damage, by pushing two dubious theories. The first strategy was to plant the suggestion, subtly and covertly, that the passengers themselves set off the explosion to avoid returning to Romania. Second, the government wanted to deflect criticism not only from itself, but also from Turkey by pointing the finger at the Romanians. Sparing Turkey was critical because the Allies were still trying to persuade Ankara to abandon its neutrality and join them. Alec Randall in the Foreign Office captured the necessity of shielding Turkey in a memo on February 26 in which he urged that "no reflection must be cast on the Turks."

The first strategy was apparent in a long piece published February 26 in the *Manchester Guardian*. The newspaper was regarded as favorably disposed toward Zionists, and the overall tone of the article was sympathetic. When it came to the cause of the sinking, however, the *Guardian* adopted a more cynical view: "Whether the *Struma* struck a mine or whether the exiles themselves took desperate measures to forestall the consequences of their arrival at a Romanian port will probably never be known."

The article was written by the newspaper's diplomatic correspondent in London, which means he probably got the suggestion of sabotage from someone in government. This possibility seems even more plausible because, the day before publication, the government sent a telegram to Lloyd's, the ship insurers, that used almost identical language in trying to shift blame to the passengers. "*Struma* later reports indicate accident not due to mine but due to explosion provoked intentionally by passengers who feared to return to Romania," said the telegram, which had been forwarded to London by the British consul general in Istanbul. "Result of explosion caused leakage which compelled the Master attempt beaching. The vessel, however, struck rock and sunk before reaching shore."

The story was a complete fabrication. The telegram also omitted critical facts well known to the British government, including absence of a working engine on the *Struma*. Like most good lies, it had the ring of plausibility—the passengers were certainly terrified of returning to Romania, and little more than eighteen months earlier desperate Jews had blown up the *Patria* in Haifa harbor to avoid deportation to Mauritius.

The next day, *The Times* of London helped carry out the second strategy in a two-paragraph article from Istanbul announcing the sinking. After asserting the ship presumably struck a mine and foundered, the article said: "The affair has much distressed Turkish people. The steamer, which was registered in 1930, was under the Panamanian flag and had a Bulgarian skipper. She arrived here from Romania two months ago, and was lying in Istanbul harbor undergoing repairs and awaiting settlement of the question of her destination, because no country had granted visas. The Turkish authorities were compelled, after vainly trying to solve the problem, to send the refugees back to their place of origin. The responsibility for this tragedy rests entirely on the Romanian government, which drove away these unfortunate people."

Like all good propaganda, the assertion contained a dose of truth; the Romanians were still killing thousands of Jews at home and in the Soviet Union. And like all the big lies, it avoided the more complicated and damning reality that Britain and Turkey had condemned the refugees more surely than if they had chosen to take their chances by staying in Bucharest.

By coincidence, British policy toward the *Struma* was scheduled for debate in the House of Lords on Thursday, February 26. Before the sinking Lord Wedgwood, a backer of the Zionist cause, had submitted a written question challenging the government's refusal to grant the passengers permission to enter Palestine. The government now considered begging off, since the issue was moot. In the end, the decision was made to respond. Finding the proper tone was a matter that went all the way to Number 10 Downing Street.

Lord Moyne was about to be replaced as head of the Colonial Office by Robert A. J. Gascoyne-Cecil, who was more formally known as Lord Cranborne. He was chosen to convey the government's response. His attitude toward Jewish immigration was more sympathetic than that of his predecessor, a position reflected in his proposed response to Wedgwood. In one particular paragraph, Cranborne wrote: "The press reports suggest that there has been a heavy loss of life. His Majesty's Government can only deplore this latest result of the inhumane traffic in illegal immigrants from ports in Eastern Europe now in enemy occupation which has caused so much suffering in the past. The circumstances of this particular case show that the mercenary organizers of this nefarious traffic, which is in direct contravention of the law of Palestine, are entirely indifferent to any consideration of humanity."

The language was emotional, even florid, though a critic could question how much blame belonged to those who organized the ship. The matter was so sensitive that Churchill himself reviewed the proposed response. The master of language saw immediately that Cranborne's response would inflame the issue, regardless of his attempt to redirect responsibility. The prime minister crossed out the entire paragraph beginning "The press reports." Lest his point be missed, he also underlined several adjectives in the offending section—"inhumane," "illegal," "mercenary," and "nefarious." Words like that could tar the British, too. At the bottom of his edited copy, Churchill added a note to Cranborne in his own hand: "This reply will get you into a lot of trouble. Anyhow I should cut out some of the adjectives."

The adjectives, and the paragraph, were duly removed, as was other explanatory language. Instead, when Cranborne took the floor of the House of Lords later that day he delivered a brief and sanitized reply, noting blandly that the ship had sunk in unknown circumstances and that the government deplored the tragic loss of life.

The deaths had not softened the British opposition to illegal immigration. Indeed, when the harshly worded statement issued by the Jewish Agency on February 25 arrived in London in early March, a Foreign Office official scrawled across it: "The Jewish Agency are trying to take advantage of the situation by bringing out this old contention that every Jew has a right to enter Palestine! This is of course an absurd contention: and it has to be refuted categorically whenever it is raised."

By this time, reaction in Britain had turned to criticism of the government's policy. Beneath the headline "New Approaches," the *Manchester Guardian* said: "The admission of refugees should be treated not with niggling state-craft but with generous humanity and a little common sense. . . . It is argued that if one refugee ship came many others would flock. That has always been said and it has not been true. If it were ever true it could be dealt with at the time. It is said that some refugees might be Axis agents. Any refugees from any Nazi country may conceivably be spies. We have taken the risk here and have not suffered for it. In Palestine itself, since the war began, several thousand refugees have been admitted and it is not suggested that Axis agents have been found among them. . . . If our policy cannot be intelligent let it be merciful."

Other voices demanded to know why the passengers had not been admitted by means of the quota of three thousand entry certificates

approved earlier in the year, which were still unused. The logical answer for many was discrimination against Jews, though few were willing to make the accusation directly. In the House of Commons debate,
D. L. Lipson raised the issue discreetly when he argued, "If the ship
had been an enemy ship, German, Italian, or Japanese, those on board
would have been interned."

In a letter to MacMichael on March 6, Moshe Shertok took Lipson's logic a step further: "Jews cannot possibly conceive that anything
of the sort could have happened if those fugitives had belonged to a
nation which has a government—be it even one in exile—to stand up
for them."

Shertok asked for an inquiry into whether all steps had been taken
to get the children off the ship before it departed, including whether
the Turks had been asked to delay the departure. He also asked that
the government give special consideration to allowing other Romanian refugees to enter Palestine. Among them were the Jews who remained in Romania, though they had been nominated for emigration
permits before Romania joined the Axis, the twenty-one passengers
from the *Dor de Val* who remained in Istanbul, and the two survivors
of the *Struma* also still in Istanbul, Medeea Salamowitz and David
Stoliar.

MacMichael saw no reason the disaster should change policy. "The
fate of these people was tragic," he cabled the Colonial Office, "but the
fact remains that they were nationals of a country at war with Britain,
proceeding direct from enemy territory. Palestine was under no obli-
gations toward them." He rejected Shertok's request for entry permits
for other Romanians, including Stoliar and Salamowitz, insisting that
the "basic principle that enemy nationals from enemy or enemy-
controlled territory should not be admitted to this country during war
applies to all immigrants."

The catastrophe had evoked a public outcry, but so far the British
were managing to contain the damage. Refusal to admit the sole survivor of the explosion and a woman who had lost a baby while onboard could have turned into a public relations nightmare. On March
21, Lord Cranborne overruled MacMichael on the two *Struma* sur-

vivors, though he upheld the refusal to allow the other Romanians into Palestine. Cranborne explained in a cable to the high commissioner that he had decided to admit Stoliar and Salamowitz "on humanitarian grounds as an act of clemency." He also pointed out that condemning them to remain in Turkey or face return to Romania "could only have exacerbated [the] intense feeling of resentment which [the] *Struma* disaster has aroused in Jewish and pro-Jewish circles in this country and [the] United States."

MacMichael was in no hurry to carry out Cranborne's directive, however. Stoliar and Salamowitz could wait. And while they waited, Stoliar in prison and Salamowitz recovering under Brod's supervision in a hotel, the Turks threatened to return both of them to Romania because they had no legal permission to be in the country.

For their part, the Turkish officials were equally adamant in defending their actions. When the Anatolia Agency wrote an article about conditions on the *Struma* and the mourning in Palestine after its sinking, a member of Parliament, Ziya Gevher Etili, denounced the article and the ungrateful Jews it depicted. "The telegraph [Anatolia Agency], instead of saying, 'Let's thank these people,' starts with the picture of hopeless conditions onboard during terrible conditions," he fumed in Parliament. "Our state fed them. Gave them even more than enough. They have even shown this ungratefulness and gave such information to the press as part of their Zionist propaganda."

Prime Minister Refik Saydam was equally defensive. "We have done everything we could, therefore carry no material or spiritual responsibility," he said. "Turkey cannot be a shelter for people not wanted by others. Turkey cannot serve as a homeland for people not welcomed by others. That's the way we choose. This is the reason we could not keep them in Istanbul. It is unfortunate that they were victims of an accident."

In the aftermath of the sinking, the Turkish government put forward a host of reasons for its refusal to allow the ship to remain or its refugees to land. The Turkish position, and that of the British, too, was summarized in a remarkably candid and chilling telegram to the Foreign Office in London from Knatchbull-Hugessen on March 8.

"The attitude of the Turkish Minister of Foreign Affairs before and since the accident has been that the *Struma* could not be allowed to stay in Turkish waters," Knatchbull-Hugessen said.

> The Turkish appeal that passengers should be allowed to enter Palestine having been unsuccessful, and Ministry of Foreign Affairs having been informed that His Majesty's Government saw no good reason why the vessel should not be sent back into the Black Sea as proposed, the Turkish government felt that they had no alternative but to send her there. The ministry said that it was intended that their action should discourage further attempts to send vessels, probably containing subversive elements, into the straits where by acts of sabotage they could mobilize themselves and remain a constant menace to the safety of Istanbul. They felt that unless the practice was at once discouraged the Turkish government might expose themselves to a large-scale influx of illegal immigrants. They said that in the case of the *Struma,* the passengers had sabotaged the ship with the idea that the Turkish authorities would be obliged to keep them in Turkey, but the Turkish government declined to be forced into receiving them and had therefore had the damage repaired and the ship sent back.

Reaction to the sinking was strongest in Palestine, where the episode was a catalyst for rising anger at the British over the exclusion of refugees and what many Zionists saw as discrimination against Jews in Palestine. Anger was inflamed when Anthony Eden, the British foreign secretary, announced the same week the *Struma* sank that Britain had agreed to readmit to Palestine Arab supporters of the mufti of Jerusalem, the city's Muslim spiritual leader and an enemy of the Jews.

March 4 was a day of fasting in honor of Purim, a holiday, beginning the following day, to commemorate the deliverance of the

Persian Jews from a massacre. Two large public banquets to end the fast were held in Jerusalem when the sun went down, both broadcast over the radio. Normally Purim is a joyous holiday. That night the mood was darkened by the fury over the loss of lives on the *Struma,* and the two banquets were interrupted by calls for revenge. The threats were directed at the British high commissioner for Palestine, Harold MacMichael.

"The blood of the *Struma* refugees will be inflicted upon MacMichael," people could be heard shouting on the radio. "MacMichael is not the representative of fighting England but the consolidators of the Nazis," raged others.

The following day, posters were plastered on walls and signposts throughout Jerusalem. Beneath a photograph of the patrician British official were the following words:

MURDER!
SIR HAROLD MAC MICHAEL
Known as High Commissioner for Palestine
WANTED for MURDER
OF 800 REFUGEES DROWNED IN THE
BLACK SEA ON THE BOAT *STRUMA*

Anger over what happened to the *Struma* coincided with rising militancy among many Jews in Palestine and a determination that it was vital to establish a Jewish homeland. They had been agitating to set up a Jewish army, with growing support from some American rabbis. Further, pamphlets had begun to appear in Tel Aviv and Jerusalem advocating creation of a separate Jewish state. The British mandate to oversee Palestine envisioned maintaining a Jewish homeland without prejudice to the Arab population, and the uneasy coexistence was in jeopardy. Within some quarters of the British government, there was an expectation that a showdown was approaching in Palestine, with the latest disaster providing momentum, as the dissent grew more violent.

The *Struma* episode marked a turning point in relations between

Zionists and the British government. MacMichael and Lord Moyne were seen by the Zionists as the primary culprits, men who had played active personal roles in blocking the ship's passage to Palestine, but the disaster had a far greater impact: It destroyed the last vestiges of what historian Bernard Wasserstein described as "the special relationship between Britain and Zionism inaugurated by the Balfour Declaration. Followed closely by the news of the full horror of the 'Final Solution' in Europe, the story of the *Struma* was to fester in Jewish minds for years as an example of British callousness and inhumanity."

Accounts of the *Struma,* sometimes exaggerated, provided part of the justification for the Jewish terrorist movements that emerged in Palestine in the later years of World War II. Among the targets of their attacks were to be the two architects of the ship's demise, Lord Moyne and MacMichael; one would be lucky, the other not. In 1944, Moyne was assassinated in Cairo, and MacMichael narrowly escaped several attempts on his life, including one in which he was wounded by gunfire outside Jerusalem. After the war ended, MacMichael was transferred to Malaysia.

Jewish organizations around the world condemned the British handling of the *Struma*. From New Zealand and South Africa to Britain and Canada, groups expressed anger and sadness. Many of the people in these groups were themselves refugees, and they identified strongly with the victims of the *Struma*.

The British officials responded with the barest facts possible, and resorted to lies in some instances. For example, the Zionist Organization of Mexico sent a strongly worded condemnation to the British ambassador in Mexico City. "Unfortunately, the attitude of the Palestinian administration has forced us to think very seriously of the unjust and unfair treatment that our people obtain in payment for their loyalty and complete cooperation," it said.

In response, the embassy rejected the accusation that the government in Palestine bore any responsibility and said it did not "accept that the government has ever acted cruelly and unjustly toward Jewish refugees." It was a categorical denial that even some colleagues in the government felt went too far.

There was no official reaction to the sinking from the Antonescu regime in Bucharest. Indeed, the primary steps taken by the Romanian government after the *Struma*'s departure the previous December had been to make sure that it was the last ship carrying Jews to leave the country, largely because the Germans had complained bitterly about the ship's having been permitted to leave. The security police officer who had officially allowed the *Struma* to depart became the scapegoat; he was dismissed from his post. To protect against more voyages, Romanian newspapers were forbidden to print any shipping or travel advertisements or notices that could be deemed helpful to Jews trying to emigrate.

Chapter 31

In the United States, reaction to the sinking of the ship lacked the fe-
rocity of the response in Palestine. However, a number of leaders
from Jewish organizations met with Sumner Welles, the acting secretary of state, and lodged a protest. Complaints were also made to the
British ambassador to Washington, Lord Halifax. A number of newspapers, including *The New York Times, The Washington Post,* and
Chicago Daily News, criticized the British government's handling of
the episode.

Rallies and memorial services were held across the country. More
than two thousand people attended a public meeting at the Cosmopolitan Opera House in New York City sponsored by the American Emergency Committee for Zionist Affairs. Among those who
addressed the meeting was Senator Edwin Johnson of Colorado, who
attacked British policy. "The most tragic thing about this mass murder," he said, "is that it need not have happened. It was the result of
acts of stupidity, callousness, cruelty. Hard-hearted colonial politicians
sent these victims to a watery grave."

American reaction concerned the British most deeply because they
feared it might encourage a return to isolationism. The United States
had entered the war reluctantly only a few weeks earlier, and some
parts of the public remained uncommitted. Even Senator Johnson,
who had torn into the British, had been an opponent of American entry into the war until the Japanese attacked Pearl Harbor.

Lord Halifax received urgent queries for information about the

Struma episode from prominent American citizens and official questions from the State Department. The official request asked pointedly whether it was true the passengers had been refused available visas because they were considered enemy aliens.

In a coded cable to the Foreign Office in London, Halifax warned that the controversy threatened to divide American opinion and had revived "agitation against the immigration policy of His Majesty's Government in Palestine and I should be grateful if you would telegraph me the facts of the case. It is alleged that Jews on the *Struma* were refused admittance because they were 'enemy aliens,' although visas were available. Is this substantially true?"

The reply to Halifax demonstrated the determination of the British to defend their policy: "Would-be immigrants on board *Struma* were all of course technically enemy aliens, and security grounds would have made acceptance of any of them at least without careful scrutiny highly questionable, but essential facts are that indiscriminate acceptance would have been against His Majesty's Government's declared policy on illegal immigration and calculated to cause extremely serious political repercussions in the Middle East at a critical moment of the war. On this aspect United States government's well-informed representatives in the Middle East will no doubt have reported fully to the State Department."

While some questions were sent to Halifax, the State Department in Washington also forwarded a more detailed request for information to the British Foreign Office in London. These questions covered the issue of considering the passengers enemy aliens and raised a host of other matters, including two that would have shifted a good portion of the blame onto the Turks.

One of these sensitive matters was whether Palestine had agreed to accept the ship's children, and whether the Turks had hauled the ship away before they could be taken off. There had been rumors to that effect circulating in Washington, but the press had not seized on the issue and the Jewish organizations did not have sufficient facts to raise it effectively.

The second was whether the Turks had buckled under pressure

from the Germans and sent the ship back to the Black Sea. This potential blockbuster was in the last paragraph of the State Department's list of questions. It reported that a secret cable from the American consulate in Istanbul said that the Americans had developed information that "the German government exerted pressure to have the ship driven from Istanbul, hoping that subsequent developments would cause adverse reactions in England and the United States."

Even if unproven, public opinion in the United States and the rest of the world would have been inflamed at the suggestion that Turkey had sent the *Struma* passengers to their graves in response to pressure from the Nazis. The ability of the British misinformation campaign to contain the angriest reaction within the predictable sectors—Jewish organizations and pro-Zionist groups—would have been threatened. A wave of negative publicity washing across a far broader group that could not be dismissed as predictable sympathizers might indeed turn a large segment of American opinion against Britain.

The Foreign Office weighed with care how to respond to the Americans. On the sensitive and emotional issue of the children, the office looked for information that might enable them to protect the Turks. Someone dug out Knatchbull-Hugessen's telegram in which he said he had notified the Turks of the decision to grant visas to the children; he asked the Turks to delay any action regarding the ship until the children could be taken off. "This tel. does not exactly exculpate the Turks," wrote Alec Randall of the Foreign Office to his colleagues. "They were informed on Feb. 18th that we had decided to admit the children. . . . But we should profoundly gloss over this."

Another handwritten note in the file prepared for responding to the Americans suggested that the United States government and British allies in the United States should be provided with as much frank information as possible, but efforts should be taken "not to incriminate the Turkish government."

The final response to Britian's ally, the United States government, was carefully crafted to defuse the potential bombshells without appearing to withhold information. It attempted to balance a sense of sorrow over the loss of life with what the British considered the necessity of limiting illegal immigration. In what could have been seen as a veiled threat, the response said: "The United States government is, of course, aware that His Majesty's Government are not alone in finding it vitally necessary, under stress of war, to place restrictions on emigration from enemy countries." No one needed to spell out that the United States, too, had imposed restrictions on Jewish immigration.

As for the potential firestorm from the intelligence report on Turkey's capitulation to Nazi pressure and the matter of the children, the British limited their reply on both matters to a single paragraph: "His Majesty's Government have no confirmation of the report mentioned in the last paragraph of the State Department's memorandum. According to their information the Turkish government, who had already expressed their inability to allow the children from the *Struma* to be landed and taken across Turkey to Palestine, were apprehensive of an attempt to force them to accept all the immigrants in their territory, and so decided to return the ship to the port from which it sailed."

The prospect that the Germans had threatened or pressured Turkey to get rid of the *Struma* never became a public issue. After the initial query to the Foreign Office, there was no indication that the American government pursued the matter either. Certainly Washington would have been cognizant of Turkey's strategic importance and therefore as unwilling as the British to stir up unnecessary trouble for Ankara.

There was, however, ample evidence that the Germans maintained a powerful diplomatic and espionage presence in Turkey, as did the Americans and British. Writing in his memoirs, *Life Line to a Promised Land,* Ira A. Hirschmann, the special representative of the United States State Department, said: "Nazi and Turkish agents were constantly on my trail. My every move was reported back to headquarters. (Later, when I was about to leave Turkey, I learned that the British Intelligence, also, had a complete dossier of my movements.) The German Gestapo, operating directly under [Ambassador Franz] von Papen, had the most active intelligence corps in Turkey."

It did not require a stretch of the imagination to envision Nazi lobbying against allowing the *Struma* to proceed to Palestine. Hundreds of thousands of other Jews were desperate to escape Europe, and Germany's extermination machinery was being perfected and getting ready to roll into high gear during the very weeks the ship sat in the harbor. The failure of the boat to make it to Palestine offered a chance to send a strong and disheartening message to anyone else willing to make such a trip, and its sinking had a profound impact on illegal immigration throughout the remainder of the war.

The British considered liberalizing the policy on illegal immigration after the disaster, primarily because Cranborne brought a somewhat more compassionate view on the issue to the Colonial Office. In the middle of March, he met with Weizmann and said that he was "personally determined to see that there should be no similar disaster in the future if it could in any way be avoided."

The Colonial Office prepared a memorandum for the cabinet favoring a modification of restrictions on illegal immigration, though it stopped short of abandoning the white paper. What Cranborne proposed instead was deducting the number of illegal immigrants from the quotas set up under the white paper. "The fate of those miserable people who do succeed in leaving enemy countries is so terrible, if we refuse them entry into Palestine, that I cannot feel that it is right to abandon them in their extremity," he said.

He described the practical effect of his proposal. A shipload of immigrants arriving in Palestine would go immediately to a detention camp. Each would be subjected to close scrutiny by the authorities on security grounds and in regard to their potential contribution to the economy. Those who passed through the two sieves, he said, would be admitted to Palestine. The remainder would be taken to another colony, such as Mauritius. "In practice, of course," he concluded, "nearly all the immigrants would be admitted, for the Jewish Agency would see that jobs were available for them. But the fact that we were maintaining the provisions of the White Paper might be used as an argument to rebut subsequent Arab criticism."

The Cranborne proposal echoed the very arguments made by the Jewish Agency to save the passengers from the *Struma:* Money was available to pay for their transportation to Palestine and to support them until they found jobs. They could go to an internment camp for security evaluation; they could even remain in the camp. Those pleas had fallen on deaf ears.

Cranborne had little success when his suggestion was discussed by the cabinet. Colleagues argued that the policy would bring a huge influx of refugees and that the shortage of available passenger vessels would make it difficult to transport them from Palestine once they arrived. The decision was made that all practical steps should be taken to continue to discourage illegal immigration and that any refugees who reached Palestine should be interned and transferred to other destinations as soon as possible.

The test of the policy came two weeks later, on March 19, with news that another ship, the *Mihai,* had reached Istanbul with fourteen hundred refugees. Cranborne approached the Foreign Office immediately and asked that Knatchbull-Hugessen be alerted to do everything possible to make sure the ship was not towed back to the Black Sea. Anthony Eden complained when he saw the request, saying it went beyond the instructions given by the cabinet. The crisis was averted when it was discovered that *Mihai* had fourteen passengers, not fourteen hundred.

In preparation for the expected arrival of the next big ship, Cranborne tried to set up a mechanism to transfer the refugees to Eritrea. He outlined the proposal in a letter to the secretary of state for war. When a copy of the letter was provided to Eden, he objected and said, "I think that Lord Cranborne is going to land us with a big problem, and that it would be more merciful to send these ships back."

Three more small boats arrived in Istanbul in April, with a total of sixty-three refugees, and the British continued to claim that "secret sources" were warning that thousands of Jews were gathering in Constanta to board ships bound for Palestine. The truth was that there was no huge congregation of potential refugees, and there were no big boats to take them toward freedom.

The sinking of the *Struma* had the effect that British hard-liners had hoped other disasters, like those of the *Salvador* and the *Patria,* would have had. The *Struma,* however, presented a different, far graver lesson for those who would venture onto the Black Sea in pursuit of freedom. The *Salvador* had suffered an accident, and the *Patria* was the victim of misguided Jewish militants. The *Struma* was the culmination of a policy of callous indifference on the part of the British and Turkish governments, carried out without interference from other Allied nations and, before the catastrophe occurred, with little outcry even from Jewish organizations.

"This was not an accident," said Turkish historian and author Rifat Bali during an interview in Istanbul. "This was a ship you could save. The world had the opportunity to save them. The British could have granted permission to enter Palestine. The permission was granted for the children to disembark. Still, Turkey did not let them off."

The magnitude of the loss of life from the *Struma* disaster, and the implacability of the British and Turkish governments, reverberated among potential refugees. The same message was heard by shipowners and potential crew members, the greedy and the humanitarian-minded alike. Other factors were at play in shutting off the flow of refugees. The Germans had tightened the noose around Europe's Jews after the Wannsee Conference, blocking emigration efforts and increasing the pace at which Jews were rounded up and dispatched to the death camps. The *Struma* was the last of the large ships to attempt to take Jewish refugees to Palestine. The escape route by sea was effectively closed on February 23, 1942, when the Turks sealed the *Struma*'s fate.

Chapter 32

Many aspects of what happened to the *Struma* remained a mystery in the weeks following the sinking. One of the most pressing questions was what had caused the onboard explosion that sent the ship to the bottom of the Black Sea. The location of the wreckage and the evidence from the Sile rescue crew and military vessels sent to the site later made it clear that the devastation could only have been caused by an explosion. While some elements continued to promote the idea of passenger sabotage, there was no evidence to support the theory.

The most credible theories were that the ship had hit a mine or that it had been sunk by a torpedo from a submarine. The latter theory was raised in a March 8 cable from the British ambassador in Ankara, who wrote: "The cause of the disaster is not definitely established. The vessel was able to proceed under her own power. Apparently she struck a mine but the possibility of her having been torpedoed is not excluded as the Turkish vessel *Cankaya* was torpedoed in the vicinity about that time."

The *Cankaya* was a small commercial fishing boat that had been sunk by a torpedo on February 23 without much warning. Most of its crew had managed to swim to shore and reported the incident to Turkish authorities, claiming that they had been sunk by a torpedo from an unseen submarine.

Stoliar had also told his Turkish captors the chief mate's story of a torpedo's telltale track coming at the *Struma*. The Turks, however, had not relayed that information, or anything else they had derived from their interrogations of Stoliar, to the British.

In neither case had anyone identified the nationality of the submarine, though naval intelligence officials reported that both Germany and the Soviets patrolled the Black Sea in the area of the Turkish coast and the Bosporus.

The cause of the *Struma*'s demise was not the only mystery surrounding the ship's final hours. Another big question was why, if the engine had been repaired as the Turks claimed, the ship had not proceeded farther up the coast in the direction of Bulgaria, the likely spot where Captain Garabatenko and the crew would want to land.

The only person who could answer at least some of the questions remained in an Istanbul jail, in danger of being forgotten as the rush of war news of German and Japanese victories pushed the disaster on the Black Sea out of the public eye.

The Turks did not know what to do with Stoliar after his release from the military hospital where he had recovered. So they put him in jail. The initial refusal by the British to allow him to proceed to Palestine had left the Turks feeling they had no choice but to send him back to Romania. The deaths of the other passengers, however, had created some disquiet in Ankara. There was no telling how the world would react to the Turks' returning the *Struma*'s sole survivor to the Nazis. Medeea Salamowitz, recuperating at the Continental Hotel under a form of house arrest, presented a similar dilemma.

Eventually, the British decision to grant entry visas to Stoliar and Salamowitz gave the Turks a painless way out. In Jersusalem, though, MacMichael was in no hurry to process the entry papers. He was angered by Cranborne's reversal of his own decision not to admit them and worried that the new head of the Colonial Office would buckle under public pressure and weaken the policy against admitting illegal refugees. He feared that providing visas to two illegal immigrants would create a loophole through which many others would try to enter Palestine. If MacMichael, who saw the wanted posters with his photograph and name on them plastered on every street corner, was not giving in to Jewish blackmail, he saw no reason Cranborne should.

In the end, MacMichael had to relent because of the pressure from

London. The tickets to freedom for Salamowitz and Stoliar arrived on April 2 in the form of a notice from the British passport control office: "To All Whom It May Concern: This is to certify that authority has been received from Jerusalem and Beirut to grant Palestine entry and Syrian transit visas to Medeea Salamowitz and David Stoliar."

In Salamowitz's case, it was only a matter of getting the British to stamp a visa in her passport and obtaining transit papers from Syria. Brod managed to take care of these details, and she was soon on a train to Palestine. Freeing Stoliar from his prison cell was a whole different challenge because of the charge that he was in the country illegally. Although he still had his passport, Stoliar had been imprisoned for six weeks. Once the British officials in Turkey received Stoliar's travel documents from Palestine, the Turks relented, and he was allowed to leave Turkey under police escort.

On April 22, after nearly two months without contact with the outside world, Stoliar was led down the stairs and into a small room. His feet and hands still ached from the aftereffects of frostbite, but he was able to walk without assistance. A stranger, a short balding man with a paunch and a serious face, waited for him. Without introducing himself or even saying a word, the man took one of Stoliar's hands and gently led him out of the prison to a waiting taxi.

"I'm Simon Brod," the man said in French as they pulled away. "You are going to stay at my house until tomorrow. Tomorrow I will take you to the railway station and I will put you on a train to Palestine."

Neither man exhibited any emotion. Both were quiet during the taxi ride, another ferry ride across the Bosporus to the Asian side, and the final leg to Brod's home. For Brod, it was a familiar routine, and he had learned to follow the lead of the tortured refugees when it came to conversation. And Stoliar had grown accustomed to silence.

At Brod's villa, Stoliar bathed and put on the clothes that Brod had bought for him. There also was a watch, for which Brod had paid 60 Turkish lira, shoes that cost 24.70, and a valise worth 11 lira.

Stoliar went into the kitchen, where he was introduced to Brod's wife and his daughter, Marta, a beautiful young woman just a few years younger than Stoliar. He sat at the table and ate slowly as Brod described what had happened over the last few weeks.

"You, you are the single survivor of the *Struma,*" Brod explained. "It's a miracle. That you survived the Turkish authorities, it's even a bigger miracle, because I expected them to eliminate you."

Certainly, Brod said, the Turks would have killed Stoliar once he was inside the hospital had it not been for the reporter who jotted down his words and wrote the story of the sole survivor of the *Struma*.

"The fact that you managed to say a few words at the entrance of the hospital and telling them your name and where you were coming from," he said, "it was known soon throughout the news media that you are a survivor of this particular vessel. Because of that, it seems, the Turkish authorities were reluctant to make you disappear. But they kept you at the police station because they didn't know how to deal with you."

Brod explained to Stoliar that he had ordered the food sent to him at the prison, hoping to help him recover from weeks without enough to eat and hoping to thwart any plans to poison him. The regular food deliveries were also a way for Brod to monitor, as best he could from the outside, the health and well-being of the inmate.

Brod's suspicion that Stoliar had been in danger assumed greater credibility nearly sixty years later. Ahmet Akarsu, one of the fishermen from Sile, remembered with great clarity that two men were rescued from the sea after the sinking of the *Struma*. He said that the first one who was brought ashore was nursed to health in the village. The second survivor, who turned up after Turkish soldiers had arrived in Sile, was taken away immediately and never seen again.

Akarsu told the stories of both survivors in the spring of 2001. He had spent all of his seventy-five years in Sile and little had escaped his notice. Nothing in all those years had left an impression as strong as the two men fished from the sea in the winter of 1942. The first man, the one he later learned was David Stoliar, had recuperated in the village before being taken away by the military.

"Two days later, another man came ashore," Akarsu said. "He

looked like the first. Tall, thin, and blond. He spoke another language. He was brought in here, though, in this cove, by a fisherman. By that time, the military had posted watchmen along the shore. He was taken away by the soldiers. We never saw him again. He had to have come from the *Struma*. There were no other boats that sank at that time. It just had to be."

There is no way to prove the second-survivor theory. Akarsu's memory of both events was equally vivid. The details about Stoliar's rescue were confirmed by others, including Stoliar himself. None of the other old-timers in the village, however, admitted knowing anything about a second survivor. The initial British reports had said there were two survivors, but the first news about the fate of the *Struma* had been notoriously unreliable.

Other factors weighed against another survivor. Chief among them was that it would have been nothing short of a miracle if someone had stayed alive for three full days in the frigid Black Sea, where the water temperature would have been sixty degrees Fahrenheit or colder. In addition, it is legitimate to ask why the Turks would have killed a second survivor if they were going to leave Stoliar alive to tell the story of what happened on the ship. On the other hand, what difference would another death have made when scores of men, women, and children had just drowned? And it is worth noting that Stoliar's rescue occurred before the Turkish military arrived on the scene.

The morning after his dinner with the Brods, Stoliar was driven to the Haydarpasa train station by his benefactor. A Turkish policeman was waiting, and Brod handed him Stoliar's travel papers. With a handshake, Stoliar said farewell to Brod and boarded the train for Aleppo with the policeman.

On the train, Stoliar could see his image in the glass of the window. He was gaunt, and his eyes looked empty and sorrowful at the same time. The train was carrying him away from the floating prison, the deaths at sea, and the rescue. Brod had paid for a first-class sleeping compartment for Stoliar, and the policeman rode in another compartment. Stoliar could eat what he chose, shave and shower at will, in that palace of a train.

At the Syrian border, the Turkish policeman gave him the papers and shook his hand. A car and driver were waiting in the town of Aleppo to take him to Haifa. They were stopped briefly at the border of Palestine, where the driver was told to take his passenger to the British security post. Stoliar spoke neither Hebrew nor English, so the police sent for a French interpreter. Stoliar was asked some routine questions—why did he leave Romania, what did he plan to do in Palestine—and surprisingly few about his recent ordeal. The border police in those hard days were accustomed to the passage of ghostlike figures with sad stories. This one was sent on his way with the wave of a hand.

The driver took him to the Tel Aviv apartment of a friend from Romania, who had been alerted to expect his guest. Stoliar had no money, and he still suffered from the effects of the frostbite that had damaged his arms and feet. He had trouble walking and could not feed himself easily.

In May, he sought financial assistance from a Romanian humanitarian group in Palestine, explaining in a letter that he was a survivor from the *Struma* and could not work yet because of injuries. With the help of the Romanians and the Jewish Agency, Stoliar underwent months of therapy to regain the use of his hands and feet.

With the exception of that plea for help, however, Stoliar tried to forget about the *Struma*. He wanted to start a new life in a new country, not dwell in a past filled with horrors and ghosts. In a place filled with survivors, no one pressed Stoliar for his personal story. The publicity on the *Struma* had died out, and Stoliar's name, which wasn't mentioned in the papers even at the height of the outcry because he was in prison, didn't come up. None of the other passengers who had come to Palestine before him—the Frenks, Martin Segal, Medeea Salamowitz—tried to get in touch with him. Nor did he reach out to them.

He lived briefly with his friend from Romania and later shared a house with another young man he met in Jerusalem. In the months that Stoliar shared a house with the man, he never mentioned the *Struma,* and the man had no idea of his friend's brush with death.

Stoliar had a number of menial jobs, working the night shift as a security guard and later driving a pickup truck.

In early 1943, Stoliar joined the British army. He later explained that he was unaware of the role the British government had played in the *Struma* catastrophe; he blamed the Turks for refusing to let the ship go on to Palestine. Joining the army seemed the best way to fight the Nazis, and he was sent off to Cairo for a short training period before joining a supply unit in Tripoli that was following British fighting troops as they marched across northern Africa in pursuit of the retreating Germans.

Another former *Struma* passenger had fought the desert wars of northern Africa, too, though he was at home recovering from a wound by the time Stoliar arrived there.

Chapter 33

When he first arrived in Palestine in February 1942, David Frenk was restless and unable to sleep. He read the few articles that were published in the Jewish press about what was happening on the *Struma*. He and his brother, Israel, were together at their parents' house in Haifa when they got the shattering news that the ship had been sunk.

"I cried all night, and afterwards I thanked God for giving me my life as a present," David Frenk said later.

Frenk's immediate assumption was that the Nazis had sunk the *Struma* to kill its passengers. They had forced him and the others to flee Romania, and he found it logical to assume the Germans were directly responsible for the deaths. He responded to the tragedy by driving to Tel Aviv to enlist in the British army.

At the recruitment office, he was told that young Jews were only being trained to remain in Palestine in case of a German invasion. He insisted that he would only sign up if he could be assured that he would be transferred immediately to a front-line unit. The recruiting sergeant consulted his superiors and eventually agreed to the demand, and Frenk signed the enlistment papers. What he knew about Britain's role in refusing to permit the *Struma* to proceed to Palestine was secondary. "I would have fought for any army that allowed me to fight the Germans," he said later.

The hard part was explaining this to his parents. Their two sons had escaped Romania and the *Struma,* and Frenk knew it would break his mother's heart if he were to leave again. His brother had already joined the Haganah, which allowed him to remain in Palestine.

Back home, Frenk stopped eating the huge meals he had consumed since arriving. His mother asked about the change, and he confessed that he had joined the British army. She fainted. When she revived, he and his father lied and said that David had joined one of the units that would remain in Palestine. Before he left, he wrote out fifty different postcards, which his father and brother agreed to send to his mother at intervals in the coming weeks to continue the charade.

Frenk was sent to northern Africa, where the British and Americans were busy routing the German tank forces. He was hit by a tank shell, and after two operations to save his leg, he was sent home to Palestine. Later, when Jews living in Palestine were changing their names to Hebrew, he and his brother changed the family name to Dinari, which meant *money,* as *Frenk* had in Romanian.

Ogen Rintzler was still on the kibbutz when the *Struma* went down. He did not read Hebrew well, so he did not pay attention to the news. The house where he lived had no electricity, so he did not hear anything on the radio. Sometime in March, however, a friend who knew he was from Romania mentioned that a shipload of Romanian Jews had been sunk in the Black Sea. Rintzler had no siblings or other close relatives, only his parents.

"I have nobody," he thought at the time. "Nobody." But it would be years before he learned the full extent of his loss.

Esthi David, Ami Atir's cousin, was getting ready to go to school the morning she heard about the sinking. "I had my backpack on," she said. "My mother accompanied me to the door and waited, just like normal. The neighbor called out to my mother, 'Oh, Bella, there is no school today. Don't you know there is a general strike by the Jewish community in Palestine? There was a ship by the name of *Struma* that sank with all the passengers onboard.'" That was how Esthi David and her family learned that eleven of their relatives had died.

The news was slow to arrive in Romania, where hundreds of

relatives remained. Even when they heard, some of the relatives refused to accept the deaths; after the war, a group of them filed a lawsuit to block using the names of their relatives on a memorial planned for those who died on the ship, insisting that they were not dead.

Another group of relatives waited. A month after Romania surrendered to the Allies on August 23, 1944, they hired three lawyers and filed suit against Jean Pandelis. A judge impounded the Greek shipowner's passport, and before the end of the year the judge, Constantin Calea, was prepared to charge Pandelis with criminal negligence.

The *Struma* was not a run-of-the-mill case, particularly in a country determined to cleanse from the history pages the crimes it had committed against its own Jewish population. The prosecutor told the judge to gather more evidence before bringing charges. When the judge presented a more complete file, the prosecutor impounded it.

Lawyers for the relatives appealed to higher authorities, right up to the Ministry of Justice. While the appeal was pending, the government of Romania passed a decree providing amnesty for crimes related to the war, including murder. Pandelis was never charged, and at the war's end he was rich from the money he had earned in the refugee trade.

Romania won a kind of amnesty, too, at least in most history books. In the fall of 1942, Ion Antonescu refused German pressure to deport the country's remaining Jews to the camps in Poland, sparing as many as three hundred thousand from certain death. As the tides of war shifted in the months that followed and Germany's certain victory turned into a predictable defeat, the Romanian officials who had overseen the earlier slaughters developed a conscience. Thousands of Romanian Jews living abroad and still in danger were protected by Romanian diplomats, and many were repatriated at the very time the German death camps were still in high gear.

"And as the vast German camp system actualized its horrific potential, the number of murders committed by Romanians decreased, as did the determination with which they enforced their country's anti-Semitic laws," said historian Radu Ioanid. "Such contradictions go a long way toward explaining the survival of at least half of Romania's Jews."

The contradictions do not constitute absolution for the fascist dictatorship of Antonescu, however. Revisionist historians during the Communist era went to great lengths to claim that Romanian officials were guilty only of moderate anti-Semitism and that they were never willing accomplices of the Nazis in organizing deportations and exterminations. The truth was far grimmer, even if it was not completely black.

The full picture of carnage in Romania is not known. Ioanid estimated more than forty-five thousand Jews, probably closer to sixty thousand, were killed in Bessarabia and Bukovina by Romanian and German troops in 1941. At least seventy-five thousand of the Jews who were deported to the camps in Transnistria died. Another one hundred thirty thousand Jews were killed in Transnistria itself, the majority in and around Odessa. In all, at least two hundred fifty thousand Romanian Jews died on orders of Romanian officials or as a result of their actions and complicity with the Nazis, though some historians put the figure as high as three hundred thousand.

Still, many of the relatives of the *Struma*'s passengers who stayed behind survived the war years. People who had not been able to afford a ticket on the ship counted themselves lucky even as they mourned those who had gone in their place.

Among those who survived the Holocaust were the wife and daughter of Horia Lobel, the *Struma*'s doctor, who died without knowing he had a daughter. He had insisted that his pregnant wife, Rosalie, remain behind because the ship was unsafe. When their daughter, Ilana, was born, she took the baby and left Bucharest and its terrors behind. She moved in with wealthy Christian friends who lived on an estate in the countryside. The family raised Ilana as their own daughter to protect her, and her mother worked as a housekeeper in the household for years. Ilana went to church on Sundays with the family and she took communion.

Safety, and knowledge, came only with the end of the war. Little by little after that, Rosalie Lobel revealed bits of her past to the child. She said that she was her mother and that her father was a physician who had not returned yet from the war. In time, Rosalie said that she was Jewish, but insisted that her daughter was Christian. Eventually they left the haven of the estate and started a new life together in Bucharest.

By the time Ilana was eleven or twelve years old, many things in her life did not seem to fit. How could her mother be Jewish and she be gentile? How could her father still be alive after all these years? Finally, after Ilana insisted on the truth, her mother admitted that Ilana was Jewish. Her mother maintained, however, that her father would return someday. Many times through the years, Ilana had heard her mother talk about her father and something called *Struma*.

"What is this *Struma*?" she finally asked.

"It was a ship," her mother replied warily.

"Why do you care about a ship?"

"Your father was on that ship."

"Okay. What happened to him?"

After a long silence, her mother told her the story of the *Struma,* about how her father had gone even though he knew the ship was unlikely to make it to Palestine, about the single postcard she had received from Istanbul and how he described the horrible conditions and the crying women and the woman who had lost her baby. She also said there were stories that the Turks had smuggled some rich people off the ship while it sat in the harbor in Istanbul. There were other stories, too, about how some people had managed to swim ashore when the ship sank and were safe somewhere in Turkey or even Palestine.

As her mother told the story she had kept bottled up for years, Ilana thought she sounded angry. Angry at her father for leaving her behind in 1941, and angry with him for not returning.

Ilana Lobel was a gifted student who won scholarships and academic prizes. She wanted to become an actress or an archeologist. Her mother insisted that she would be a doctor. Mother and daughter emigrated to Israel in 1958, where Ilana enrolled in medical school and became a doctor like her father. Even years after finishing medical school and becoming a practicing physician and professor, like her mother, part of Ilana kept waiting for her father to appear one day.

For years she searched for people who might have known her father, in an effort to establish a connection, even a tenuous one. When she first heard of Greg Buxton and his efforts to find the ship and the growing list of passengers, she questioned David Stoliar and David Frenk about her father, but they had never met the ship's doctor. "They were young at the time," she said sadly. "I guess they wouldn't have needed him."

Michael Bucspan was an engineer, a pragmatic man who harbored no illusions about life or death. He had been in engineering school in England when his parents left for Palestine on the *Struma*. He had no desire to go to Palestine.

"My idea was that you must fight the Nazis," he said later. "The Jewish people were not strong enough. But in the British army you could fight them. So when the war broke out, I volunteered and joined the army right at the start of the war. I was not fighting for the British. I was fighting against the Germans. To me, the essential thing was to destroy the Nazis."

He was stationed with a unit of engineers near Oxford when he saw a newspaper article about the sinking of the *Struma*. He had just received the postcard his father had sent to him on February 17, one of two he had received from onboard the ship. He tore the article from the paper and took it, along with the postcard, to his commanding officer.

"I must go to London to sort things out," he sobbed.

He was given two days leave. He stayed away for a week. Partly, he was in shock. It had been a brutal way to find out about the death of his parents, his only relatives, and he harbored no illusions that two people in their middle fifties had survived the sinking. Almost as bad, the thought of the conditions described in his father's postcards gnawed at him and increased his bitterness that the world might not ever know what horrors the passengers of the doomed ship had suffered.

"I was very angry," he said. "I did that on purpose, stayed away a week. I had an idea that if they made a case, let's say a court-martial, I could expose the whole thing—what happened to the *Struma*. Unfortunately, as a soldier I had no right to contact the press, to speak out. Had they charged me with being absent without leave, however, I would have been able to present the whole case to the authorities."

Bucspan would not have his chance to speak out. His fellow soldiers had covered for their grieving colleague the entire week he was away, performing his duties and pretending he was there. The commanding officer never discovered the length of his absence. A few weeks later, Bucspan transferred to the glider corps and became a pilot. He was injured and returned to a mechanical engineering unit. He landed on Normandy Beach in 1944 and fought alongside men who died in action and men who became lifelong friends.

After Normandy, someone discovered that he spoke Romanian and German, so he was transferred to the intelligence service as a translator. As the war wound down, Bucspan was assigned to a prisoner-of-war camp on the Rhine River in Germany. Many of the prisoners were not Germans, but foreign nationals whose countries had been aligned with Germany, and many of them claimed they had been conscripted against their will and should be freed.

"One of the groups incarcerated in this camp was a bunch of Romanians who were in the German SS," he said. "I interrogated them in German and asked why they were in the SS. They said they were forced to join because they were afraid they would be killed by the Germans. They said they could prove they were all Romanian citizens."

As proof, the soldiers handed Bucspan their Romanian identity cards. Only then did they discover, to their dismay, that their interrogator also spoke Romanian. The soldiers had given him their membership cards from the Iron Guard.

"I told them that I was a Jew and I was from Romania," he said. "They were very upset. I made sure that they stayed upset."

After the war, Bucspan changed his name to Buxton, married an English woman, Patricia Stevens, and closed the part of his life that was scarred by war and losses. His two treasured postcards were placed in a box and put on a shelf. He and Patricia settled outside London and had a daughter, Candida, and a son, Gregory, named after his grandfather. Little was said within the family about the tragedy surrounding the deaths of Grigor and Zlata Bucspan. It seemed distant, painful, and closed.

Chapter 34

In the months after the *Struma*'s sinking, Turkish people faced their own hardships. Nazi troops were on the border with Greece, less than fifty miles from Istanbul, and the government faced a depressed economy, food shortages, and the continuously rising costs from mobilizing its armed forces in case of invasion. When price controls and rationing did not ease the pressure, the government introduced a series of drastic tax increases in late 1942. The last of the taxes, known as the Varlik Vergisi, or "capital levy," was enacted on November 11, 1942, to raise $360 million. Though ostensibly aimed at anyone who owned property and was thought to be making inordinate profits as a result of the war, its implementation fell hardest on non-Muslim merchants, who were suspected of having the most ready cash on hand.

Local assessment councils were established to determine who owed the tax and how much they owed. Officials from the Finance Ministry, local merchants, and prominent citizens formed the councils, virtually all drawn from the majority Muslim population. Their decisions could not be appealed, and the taxes had to be paid in full in a short time, often within two weeks.

"As it turned out, the assessments were based on very limited information and were therefore often crudely assessed and collected, taxing some far more than they had and others far less," wrote Stanford J. Shaw, a historian otherwise inclined to praise Turkey's attitude toward Jews and other minorities.

The result was an atmosphere of economic terror. Those who were taxed more than they had were invariably Jews or members of the Christian Greek and Armenian minorities, who formed the strongest part of Istanbul's merchant class. People who could not pay immediately were forced to sell everything they owned and declare bankruptcy. If they still could not pay, they were sent to work on government projects or loaded onto trains and taken to a labor camp in eastern Turkey. Out of 1,400 people sent to the camp in 1943, 1,229 came from Istanbul and 21 died while there, according to Shaw.

Ishak Alaton was barely fifteen years old when the capital levy was imposed. His father, a wealthy businessman, was assessed far more than he could pay. The family moved from their villa to a tiny apartment, and they sold all of their furniture. Still his father could not pay it all, and so in late 1942 he was sent to the labor camp, where he remained for ten months.

"My father came home from the camp one evening," his son remembered. "The apartment was in semidarkness. We didn't use lights to avoid spending money on electricity. There was no furniture because it had all been sold. We were sitting on the bare floor. He came in and he was an old man, with white hair. I didn't recognize him. I thought, 'Why is he in the house? Who let him in?' And then he started speaking and I recognized his voice. He left with black hair. He came back with white hair, and I didn't recognize him any longer."

Like many Jews and Christians crippled financially by the tax and disheartened by the way their country had treated them, Alaton sent his son away. Ishak Alaton went to Sweden, where he studied engineering, eventually returning as a young man to rebuild and redouble the family fortune. Most who left, however, did not come back.

Another person who suffered in the economic crisis was Simon Brod. His textile business was already weakened by the general economic stagnation and the time and money Brod had spent helping refugees. When the capital levy was imposed, he was forced to sell everything, his daughter, Marta, said later. The irony was that the family had only recently revoked their Polish citizenship and become Turkish, she said. "I remember, I was at school, and all the girls came

246 / DEATH ON THE BLACK SEA

over to congratulate me on my new citizenship," she said. "Actually, it was the beginning of the end.

"We had a building, Brod Han, and he sold that for nothing," she said. "He sold our textile shop. We had a villa on the Asian side of the Bosporus. He sold that as well."

Eventually, Brod was arrested and sent to prison. There are many who think his arrest was actually to prevent his work on behalf of the refugees. His wife took food to him throughout his stay. Eventually he was freed, and the family left Turkey.

The number of Jews in Turkey dropped steadily after the war, dwindling to twenty-seven thousand by the late 1990s. Some, like Alaton, eventually prospered. Rich or not, most who remained kept their heads low, attending a handful of synagogues but largely assimilating into the secular country. The politics of the Jewish leaders in Istanbul, where most of the Jewish population lived, was to maintain good relations with the state. Like the rest of the people in modern Turkey, they learned to forget and to promote the idea that Turkey had been tolerant of its religious and ethnic minorities.

"In this complex world, *Struma* was something everyone wanted to forget about," said Rifat Bali, a Jewish businessman in Istanbul who has written extensively about the history of the country's Jews. "Jews wanted to forget because how else can you go on with your rhetoric of tolerant Turkey when almost eight hundred people died?"

When the war ended, Stoliar wanted to forget, too, though his reasons were different. "At that time, my mind was already completely blank of it," he said. "I already put it way behind. Those had been dark days, my darkest days. There was no reason whatsoever to mention it. Talking about it, you don't get any relief."

Much like Michael Buxton, he closed a chapter of his life to start on a new one. His mother had died in the gas chambers of Auschwitz. He had discovered that his father, Jacob, had survived in Bucharest. They corresponded, but Stoliar vowed he would never again set foot on Romanian soil. His father would have to come to him.

Stoliar arrived in North Africa near the end of the campaign there. After a stint driving a supply truck on the battlefield, he had been transferred to Cairo in the middle of 1943. For the first time in years, he was able to relax. The battlefield had shifted to Europe, the Germans were on the run, and Stoliar rented a room in a house. At a dinner party one night, he met Adria Nacmias, a young Jewish woman from Alexandria. She was twenty-one and had left home for Cairo with her parents. They courted, and in 1945 they were married. Stoliar wore his British army uniform.

He told his wife little about his background. He was born in Romania, his mother was dead, his father still there. He had fled on a refugee ship and later joined the army. He did not mention a word about the *Struma* or his survival.

After the war ended, Stoliar stayed on in Cairo as a civilian employee of the army for another six months. In late 1946, when he decided it was time to move on, his service had earned him a generous offer from the British. He was told he could live anywhere in the commonwealth—Britain, Canada, Australia. He chose Palestine so his wife could remain near her family. By the time he returned to Palestine, he was just in time for another war.

Britain had never managed to reconcile the conflicting demands of the Jewish and Arab people who tried to share Palestine under the mandate. There had been constant violence, much of it aimed at the British from the increasingly effective Jewish underground army. In April 1947, the beleaguered British government asked the United Nations General Assembly to determine the fate of the strife-torn country. On November 29, 1947, the assembly approved partitioning Palestine into two states, one Jewish and one Arab. The Jewish community accepted the plan; the Arabs rejected it.

The violence increased, the Jewish underground forces were replaced with an organized army. As an experienced soldier, Stoliar was among the first drafted. He had worked for a few months for Esso Oil Company in Haifa, but he left his wife there and soon found himself fighting Arabs. The Jewish forces managed to take hold of the entire area that the United Nations had allocated to them. On May 14, 1948, when the British mandate came to its official end, the State of Israel was officially brought into existence. Less than twenty-four hours later, the regular armies of Egypt, Iraq, Jordan, Lebanon, and Syria invaded the country. In what became known as the War of Independence, the Israelis fought for fifteen months until the United Nations negotiated an armistice agreement.

Stoliar returned to his job with Esso in Haifa and soon became manager of the company's plant there. In 1950, he brought his father and his stepmother to Israel to live. The following year, Stoliar and Adria had a son, Ronnie.

In 1953, the American oil companies began pulling out of Israel. They were under pressure from the Arab states, and their investments in the Persian Gulf were far more valuable than the operations in Israel. Stoliar was offered a job with another American company in Tokyo, and he and his family moved there.

Japan was working tirelessly to rebuild an economy devastated by the war and its humiliating loss. For Stoliar, it was a perfect place. He could do his job, which involved arranging barter deals for the American company, and be left alone. Nobody asked about his past. Nobody stirred up memories he was busy burying. "Basically, the Japanese live and let live," he said. "They don't understand foreigners, so they think that the foreigner does not exist. They just ignore you completely. It's a very pleasant feeling that nobody pays any attention to you."

Stoliar remained there for eighteen years. Adria died of lung cancer in 1961, leaving him to raise their son. Amazingly, she died not knowing that her husband was the sole survivor of the *Struma* tragedy. In August 1968, he married Marda Emslie, an American from Portland, Oregon. She was a shoe designer living in New York and working all over the world. They had been introduced by Stoliar's boss. After several years in Japan, they moved to the United States and settled in Oregon, not far from Marda's childhood home.

They were married for nearly three years before Stoliar mentioned the *Struma,* and then it came up only because a television crew from Britain had tracked him down and wanted to interview him. To his surprise, Marda told him she already knew. Before their first date, she had gone to the New York Public Library and checked his name in the databases out of curiosity. She had seen a couple of articles about the ship and the sole survivor, but she was not going to mention it if he didn't.

Over the years, a handful of newspaper and magazine articles reconstructed the saga of the *Struma*. A number of books dealt with it, too, mostly scholarly assessments. The best of the books, works such as Bernard Wasserstein's *Britain and the Jews of Europe 1939–1945* and Dalia Ofer's *Escaping the Holocaust,* were based on extensive archival research and provided a compelling portrait of British attitudes at the time.

By and large, however, the *Struma*'s story was lost among the larger cataclysms of the death camps. Why some deaths were remembered so vividly and others were forgotten is impossible to figure out entirely. Part of the reason was the horrific drama of the liberation of Auschwitz and Bergen-Belsen, names that became synonymous with Nazi evil. The searing images were impossible to forget. Beyond the images, however, were the people who had been in those camps and survived, and they described the atrocities they had suffered. Belzec, on Poland's eastern border with Russia, was a prototype for the death camps. The world remembers little of the six hundred thousand who died there because only a handful of people survived to tell its story.

"Who ever goes to visit Belzec?" said Rabbi Barry Marcus of the Central Synagogue in London. "The irony of our relationship with the Holocaust, and let's talk about the *Struma* in that context, is that the places that have become symbolic are only so because there were survivors."

The *Struma* sank out of sight, without leaving a photographic record of the horror endured by its passengers. The ten people who survived the *Struma* were widely dispersed, and they chose silence. Leon Uris, who romanticized the exodus, never wrote about the *Struma*. When the United States Holocaust Memorial Museum opened in 1993 in Washington, D.C., there was no mention of the *Struma* and the 768 Jews who went down with the ship.

About the only place where the *Struma* was remembered regularly was in Tel Aviv, where each February the members of its sizable population of Romanian immigrants gathered in a small synagogue for a memorial service honoring its passengers.

The synagogue was founded by Rabbi Hersh Guttman after his arrival in Israel in 1961, many years after he survived the Iron Guard death squad that killed his two sons. People still marveled at his survival, and they still told the story of the blessing he bestowed on David Stoliar before the voyage of the *Struma*. Rabbi Guttman wanted the synagogue to remain a living commemoration of the victims of the Romanian Holocaust, which like the *Struma* is too often relegated to history's footnotes. Throughout the community room were memorials to many of the numerous tragedies from his homeland—the Jassy and Bucharest pogroms, the death marches in Bessarabia and Bukovina, and the *Struma*.

Occasionally when people congregated for one of the memorial services, an old debate was renewed among those who remember the events of the war years. Some argued that the sinking of the *Struma* was not part of the Holocaust. They reasoned that it was not an organized event, like shipping trainloads of people to gas chambers. Instead, they saw it as people fleeing one country for another to save their lives.

It is really a debate over semantics, but the rationale for considering the *Struma* part of the greater Holocaust seems to outweigh the reservations. "It is the Holocaust because they died because they were Jews," said Ruth Ben-Zvi, who lost a childhood friend on the ship. "They died because they were Jews. There were Jews who died by starvation. There were Jews who died on forced marches to Transnistria. There were Jews who were killed in police stations. It was a Holocaust. The means of killing doesn't matter."

For many years, Ami Atir, who lost eleven family members on the *Struma,* including his grandparents, never thought of them as Holocaust victims. He knew little about the *Struma*. But that changed. "For me the whole thing began when my mother died," he said. "She didn't leave us much because she didn't own much. But she did leave a piece of paper asking that all the names of her perished family be inscribed on her grave. The words are, 'In memory of my family Reichman and Rosenzweig who perished in the disaster of the *Struma* and the Bucharest pogrom.' For all those years she had said nothing about it. I don't know why. I never asked her. Maybe it was because there were so many stories that the individual stories seem so little."

Years after his mother's death, Atir saw a Yad Vashem Holocaust Memorial Authority advertisement in the newspaper inviting Holocaust survivors and their relatives to tell their stories. It hit him then. He had lost his family to the Holocaust. "As a child, I knew that my family was murdered by the British government. Two years ago, I opened the paper, and I said, wait a minute. My family was also victim to the Holocaust."

Chapter 35

Summer, 2000

The best account of the cause of the *Struma*'s sinking was Stoliar's recollection of the chief mate describing the torpedo that he saw approaching ship. Stoliar had recounted the story in various interviews, including the earliest ones with the Turkish police. The sinking of the fishing vessel *Cankaya* in the vicinity at about the same time gave credence to the hypothesis. But for years there was no proof, and a nagging question remained: If it was a submarine, was it German or Russian?

Both countries had enough diplomats and spies in Turkey during the war to have known precisely who was onboard the *Struma* and to have monitored its departure. The Germans were thought by many to be the best bet, since they would have had a reason for sinking a ship filled with Jews. But there was no indication that German U-boats were operating in the Black Sea at that time. The Soviets, on the other hand, did patrol the sea with submarines in order to protect their southern flank. Still, the prospect that a Soviet submarine sank an un-armed shipload of refugees seemed illogical—until the discovery of Stalin's secret 1941 order to destroy all shipping headed toward Germany in the Black Sea and the logs of a particular Soviet submarine.

The first piece of the puzzle was discovered in the early 1960s by a German investigator, Jurgen Rohwer. He had been asked by German courts to investigate a number of sinking incidents during World War II. The cases were opened after victims' relatives petitioned the German government for compensation.

In his inquiry into the sinking of the *Struma*, Rohwer determined that no German submarines were operating in that part of the Black Sea in February 1942. In fact, he concluded, the Germans had removed their submarines as a result of a dispute with the Turks over the accidental sinking of a Turkish boat.

Rohwer concluded that the Germans had not sunk the ship. The next step was finding who was responsible. His search led him to Soviet naval archives from the war. There, he found the log of a Russian submarine, SC 213, that had been operating in the Black Sea in early 1942. The log provided the coordinates for targets and a list of operations in the Black Sea. Among them was a listing for the sinking of a ship identified as the *Struma*.

Rohwer published his findings in 1964 in a book called *Die Versenkung der Judischen Fluchtlingstransporter Struma und Mefkureim Schwarzen Meer*. But his exoneration of the Germans and blaming the Soviets was considered suspect by some experts because he was, after all, in the pay of the German government.

The next piece came from an unlikely source. In the early 1980s, Yosef Govrin, an Israeli diplomat and scholar, was completing research for his doctorate in Soviet-Israeli relations at Hebrew University in Jerusalem. Fluent in Russian, he was reading through technical publications from the Soviet Defense Ministry when he noticed a reference to the *Struma* in one of the books, *Soviet Fleet in the Black Sea During the Great Patriotic War*. Because he had been born in Romania, the ship's name meant something to Govrin. Why, he wondered, would something about that ship be in a book about Soviet naval tactics?

The book was written by G. I. Vaneyev and drawn from records in the Soviet military archives, which were closed to the public. In dry language, Vaneyev had listed every significant action taken by the Soviet navy in the Black Sea. On his list was an entry detailing how a submarine identified the *Struma* at first light on February 24, surfaced, and fired a single torpedo at the unaccompanied ship.

On the morning of 2/24/1941 the sub SC 213 under the command of Lieutenant D.M. Denezhko and Political Commissar A.G. Rodimatzav sighted the enemy freighter *Struma*, of 7,000 tons and no defences. The submarine launched a torpedo from a distance of 1111.8 meters that found its target and sunk the ship. Sergeant Major V.D. Tchernov, unit leader Sergeant G.G. Nusof, and torpedo operator Sailor I.M. Filtov showed courage during the operation.

It was clearly a second confirmation that the Soviets had sunk the ship. But the records did not provide a reason for Denezhko's action, though they noted that he and another senior officer were later given citations for sinking the ship. Perhaps, Govrin reasoned, they mistook it for a military transport. Perhaps the commander needed another kill; the log recorded three other boats sunk by the same sub in the area about that time. The motive seemed likely to remain a mystery, because a month after he ordered the torpedo fired at the *Struma,* Denezhko died when another submarine under his command was sunk.

"The riddle is, what prompted the Soviets to torpedo that boat?" said Govrin, who later spent four years as Israel's ambassador to Romania. "This is a key question. Taking into consideration that the Soviets had their spies in Turkey at that time, they probably knew it was a boat of immigrants. You didn't even have to be a spy to know that this was a boat of immigrants."

It took the fall of the Soviet Union and the efforts of Gennadi Kibardin, a Latvian researcher, to discover the key that unlocked the mystery and provided the motive. In the late 1990s, Kibardin was examining documents about Soviet submarine tactics in World War II that had been declassified after the fall of the government in 1989. Among the records he found Stalin's secret order to destroy all neutral shipping in the Black Sea. One of the documents in this particular file was another report about the submarine SC 213 and the destruction of an enemy ship on February 24, 1942; a footnote identified the vessel as the *Struma*. The discovery clarified the mystery of why the rickety ship filled with nearly eight hundred hapless refugees was sunk. It also explained why the smaller *Cankaya* had been sunk nearby.

The tragic events that led to the sinking of the *Struma* had unfolded not only on the Bosporus, but in the marble corridors of power in London, Ankara, and Moscow. The passengers were victims of the British geopolitical strategy of keeping the Arabs pacified, the Turkish insistence on maintaining the façade of neutrality, and the heartless pragmatism of the policy of Stalin and the Soviets to starve the German war machine. All three of these countries sacrificed the men, women, and children of the *Struma*.

Over time the *Struma* had faded from memory in most places. The sinking and events that led up to it had been included briefly in a few excellent books about the Holocaust and Jewish immigration during World War II, but the story never made it into the mainstream teaching about the Holocaust, despite the fact that it was the largest naval civilian disaster of the war. The *Struma* had been omitted from the history books in the involved countries—in Britain, Turkey, and Romania.

Though mostly forgotten elsewhere, the *Struma* was still a sensitive subject when Buxton arrived on the scene in Turkey in early August 2000 to begin dive preparations. The Turkish divers, like their government, were defensive about the circumstances surrounding the sinking of the ship and the rights to discovering its remains. When Buxton made a thinly veiled accusation that the Turks might be anti-Semitic because they were at least partly responsible for the fate of the ship, the divers had been understandably offended.

They regarded the British diver as high-handed and feared that he and his filmmaker buddy intended to embarrass Turkey. So the Turkish divers had decided several weeks earlier to go ahead with their own project without informing Buxton. They had researched the possible location of the wreck off and on for several years, using much of the same data that Buxton had found. They also had talked with local fishermen, who said they had caught their deep nets for years on wreckage they believed to be "the Jew ship." In late 1999, not long after meeting Buxton, the Turks had done some exploratory dives, when the water on the bottom of the Black Sea was a frigid forty-three degrees. When they broke with the British diver in the summer of 2000, the Turks resumed their diving in earnest, feeling that a race was on.

"It is part of our history," said Murat Draman, one of the lead Turkish divers. "For years, people have talked about this ship. The fishermen knew about the *Struma*. They fish all around there. They like to fish there because the fish like to live near the wrecks. All the Turkish divers knew about the *Struma*, but no one liked to talk about it. There were bad feelings. It was a tragedy. It was not just a Jewish tragedy, but an important part of history that shows the mistakes made by many countries."

When the Turks resumed diving for the ship in June 2000, they examined three possible sites in a series of twelve dives with a team of seventeen to eighteen divers. The first site turned out to be a tugboat, and the second was much larger than the *Struma*'s dimensions, possibly a cargo ship. The third site, they believed, was the lost refugee ship. It was lying on its side at a depth of about two hundred fifty feet, about six miles from shore.

The initial dives were inconclusive. The Turks said the dimensions seemed right—about one hundred fifty feet long, eighteen feet wide. The wreck was covered with seaweed and mud, and the visibility was low, which made it difficult to make out details and impossible to photograph from far enough away to get a good image of the entire site.

On July 16, the team returned for a final dive at the same site. When the dive team reached the bottom, they found that an unusually strong current had cleared away much of the sediment in the water. They were able to get a good view of the ship, and the divers took photographs and video footage. They could make out features that they thought indicated it was the *Struma:* The wooden superstructure built at the stern for the captain appeared to be visible, and the shape of the hull and number of decks seemed to match photographs and descriptions of the ship. The Turks were convinced they had found the *Struma*, fifty-eight years after it had disappeared.

However, the final steps that would have confirmed the identity of the vessel were not taken. Because they considered the wreck a grave site, the Turks said they decided not to touch anything. They did not search for artifacts, such as luggage, that would have made the discovery conclusive. Nor did they attempt to scrape away the barnacles and sediment accumulated on the hull where the name could have been found.

"We did not enter the ship and we did nothing to disturb it because it was a grave site," said Levent Yuksel, the leader of the Turkish expedition.

There were inconsistencies between what they discovered and what most experts would have expected the condition of the *Struma* wreck to be. An illustration prepared by the expedition's artist showed the wreck almost completely intact, resting deck up on the bottom. The Turks said a small rupture was visible in the front of the ship. They said it could have been caused by a torpedo, though they acknowledged it appeared too small, so they speculated that the ship might actually have hit a mine.

Certainly, the *Struma* was so old and rickety that a torpedo would have been expected to destroy the vessel, not send it to the bottom almost intact, with a single gaping hole near its front. Stoliar was clear on this point—the ship had virtually disintegrated when it was hit. And the Soviet submarine log had recorded the hit with a torpedo. Finally, even if the ship had hit a mine, the explosion would have almost certainly been more devastating than the small hole described by the Turks.

Even with the blessing of a strong current the day of the last dive, the photographs taken by the team and posted on its web site (www. sad-uwrs.org/bag) were not clear enough to provide conclusive proof of the vessel's identity. One of them showed what appeared to be portholes on the wreck, something that the *Struma* did not have.

Despite the inconsistencies, the Turks were confident they had located the *Struma,* and they trumpeted the discovery to the public in late July 2000. "To us, this is finished business," Draman said later. "It is the *Struma*."

Buxton was by no means certain the Turkish divers had found the ship. He was sure, however, that he had been betrayed. From his perspective, the Turks had pushed ahead and publicized their discovery prematurely, before they had the proper confirmation, in order to damage his expedition. He decided he could not work with the Turkish divers when he arrived in August 2000. This meant finding new equipment, hiring another dive boat, and most difficult of all, though he would not find this out until later, getting permission from the Turkish government to dive. With only days to go, a challenging expedition had just gotten much more complicated.

Buxton did not know how complicated things were going to become. When he and the Turks dissolved their partnership, it meant that verbal permission from the Turkish government to conduct the dive was invalid, since Turkish citizens were no longer involved. The biggest scramble was to find a ship to tow the side-scan sonar equipment necessary to locate wrecks on the seabed. The Black Sea, which the Greeks called Axenos, meaning "inhospitable," was notoriously murky and prone to fierce storms that kicked up the bottom and reduced visibility to nearly zero. Without using sophisticated sonar gear, it would be like looking for a needle in a haystack, impossible to identify suspected wreck sites.

The use of sonar to search the sea bottom was developed in the 1970s, and it revolutionized underwater exploration. The sonar is similar to radar, though it uses sound echoes instead of electromagnetic pulses. The sound pulses are usually on frequencies between 100 and 500 kHz: the higher the frequency, the better the resolution but the lower the range. The sonar pulses are usually sent from and received by a sonar sled towed behind a boat. The sled covers broad swaths of the sea bottom, sending pulses in a wide angular pattern down to the bottom. The returning pulses are displayed on a monitor on the ship.

To narrow the search area, Buxton had gathered as much information as possible about the paths of the *Struma* and of Stoliar's makeshift raft. Using a global positioning satellite and video plotter, he could identify the most likely areas. It was essential to have reliable sonar equipment to scan the bottom in those areas. Without access to the gear from the Turkish divers and Sadi Tanman's dive shop, the question was where to get it.

The Turkish divers had tried unsuccessfully to get funding for their own expedition from the Kocs, one of Turkey's wealthiest and most influential families, with extensive business holdings throughout Turkey and surrounding countries. The family had its own connection with the *Struma*—the family's late patriarch, Vehbi Koc (pronounced "coach"), had been the Turkish businessman who helped rescue the Segal family in 1942. The family also happened to operate a museum and research center in Istanbul devoted to marine archeology. Best of all, the center had a ship, the *Saros,* which was suitable for use as a diving platform.

On July 5, Buxton made another quick trip to Istanbul to meet with Mustafa Koc, one of the patriarch's two grandsons, and Selcuk Kolay, the director of the Koc museum and an experienced diver himself. They agreed to allow the expedition to use the *Saros* and to share its search data and underwater surveys of the area conducted previously by the center. Kolay confided that he thought he had already located the site of the *Struma*. However, both men cautioned Buxton that none of the center's equipment could be used for actual dives until the expedition received written permission from the Turkish government.

On August 7, Buxton arrived in Istanbul with three other team members to begin conducting a side-scan sonar survey of the seabed areas where they believed the *Struma* had sunk. With him was veteran diver Nick Hope, whom he'd met in 1993, close diving buddy Jonathon Lewis, and Dr. John Roberts, an underwater archeologist with a respected firm called GeoTek. Roberts would conduct the actual survey. Also in tow was a good-sized film crew.

The group first set up operations in a hotel in Tarabya, a village on the European side of the Bosporus north of Istanbul, before moving to the smaller, quieter, and, most important, cheaper Hotel Eysan on the Asian side of the city. The difficulties began piling up immediately. First, they had difficulty getting their sonar and other equipment through Turkish customs. Buxton went to the airport with a shipping agent from the Koc businesses, and they tried to persuade the Turks to release the equipment. The Turks refused, and Buxton was convinced that someone had told them to stop the gear coming into the country. At one point, Buxton was asked to put up a ten-thousand-dollar deposit to get the equipment, but this was later forgotten.

Still missing was written permission to dive from the government, and the group started to hear rumors through the Koc contacts and others that the government was going to try to block the dive. Buxton felt that he had powerful allies in the Koc family, Jeff Hakko, and Ishak Alaton. He decided to buy some insurance and called in the international press. He figured that a healthy dose of publicity about the expedition and the sad story of the *Struma* would make it harder for the Turks to halt the project.

For almost an entire day, foreign reporters and a handful of Turkish reporters from newspapers and television networks trooped through the hotel suite where Buxton had set up camp. The story was picked up around the world. After more than fifty-eight years of being almost ignored, the *Struma* was back in the news. Buxton was great copy—the soft-spoken, self-effacing grandson of two of the ship's passengers who had come to identify their resting place and say a final good-bye.

Buxton found that he enjoyed the limelight. Overnight a guy who described himself as distinctly average was a star. He got a thrill out of being interviewed on BBC TV and local stations in Turkey. When *The New York Times* ran an article about the expedition, with Buxton's photograph, his mother got a congratulatory letter from an old friend in the States whose own children had achieved enormous success, one as a writer for *The New Yorker* and the other as a nuclear physicist.

"Suddenly people were saying that I had done something really good, and I got a lot of satisfaction from that," Buxton said later. "I liked it even though I didn't like liking it."

Publicity can be a double-edged sword. The coverage stirred resentment among the Turkish divers who had received little attention for their efforts. They would find a way to try to tarnish his success.

Chapter 36

Though the cause of the sinking was established, no one was certain where the *Struma* had gone down. In those harried days of 1942, there was no reason to mark the spot where rescuers had found the flotsam and debris of the sunken ship. And the location in which they found the remains was miles away from where the ship was struck initially. But there were hints from many sources, and relying as much on guesswork as science, Greg Buxton and his technical team narrowed the search area to a fraction of the immense Black Sea. They planned to concentrate their search for the wreckage in a section about thirty miles square that started about five miles offshore. Within that grid, they had identified a couple of possible wreck sites based on anecdotal information from previous research by Selcuk Kolay, the director of the Koc museum in Istanbul.

The group expected to spend ten days trolling for the wreck with their sonar sled, mapping the grid, evaluating the known sites, and identifying others in preparation for the dive team's arrival. The clock was running because the memorial service planned for the site of the shipwreck was set for September 3, and relatives of the victims were coming from Israel, Britain, and the United States for the service.

What they still lacked when the scanning started was an accurate location for the site identified by the Turkish divers, who had gone from being collaborators to competitors. The location listed on the web site put up on the Internet by the Turkish dive team was not specific enough to allow others to find the site. Normally wrecks are identified with precise coordinates of latitude and longitude, which allow anyone with a good global positioning satellite receiver to locate the spot within a few yards. The only reference the Turks had provided, however, said the ship was six miles off of a particular shore point on an approximate bearing. Buxton was convinced the vagueness of the information was a deliberate attempt to keep others from exploring the site, a violation of the unwritten code of ethics that governed the world of amateur deep-water diving. Others with a more charitable attitude thought the omission might have been inadvertent.

The first day of scanning was disappointing for the Buxton team. The tow sled, pulled just above the seabed, relayed its information to computers on the boat, and it appeared as an image on the monitor. The sonar had picked up some objects that could have been debris from a wreck: the sharp edges of one object appearing on the shipboard monitor were promising. After several passes over the site, John Roberts, the dive's underwater archaeologist, and the others determined that it was too small to be a ship anywhere near the size of the *Struma*. More likely it was debris thrown overboard from a passing ship. The maneuvering was difficult because the *Saros* did not have an autopilot to follow the precise coordinates of the grid plotted out in advance, so the captain had to try to keep the boat on a straight course manually.

The second day, they were about 5.7 miles off the shore, as near as they could get to the site identified by the Turks, when the sonar picked up distinct images of something large on the bottom. It was clearly a wreck of some sort. After several passes, they were disappointed. This wreck was at least three hundred feet long, nearly twice the length of the *Struma*. They had eliminated another possibility.

Kolay had pushed from the start to examine the site where his own previous sonar tests had indicated a possible wreck. The *Saros* went there on the third day. Buxton did not have much confidence in Kolay's judgment on the matter, partly because the Turk had not dived the spot where he thought he had found the ship. Seeing something on sonar was only the first step, and Buxton only trusted people willing to go down and take a look for themselves.

About eleven o'clock that morning, the sonar picked up a couple of large objects in Kolay's area. The ship turned again and again, and with each pass, more eyes were riveted to the monitor, where the images were dancing across the screen. Lying on the bottom appeared to be hard, straight edges of steel, possibly from the *Struma*'s metal-plated sides. They were clean and the dimensions seemed to fit. Buxton's pulse raced and he told the other divers, "That looks for sure like a forty-five-meter long hunk of broken metal down there." Roberts and the others agreed that they had found something. There was a lot of debris in the area, and Buxton speculated that it might be fishing nets snagged on pieces of the wreckage. No one was ecstatic, but they felt they had identified a promising site for the divers to examine.

The process continued for several more days, interrupted by bad weather on several occasions. As they neared the end of the allotted time, they had found four likely locations. Buxton was determined to find the spot where the Turks said the wreck rested, despite his reservations about their claim. "I was going to be very unhappy if we didn't manage to dive the same wreck that the Turkish divers had, because then we could not say yes it is or no it is not," he explained. "And they might have been right. Looking at all their photos, I thought, boy, this is such an intact ship that it can't be the *Struma*. But, unless we went to see it ourselves, we couldn't really comment. So I had to know that I was going to dive the same shipwreck, and I knew that time was running out."

The expedition still did not have its dive permits, despite wrangling with the Turkish government and the intercession of Ishak Alaton. Buxton feared they could be arrested the minute they went into the water, so he was determined that the first dive they made would be at the wreck identified by the Turks, if they could find it.

From his earlier conversations with the Turkish team, Buxton knew that they usually hired fishermen from some of the small ports on the Asian side of the Bosporus to take them to their dive sites. He began to ask around in some of the villages, and he was soon directed to a group of fishermen who said they had taken the divers to the site of the *Struma*. They demanded four thousand dollars to go along on the *Saros* and point out the location. Buxton, already running low on cash even before the divers arrived, did not want to pay anything. Simcha Jacobovici, the filmmaker, convinced him that the opportunity was too good to pass up. They bargained the price down to twenty-five hundred dollars, with Jacobovici kicking in one thousand dollars of it.

Cash in hand, the fishermen guided another fishing boat that Buxton chartered the next day, in hopes of diving, the *Saros* being off limits for diving until permits were in hand. The Turks directed its captain to the same spot where Buxton and his team had discovered the three-hundred-foot wreck on their second day of searching. The fishermen insisted it was the site where the Turks had claimed to have found the *Struma*. Buxton was furious. He was out precious money, and the team had wasted a half day's searching on a site they had already found and dismissed. He could not decide whether the Turkish divers had lied about the dimensions of the ship they had found or his own sonar was somehow misreading the size of what lay on the bottom. He put the site on the dive list: it would be the first spot they hit.

The fishermen asked Buxton not to tell their comrades how much they had been paid, and he agreed, assuring them it was a private transaction and should stay that way.

Within a day or so, however, one of the fishermen must have telephoned the Turkish diving group and said the British team had been led to their site. Still angered by the last encounter with Buxton, someone from the group probably made sure the government knew what was going on. Letters were sent to several departments, criticizing Buxton and accusing him of cooperating with a film crew planning to make an anti-Turkish movie.

In mid-August, when the divers started to arrive, the expedition faced a serious problem. The government still refused to grant the dive permit, despite pleas made through the British and Israeli delegations to Ankara. Without the permission, the Koc center had withdrawn its boat, not wanting to risk either the coast guard confiscating the vessel or ruffling the feathers of senior government officials. For the team, carrying out the diving meant finding new transportation and risking their own arrest.

"I didn't figure we would get thrown in jail," Buxton said, "but if it got anywhere near that, we had some powerful names to start throwing out—Koc, Alaton, the ambassadors we'd dealt with. On the larger scale of things, it was not exactly the crime of the century. Are you stealing anything? No. Are you damaging anything? No. You're just diving."

The decision was to proceed with the diving, but to keep everything as secret as possible to avoid attracting the attention of the authorities. To keep its profile low, Buxton asked the divers not to wear the T-shirts prepared for the expedition and to avoid talking about what they were doing in restaurants and other public places. The restrictions reflected the mild paranoia running through the group as they prepared for the rigors of deep-water diving.

There were also minor problems. The tons of diving gear was stored in a former sweatshop that a Turkish friend, Atil Gelgor, had found for them. They still had not found anyone to supply the gases for the air tanks, and they had not found a boat to replace the *Saros*. For a change, the expedition got lucky. Gelgor proved a resourceful ally. He found a dive shop that agreed to let the expedition rent its compressor for filling tanks, and through his wife, he located a place that could sell them the necessary oxygen and helium. Pressing his luck, Buxton asked if he knew anyone with a boat.

"Oh, yeah," said Gelgor. "I know these fishermen up the way. I'll give them a call and we can go see them. I'm sure they have a boat you can use."

Some of the divers went to check out the offerings. They wanted to make sure that the boat they chose was safe and that they would be able to dive from it. Most of the commercial fishing boats based along the Bosporus sit high out of the water, making it potentially difficult for divers to get in and out safely. The report came back that a couple of available boats looked like they would work. Pressed for money and worried about being overcharged, Buxton chose a less expensive wooden boat over a larger steel vessel. It also looked as if it would be easier for exits and entries.

On August 22, the dive team packed their gear into a truck and drove to the dock. As they loaded the fishing boat and covered the gear with tarpaulins, keeping an eye out for the police, emotions were running high. The first dive was planned for the wreckage located by the Turkish divers. It was not necessarily the most promising site, but Buxton was anxious either to confirm the find so they could concentrate on discovering artifacts or eliminate it. It was to be the day's only dive to avoid tiring the divers before they got accustomed to the water and shed their jet lag. The captain found the location of the shipwreck, and a line was dropped to the bottom as a guide for the divers on their way down and to give them something to follow and hold as they returned.

Eight people had been chosen to make the two-hundred-fifty-foot dive to the bottom. Two more divers would be stationed with additional air cylinders at one hundred twenty feet and twenty feet, where the bottom divers would stop for decompression. The plan called for the divers to divide into four pairs, each with a video camera and measuring devices, and descend in ten-minute intervals. They would remain on the bottom for no longer than twenty-five minutes, the maximum safe time, photographing the ship and taking down its dimensions in as much detail as visibility and time allowed.

Before the group had left the hotel, Buxton had talked to them. He was emotional. For him, this was a dive that bore the weight of history. In the months of preparation, he had made an intimate connection with the grandparents he had never met. He had come to see this expedition as way of honoring them, of imbuing their deaths with the significance that had eluded them for nearly six decades.

"My grandparents have only the existence that I can give them," he had explained late one night to his friend and dive partner, Jonathon Lewis. "I can create a memory of what they were and I can try to live up to that reality."

As the divers gathered quietly in the hotel lobby, Buxton tried to convey his feelings. "There's a chance that you are about to dive on the *Struma*," he said in a choked voice. "There's a chance you are. I want you to please think a little bit about what that means and where you are going. You may be the first people to go and see my grandparents. I'm not going down there for the first dive. You will be there for me."

Even for experienced divers, depths of two hundred fifty feet or more are extremely hazardous. The slightest mistake can turn into a catastrophe unless a diver remains calm and controlled, practicing the lessons and techniques that have become second nature in hundreds of hours beneath the water. When something goes wrong, the natural reaction is "Get me out of here." People die when they panic and hit the eject button at two hundred fifty feet, rocketing to the surface without any time to decompress. Buxton felt he would be too emotional and under too much stress to make the dive safely, and one unsafe diver jeopardizes himself and everyone else on the team. He decided to wait on the boat for news of what the divers found at the first site.

Conditions in the water were better than anticipated. The top one hundred feet of the surface was very warm, nearly eighty degrees, with good visibility. At one hundred feet the divers encountered a three-foot layer of sea swarming with jellyfish. Wrapped in their dive suits, they were in no danger. Just below the jellyfish they hit a dramatic drop in temperature. The temperature plunged to forty-six degrees and remained that cold all the way to the bottom.

The bottom was much darker because sunlight does not penetrate to that depth, but visibility and overall conditions were better than the divers had expected. They went immediately to the wreck and spent nearly twenty-five minutes videotaping and measuring the metal plates, the wooden superstructure, and the rest of the site. Even at first glance, it appeared to be better preserved than they had expected from Stoliar's descriptions of the *Struma*'s disintegration, and it appeared far larger, too.

Though the bottom time was less than half an hour, it had taken nearly an hour to get to the site and the ascent required nearly two hours. Their bodies had absorbed nitrogen from the air on the scuba gear at levels far greater than those found in a body at sea level, and they had to ascend slowly enough to allow the pressure to equalize and avoid decompression sickness.

The eight divers and their two support divers in the water emerged at intervals with their thumbs up and clambered onto the boat for the return to shore. The trip back was an omen: the boat's engine quit and it had to be towed back to port. They were told it would be out of commission for several days.

The news was no better when the group gathered to make its report to Buxton. "It's not the *Struma*," said Jeannette Plant, one of the divers who had gone to the bottom. "The dimensions are all wrong."

"Yeah, it looks like a coastal freighter," said John Chatterton, the team's lone American and its only professional diver. "The construction is similar to the *Struma*. It probably had steel plates on the sides, but this ship was very intact. The only damage was along one side."

Alex Vassallo, another of the divers, had the final say: "Well, I ran the tape measure out to its full length, fifty meters, and I think I got halfway down the side of the wreck. It's much bigger than the *Struma*."

Several other discoveries convinced the divers that they had not found their shipwreck. The boat definitely had portholes and a very ornate compass, neither of which would have been likely to be found on a converted river barge like the *Struma*. Everyone was unanimous that what they had seen, and what the Turks called the *Struma*, was in fact a reasonably well fitted out coastal freighter of some sort at least twice the length of the *Struma*.

Buxton tried to be philosophical. "It would have been very nice to have said, 'Yes, this is definitely *Struma*.' Forgetting the Turkish divers for a moment, if we had hit the wreck right the first time, we could spend seven or eight days doing good, detailed archeological work. Life would be easier and I'd just have to swallow and congratulate the Turks for locating the *Struma*."

Life was not going to be that easy. Buxton found himself disappointed and in urgent need of a boat for the next day's dive. He contacted the captain whose steel boat he had rejected earlier and agreed to pay the asking price of seven hundred dollars a day if it could be ready in the morning. With fishing season still weeks away, the captain said he would be ready at first light. The boat was not ideal. The bridge where the captain sat was high and near the front of the boat, too far for easy communication as he maneuvered the boat into position and the divers suited up in the stern to enter the water. Buxton solved the problem by assigning the Turkish-speaking assistant from the film crew to a post between the bridge and the back of the boat from which she could relay messages between the crew and the captain.

The next day, the boat went to Kolay's site where the sonar had picked up some promising images. Buxton stayed behind again, this time to do an interview with a Turkish television station and to distract any curious authorities. "The idea was that if I was talking to the TV people, I couldn't be diving," he said. "We were still expecting someone to nab us any minute."

It was another disappointing dive. Within minutes of getting to the bottom, the first four divers sent up the signal—"no wreck." The remaining four did not bother to get wet. When they surfaced, the divers who had gone down said they had seen a few pieces of wood and some very large boulders. The weather was bad and the seas were rough, so they decided to return to port. On the way, however, the captain had steered the boat to a nearby spot. "There's a wreck over here that I lost some nets on a few years ago," he said. The boat had a less sophisticated sonar system for spotting schools of fish, but it picked up a distinct echo over the spot where he had marked a wreck on his chart. The water was three hundred feet deep, more than the diving equipment was set up to handle that day, but the discovery gave the divers a glimmer of hope after the disappointment of the discovery at what they quickly dubbed "the boulder site."

A smaller boat mounted on the back of the fishing vessel was used for distributing the large, heavy nets for fishing. The divers had tried to use it to set up the line to the bottom and hover over the dive site. In the rough weather, the boat proved too light and it was rocked heavily by the waves. What the divers needed was a small, maneuverable craft that would hug even rough water, so Buxton called Kolay and asked if

270 / DEATH ON THE BLACK SEA

he could borrow the *Zodiac,* a small inflatable boat from the *Saros.* Ko-lay pondered for a bit before agreeing to meet the fishing boat on its way out the next day and send over the *Zodiac.* The exchange took place just off the dock the next morning, close enough that someone spotted what was going on. The weather the third day was too rough for safe diving. That evening there was more bad news. A Turk who had helped the group earlier telephoned Buxton with a warning: "If you carry on diving, you're going to get in trouble."

Chapter 37

The morning of August 26, the fourth dive day in the search for the *Struma,* was clear and calm, a promising start to what had so far been a disappointing process. Everyone was aware of the warning call; no one was willing to back down. Greg Buxton's passion had infected the entire expedition, and they were determined to find the shipwreck.

Two dives were planned. The first would be an exploration of the wreck at three hundred feet that the captain had identified the previous day, and the second would be a second look at the Turkish divers' location. Buxton had viewed the video taken the first day and wanted another examination to be one hundred percent certain that it was not the *Struma*.

As the first of the two teams of divers was entering the water at the deep site, someone spotted a boat approaching from the distance at a fast clip. It was just a speck, but it raised alarm bells. By the time the second team was in the water and headed down the dive line, the speck had pulled alongside. It was a Turkish coast guard boat, bristling with sailors toting machine guns. They radioed and ordered the divers to pack up and accompany them to the coast guard station for questioning. Buxton had come along this time, and he explained that they had divers in the water. The commander insisted that they be brought up immediately.

"Well, if we do that, they will all die," Buxton said, explaining the decompression requirements.

He convinced the coast guard to wait until the dive was completed. When the commanding officer asked to see the written diving permission required by Turkish law, Buxton feigned ignorance and said he thought they were diving in international waters and did not require permission. It was, he hoped, a plausible denial. The commander was not buying, and he took the passports of all the divers and the identity papers of the Turkish captain and his crew members.

While the divers in the water finished their work and decompression, the coast guard boat patrolled in circles around the dive boat, young sailors standing at the rails with their machine guns ready. Two other sailors videotaped the fishing vessel and the divers as they emerged from the water. Buxton and his expedition members found more humor than danger in the display of bravado. The fishermen were clearly very frightened, however. The captain was afraid his boat would be confiscated and that he and his crew both faced the distinct possibility of going to jail.

August 26 was a Saturday, and Jacobovici, who is an orthodox Jew, had forbidden anyone on the film crew to work on the Sabbath. He had even tried unsuccessfully to persuade Buxton that no diving should be done. Buxton telephoned one of the filmmaker's assistants and told her to get in touch with Mustafa Koc, the family member who had been their contact from the start. Explain what is happening, he told her, and get him to make some telephone calls.

Buxton also telephoned Kolay and told him what had happened. "How about calling up your cousin who is head of the navy?" he asked.

"Oh, this is very bad," Kolay said. "I don't want to get involved. And the Kocs can't be dragged into it either."

Buxton insisted that Kolay make some telephone calls.

The fishing boat was escorted to a coast guard station on the European side of the Bosporus. A senior officer boarded and started to question the divers, who faced the only real jeopardy, since diving was illegal and being on the boat was not. The officer held a thick book of regulations and he kept pointing to a page and saying that the law required written permission to dive in Turkish waters. While he talked to them, other sailors took a complete inventory of all the equipment onboard and demanded the videotapes. In anticipation of this demand, the crew had copied the tapes before they were asked to turn them over.

Atil Gelgor, the resourceful Turk who had helped with equipment, had become an unofficial member of the expedition, and he tried to keep the divers calm. "Make sure they talk to you, even if you can't understand what they are saying," he urged the Brits. "When you see them start to fill out forms, you're lost." From years of experience with traffic police, he knew that once someone started to write, it would prove a lot harder, or more expensive, to undo the damage.

The situation seemed to be going smoothly until the film crew arrived and the Turkish authorities saw them heading toward the boat. Jacobovici had not broken Sabbath, but when his assistant told him what was going on, he had sent his crew to record the excitement.

For days, as the divers failed to find the wreck, Jacobovici had grown more concerned. His film needed a dramatic ending. If the conclusion would not be filming the discovery of the *Struma,* maybe it would be footage of the Turkish authorities firing their guns or hauling the crew off to jail.

"Either we had to find the *Struma* or be shot in the ass trying," Buxton said later.

Buxton had a different agenda at the moment. He was desperate to keep the stress level from rising to a point where the coast guard would feel compelled to throw someone in jail or confiscate tens of thousands of dollars worth of equipment. The arrival of the film crew threatened to disrupt the peace he was working to establish with the Turkish authorities. Urgently he waved at the cameraman and sound guy to get away from the coast guard station. He called Jacobovici's assistant, Deborah Weiss, on her cellular phone.

"Just go away," he insisted. "Just take the stress out of the situation. Leave. It might be nice for the drama, but we want to walk away from this without any problems. No fines, no bribes."

The cameraman and soundman slipped into a café and filmed through the window as the senior officer stepped off the fishing boat and went inside the station office. When the officer returned, his demeanor had changed. The swagger was gone from his step and the tone in his voice had softened considerably. He could not bring himself to apologize, but he wrapped up the questioning quickly, returned the passports to the divers and the identity cards to the Turks, and left the ship. "No more diving," he said as he stepped off. "No more diving."

Someone among their protectors had come through, though the nature of these sorts of calls meant no one would step forward to claim credit. A call had been made, and another call or two. Finally the senior officer had been told this was an event that had never happened.

But the Turkish captain and crew knew it had happened, and they refused to take the divers out again until they received written permission from the authorities. To underscore the danger they had just escaped, a coast guard patrol boat escorted them back to port at Kadikoy on the Asian side to make sure that the equipment was taken off the boat. The tension was gone, arrests averted for now. As the young sailors watched, machine guns cradled in their arms, some of the divers offered them customized dive hats with logos. The Turks happily accepted and said thank you.

By evening the adrenaline rush of escaping arrest had dissolved into depression. The fishing captain still refused to take them back out, and no one could blame him. The boat was his livelihood, and if they were caught a second time, nobody expected the same leniency, regardless how high the intervention went. For his part, Buxton was reluctant to ask anyone on the expedition to put himself at risk. They had come to help him, spending time and their own money, and the last thing he wanted was for any of them to wind up in prison. They were no closer to finding the *Struma* than when Buxton had arrived three weeks earlier, and the diving seemed to be over.

Instead of diving, they spent the following day reviewing video footage from the earlier dives. The divers had found something the previous day, before the coast guard interrupted things. It was not the *Struma,* but a World War II–vintage Russian submarine. Some intriguing elements showed up in the first day's footage from the wreck at the Turkish dive site. No one thought it was the *Struma.* But Buxton and Geraint Ffoukes-Jones, the technical chief, believed they should take a second look at the hull if possible. Possibilities also emerged in viewing the video of the "boulders site." They may have been nothing more than wishful thinking. Still, it seemed possible on close inspection that the boulders could have been covering pieces of a ship. Given more time, the team would have liked to revisit both the Turkish and the boulders sites.

The next day a small group from the team drove to Sariyer, a village on the Bosporus. They found an elderly man who said he had seen the *Struma* in Istanbul harbor as a child, and he knew where the wreck was. Some of the old man's relatives promised to take the divers out to the site in a large fishing boat the next day, though they had no intention of diving.

Buxton refused to give up completely on diving. He had gotten word of his difficulties to David Logan, the British ambassador in Ankara, and to Uri Bar-Nev, the Israeli ambassador. There had been earlier conversations with representatives of the Israeli government in Turkey, and the divers felt the Israeli representatives had not been helpful, given the history of the *Struma*.

Israel and Turkey are the odd couple of the Middle East, a Jewish nation and a secular Muslim country both considered outsiders by the region's Arab nations. As a result, they had formed a close alliance over the years, exchanging military delegations and expanding commercial ties. Israel won contracts to sell military equipment to Turkey, and the Turks developed an ambitious plan to sell excess freshwater to parched Israelis. Because of this closeness between the countries, the divers thought that the Israeli government could have pressured the Turks from the outset to grant permission for the dive, and they were bitter that nothing appeared to have been done.

The latest round of pleas had come at an opportune time. Israeli prime minister Ehud Barak was coming to Ankara for meetings with the Turkish prime minister, Bulent Ecevit, in late August. Before the prime ministers met, Bar-Nev, who had lost fifty members of his extended family in the Holocaust, discussed the search for the *Struma* and its difficulties with one of Barak's senior advisers, Ephraim Sneh. Sneh, in turn, raised the issue with Ismail Cem, Turkey's foreign minister. The two of them laid the groundwork. It would be up to Barak to raise the subject with Ecevit, and there was no guarantee he would do so. The two leaders met on August 28, and amidst the discussion of strategic and economic issues Barak mentioned the *Struma* dive gently to Ecevit. It was just a sort of passing reference that would allow the Turkish leader to reverse his government's position without appearing to succumb to anything resembling pressure.

Most of the divers had decided against staying on for the memorial service, and they were scheduled to return to Britain on August 30. The day before, they were packing their gear while Buxton and a few others went back to Sariyer for their boat ride to the old man's site. Buxton was already on the water headed for the site when he got a call on his cellular phone. The Turkish government had granted permission for the dive. Oddly, the okay had come from the embassy in London, where Buxton had applied months before. It was clear that the order had come from the top because within two hours the written okay was faxed to the divers' hotel.

Buxton was drained, though he still had not gone to the bottom on a dive. The stress and the wasted time had eaten at him, and he was seriously out of money. Most of the divers had to honor their return tickets or buy new ones, so they went ahead with plans to leave. With the written permission in hand, Buxton telephoned Kolay and asked for the use of *Saros* for the final two days of diving allowed by the permit and time. Kolay agreed to the request and promised to meet them in the harbor early the next morning. The frustrations were not over yet. It was nearly ten o'clock by the time the *Saros* arrived, and it took another hour to load all the gear. Buxton and the remaining six divers, with one video camera and one still camera between them, had decided to take one more look at the Turkish divers' site.

"I'm still not convinced we have enough evidence to say for sure this isn't the *Struma*," he explained to his colleagues. "If no one had ever suggested it was the *Struma,* we wouldn't be going back, because there is nothing to suggest that it is. But we have to be very sure, and I'd like another look at the bow where the hole is."

A coast guard boat shadowed the *Saros* on its journey out, and two Turkish navy divers were aboard to monitor the dive. The day didn't go well. The captain had difficulty following the coordinates, and the *Saros* proved to be a difficult boat from which to dive. They ran out of daylight and had to head back to port without anyone getting wet. Before getting off the boat, however, Buxton insisted to the captain and Kolay that the *Saros* be at the dock and ready to go at seven o'clock the next morning. He wanted to get in two dives on what he expected to be the final day of searching for the *Struma*. On tap was a final look at the Turkish dive spot and another at the boulders site.

The ship was on time, and they arrived at the site quickly. Buxton had decided finally to make his first bottom dive, and he had brought with him a brass plaque commemorating the passengers of the *Struma* that he intended to leave at the site of the wreck. He did not imagine that it would be the Turkish divers' spot. He had brought the plaque for luck as much as anything.

Buxton went down with Chatterton, the American and the most experienced video cameraman on the team. Buxton had been so consumed with the logistics of the expedition and managing the chaos in Turkey that he had not been diving in nearly two months. He was a little wobbly on the seabed, but quickly sorted things out. While Chatterton videotaped the wreck, Buxton repeated the measurements done by others and examined the hole in the bow. Having seen the vessel himself, he was finally convinced it was not the *Struma*.

Jonathon Lewis and Mark Brill were scheduled to be the bottom divers at the boulders site, with Louise Trewavas and Rosemary Feenan providing support at the decompression station and on the surface. Trewavas, Buxton's girlfriend, was a diver who had helped him in many aspects of the planning. Feenan, though a diver, was not part of the original team, but she and Jonathon had lived together for years. She knew that Lewis had become almost as committed to the expedition as his closest friend, Greg Buxton. She had grown so con-cerned by the despair she heard in Lewis's voice over the telephone as he described the obstacles and frustrations of the expedition that she had packed a bag and come to Istanbul to be with him.

Chatterton was on the bridge as the ship approached the boulders site, watching for the landmarks. Just before they got to the location, he spotted something on the sonar. From the outline and shape, he thought it was a wreck. The ship turned and made another pass. With Buxton and the others watching the screen, the ghostly image of a ship appeared. Daylight was fading and there was only time for one last dive. It would be the new spot, just short of the boulders. The position was still right, and the thought ran through Buxton's mind that the team's luck might have changed.

Lewis and Brill donned their suits, tanks, and other equipment. Both were veteran divers, but they had less experience in deep water than the rest of the expedition. For his part, Lewis had never gone this deep before and he was nervous. In a pre-dive conference, Chatterton and Buxton stressed the rigid time schedule. They gave Lewis and Brill strict orders to look around quickly on the bottom and head back for the surface so they could be safely back onboard before dark. Once they reached bottom at two hundred fifty feet, the divers saw the out-line of the wrecklike object a few yards away. It was angular, like the bow of a ship. They circled it slowly, really hoping that it was a wreck. When they got close enough, they could see that it was another huge boulder. After Brill took a few photographs, the disappointed divers headed back to the surface.

At some point during the slow ascent, Lewis got a nosebleed. By the time he got to the surface, his mask contained a fair amount of blood, and Feenan, who had never seen it happen before, was horri-fied. "All I could see was his mask and it was full of blood," she said later. Lewis was hauled from the water and his mask was stripped away. He explained that it was a common occurrence because of prob-lems with his sinus cavities.

As darkness fell on the ninth and final dive day, the ship headed back to port. The divers talked about the hints of wreckage at the boulders site, refusing to let go of the possibility of finding the *Struma*. "We only had ten minutes of bottom time and we didn't see any wreckage," Lewis explained, holding out hope that a longer dive might be more productive.

The dives were over, at least for this expedition. After the weeks of planning, the fallout with the Turkish divers, and the cat-and-mouse game with the Turkish authorities, after ten days of sonar scans and nine days of interrupted diving, they were certain only that the Turks had not found the right site. Some sites held promise, including the last one. Nobody knew when they might be allowed to dive again, or whether it would be worth the effort. The divers patted Buxton on his broad slumped shoulders, praising him for the effort. None would call it a failure, despite the fact that they had not found the ship.

Part of Buxton saw it as a failure, however. People had believed in him and he had failed them, he thought. He should never have started this expedition. He should never have persuaded his friends to risk their lives diving or raised the long-buried hopes of the relatives of those who had gone down with the *Struma*.

To Buxton, it seemed that the same political self-interests that had condemned the *Struma* in 1942 had thwarted his expedition. He felt that the Turkish government had thrown up roadblocks at every juncture. Rightly or wrongly, he believed the Turkish divers had obstructed his effort. The British government had not pushed hard enough, and the Israelis had come to the table too late.

There was a time when Buxton might have given in to the self-pity and recriminations. He would have called the project a failure and slipped back into his routine. But the months of planning, the challenges he had faced and surmounted in merely getting the chance, had changed him. And then there was the newfound intimacy with the grandparents he had never met, but felt as if he had come to know. In the end, he had the strength and character to see the victory, not the defeat.

Finding the pile of wood and metal that had carried his grandparents and so many others to their deaths was not what was most important about this expedition. Buxton was convinced that the significance lay in remembering those people and the events that led to their end. Just as the tomb of an unknown soldier represents the sacrifices of thousands, he thought, the effort to discover the resting place of the *Struma* and its passengers honored their lives.

It was well past dark when the *Saros* pulled into port in Kadikoy that night. As he got off the boat, Buxton still carried the commemorative plaque, in addition to his dashed dreams of finding the final resting place of his grandparents. He had reached an inner peace, but his worries were not over: with sixty or more relatives arriving from around the world in the coming days, there was no wreck site for the memorial service.

Chapter 38

In certain weather, when the sky is swept clean of clouds and the sun is bright, the Bosporus shimmers like a softly rolling carpet of blue-green gems. On the morning of September 3, a Sunday, the water sparkled just that way as a one-hundred-foot yacht called *Leaf in Love* left the dock in front of the Tarabya Hotel about two thirds up the waterway from Istanbul's main harbor. Onboard were more than sixty people whose relatives and friends had passed this same spot some fifty-eight years earlier on the way to meet their fate in the Black Sea. As the yacht headed up the straits to its rendezvous with the memories of those people, Greg Buxton paced nervously in the stern of the boat, wondering if he had chosen the right words to convey the combination of sorrow and peace that had washed over him like a gentle wave in the past few hours.

In the days after the last dive, Buxton had undergone moments of disappointment bordering on depression, followed by periods of calm and satisfaction. The expedition had not found the ship, and he was worried that he had failed to live up to the expectations of the relatives and the memory of his own grandparents. On the other hand, he had rekindled worldwide interest in a long-forgotten tragedy and, with the memorial service, was about to honor those who died.

The pressure and emotion had taken a heavy toll. The first day after the diving ended, Buxton had collapsed on the sidewalk outside a small restaurant in the evening. Louise Trewavas and John Chatteron were with him. Fearing a delayed onset of decompression sickness from the previous day's dive, they had insisted that Buxton go to the emergency room at a nearby hospital. The diagnosis was exhaustion and dehydration. In the pressure-cooker atmosphere surrounding the days of searching and diving, Buxton had not eaten properly or taken enough liquid. Within hours, he was feeling better and returned to his hotel in Kadikoy. For the first time he understood the physical toll the past few months had taken on him.

Other aspects were more concrete: Buxton had borne the bulk of the costs of the dive. He had sold his house and maxed out his credit cards to raise most of the sixty-three thousand dollars in expenses. The Holocaust Museum had contributed ten thousand dollars, and Simcha Jacobovici had kicked in ten thousand dollars from the money he got for his film. Greg's father and a handful of close friends, like Jonathon Lewis, helped out, too. The divers had covered their own personal expenses, but Buxton was left to pick up the remainder of the tab for the dive boat, the equipment, and the like.

In the three days between the last dive and the day of the memorial, as he worked on the final plans for the service, Buxton thought back over the experience. The expedition had not found the wreck, though the last site remained a tantalizing possibility. He did not think the effort had been a failure. It would have been good to lay the plaque and bring up some artifacts for museum exhibits, though Buxton shuddered at the potential bureaucratic challenge of getting them out of Turkey. He thought that the larger goal, remembering the ship's passengers, their lives and their wasted deaths, had been achieved.

Through his research and the wave of publicity that accompanied the search, Buxton had heard from hundreds of people who had lost relatives or loved ones on the ship. They had sent him their stories and prayers and photographs. His expedition was a catalyst for the revival of memories, a focus for rekindling those memories and stimulating new ones. By that shiny Sunday morning, as the boat headed out toward the Black Sea, he left his disappointment behind him.

"We didn't find the *Struma,* but we found the memories of the people on it," he said. "The *Struma* turned out not to be a physical pile of mud and steel plates in the seabed. It is the politics that caused its sinking and the unfulfilled ambitions of all the people who were going to a new land. These were soldiers going to fight for a new homeland. The *Struma* encompasses so many things from that time, the ruthlessness of it and the hopefulness, the wickedness of some people's actions and inaction. A lot of that has not changed much either."

Buxton had reached an understanding of what the *Struma* was and was not. He was not sure that those who had come from Israel and the United States and other countries for the service had reached the same conclusion. A couple of people had decided not to attend unless the actual shipwreck was located, and some of those who had arrived in recent days had told Buxton that they knew he must have been disappointed not to find the ship. He worried that the disappointment was more theirs than his.

Leaf in Love was docked up the Bosporus, near the harbor at Tarabya. Once a small fishing village, Tarabya's waterfront is now dominated by a dozen traditional fish restaurants and the unattractive, boxy hotel. A large crowd of press had gathered at the dock. Only a few reporters were allowed onto the yacht, in order to leave room for the relatives and dignitaries.

Jacobovici, the filmmaker, insisted that no television cameras be allowed on the ship. He wanted to preserve the exclusivity of the moment for his documentary. When a young man whose grandmother had perished on the *Struma* tried to bring his personal video camera aboard, Jacobovici objected loudly and tried to force the young man off the boat. The ruckus drew Buxton, who rushed over.

"Calm down," he said to Jacobovici. "Come on. We can sort it out."

The young man said he had no intention of making a commercial film. He simply wanted to record the event for other relatives who had been unable to attend. Buxton told Jacobovici that the young man had a right to tape the service. The filmmaker stalked off toward the bow of the boat.

As *Leaf in Love* made its way up the Bosporus and into the Black

Sea, Buxton's last fears dissolved as he watched what was taking place around him. Many of those who came were elderly people who had lost parents, sisters, brothers, or cousins. They were finally saying farewell. Some had brought their adult children and young grandchildren, hoping to pass to the next generation the memories of relatives and the circumstances in which they died. People spoke quietly, sharing recollections and leafing through photographs.

Standing at the rail in the front of the ship, his white hair whipped by the breeze, seventy-four-year-old Ogen Rintzler held three photographs of his parents. He had come with his wife, Miyriam, to say good-bye to them. "People in Israel, if you ask them what is *Struma,* most don't know," he said quietly. "It is important that we convey the feelings and memories to the next generation so that we will not forget the victims."

The loss that Rintzler suffered on the kibbutz when he learned of the death of his parents had been compounded many years later. In 1967, an aunt from Romania visiting Israel told him that his mother was pregnant when she boarded the ship. After years of unsuccessful attempts, Aron and Fani Rintzler were going to have a second child. He said the news resurrected the old pain and nearly broke his heart. "This was the heaviest blow," he said with great sadness in his voice. "Knowing what they suffered, what my mother suffered while she was pregnant, it was worse than the deaths."

Stroking her husband's hand, Miyriam Rintzler said, "I knew this for many years from relatives, but I didn't want to tell him. I knew it would make things worse. It was a great tragedy. His mother's parents did not want her to go on the *Struma.* The family members who stayed behind, they all lived."

Not far from the Rintzlers, Ilana Blum, Horia Lobel's daughter, stood between her two grown sons. She wore a floppy gray hat and clutched a spray of flowers. Though nearly sixty years old, part of her had never accepted her father's death, and she had waited for the ship's doctor to reappear miraculously. "I know it's ridiculous," she said with a half-smile, "but all those years I still hoped that somewhere, somehow he could still be alive. I remeber daydreaming as a kid that he would come back, that he had been stranded somewhere after being smuggled off the ship. Now I know that he's dead and it's over."

Others found a beginning in the end. Some people had arrived two or three days earlier to visit Istanbul. Buxton had arranged for small buses to take them to the various sites, since most were staying at the Tarabya Hotel, far from the city's many historic buildings. One morning several of them boarded the bus for a trip to Dolmabahce Palace, the extravagant home that the sultans built for themselves on the Bosporus in 1856.

"Did you lose someone on the *Struma?*" Tami Barak asked the woman sitting next to her. Barak had come with her father, Tudor Chefner, who had been scheduled to take the *Struma* with his brother. They had been spared because, before the *Struma* departed, they had left for Palestine on the *Darien II*. Chefner had still come to the memorial service with his daughter to honor his best friend, Norbert Storfer, who had waited for the *Struma*.

"Why, yes," replied the woman. "I lost my cousin. Her name was Silvia Mayer. She had just gotten married and was on the ship with her husband. All I know is that his name was Ionas. My family all died, and I have never been able to learn any more about them."

The woman then introduced herself as Rifka Gefner. From her purse, she pulled out a photograph of the newlyweds from 1941, turned it over, and showed Barak what her cousin had written: "This is her lover, Ionas." She said she had carried the photograph with her for years in a fruitless search to find the family of her cousin's husband.

"Listen," said Barak, "I have brought a friend from Haifa to Istanbul. I know only that she had a brother on the *Struma* and that their family name was Ionas. I'll get her to meet with you at the hotel when we get back. What do you have to lose? Show her the picture and see what happens."

Once they returned to the hotel, Barak introduced Gefner to her friend from Haifa, Betty Rosenblatt. When Gefner showed her the picture and told the story of her cousin, Rosenblatt went white. Finally she said her brother, Joseph Ionas, had been married on September 7,

1941, his wife's name was Silvia Mayer, and they had been on the *Struma*. From her purse she withdrew the couple's wedding photograph, which she had brought as part of her remembrance. It was identical to the photograph Rifka Gefner had kept with her for so many years. The two women collapsed into each other's arms and sobbed. Later, Betty Rosenblatt said of the encounter, "After sixty years, I have met a part of my family. And now, all three of our families, we are like one."

At her home in Spain, Marta Brod paused that day and thought about the ceremony on the Black Sea. She had shared some of her memories of her father, Simon, with Greg Buxton, but she did not feel well enough to attend the memorial in Istanbul. She knew, however, that her father had played a role in making it possible for David Stoliar, the Frenks, Medeea Salamowitz, and many other Jewish refugees to survive during the war years, even if he had not been able to save all those on the *Struma*.

In Jerusalem, the Central Zionist Archive has fifteen folders labeled with Simon Brod's name. One third of them are filled with the small, letter-size envelopes, each one containing dozens of tiny photographs. Few of the hundreds of photographs are identified. Brod was known for taking photographs of those he helped, and he was also, according to his daughter, Marta, known for being disorganized. It seems quite likely that these are the photographs of those who passed through his hands on their way to safety. Tucked into one of those envelopes is a rare photograph of Brod with his arm around the shoulder of one of those he helped—David Stoliar.

Teddy Kollek was one of the leaders in the Jewish immigration effort during the war. He went on to become mayor of Jerusalem and one of Israel's most influential and respected political figures. During the war, Kollek spent several months in Istanbul, working undercover to try to help refugees slip past Turkish authorities in groups of twos and threes. Kollek did not arrive until after the *Struma* had met its end, but Brod was still working tirelessly and Kollek remembered him decades later as someone who helped refugees in Istanbul at a time when few others would.

"I met with him frequently and he was a wonderful man," Kollek said. "He somehow got access to people who were prisoners and provided them with food and everything else. He was very careful, but he had some friends among the Turks whom he paid a little. They wouldn't have accepted bribes from us. Brod was a devoted person, as devoted as he could be."

Kollek was less enthusiastic in his assessment of the role played by the larger Jewish community in Istanbul. "They were of no consequence whatsoever," he said. "There was a representative of the Jewish Agency there, Chaim Barlas. We were unofficial, with two or three people working under all kinds of disguises. I was a newspaperman for a nonexistent newspaper in Palestine. The others were representatives of trade and industry. We had relations among the Turkish Jews, but they remained very careful to remain neutral. Brod was the one who had all the connections. No one exerted themselves to the same extent as Brod."

Joel Ives had a loose connection to the *Struma,* but the story of the ship had touched him deeply. An amateur genealogist from Fairlawn, New Jersey, he was researching thirty-eight people from an old family photograph when he had discovered that his grandfather's uncle, Itic Iancu, had died on the *Struma.* Ives had never heard of the ship, but he soon found himself immersed in its story. In time, he learned so much about the ship's passengers that he wrote an article about them for a Jewish genealogy magazine for Romanians. The article, with its complete list of passengers, was posted on the Internet, and Ives soon found himself corresponding with dozens of people trying to discover what had happened to their relatives or looking for information about the *Struma.* Ives and his wife, Sheryl, had met Buxton at the Holocaust Memorial Museum in Washington in early 2000, and they had developed a bond with Buxton and the story that had compelled them to attend the memorial service.

Before they left New York for Istanbul, Ives had received an e-mail from JoAnn Kindler in California. She said her mother-in-law, Elena Kindler, was planning to go to the ceremony because she had lost her brother, Sami Kaufman, on the ship. Mrs. Kindler was eighty-four years old and her daughter-in-law asked Ives to look after her. It turned out all three were on the same flight to Istanbul, and Ives had no difficulty picking out the eighty-four-year-old woman in the boarding area. On the flight, she showed them photographs of her brother, including one in which he was wearing a military uniform and sitting atop a magnificent horse. She described the frightful days of the pogrom in Bucharest, her narrow escape, and her brother's insistence on going to Palestine.

Kindler turned out to be quite able to take care of herself, and the day before the ceremony she had joined the film crew for a trip to Sile, the village where Stoliar had been brought ashore. While interviewing villagers, the crew learned that several bodies had later washed ashore and had been buried in unmarked graves near the water. Kindler picked her way down the slopes with some help and visited the crude graveyard with the film crew. The graves were scarcely visible beneath a fruit tree. They said kaddish, the mourner's prayer, and left in silence.

Sitting in the stern of *Leaf in Love* that morning, sipping juice, was Michael Buxton, who had taken a little persuading from his son to make the trip. Buxton had tucked away his emotions about the *Struma* decades ago, and he saw no reason to dust them off at the age of eighty-three. No reason except pride in his son. "Once the *Struma* was a thing of the past, I lost interest," he explained. "I won't stay in touch with these people. Sharing a similar loss is not the basis for a future relationship."

Still, he was proud of what his son had accomplished. "Greg is very much his own person," he said. "We brought him up to be independent. And he did this almost completely on his own."

About five miles into the Black Sea, *Leaf in Love* pulled alongside the *Saros,* which had been waiting at the site chosen for the memorial service. The spot Buxton had selected was the one where they had made the final dive. It seemed, he explained later, as good a spot as any, and as likely a spot as any to someday begin the search again.

The Israeli flag was raised over the ship to mark the start of the ceremony, and Israel's ambassador, Uri Bar-Nev, dropped a wreath into the water. David Logan, the British ambassador to Turkey, and his wife, Judith, had also come, and brought a large memorial wreath. Logan's presence was a bit brave, given his government's role in the tragedy, and he made no excuses when people asked him about it.

"We had a very clear policy of restricting immigration to Palestine," he said shortly before dropping his wreath over the side. "In retrospect, we could obviously have adopted a more humane attitude. In pursuit of our policy, we lost sight of the humanitarian situation."

The deputy rabbi for Istanbul and a cantor had come to lead the memorial service. The cantor blew the ram's horn, known as a shofar, and its plaintive wail echoed across the water. Rabbi Yishak Haleva said he had come in the name of the Jews of Turkey to mourn the deaths of those on the *Struma* and all who had died in the Holocaust. As he finished reciting the mourner's prayer, dozens of people who had brought flowers tossed them gently onto the water, and the carnations, mums, roses, and lilies drifted slowly away on the current.

"The sea had its say," said Elena Kindler as she stood to read a poem she had written in memory of her brother. "And now we have had ours." When she finished her poem, she collapsed weeping into the arms of another mourner.

Finally it was Greg Buxton's turn. His own fated journey had come to an end not far from where his grandparents had perished. What had begun fourteen years earlier as a search for a piece of property had concluded as an exploration in which he discovered part of his past and part of himself. His motives were cloudy in the beginning, and the trip endured many starts and stops on the way to an inconclusive end. But Buxton had found clarity and purpose along the way, and that was going to be enough for him.

In many ways, Buxton remained a closed and private man, much like his father. The events of the past few months, however, had stirred him in unexpected ways, and he wanted to thank those who had come and honor those who had died. First, he had to overcome a deep-seated fear of speaking in public. Plus, he still had difficulty shaking the bitterness of failure when he looked at the warm smiles of the relatives and friends. These people had believed in him and in his ability to find the ship. Sometimes he thought he should never have raised the long-buried hopes of so many people.

Yet he knew that he had also succeeded. He had created a place where people could pour out the long-held sorrow and mourn for lost relatives and friends. They had come to pay respects to the dead because Buxton had made it possible. He had brought it this far. Now he would recognize his victory and deliver his speech.

He wore a casual white shirt and blue jeans. His open face was sunburned from the recent days on the water. He smiled as he walked toward the front of the boat, holding a slip of paper on which he had written the verses from the Bible that he thought appropriate for the occasion.

His voice broke as he read the familiar passage from Ecclesiastes about a time for all things, and again as he spoke of the untimely deaths of those they had come to remember. He managed to complete the reading. Everyone on the ship was silent. The only sound was the thwack-thwack of a helicopter circling the ship, with Jacobovici's cameraman hanging out the open door. Buxton did not look up at the sound. He tried to concentrate on the faces of everyone before him— the relatives of the dead, their friends, his own father—as he thanked them for coming and thanked his comrades who had dived for the wreck.

One notable was missing that day on the Black Sea. David Stoliar, the only survivor of the *Struma,* had sent a letter of regrets. He said family troubles at his home in Oregon had kept him from attending. One of the other divers, Jonathon Lewis, read Stoliar's words. "For fifty-eight years," Stoliar had written, "no one asked me anything about the *Struma,* and I felt that no one cared. It was forgotten until Greg decided to remember it."

Epilogue

David Stoliar is a private man. Like Michael Buxton, he found no common bond in common suffering. Had he attended the memorial service, he would have been ill at ease among grieving relatives, unwilling to relive the sinking, unable to explain why he had survived when their loved ones had perished. He had been honest in his letter when he said that family problems had kept him away; his father-in-law was gravely ill.

But there was another reason. Stoliar expected that his very survival might have been thrown in his face by some of the relatives attending the service. Emotions would be high, recriminations impossible to escape. He was certain of this because on a regular basis over the years, no matter where he lived in the world, people had tracked him down and sent him letters asking how he had stayed alive when their brother, mother, cousin, father, or sister had perished.

Stoliar had lived with a moat around the *Struma*. Greg Buxton had dropped a bridge across the moat, and memories had swarmed in uninvited. But after waiting all those years, they refused to leave, and Stoliar, despite his best efforts, could not turn away from those painful memories and walk away again. Part of him welcomed the attention to the *Struma*. It validated the deaths of his fellow passengers. Marda, his wife, had agreed with his decision not to go to the memorial service. When he began to talk about making a trip of their own to Istanbul, she encouraged him.

In May of 2001, nearly a year after the service and well after interest had quieted again, they flew to Istanbul. It was Stoliar's first visit since he had left by train six decades earlier. This time he visited the city's magnificent monuments and overflowing bazaars and marveled at the friendliness of the Turks. At Dogan Bilgili's shop, one of the four thousand beckoning in the city's venerable Grand Bazaar, Stoliar bought a leather jacket. It was nothing like the thick one that had saved his life; this jacket was thin and supple goatskin.

Buxton and Jonathon Lewis flew to Istanbul from London. They said they were contemplating another expedition to search for the wreck, but mostly they wanted the chance to see the place through Stoliar's eyes. On a Friday afternoon, they piled into a small van, crossed one of the two graceful bridges spanning the Bosporus to the Asian side, and went to Sile. Stoliar was curious to test his memories of the village where he had been brought ashore. He was intrigued after being told people there still remembered the tall blond foreigner saved from the Black Sea in the winter of 1942.

The village had changed little in more than half a century. There were a few newer homes used as summer places by people from Istanbul. The watchtower still stood by the sea, and the boathouse was just as Stoliar remembered it. They stopped at a bakery that still baked bread in a wood-fire oven. Stoliar was amazed at how something as simple as a taste or smell can traverse decades.

They stopped the van on a narrow road, and everyone watched as Stoliar crossed into the small yard of Ismail Aslan's cottage. A wizened man in his seventies gazed curiously at the strangers. He smiled warmly when Sebnem Arsu, the young Turkish translator accompanying Stoliar, identified his visitor. The man who had been pulled from the sea and the fisherman who had watched grabbed each other by the arms and both men smiled broadly.

"When the *Struma* sank in the Black Sea, a stranger came to our town," Aslan said. "Today, almost sixty years later, I am a stranger in this town, which has changed so much. And the stranger from far away has returned. Right now, I feel a little more at home," Aslan said.

The two men had a very private and intense conversation while the translator and the others fluttered on the periphery. Although they had never spoken before, and still could not converse in a common language, the two men shared a bond. They posed for photographs, and when they said good-bye, they knew it was not likely that they would see each other again. Neither would forget the encounter, ever.

As she watched her husband walk away from the fisherman, Marda Stoliar remembered a serendipitous encounter she had had a quarter century earlier. She had been in Hong Kong on business and her name was posted on the welcome board at her hotel. When she went down for dinner that night, a stranger was waiting at her table.

When she approached, he stood and asked, "How did you come by that name, Mrs. David Stoliar?"

"Well, I married it," she said.

"Sit down, please, and let me tell you how I saved your husband's life," he said.

As she listened raptly, the Swiss journalist whose newspaper article may well have saved the life of her husband told how he had encountered a frail young man being helped up the steps of an Istanbul hospital. He described how, upon seeing the police escort, he sensed that something was wrong. Then, when he realized that despite the early reports that no one had survived the *Struma* explosion, there was one man who had, he rushed to his office to file his story. It moved quickly across the wires.

"I had to get it on record that this man had survived, so the world would know, and that he might have a chance of surviving the next few days in Turkey while they contemplated what to do with the only witness to this disaster," he told Mrs. Stoliar.

Remembering that chance encounter with a journalist whose name she had long ago forgotten, Marda Stoliar marveled at the way the world had come full circle for her husband, at the quiet dignity of his survival, and at the warmth of his reception in this tiny village. Pausing in the street to watch the foreigners, a tiny woman in a flowered head scarf asked how they had come to her village. When she heard the mention of the *Struma,* she launched into her own telling of the story of the young man who had survived the Black Sea. "He was such a handsome young man," she said, gasping and covering her face with her hands when she realized that the same man was in fact standing before her that day.

Later that day, visiting the watchtower, the crew took Stoliar from room to room, looking for the place he had stayed. Nothing looked familiar. "The room had a high wooden ceiling," Stoliar said again and again. Finally, the watchtower chief understood. He took Stoliar by the arm and walked him down the hill into the boathouse. There, in the shadows of the cavernous structure, Stoliar found his first refuge after *Struma*. He walked around the huge room, standing silently and staring up at the thirty-foot ceiling. Moving outside and standing apart from the others, while his wife watched carefully, he stared at the sea and said nothing for several minutes.

In the late afternoon sunshine, the watchtower crew served tea in the garden beneath the Ataturk statue. Someone in the crew asked Stoliar how it felt being back. "Well, it is good to be able to come back like this," he said politely.

A private man had said his hello, and farewell, to a place and people he had encountered under the direst circumstances, in his own private way. There were no tears, no visible emotion. David Stoliar, the survivor, had accepted his good fortune many years earlier, and he had lived a full life.

Who Perished on the *Struma* and How Many?

Samuel Aroni, Ph.D., Professor Emeritus UCLA, California, USA

Introduction

Sixty years have passed since so many men, women, and children died in the sinking of the *Struma*. Much has been written about it, and the years have not diminished either the interest in it or the horror of it. We know that this tragedy was caused by a combination of factors: the British white paper of 1939 and their insistence on closing Palestine to Jewish refugees, the Turkish refusal to help them, and the Soviet war against all vessels in the Black Sea. But how many people perished, and who exactly were they?

Apparently, there have been over one dozen lists compiled of the passengers of the *Struma,* dated from 1941 to 2002, some official and some not. A "classic figure" of 769 passengers has emerged. However, since the lists do not agree with one another, how accurate is this figure? In order to get closer to the truth, a composite list was developed, incorporating the information from six previous sources. This paper describes and presents the composite list, and includes a brief analysis of its contents. The truth may never be known, but the search for it will probably persist.

The Lists

The six lists providing the information for the composite list are as follows:

[A] List of the Constanta Port Police

Prepared by the Constanta Port Police at embarkation, December 8–11, 1941, it is numbered and contains 765 names. No sex or age is given, and the list is neither alphabetical nor does it always group families together. The names of the nine passengers who were later allowed to disembark in Istanbul and that of the sole survivor (David Stoliar) are included, and so is the name of only one Jewish member of the crew (Nadar Molnar); the names of three other Jewish members of the crew are not on this list.

The list used was published, in the year 2000, in the manuscript of Touvia Carmely (Carmely, 2000). The manuscript includes a photographic reproduction of one original page of the list and provides the 765 names in their original numerical listing.

[B] List of the American Consul General in Istanbul

On March 7, 1942, Samuel W. Honaker, the American consul general in Istanbul, sent this alphabetical list of 768 names to the United States secretary of state in Washington, D.C. The names included those of six of the nine persons who disembarked, and also that of the sole survivor. In addition to noting age and sex, the list also indicated the nationality of each person. Most were Romanian (a few of them were shown as having "collective passports" or traveling under a "certificate of voyage"). There were also six German, one Greek, three Nansen, four Polish, and four Polish Chilean (?) passports. Finally, one Romanian passport was indicated as "lost."

The list that was used is a copy of the original, including the consul general's cover letter. Where the consul general obtained the list is not mentioned.

[C] The Romanian List of Serban Gheorghiu

This list is from a Romanian book published in 1998 (Gheorghiu, 1998). It presents, alphabetically and numerically, 767 names and ages. Mistakenly, it also included those of three people who disembarked in Istanbul. The sources for the list were stated by the author to be as follows:

The list of the *Struma* passengers was taken and checked from the following lists:

1. The list of the International Red Cross of Geneva,
2. The list of the General State Security of Bucharest,
3. The list of the Constanta Port Police, and
4. The list published in 1942 in the book *Meghilat Struma,* in Jerusalem.

[D] The List of Struma Victims for the Holon Monument

This list was prepared in connection with the *Struma* monument, erected in Holon, Israel, in 1968, and published in the special brochure prepared for the occasion. (*The Struma Monument,* 1969). It contains 801 names, without ages, again mistakenly including those of three people who disembarked in Istanbul.

[E] The List of Efhraim Ofir

Ofir's Hebrew book contains an alphabetical and numerical list of 767 names and ages, in addition to a separate list of the crew (Ofir, 1999). It also includes much additional information and photographs, for over 160 people. The names are not in Hebrew and did not need translation.

[F] and [F1] The Lists of Touvia Carmely

Touvia Carmely produced two distinct manuscripts, the first in Romanian and the second in English (Carmely, 2000, and Carmely, 2002). Each contains a list of drowned *Struma* refugees, arranged alphabetically and separated into single persons and families. The first list has 760 names ([F]), and the second list, the so-called "Register of the Drowned Refugees," has 766 names ([F1]). Both lists include three of the four Jewish members of the crew. Beyond age and sex, Carmely provides a great deal of additional information for most of the listed names, such as family relations, occupation, passport numbers, city of origin, and addresses, which are restricted to the first manuscript.

The Composite List

The combination of names from the above six independent lists resulted in the composite list shown in Table 1. It is alphabetical according to what was assumed to be the most probable surname of each of the 781 listed drowned passengers. Where available, ages are also indicated. Where a different surname is shown in certain lists, the information is indicated in parentheses. The letter of each list ([A] to [F] or [F1]) follows the data obtained from it.

The convention in the table with respect to age is to indicate it again only when there is a change from the previously given age. Thus, it is to be assumed that all lists shown after a given age have the same age. Obviously, this does not apply to the two lists that did not contain ages, namely lists [A] and [D]. However, when all four of the lists with ages have the same age, it is shown at the very beginning, even if lists [A] or [D] are noted.

We have considered list [F1] to be a corrected version of [F]. Thus, when the [F1] version differs from the [F] version, the [F1] version is given.

Table 2 shows the details of the ten members of the *Struma* crew, four of which were apparently Jewish. Table 3 summarizes the names and ages of the nine passengers who were allowed to disembark in Istanbul. They, together with David Stoliar, the sole survivor of the sinking, were the only ten persons who remained alive of those who sailed with the *Struma* from Constanta.

Analysis

Composite List

The composite list contains 781 passengers, or individual names. Ideally, each passenger would be listed identically in each of the six separate lists investigated.

Obviously, this is not the situation. The following classification can be made of the 781 passengers:

Description	Number of Passengers	Percentage
Identical (surname, name, age)	50	6.4%
Minor differences (except in surname)	183	23.4%
Missing (from either one or more lists)	39	5.0%
Missing (appear in ONLY ONE list)	10	1.3%
Cases with duplicates (in one or more lists;		
including some surname variations)	43	5.5%
Surname variations	456	58.4%
Total	781	100%

In the cases indicated as "Minor differences," the surnames of the passengers are the same in all six lists. However, there are various differences in personal names, and possibly also in the indicated ages. Usually, age differences are of one year, but in some cases more significant variations exist.

Missing Names in Lists

In ten passenger cases, the name appears in only one list and is missing from the other five lists. This occurs three times in list **[F]** or **[F1]** (passengers 101, 510, and 726), and seven times in list **[D]** (passengers 198, 244, 316, 358, 428, 456, and 678).

There are a total of thirty-nine passengers with names missing from one or more lists. Twenty-seven of these are from single lists, as follows:

List **[A]**:   10 (passengers 109, 333, 499, 501, 502, 577, 584, 599, 730, and 731)

List **[B]**:   9 (passengers 261, 269, 270, 271, 402, 603, 604, 776, and 779)

List **[C]**:   1 (passenger 514)

List **[D]**:   2 (passengers 44 and 466)

List **[E]**:   2 (passengers 55 and 732)

List **[F]** or **[F1]**:   3 (passengers 336, 337, and 760)

Twelve passengers have names missing from more than one list, resulting in a total of thirty-four missing names. The missing passenger names and the lists from which they are missing are as follows:

List [A]	List [B]	List [C]	List [D]	List [E]	List [F] or [F1]
255	255				
449	449				
		450	450	450	
	481	481	481	481	
522		522		522	
523		523		523	
524		524		524	
590	590				
	591	591	591	591	
672	672				
739	739				739
741	741				741

Duplicates

Some lists have duplicate names of the same passenger. This has been discovered in the case of forty-three passengers—five of which have duplicates in more than one list for a total of forty-eight duplications—and is indicated in the composite list by the sign &. Most duplicates have variations in both surname and personal names. In only eleven duplications are the surnames identical, and in only two cases are both surname and personal names the same. The identification of duplicates has, therefore, been based partly on judgment, introducing the possibility of additional errors.

The forty-eight duplicates are distributed among the six lists as follows. Duplicates in more than one list are indicated in **bold**:

List [A]: 3 (passengers **61**, 108, and 280)
List [B]: 3 (passengers 115, 116, and **235**)
List [C]: None
List [D]: 24 (passengers **38**, **61**, 73, 94, 132, 147, 163, 176, 177, 201, 254, **407**, **408**, 425, 521, 536, 551, 557, 560, 561, 575, 586, 623, and 631)
List [E]: 4 (passengers **38**, 84, **235**, and 708)
List [F] or [F1]: 14 (passengers 15, **61**, 277, 278, 353, **407**, **408**, 419, 420, 452, 482, 593, 594, and 599)

In six cases, duplicates occur for two members of the same family: Husband and wife: 115 and 116, list [B]; 277 and 278, list [F]; 407 and 408, lists [D] and [F1]; 593 and 594, list [F1]; 623 and 631, list [D]. Father and daughter: 557 and 560, list [D].

Surname Variations

As indicated above, there are a great number of surname variations between the lists, seemingly for the same person. There are many possible reasons for these differences, including typographical errors, different spellings in Romanian and other languages, such as German, various possible versions of a given name, and errors made in the original recording. The same applies to variations of personal names.

Conclusions

There remains an uncertainty about the number and exact identity of the victims of the *Struma* tragedy. If the composite list is fully accurate, the number of victims, including the crew, was 791, of which 785 were Jewish.

However, doubts remain and may not be easily resolved. If every one of the ten people shown in only one list was a *Struma* passenger, why were they missed in the other lists? While contamination of mistakes between lists is to be expected, why did the list of the Constanta Port Police miss nineteen passengers? The Holon Monument list, **[D]**, seems the most inaccurate, with seven unique names and half of all the duplicates.

Acknowledgments

Sincere thanks are expressed to Mr. David Stoliar and Mr. Rifat Bali, for supplying copies of lists **[B]** and **[C]**, and to Mr. Touvia Carmely for copies of his two manuscripts.

References for "Who Perished on the Struma and How Many?"

Carmely, Touvia. "STRUMA Periplul Pierzaniei" (in Romanian). Haifa: 2000.

Carmely, Touvia. "The Real Story of "Struma" or Breaking Down a 60 Years Old Conspiracy of Silence." Haifa: 2002.

Gheorghiu, Serban. *Tragedia Navelor "Struma" si "Mefkure"* (in Romanian). Constanta: Editura Fundatiei Andrei Saguna, 1998.

Ofir, Efhraim. *With No Way Out, Story of "Struma"* (in Hebrew). Tel Aviv: A.C.M.E.O.R., 1999.

The Struma Monument (in Romanian and Hebrew). Bat Yam, Israel: The Committee for the Erection of the Struma Monument, 1969.

Table 1

COMPOSITE LIST
OF DROWNED PASSENGERS ON S.S. *STRUMA*

1. ABRAMOVICI Ghizela [A] 29 [B] [C] [D] [E] 28 [F]
2. ABRAMOVICI Iosef 33 [A] Iosif [B] [C] [D] [E] [F]
3. ABRAMOVICI Jean 30 [A] [B] [C] [D] [E] [F]
4. ABRAMOVICI Matei 21 [A] [B] [D] [E] [F] (ABAMOVICI Matei [C])
5. ABRAMOVICI Moise [A] 32 [B] [C] [D] [E] 31 [F]
6. ADANIA Silvian 25 [C] [D] [E] [F] Silvain [B] (SILVIAN Adania [A])
7. ADLER Gustav 38 [A] [B] [C] [D] [E] [F]
8. ADLER Israel 19 [A] [B] [C] [D] [E] [F]
9. ADLER Oswald 45 [C] [D] [B] [E] [F] (OSVALT Adler [A])
10. ADLER Tilia 37 [A] [B] [C] [D] [F] Tilia Otilia Tuca [E]
11. AGAR Simon Zeilig 33 [B] [D] [E] Simon (Zelig) [F1] Zeiling [C] (AGAD Simon Zeilig [A])
12. AIZIG David 22 [A] [C] [E] [F] (AIZIC David [B] [D])
13. ALCALAY Sara [A] 39 [B] [C] [D] 38 [E] 39 [F]
14. ALTER Bention 37 [E] [F] Bentin [B] Nentin [C] Bentzin [D] (BEN-TION Alter [A])
15. ALTER Betty 20 & SIN ALTER Betty [F] (SIN ALTER Betty [A] ALTER Betty Sin [E] Betty [B] [C] [D])
16. ALTER Esther 11 [A] Estera [B] [C] [D] [E] [F]
17. ALTER Iacob 5 [A] [B] [C] [D] [E] [F]
18. ALTER Taube (Toni) 35 [F] Toni [B] Toni Tauber [C] Toni Taube [D] [E] (BENTION Tauba [A])
19. ANTONIER Jacques [A] 31 [B] Jaques [C] Jacques [D] [E] 30 [F]
20. ANTONIER Rodica [A] 20 [B] [C] [D] [E] 19 [F]
21. APFELBERG H. Solomon 31 [C] [D] Solomon [E] H. Solomon (Solo) [F1] (AFELBERG Solomon [A] APPLEBERG H. Solomon [B])
22. APOGI Maximilian August 20 [E] (Mickey) 21 [F1] (MAXIMILIAN August [A] Apogi 20 [B] August Apogi [C] [D])
23. APOTHEKER Aurel 44 [C] [D] [E] Aron [F] (APTEICHER Aron [A] APOTEKER Aron [B])
24. APOTHEKER Dina 38 [C] [D] [E] [F] (APTEICHER Dina [A] APOTEKER Duca [B])

25. APOTHEKER Puiu Julius 17 [C] [E] [F] Puiu Iulius [D] (APTEICHER Iulius [A] APOTEKER Julius [B])
26. APPEL Aron Alexander [A] Avram Alex 21 [B] Aron Alexandru [C] 19 [D] 21 [E] Alexandru (Aron) 19 [F1]
27. APPEL Emanuel [A] 19 [C] [D] [E] Emanoil 18 [F] Emanueal 19 [B]
28. APPEL Feiga [A] 41 [C] [D] [E] 40 [F] Ferga 41 [B]
29. APPEL Israel [A] 52 [C] [D] [B] [E] 51 [F]
30. APPEL Zoltan 16 [A] [C] [D] [E] [F] Loctan [B]
31. ARONESCU Mina [A] 25 [B] [C] [D] Mina Madeleine 25 [E] 24 [F]
32. ARONESCU Siegfrid [A] 31 [E] Siegfried 32 [F1] 31 [B] [C] [D]
33. ARONOVICI Lulu 30 [C] [D] [E] 29 [F] Lula 30 [B] (ABRAMOVICI Lulu [A])
34. ARONOVICI Natalia 20 [A] [C] [D] [E] [F] (ARONONCI Natalia [B])
35. AURELIAN Alexandru 31 [C] [D] [B] [E] 20 [F] (ALEXANDRU Aurelian [A])
36. AVNER Berthold 34 [B] [C] [D] [F] Bertold [E] (BERTHOLD Avner [A])
37. AVNER Mesalina Linzi 28 [E] Mesaline [B] Messalina [C] [D] Mathilde (Messalina) [F1] (ANDER Mesalina [A])
38. AVNER Saia Mendel 24 [C] AVNER Saia Mendel & AVRAM Iesaiahu [D] AVNER Saia Mendel & AVRAHAM Iesaiahu [E] (AVRAM Sare [B] MENDEL A. Saie [A] [F])

39. BACALU Ihil 33 [E] [F] Iehiel [A] Ichil [B] [C] [D]
40. BACALU Marian [A] Miriam 1 [B] [C] [D] [E] [F]
41. BACALU Seina-Tvia [A] Sena Tivia 37 [B] [C] [E] Seina Tivia [D] Sema-Tivia 34 [F]
42. BACH Iuster Octav 24 [C] [D] [E] Iuster Octar [B] Juster-Octav 23 [F1] (OCTAV Juster Back [A])
43. BANC Baruch Debora 50 [E] [D] (BANC or BANK or BARUCH Debora [F] BARUCH Debora [A] [C] BANCK Debora [B])
44. BANC Baruch Iosif Jose 20 [E] (BANC or BANK or BARUCH Jose [Josef]) [F] BARUCH Jose [A] [C] BANCK Jose [B] BANK-BARUCH Iosef)
45. BARAT Eli Elias (Perets) 27 [E] Elias 26 [D] [F] (PERET Elias [A] ELIAS Barat 27 [B] [C])
46. BARAT Sofia 20 [F] (ELIAS Sofia [A] 21 [B] [C] [D] [E])
47. BARBER Rita [A] Lica 38 [B] Rica 38 [C] [D] [E] Rica (Litta) 37 [F]
48. BARBER Siegfried [A] 37 [B] [C] [D] [E] 36 [F]
49. BARON Adolf-Herbert [A] 17 [B] [D] [E] Ad. Herbert [C] 16 [F]
50. BARON Gusta [A] 41 [B] [C] [D] [E] 40 [F]

51. BARON Marcel [A] 40 [B] [C] [D] [E] 39 [F]
52. BARON Richard [A] 12 [B] [C] [D] [E] 11 [F]
53. BARTFELD Martin [A] 15 [B] [C] [D] [E] 16 [F]
54. BARUCH Cecilia 31 [A] [B] [C] [D] [E] [F1]
55. BARUCH Josef [A] Iosif [C] 35 [B] Jose [D] Iosef [F1]
56. BEER Ionel 21 [A] [B] [C] [D] [E] [F]
57. BEILICH Egon 17 [B] [C] [D] [E] [F] (BEILIK Egon [A])
58. BERCOVICI Alfred [A] 9 [C] [D] [E] 8 [F] (BERCONCI Alfred 9 [B])
59. BERCOVICI Cornel Adrian 2 [C] [D] [E] 1 [F] Carmel Adrian [A]
    (BERCONCI Cornel Adrian 2 [B])
60. BERCOVICI Ignat [A] 42 [C] [D] [E] 41 [F] (BERCONCI Ignat 42 [B])
61. BERCOVICI Iona 33 [F] & Ionas [F1] Iona & Ioinia [A] Ioina [B] [C]
    Ioina 23 [E] Ioine & Toni [D]
62. BERCOVICI Margareta [A] 31 [E] [D] 28 [F] Margarete 31 [C]
    (BERCONCI Margareta 31 [B])
63. BERCU Betty 26 [B] [C] [D] [E] [F] Berry [A]
64. BERCU Iosef 29 [A] [D] [E] [F] Iosif [B] [C]
65. BERLAND Eduard [A] 57 [E] 56 [F] 56 (BERLANDT Eduard 57 [B]
    [C] [D])
66. BERLAND Lazar Lulu 19 [E] Lazar [A] Lazade Lulu [F] (BERLANDT
    Lazar Lulu [B] Lazar [C] [D])
67. BERLAND Lea Liza 49 [C] [E] Eliza [A] Elise [F] (BERLANDT Eliza
    [B] Lea Liza [D])
68. BERMAN Fichel 29 [A] Fischi [B] [C] Fischel Filip [D] [E] Fishel (Fisii)
    [F1]
69. BERRY Waldi Willi 20 [C] [E] Waldi Willy [D] (BARY) Willy [A] Waldi
    [B] Willy Waldi [F]
70. BINDER Iosef 47 [A] [C] [D] [E] [F] Yosif [B]
71. BINDER Marcu 14 [A] [B] [C] [D] [E] [F]
72. BINDERER Leopold 23 [A] [B] [C] [E] [F] (BINDER Leopold [D])
73. BIRSTEIN M. Samy [A] M. Samuel (Sami) 22 [E] 31 [F] (BITESTEIN M.
    Samuel 22 [B] BIRNSTEIN M. Samuel [C] BIRNSTEIN M. Samuel &
    BORNSTEIN M. Shmuel [D])
74. BLANK Osias [A] 28 [D] [E] Osias (Jehoshua) 29 [F1] (BLANCK Osias
    28 [B] BLANK Osias [C])
75. BLUMENFELD Leiba 27 [A] [B] [D] Leiba-Leon [F1] Leiba Leibu Leon
    [E] (BLUMFELD Leiba [C])
76. BRAUN Eugen [A] 37 [B] [C] [D] Eugen Itzhac [E] 38 [F1]
77. BRAUN Judit 3 [A] Judita [B] Iuditha [C] [D] Juditha [E] Judith [F]
78. BRAUN Maria 37 [A] [B] [C] [D] [F] Maria Miriam [E]

79. BRILL Frida [A] [C] Freida 39 [B] Frieda 39 [E] [D] 38 [F]
80. BRILL Marcel [A] 39 [B] [C] [D] [E] 38 [F]
81. BRILL Sonia [A] 11 [B] [C] [D] [E] 10 [F]
82. BRIRER Zoltan 39 [A] (BREYER Loctan [B] Zoltan [C] [D] BROYER Zoltan [E] BRAYER Zoltan [F])
83. BUCSPAN Enta-Zlata 55 [A] [B] [C] Anita Zlata [D] Zlota Liza [E] Anita, Zlota-Lisa [F1]
84. BUCSPAN Grigore 54 [A] [B] [C] [D] BUCSPAN Grigore & BUKSPAN Mirel Gr.[E] BUCSPAN Grigori [F1]
85. BUTNARU Elias 20 [A] [B] [D] Elliss [C] Elias Eliahu-Alecu [E] Elias (Elli) [F]
86. BUTTER Alexandru [A] 33 [B] [C] [D] [E] 32 [F]
87. BUTTER Bertina [A] 27 [B] [C] [D] [E] 26 [F]

88. CALICHMAN Avram 50 [A] (CALIHMAN Avram [B] [C] [D] [E] [F])
89. CALICHMAN Beila-Liula 45 [A] (CALIHMAN Bela Luiba [B] Bela-Liuba [C] [D] [E] [F])
90. CAMERMAN Solomon 23 [A] [B] [F] (CAMMERMAN Solomon [C] [D] [E])
91. CANETTI Isac 40 [B] [C] [E] Itzhac [D] Itzah [F1] (CANCITI Isac [A])
92. CANETTI Jose Moise 7 [D] [E] Jose [B] [F] Iose Moise [C] (CANCITI Moise [A])
93. CANETTI Virginia 35 [B] [C] [D] [E] [F] (CANCITI Virginia [A])
94. CASSEL Mordehai 27 [E] [F] Mordnei [C] (CESEL Mordehai [A] CHESSEL Mordhai [B] CASSEL Mordehai & SCHESSEL Mordehai [D])
95. CIOBOTARU C.Z. Alfred 34 [A] [F] Alfred [C] [D] [E] (CISBOTARU Alfred [B])
96. CIOCANILE Jean-Marcel [A] 38 [B] [C] [D] (CIOBOTARU Jean Marcel 38 [E] CIOCANIDE Jean-Marcel 37 [F])
97. CLARFELD Motel 41 [D] [E] Matta [B] Motel (Mathe) [F] (CHARTFELD Motal [A] CLARFRED Motel [C])
98. COGANSCHI Adela-Ana 17 [A] [C] [D] [E] Ana [B] (CAZANSKI Ana-Adela [F1])
99. COGANSCHI Haia 45 [A] [C] [D] [E] Haia or Ilaia [B] (CAZANSKI Haia [F1])
100. COGANSCHI Iosef 57 [A] [C] [D] Iosif [E] Iosof [B] (CAZANSKI Iosif [F1])
101. COHAN Izhac 22 [F1]

102. COHEN Adof 59 [C] [E] Adolf [D] Adolf 58 [F] (KOHN Adolf [A] COHN Adolf 59 [B])
103. COHEN Rosa 59 [E] Roza [C] [D] 58 [F] (KOHN Raza [A] COHN Roza 59 [B])
104. COHEN Simon [A] Simona 32 [B] [D] Simone [C] Simona Simone [E] Simone [F1]
105. COHN Bercu [A] 12 [F1] (COHEN Bercu [B] [C] [D] [E])
106. COHN David Dudu 21 [E] [F] David [B] (COHEN David [A] [C] [D])
107. COHN George Gigel 1 [A] [E] [F] Giorgio [B] Gigel [C] [D]
108. COHN I. Zalman & Zanas 35 [A] J. Zalman [B] I. Zalman [C] [D] [E] I. Zalman [F]
109. COHN Ionas 21 [E] 19 [F] (IONAS Cohn 21 [B] [D] IONSS Cohn [C])
110. COHN Ionel 19 [A] [C] [D] [E] [F] (COHEN Ionel [B])
111. COHN Touba 34 [A] Toba [B] Tony [C] Tony (Tova) [D] Toni Tova [E] Tova [F]
112. COIFMAN Paula-Haia 54 [A] Taube Haia [C] [D] [E] Tauba-Haia [B] [F]
113. COIFMAN Struli 53 [A] Strul [B] [C] [D] [E] [F]
114. COJOCARU Carol [A] 19 [B] [C] [D] 20 [F] Carol-Haim Natan 19 [E]
115. COTIGARU Debora 23 [A] (COTTINGARU Debora & COTINGARU Debora [B] COTIUGARU Debora [C] [D] [E] [F])
116. COTIGARU Lupu [A] (COTTINGARU Lupu 26 & COTINGARU Lupu 24 [B] COTIUGARU Lupu 26 [C] [D] [E] [F])
117. CRAMER Iosif 18 [C] [D] [E] (KRANER Iosef [A] CRAMMER Iosif [B] RAINER Iosif [F])

118. DAIAN Haim Abraham 55 [E] (DANI Haim Abraham [A] DAIN Haim-Abraham 55 [B] [D] Haim Abraham [C] 52 [F])
119. DAIAN Olga 13 [E] (DANI Haim Olga [A] DAIN Olga [B] [C] [D] [F])
120. DAIAN Sara 50 [E] (DANI Haim Sura [A] DAIN Sura [B] [C] [D] [F])
121. DAVID Etty [A] Etti 27 [F] 28 [B] [C] [D] [E]
122. DAVID Rifca 61 [A] Rifca Amalia [B] [C] [D] [E] Rivka-Amalia [F1]
123. DAVIDOVICI Sofia 22 [A] [B] [C] [D] [E] [F]
124. DIAMAND Ghizela [A] 33 [C] [D] [E] 32 [F] (DIAMANT Gluzella 33 [B])
125. DIAMAND Nicu [A] 37 [C] [D] [E] 36 [F] (DIAMANT Micu 37 [B])
126. DIAMAND Simona [A] 8 [C] [D] [E] 7 [F] (DIAMANT Simona 8 [B])
127. DICHTER A. Ionel [A] 41 [B] 31 [C] [D] 41 [E] 40 [F]

128. DITZ Eugen 27 **[A]** **[B]** **[C]** **[D]** **[E]** **[F]**
129. DRATH S. Danil **[A]** S. Daniel 40 **[C]** Daniel **[D]** S. Paul 39 **[F1]** (DRAHT Paul S. 40 **[B]** S. Daniel Paul 40 **[E]**)
130. DULITZCHI Rachil **[A]** (DULITCHI Rachil 40 **[B]** Rahil **[C]** Rahel 42 **[D]** **[E]** DULITCHI Rachel 42 **[F1]**)

131. EDELSTEIN Clara 29 **[A]** **[B]** **[C]** **[D]** **[E]** **[F]**
132. EDELSTEIN Jack 25 **[A]** Jean **[B]** Jaques **[C]** **[E]** Jacques **[F]** Jacques & Jean **[D]**
133. EDELSTEIN Leo 32 **[A]** Leon **[B]** **[C]** **[D]** **[E]** **[F]**
134. EISIC Louis 20 **[C]** **[D]** **[E]** **[F1]** (ESYG Louis **[A]** EISIG Louis **[B]**)
135. EISIC Mircea 18 **[C]** **[D]** **[E]** **[F1]** (ENIG Mircea **[A]** EISIG Mircea **[B]**)
136. EKELSTEIN Roza **[A]** (ECKSTEIN Rosa 22 **[B]** **[C]** **[D]** EKSTEIN Rosa 22 **[E]** WEGNER (ECKSTEIN) Roza 23 **[F1]**)
137. ELCOVICI Naftali 24 **[A]** Naftuli **[B]** **[C]** **[D]** Naftali Tuli **[E]** (ELICOVICI Naftuli (Tuli) **[F1]**)
138. ELIAS Avram-Bernard **[A]** 10 **[B]** 9 **[E]** 8 **[F]** Avr. Bernard 10 **[C]** Avraham Bernard **[D]**
139. ELIAS Iosif **[A]** 37 **[C]** **[D]** Iosef **[B]** **[E]** **[F1]**
140. ELIAS Medea **[A]** 34 **[B]** **[D]** Medes **[C]** Medea Malvina **[E]** Malvina-Magda 37 **[F1]**
141. ELIAS Rozi **[A]** 13 **[C]** **[D]** Rosy **[E]** Rozi 12 **[F1]** Roji 13 **[B]**
142. EPSTEIN Matias 37 **[A]** **[B]** **[C]** **[D]** **[E]** **[F1]**
143. EPSTEIN Sara Rebeca 26 **[B]** **[C]** **[D]** **[E]** **[F]** Oarah Rebeca 26 **[A]**
144. ERBST Matei 21 **[B]** **[C]** **[D]** **[E]** **[F]** (ERBIS Matei **[A]**)

145. FARHI Henry 22 **[A]** Henri **[E]** (FARCHI Henry **[B]** Henri **[C]** **[D]** FARCHI Henry (Bubi) **[F1]**)
146. FEIGHENBAUM Elias 29 **[B]** **[C]** **[D]** **[E]** **[F1]** (FEIGHEIMAN Elias **[A]**)
147. FEIGHENBAUM Estera Liza 23 **[E]** Liza **[B]** **[F1]** Estera **[C]** **[D]** (& FEIGHENBOIM Liza **[D]** FEIGHEIMAN Lisa **[A]**)
148. FEIGHENBAUM Ruhla 53 **[E]** **[F]** Ruhea **[B]** Ruchla **[C]** **[D]** (FEIGHEIMAN Ruhlea **[A]**)
149. FEINGOLD Otto **[A]** Otto Jacques 21 **[B]** **[D]** **[E]** 20 **[F]** (FELINGOLD Otto Jaques 21 **[C]**)
150. FELD Margareta **[A]** 28 **[B]** 26 **[D]** **[E]** 30 **[F]** (FLRD Margareta 28 **[C]**)

151. FELD Nicolaie [A] Nicolas 36 [B] Nicolae [C] [D] Nicolae Miclos 32 [E] 31 [F]
152. FELDMAN Estera 40 [A] Esther [B] [C] [D] Ester Ernestina [E] Ernestina-Esther [F1]
153. FELDMAN Isak [A] Isac 18 [B] [C] [D] Isac Itzhac-Gutu [E] Isac 15 [F1]
154. FELDSTEIN Avram [A] 2 [B] [C] [D] [E] 1 [F]
155. FELDSTEIN David [A] 34 [B] [C] [D] [E] 33 [F]
156. FELDSTEIN Ghedrich 31 [A] Heinerich [C] Heinrich [D] Henrich [E] Ghenrich [B] [F]
157. FELDSTEIN Gheorghe [A] Ghenghe 33 [B] George 33 [C] [D] [E] 38 [F]
158. FELDSTEIN Ghizela-Luisa 28 [A] [B] [C] [D] Ghizela-Luiza [F1] Ghiz Louiza [E]
159. FELDSTEIN Nely 23 [A] [C] [D] [E] Nelly [F1] Nelli [B]
160. FELDSTEIN Robert 28 [A] [B] [C] [D] [E] [F]
161. FELDSTEIN Rozica 23 [A] [B] [C] [D] [E] [F]
162. FELDSTEIN Schefie [A] Sure 33 [B] Sura [C] [D] Sara [E] Sura 32 [F1]
163. FELL Solomon 22 [C] [E] [F] (FEL Solomon [A] FELD Solomon [B] FELL Solomon & PAL Solomon [D])
164. FELLER Gustav 29 [A] [B] [C] [D] [E] [F]
165. FICHER Lanca 40 [E] Leanca [A] (FISCHER Lenea 35 [B] Lanea [C] Lina (Lanca) [D] Lanca-Lina [F1])
166. FISCHER Jacob 40 [B] Iacob [C] [D] [E] Iacob-Eugen [F] (FICHER Iacob Eugen [A])
167. FISCHER L Roszica [A] Rozica 44 [B] [C] [D] Rosica 44 [E] Rosica 43 [F1]
168. FISCHER Rudy [A] Rudi 16 [E] 14 [F] 16 [B] [C] [D]
169. FISCHER Silvia [A] 18 [B] [C] [D] [E] 16 [F]
170. FISCHER Zoltan 9 [C] [D] [E] [F] Loctan [B] (FICHER Zoltan [A])
171. FISCHMAN Maletta (Moleta) 36 [F1] (FLICHER Moleta [A] FLEISCHER Maletta [B] [C] [D] [E])
172. FISCHMAN Nissem 22 [E] Nissem (Niscu) [F1] Nisen [B] Nissen [C] [D] (FICHMAN Nisim [A])
173. FLEISCHER Anna 33 [E] Ana 33 [B] [C] [D] Sonny-Ana 37 [F1] (FLEICHER Ana [A])
174. FLEISCHER David Sami 44 [E] David 44 [B] [C] [D] David-Sami 42 [F1] (FLEICHER David [A])
175. FLEISCHER Robert 7 [E] 8 [B] 3 [C] [D] Norbert 7 [F1] (FLEICHER Robert [A])

176. FLIGHELMAN Haim 18 **[A] [C] [E] [F]** (HIGHELMAN Haim **[B]** FLIGHELMAN Haim & FEIGHENBOIM Haim **[D]**)
177. FLIGLER Max 31 **[B]** Maximilian (Max) **[F1]** (FLIGHER Max **[A]** FLICKER Max **[C]** FLINKER Max & REGLER Max **[D]** FLINCKER Max (Regler) **[E]**)
178. FLINCKER Jeanette 51 **[E] [F]** (FLICHER Jeanata **[A]** FLINKER Jeanette **[B]** Janeta **[D]** Janeta **[D]** FLICKER Janeta **[C]**)
179. FLINCKER Klaus Zoltan 15 **[E]** (KLAUS Zoltan Flicher **[A]** FLINKER Claus Lola **[B] [F1]** Klaus Zoltan **[C] [D]**)
180. FLINCKER Richard 17 **[E]** Richard-George **[F]** (RICHARD Flicker **[A]** FLINKER Richard **[B] [D]** FLICKER Richard **[C]**)
181. FRANGHIERU Aron 17 **[A] [E] [F]** (FRANGHIEN Aron **[B]** FRANGHERU Aron **[C]** FRINGHIERU Aron **[D]**)
182. FRIEDMAN Desideriu 42 **[A] [B] [C] [D] [F]** Dezidoriu **[E]**
183. FRIEDMAN Ileana 19 **[A] [B] [C] [D] [E] [F]**
184. FRIEDMAN Nicolae 13 **[A] [B] [C] [D] [E] [F]**
185. FRIEDMAN Sofia 38 **[A] [B] [C] [D] [E] [F]**
186. FRUCHTER Iehuda 16 **[C] [D] [E]** Jendha **[B]** Eugenie **[F1]** (FRICHTER Iehuda **[A]**)
187. FRUCHTER Isac 18 **[B] [C] [D] [E]** Jean **[F]** (FRICHTER Isac **[A]**)
188. FRUCHTMAN Henrieta 26 **[A]** Herscovici H. **[C]** Rabinovici Henriette **[E]** R. Henrietta 27 **[F]** (FRUCHMAN Henriette **[B]** FRUCHTMAN-RABINOVICI Henrieta **[D]**)
189. FRUCHTMAN Solomon **[A]** 22 **[C] [D]** 27 **[E]** 28 **[F]** (FRUCHMAN Solomon 27 **[B]**)
190. FUCHS Mauriciu 29 **[A] [B] [D] [E] [F]** (FUCHA Mauriciu **[C]**)

191. GALATAN Moise **[A]** 47 **[B] [C] [D] [E]** 46 **[F]**
192. GALATAN Posina 45 **[A]** Rosina **[B] [C]** Rozina **[D] [E]** Rosina **[F]**
193. GALIA Jean Haralambie **[A]** 22 **[C] [D] [E]** 21 **[F]** Haralambe 22 **[B]**
194. GANBIS I. Emanuel **[A]** (GLAUBES I. Emanuel 23 **[B]** Emanuel **[C] [D] [E]** 22 **[F1]**)
195. GARTENBERG Arnold 33 **[B] [D] [E] [F1]** (GARTHENBERG Arnold **[A]** GARTEMBERG Arnold **[C]**)
196. GARTENBERG Felix 31 **[B] [D] [E] [F]** (GARTENBEG Felix **[A]** GARTEMBERG Felix **[C]**)
197. GARTENBERG Rifca 28 **[B] [D] [E]** Rivca **[F1]** (GARTHENBERG Rifca **[A]** GARTEMBERG Rifca **[C]**)
198. GHELBER Batia **[D]**

199. GHELBER Heinrich 44 [E] [B] [D] [Fl] Heirich [C] (GHELBERT Heinerich [A])

200. GHELBER Lea-Hude 39 [C] [D] [E] [Fl] Leia Hude [B] (GHELBERT Leia Hurle [A])

201. GHELBER M. Danil [A] M. Paul 18 [B] M. P. Daniel [E] (GHELBERG M. P. Daniel [C] GHELBERG M. P. Daniel & GHELBER Marcel Moshe [D] M. F. Paul 17 [Fl])

202. GHELMAN Alexandru [A] 28 [C] [D] [E] 27 [Fl] Alexander [B]

203. GHELMAN Fania [A] 21 [B] [D] [E] Leigha 22 [Fl] Fanea 21 [C]

204. GHELMAN Feiga-Fanea [A] 26 [B] Fanea [C] [D] Fanes Genia [E] Fania (Genia) 20 [Fl]

205. GHELMAN Moise [A] 29 [B] Moses 29 [D] [E] Moses-Mose 38 [F] (GHERMAN Moses 29 [C])

206. GHENTZER Ernestina [A] 37 [F] (GHENZER Ernestine 39 [B] [C] [D] [E])

207. GHENTZER Magdalena [A] 8 [F] (GHENZER Magdalena 7 [B] [D] [E] GHEZNER Magdalena [C])

208. GHETEL Frida 32 [A] Basia Frieda [B] [D] Basia Frida [E] [C] (GHETZEL Basie-Frieda [Fl])

209. GHETEL Solomon 45 [A] Moritz [B] Mor. Solomon [C] Moritz Solomon [D] [E] (GHETZEL Moritz-Solomon [F])

210. GHETLER I. Macas [A] J. Macas 18 [Fl] (GHETTLER Macas 19 [B] I. Macas [C] I. Mathias [D] [E])

211. GHETLER Iosif 49 [F] (GHETLAR Iosef [A] GHETTLER Josef 50 [B] Iosif [C] [D] [E])

212. GHETLER Leah-Lia 44 [F] (GHETLAR Leia-Liza [A] GHETTLER Lya 45 [B] Lea Liza [C] [D] [E])

213. GHINSBERG Adrian 7 [A] [B] [C] [D] [F] (GHINZBERG Adrian [E])

214. GHINSBERG Evelina 32 [A] [B] Evelina-Marcus [C] [D] [F] (GHINZBERG Evelina (Marcus) [E])

215. GHINSBERG Marcu [A] 32 [B] Marcu Beniamni [C] Marcu-Beniamin 35 [D] [F] (GHINZBERG Marcu Beniamin) 32 [E])

216. GLANOVSCHI Gherson 30 [E] (GRANOSCHI Ghers [A] GRANOVSCHI Ghers [B] GLANOVOKI Ghers [C] GLANOVCKI Gherson [D] GRANOVSKY Ghers [Fl])

217. GLICKMAN Avram 48 [C] [D] 47 [F] (GLIMAN Avram [A] GLICMAN Avram 48 [B] [E])

218. GLICKMAN Evghenia 33 [F] Eugenie 34 [C] Eugenia [D] (GLIMAN Eugenia [A] GLICMAN Eughenia 34 [B] Eughenie 34 [E])

219. GLICKMAN Iacob 7 [C] [D] 6 [F] (GLIMAN Iacob [A] GLICMAN Iacov 7 [B] Iacob 7 [E])

220. GLICKMAN Liza 70 [C] [D] [F] (GLIMAN Lisa [A] GLICMAN Liza
[B] [E])

221. GLICKMAN Rita 10 [C] [D] 9 [F] (GLIMAN Ritta [A] GLICMAN
Rita 10 [B] [E])

222. GLUCKMAN Alfred 30 [B] [C] [E] (GLUKMAN Alfred [A]
GLUECKMAN Alfred [D] 40 [F1])

223. GLUCKMAN Sophie 24 [B] Sofia [C] [E] (GLUKMAN Sofia [A]
GLUECKMAN Sofia [D] 23 [F1])

224. GOLDENBERG Iossi 26 [A] Jassy [B] Iosef [C] [D] [E] Iassy [F1]

225. GOLDENBERG Osias 24 [A] [B] [C] [D] [E] [F]

226. GOLDMAN Alexandru 40 [A] Alex [B] Alexandru [C] [D] [E] [F]

227. GOLDMAN Hans 4 [A] [B] Hana [C] [D] [E] Heinz [F]

228. GOLDMAN Racla 7 [A] Rachela [B] [C] [D] [E] [F1]

229. GOLDMAN Tivi 32 [A] Turia [B] Tivia [C] [D] [E] [F]

230. GOLDSTEIN Ana [A] 26 [B] 27 [F1] Anna 26 [C] [D] [E]

231. GOLDSTEIN Armand 25 [A] [B] [C] [D] [E] [F]

232. GOLDSTEIN Eliezer 31 [A] Eliazar [B] Elazar [E] (GOLDENSTEIN
Eliszar [C] Eliazar [D] Eleazar [F1])

233. GOLDSTEIN Marcu 50 [A] [B] [C] [D] [E] [F]

234. GOLDSTEIN Moise Haim [A] 19 [B] [D] [E] 18 [F] Moise H. 19 [C]

235. GOLDSTEIN Simon [A] 40 [C] [D] L. Simon [F] (GOLDSTEIN Simon 41 & GOWSTEIN Simon L. 40 [B] GOLDSTEIN Simon 41 &
GOWSTEIN Simon 40 [E])

236. GOLDSTEIN Stefania 29 [A] [B] [C] [E] (GOLDENSTEIN Stefania
[D] [F1])

237. GOTLIEB Bronislava 52 [E] Bronislawa [F1] Bratislava [A] (GOT-
TLIEB Bronislava [B] [C] [D])

238. GOTLIEB Heinrich 54 [A] (Henry)[F1] Henry [E] (GOTTLIEB Henry
[B] [C] [D])

239. GOTLIEB Paul-Norbert 21 [A] [E] [F] Paul [C] (GOTTLIEB Paul
Norbert [B] [D])

240. GOTLIEB Thea-Ruth [A] 18 [F] Ruth Thea 19 [E] (GOTTLIEB Tea
Ruth 19 [B] Ruth [C] Thea-Ruth [D])

241. GOTTESMAN Iacob 33 [D] [E] [F] (GOTESMAN Iacob [A]
GOTTESMANN Iacob [B] GOTTEAMAN Iacob [C])

242. GREIF Calman 24 [C] [D] [F] (GRIF Calman [A] GRIEF Calman [B]
[E])

243. GROBDRUG Alexandru 22 **[E]** Alevei 21 **[B]** (GROBVDRIC Alexandru **[A]** GRODBURG Alexandru 22 **[C]** GROBDRUCK Alexandru **[D]** Alexandru (Alex) **[F]**)

244. GROPPER Marcel **[D]**

245. GROSS Nora 26 **[B]** **[C]** **[D]** **[E]** (GAVAS Nora **[A]** GRASS or GROSS Nora 25 **[F1]**)

246. GROSS Victor Paul 16 **[B]** Victor Daniel **[C]** **[D]** Vict. Daniel **[E]** (GAVAS Victor Danil **[A]** GRASS or GROSS Victor-Paul **[F1]**)

247. GROSSMAN Marcel **[A]** 20 **[C]** **[D]** **[E]** 19 **[F]** (GROSSMANN Marcel 20 **[B]**)

248. GRUBER Isac 34 **[B]** **[C]** **[D]** **[E]** **[F]** Isach **[A]**

249. GRUENBERG Gabriel 25 **[D]** Daniel Gabriel **[E]** (GRINBERG Gabriel **[A]** **[B]** Gabriel (Gabi) **[F1]** GRUNBERG Gabriel **[C]**)

250. GRUENBERG Efraim 30 **[D]** **[E]** (GRINBERG Efraim 37 **[F1]** GRUS-BURG Efraim **[A]** GRUNBERG Epraim **[B]** Efraim 30 **[C]**)

251. GRUENBERG Ferdinand-Lica 24 **[D]** Ferdin.-Lica **[E]** (GRINBERG Ferdinant **[A]** GRUMBERG Ferdinand **[B]** GRUNBERG Ferdinand Lica **[C]** GRINBERG Ferdinand (Lica) **[F1]**)

252. GRUENBERG Irina 21 **[D]** **[E]** **[F]** (GRINBERG Irina **[A]** GRUM-BERG Irina **[B]** GRUNBERG Irina **[C]**)

253. GRUENBERG Jean 21 **[D]** **[E]** **[F]** (GRUNBERG Jean **[A]** **[B]** **[C]**

254. GRUENBERG Leon 19 **[E]** (GRUENBERGER Leon **[A]** GRIN-BERGHER Adolf **[B]** GRUNBERG Leon **[C]** GRUENBERG Leon & GRUENBERGER Adolf **[D]** GRUEN(S)BER(ER) Leon **[F1]**)

255. GRUENBERG Moritz 42 **[D]** **[E]** **[F]** (GRUNBERG Moritz **[C]**)

256. GRUENBERG Otto **[D]** 27 **[E]** 26 **[F]** (GRINBERG Otto **[A]** GRUN-BERG Otto 27 **[B]** **[C]**)

257. GRUENBERG Stella 19 **[D]** **[E]** (GRINBERG Stela **[A]** **[B]** **[F1]** GRUNBERG Stella **[C]**)

258. GRUENBERG Wolf-Zeev 28 **[D]** Wolfi (Zeev) **[E]** **[F]** (GRINBERG Wolf **[A]** GRUNBERG Wolfy **[B]** Wolfi **[C]**)

259. GRUENFELD Itzhac-Eizig **[D]** I. Aizic 29 **[F1]** (AIZIC Grunfeld **[A]** GRUNSFELD Eisig 30 **[B]** GRUNFELD Eizig **[C]** GRUNNFELD Eizig Ithac **[E]**

260. GRUENFELD Laszlo 38 **[D]** **[E]** **[F1]** (FRIEDMAN Laslo **[A]** GRUN-FELD Laszlo **[B]** Lasslo **[C]**)

261. GRUMER Fritz **[A]** **[C]** **[D]** 38 **[E]** 51 **[F]**

262. GRUNSTEIN Herman **[A]** (GORNSTEIN Herman 30 **[B]** GRUEN-STEIN Herm. Lica **[C]** **[E]** Hermann-Lica **[D]** Herman (Lica) 34 **[F1]**)

263. GRUPPER Filip 27 **[B] [C] [D] [E]** 26 **[F]** (GRUPFER Plipi **[A]**)

264. GRUPPER Rachella 36 **[E]** 35 **[F]** Rachila 36 **[B]** Rachela **[C] [D]** (GRUPFER Rachele **[A]**)

265. GUTMAN Adeline 25 **[E]** Adelina (Adina) **[F1]** (GUTTMAN Adelina **[A] [C] [D]** GUTTMANN Adeline **[B]**)

266. GUTMAN Alexandru 27 **[E]** (Sandu) **[F1]** (GUTTMAN Alexandru **[A] [C] [D]** GUTTMANN Alexander **[B]**)

267. GUTTENMAHER Smil 21 **[A]** Smil Zanviel **[E]** (GUTTENMAEHER Smil **[B]** GUTTERMACHER Smil Zanvel **[C]** Smi-Zanvel **[D]** GUTTENMACHER Smil-Zamvel (Michey) **[F1]**)

268. HAFNER Luci 20 **[A]** Lucy **[B] [C] [D] [E] [F]**

269. HAIM Denise 6 **[A] [D] [F]** Denisa **[E]** Danisa **[C]**

270. HAIM Iacob 32 **[A] [C] [D] [E] [F]**

271. HAIM Nahoma **[A]** Nehuma 31 **[E]** Nehama **[D] [F]** Nehuma 32 **[C]**

272. HAIM Sabina 30 **[C] [D] [E] [F]** Sabine **[B]** (SABINA Haim **[A]**)

273. HAIMOVICI Angelina 20 **[A]** Angelica **[B] [C] [D] [E]** Angela (Angelica) **[F]**

274. HAIMOVICI Carol 19 **[A] [B] [C] [D] [E] [F]**

275. HAIMOVICI Virgil **[A]** 30 **[C] [D] [E]** Vergil 30 **[B]** Virgiliu 29 **[F]**

276. HALFIN Ida 55 **[B] [C] [D] [E]** 57 **[F]** (HALFIM Ida **[A]**)

277. HALISCH Alfred 35 **[C] [D] [E]** (HOCH Alfred **[A]** HOLICI Afred **[B]** HOCH & HALISCH Alfred **[F]**)

278. HALISCH Jeannette 28 **[E]** Janeta **[C] [D]** (HOCH Zelda **[A]** HOLICI Jeanatte **[B]** HOCH & HALISCH Zelda **[F]**)

279. HARAS Sergiu **[A]** 15 **[B] [D] [E] [F]** 16 **[C]**

280. HASCALOVICI Iosef & Iosef **[A]** 26 **[E]** Iosif 36 **[B] [F]** 26 **[C] [D]**

281. HASCALOVICI Rachela 30 **[B] [C] [D]** Rachella **[F1]** Racha **[A]** Raschella **[E]**

282. HASCALOVICI Sergiu 6 **[A] [C] [D] [E] [F]** (HASCALOVICHI Sergin **[B]**)

283. HASSAN Eduard 20 **[B] [C] [D] [E]** 19 **[F]** (EDUARD Hassam **[A]**)

284. HASSAN Iuditha 17 **[C] [D] [E]** Juditha 17 **[B]** 16 **[F]** (HASSAM Judita **[A]**)

285. HEFTER Harry 21 **[B]** Henry Ernest **[C]** Henry-Ernst 19 **[F1]** Henry Ernest (Hary) 21 **[E]** (HERFTER Ernest Hary **[A]** HAFTER Henry Ernest **[D]**)

286. HEINIS Boris 21 **[E]** Beris **[A] [B] [C] [D]** (HEINNIS Beris **[F]**)

287. HELENBRANT Louis 21 **[E]** (HERENBRAND Luis **[A]** HELLEN-

BRANDT Louis **[B]** HELENBRANDT Louis **[C] [D]** HE-
LENKRAUT Louis **[F1]**)

288. HELLER Bertha 36 **[C] [D] [E] [B]** 25 **[F]** (HELTER Berta **[A]**)

289. HELLER Henic 22 **[E]** (HENIC Henic **[A] [B] [C] [D] [F]**)

290. HELLER Leon 36 **[C] [D] [E]** 46 **[B]** 45 **[F]** (HELTER Leon **[A]**)

291. HELLER Oswald 2 **[B] [D] [E]** 1 **[F]** Osvald 2 **[C]** (HELTER Leibu-
Osvalt **[A]**)

292. HELLER Pepi 54 **[E]** Pepy **[C] [D]** (HALTER Pepi **[A]** HALLER Pepi
[B] HOLLER Pepi **[F]**)

293. HERSCOVICI Edith 10 **[A] [B] [C] [D] [E] [F]**

294. HERSCOVICI Hary 22 **[A]** Harry **[C] [D] [E] [F]** (HIRSCOVICI
Harry **[B]**)

295. HERSCOVICI Marcel 44 **[A] [B] [C] [D] [E] [F]**

296. HERSCOVICI Maximilian 39 **[A] [B] [C] [D] [E]** (Max) **[F1]**

297. HERSCOVICI Moise 18 **[A]** Mosias **[B]** Mozis **[C] [D]** Mozis Musia **[E]**
Matilda **[F1]**

298. HERSCOVICI Saly 41 **[A]** Sally **[B] [C] [D] [E]** Sali **[F]**

299. HERSCOVICI Teodor 21 **[A]** (HEROVICI Feodor **[B]** Theodor **[C] [D]**
[E] Teodor **[F]**)

300. HERSCU Eva **[A]** 45 **[C] [D] [E]** 35 **[B] [F]**

301. HERSCU I. Herscu **[A]** 40 **[B] [D] [E]** 35 **[F]** H. Herscu **[C]**

302. HERSCU Sali **[A] [F]** Zonenreich Sali 28 **[C] [E]** Sonnenreich Sali **[D]**
(HERSIU Sali **[B]**).

303. HERSCU Sofia **[A]** 4 **[B] [F]** 28 **[C] [D]** 42 **[E]**

304. HERSER Malca 30 **[D] [E] [F]** (HERCHER Malca **[A] [B]** HERSAR
Malca **[C]**)

305. HERSER Samuel 34 **[C] [D] [E]** Samoil **[F]** (HERCHER Samoil **[A]**
Samuel **[B]**)

306. HERZBLUT Matilda 53 **[B]** Mathilda **[D]** Matilda Natalia 33 **[E]** Matilda
35 **[F1]** (HERTHBLUTH Matilda **[A]** HELZBUT Matilda 33 **[C]**)

307. HIRSCH Adalbert 38 **[B] [C] [D] [E]** 37 **[F]** (HIRS Adalbert **[A]**)

308. HIRSCH Gabriela 2 **[B] [C] [D] [E] [F]** (HIRS Gabriel **[A]**)

309. HIRSCH Roza 34 **[B] [D]** Rosa 34 **[E]** 33 **[F]** (HIRS Rosa **[A]** HIRCH
Rosa 34 **[C]**)

310. HONIGSBERG Berta 20 **[A] [B]** Bertha **[E] [F1]** (KOENISBERG
Bertha **[C]** KOENIGSBERG Bertha **[D]**)

311. HONIGSBERG Fritz 18 **[A]** Fritzi **[B] [E] [F1]** (KOENISBERG Fritz
[C] KOENIGSBERG Fritz **[D]**)

312. HONIGSBERG Lisa 43 **[A]** Luiza **[B] [E] [F1]** (KOENISBERG Luiza
[C] KOENIGSBERG Luiza **[D]**)

313. HONIGSBERG Ozias **[A]** Osias 48 **[B]** Osias-Oscar **[E]** Oscar-Stanislav 50 **[F1]** (KOENIGSBERG Osias **[C]** **[D]**)
314. HORENSTEIN Carol 30 **[A]** **[D]** **[E]** **[F]** (HORNSTEIN Carol **[B]** **[C]**)
315. HOROVITZ Daniel **[A]** 19 **[D]** **[E]** **[F1]** (HOROWITZ Daniel **[B]** HORVITZ Daniel **[C]**)
316. HOSIN Sami **[D]**

317. IACOBOVICI Bernard **[A]** 19 **[C]** **[D]** (Benu) 18 **[F1]** (IACOBIVICI Bernard 19 **[B]** IACUBOVICI I. Bernard Benu 19 **[E]**)
318. IACOBOVICI Fainaru Pincu 46 **[C]** **[D]** **[F]** (FAINARU Pincu **[A]** JA-COBIVICI Fainaru Pinca **[B]** IACUBOVICI Fainaru Pincu **[E]**)
319. IANCHELOVICI Etti 10 **[A]** Eti **[E]** (IANCHELEVICI Ety **[B]** Eti **[C]** **[D]** Ieti **[F1]**)
320. IANCHELOVICI Frida **[A]** 37 **[E]** (IANCHELEVICI Frieda 37 **[B]** Frida **[C]** **[D]** Frida 36 **[F]**)
321. IANCHELOVICI User **[A]** Nissen User 40 **[E]** (IANCHELEVICI Nisen 48 **[B]** Nissen Usar 40 **[C]** Nissem User **[D]** Niscu-User 48 **[F]**)
322. IANCOVICI Moritz **[A]** 30 **[B]** **[D]** **[E]** 31 **[F]** (INACOVICI Moritz 30 **[C]**)
323. IANCU Clara **[A]** (IONAS Clara 25 **[B]** **[D]** **[F1]** Clara Iancu **[E]** IONSS Clara **[C]**)
324. IANCU Ioines 34 **[A]** (IONAS Iancu **[B]** Jacques-Iancu **[D]** Iancu Jacques **[E]** **[F1]** IONSS Jaques 4 **[C]**)
325. IANCU Itic 68 **[A]** **[B]** **[C]** **[E]** **[F]** Itzic **[D]**
326. IANCU Moise 30 **[A]** **[B]** **[C]** **[D]** **[E]** **[F]**
327. IANCU Sofia **[A]** 40 **[B]** **[C]** **[D]** **[E]** 64 **[F]**
328. IOINA Iosif 28 **[A]** (IONA Iosif **[B]** IONSS Iosif **[C]** IONAS Iosif **[D]** **[E]** Jose (Iosif) **[F1]**)
329. IOSUBAS Itic 32 **[A]** **[B]** **[C]** **[D]** **[E]** (IOCUMBAS Itic **[F]**)
330. IRMAN Haia 27 **[A]** **[F]** Haim **[B]** **[C]** **[D]** **[E]**
331. ISTACESCU Adela **[A]** 57 **[C]** **[D]** **[E]** (ISTAVESCU Adela 57 **[B]** IS-TACEANU Adela 56 **[F1]**)
332. ISTACESCU Alfred 8 **[A]** **[C]** **[D]** **[E]** **[F]** (ISTAVESCU Alfred **[B]** IS-TACEANU Alfred **[F1]**))
333. ISZAC I. Emerio 24 **[C]** I. Emeric **[D]** **[E]** L. Emeric **[F]** (ISZAK I. Emeric **[B]**)
334. ITCOVICI Adela 24 **[A]** **[F]** (ITICOVICI Adela **[B]** **[C]** Adelina **[D]** **[E]**)
335. ITIC Avdel **[A]** Aurel 27 **[B]** 24 **[C]** **[D]** **[E]** 23 **[F]**
336. ITIC Avram 21 **[E]** **[B]** **[C]** **[D]** (AVRAM Itic **[A]**)

337. ITICOVICI Adela [A] Adila 61 [B] Adela [C] [D] 51 [E]
338. ITICOVICI Cornelia 18 [A] [E] Corneliu [B] [C] [D] (ITCOVICI Corneliu [F])
339. ITICSON Albert [A] 22 [F] (ITICSOHN Albert [B] [D] [E] ITICSHON Albert 21 [C])

340. JUSTER Harry 20 [A] [B] [C] [F] Harry (Feinstein) [E] (IUSTER-FEINSTEIN Harry [D])
341. JUSTER Mircea 22 [A] [B] [C] [F] Mircea (Feinstein) [E] (IUSTER-FEINSTEIN Mircea [D])

342. KAFRISEN Moise 27 [A] Moise (Marci) [F1] (KAFFRISEN Marcus [B] KAFRISSON Marcu Moise [C] [D] KAFRISSEN Marcu Moise [E])
343. KAHANE Ilie 22 [C] [D] Ilie Elie [E] Elias (Ilie) [F1] (CAHAN Itic [A] Ilie [B])
344. KAHANE Julius Ilie 35 [E] Julius [B] [F] Iulius Moise [C] Iulius Ilie [D] (KAHAN Julius [A])
345. KANIUK Ernest 30 [C] [E] 32 [F] Ernst [D] (RAMIK Ernest [A] KANINK Ernest 30 [B])
346. KANNA Gustav 20 [B] [F1] Gusta [C] (CANA Gustav [A] KANNE Gusta [D] [E])
347. KATZ Armand 19 [A] [B] [C] [D] [E] [F]
348. KATZ Friederike 39 [B] Friederica [C] [D] Frederica [E] Frederika (Ilse) [F1] Frederich [A]
349. KATZ Sigmund 45 [A] [B] [C] [D] [E] [F]
350. KATZ Zelig 20 [A] Zeilig [B] [C] [D] Zelig [E] [F]
351. KAUFMAN Sami 27 [F] Seni [A] (CHUFMAN Samie [B] CAUFMAN Seni [C] Sonia [D] CAMMERMAN Sonia [E])
352. KELEN Nicolae [A] 38 [B] [C] [D] [E] (KELLEN Nicolae 37 [F1])
353. KELMAN Matilda 20 [B] [C] [D] [E] (KEHNAN Mathilda [A] KALMAN Matilde [F] & BEHAR Matilda [F1])
354. KESSELBRENNER Ghitel 55 [E] [F1] Ghittel [B] (CHESELBRINER Ghitel [A] KESSELBRENER Ghittel [C] [D])
355. KLEIN Herman [A] 25 [B] [C] [E] 20 [F] Hermann [D]
356. KLEIN Josef 38 [A] [B] Iosif [C] [D] [E] [F]
357. KLEINBERG Mendel 28 [C] [D] [E] 27 [F1] (CLEINBERG Mendel [A] CLEINBURG Mendel 28 [B])
358. KOERNER Zighi [D]

359. KORN Malvina 20 **[B] [C] [D] [E] [F1]** (CORN Malvina **[A]**)
360. KORNBLUTT Mauriciu 27 **[A]** (CORNBLUTT Maivriciu **[B]** CORN-BLUT Mauriciu **[C]** CORNBLUET Mauriciu **[D]** KORENBLUT Mauriciu Marcel **[E]** KORNBLUT Mauriciu **[F1]**)
361. KORNBLUTT Zela 20 **[A]** (CORENBLUTT Lela **[B]** CORNBLUT Zela **[C]** CORNBLUET Zela **[D]** KORENBLUT Zela **[E]** KORN-BLUT Zela **[F1]**)
362. KRAUS Clara **[A]** 30 **[B] [C] [D] [E]** Clara (Segal) 30 **[F1]**
363. KRAUS Marcel 37 **[A] [B] [C] [D] [E] [F]**

364. LANDAU Emil 31 **[A] [C] [D] [E] [F]** (LANDAN Emil **[B]**)
365. LANDAU Hortensa-Silvia 33 **[A] [F1]** Hort. Silvia **[C]** Hortansa Silvia **[D]** Hert Silvia **[E]** (LANDAN Hortansa Silvia **[B]**)
366. LANDAU Ruhla 30 **[A] [B] [C] [D] [E] [F]**
367. LANDMAN Heinerich **[A]** Harry 33 **[B] [C] [D]** 35 **[E]** Heinrich **[F]**
368. LANDMAN Jose **[A]** Joze 10 **[B]** Iose **[C] [D]** Jose **[E]** 9 **[F]**
369. LANDMAN Liza **[A]** 36 **[B] [C] [D] [E]** 35 **[F]**
370. LANDMAN Willy **[A]** 39 **[B] [C] [D] [E]** Willi 38 **[F1]**
371. LANGENMAS Dvora 49 **[E]** (LANGENAS Dora **[A]** LANGEMASS Dvora 49 **[B]** Dora 45 **[F]** LANGENMASS Dvora **[C] [D]**)
372. LANGENMAS Ruth 17 **[E]** (LANGENAS Ruthla **[A]** LANGEMASS Ruth **[B] [F]** LANGENMASS Ruth **[C] [D]**)
373. LANGMANTEL Armand 36 **[D] [E] [F]** Herman **[A]** (LONGIN Armand **[B]** LANGEMANTEL Armand **[C]**)
374. LANGMANTEL Eduard **[A] [D]** 8 **[E]** Ervard 6 **[F]** (LONGIN Eduard 8 **[B]** LANGEMANTEL Eduard **[C]**)
375. LANGMANTEL Margareta 10 **[A] [F]** Margherita **[D]** Margerita **[E]** (LONGIN Margarite **[B]** LANGEMANTEL Margherita **[C]**)
376. LANGMANTEL Rachel 31 **[A]** Rica-Rachel **[D]** Rachel Rica **[E] [F]** (LONGIN Rica **[B]** LANGEMANTEL Rachel **[C]**)
377. LAXER Adolf **[D]** 35 **[E] [F]** Acolf **[C]**(LAXIR Adolf **[A]** LAURER Adolf 32 **[B]**)
378. LAZARESCU Bernard David 28 **[A]** David **[B]** Dvs. Bernard **[C]** Bernard Dov **[D]** Dov Bern **[E]** B. David **[F]**
379. LAZARESCU Heinerich **[A]** Heinrich 30 **[B] [C] [D]** 39 **[E] [F]**
380. LAZARESCU Henta **[A] [F]** Hentia 21 **[B] [C] [D] [E]**
381. LAZARESCU Paulina 29 **[A]** Pauline **[B]** Paulina **[C] [D] [E]** Paula (Paulina) **[F]**

382. LAZAROVICI Leibu [A] Milu 18 [B] Iuliu [C] [D] Juliu Milo [E] Julius (Milu) 17 [F]

383. LAZAROVICI Rene [A] 20 [C] [D] [E] 19 [F] (LAZAROVIC Renee 20 [B])

384. LAZAROVICI Severin [A] 54 [D] [E] Sev [C] (LAZAROVICZ Severin 34 [B] LAZAROWICZ Severin 54 [F1])

385. LECKER Leon Leib 34 [B] [D] [E] Leon Leib (Arie) [F1] (LEKER Leon [A] LACKER Leon Leib [C])

386. LEIBOVICI Leonido Corucli [A] Lemida Cornelius 40 [B] G. Corn [C] Cornel [D] L. Corneliu [E] (Leonida) Corneliu 28 [F1]

387. LEIBOVICI Basia 30 [A] [F] Basse [C] [D] Base Batia [E] (LABONCI Basa [B])

388. LEIBOVICI D. Iacob 27 [A] Jacob [B] Iacob [C] [D] [E] D. Iacov [F]

389. LEIBOVICI Haia [A] Ilaia 38 [B] Haim [C] Hava [D] Haia [E] 37 [F]

390. LEIBOVICI Heinerich [A] Henrich 21 [B] Heinrich 20 [C] [D] Heinrich Antoren [E] Heinrich [F1]

391. LEIBOVICI Silvia (Leonin) 51 [B] Silvia [C] [D] L. Silvia [E] (LEONIN Leibovici Libu [A] L. Silvia [F1])

392. LEIBOVICI Leib-Itic [A] Leib Itic 49 [B] Leibiti [C] Leib [D] [E] L. Itic 48 [F]

393. LEIBOVICI Lizica (Leonin) 44 [B] Lizica [E] 41 [C] [D] (LEONIN Leibovici Lizica [A] L. Lizica 45 [F1])

394. LEIBOVICI Luis 27 [A] G. Louis [B] [C] [D] [E] [F]

395. LEIBOVICI Marcu 25 [B] [C] [D] 23 [E] 24 [F] Maria [A]

396. LEIBOVICI Simon [A] 22 [B] [C] [D] 20 [E] 21 [F]

397. LEIBOVICI Solomon 37 [A] [B] [C] [D] [E] [F]

398. LEON Marcu 21 [B] [C] [D] [E] [F] (LEORA A. Marcu [A])

399. LEVI Haim 23 [A] [E] [F1] (LEWY Haim [B] LEVY Haim [C] [D])

400. LIUBARSCHI David 57 [C] [D] [E] [F] (LEIBARSCHI David [A] LINBARSKI David [B])

401. LIUBARSCHI Dora 54 [C] [D] [E] [F] (LEIBARSCHI Dora [A] LINBARSCKI Dora [B])

402. LIVESCU Matilda [A] [C] [D] [E] [F]

403. LIVOVSCHI Basia 60 [B] [D] [E] (LVOVSCHI S. Basia [A] LVOVSCHI or LIVOVSKI S. Basia [F1] LINOVSCHI Basia [C])

404. LIVOVSCHI Sara 29 [D] [E] (SVORSCHI Sara [A] LIVOWSKI Sara [B] LINOVSCHI Sara [C] LVOVSCHI or LIVOVSKI S. Sara [F1])

405. LIVOVSCHI Smil Wolf 69 [B] [D] [E] (LVOVSCHI Smil Wolf [A] LVOVSCHI or LIVOVSKI Smil-Wolf (Smil) [F1] LINOVSCHI Smil [C])

406. LOBEL Horis [A] Horia 30 [B] Horia Luca [D] [E] (LEBEL Horia [C] LOEBEL Horia-Luca 40 [F])

407. LOCKER Gerta Marta & SCHOR Greta Marga [D] LOCKER SCHOR Gerta Marta 24 [E] LOCKER Gerta Maria [C] LOCKER or SHORR Gerta-Martha & SCHOR Greta-Magda Maria [F1] (LOCHER Getta-Marie [A] SCHOR Gherta Marga [B])

408. LOCKER Siegfried & SCHOR Siegfried [D] LOCKER Siegfied [C] LOCKER SCHOR Siegfr. 42 [E] LOCKER or SHORR Siegfried & SCHOR Siegfried [F] (LOCHER Siegfried [A] SCHOR Siegfrid [B])

409. LORIAN Silvian 27 [A] [C] [D] [E] [F] (LORIN Silvin [B])

410. LOTHRINGER Ilse 20 [B] [C] [D] [E] (LOTINGHER Ilse [A] LOTHRINGER or LOTTINGER Ulse (Ilse) 18 [F1])

411. LOWENSTEIN Carol 18 [C] [E] (LEVENSTEIN Carol [A] [F1] LOEWENSTEIN Carol [B] [D])

412. LUCIAN Hana Mayer 31 [D] [E] Chena Mayer [B] G. Mezer [C] (MAYER Ghena [A] MAYER (MARCUS) Kenna (Hanna) [F1])

413. LUCIAN Ilie Mayer 8 [E] Julian Meyer [B] Iul. Mayer [C] Iulius Mayer [D] (MAYER Julian [A] MAYER (MARCUS) Juliu (Iulian) [F1])

414. LUCIAN Mayer 32 [B] [C] [D] [E] Gr. Maier [F] (MAYER Lucian [A])

415. LUDOVIC Eduard 39 [B] Eduard Edi [C] [D] [E] Eduard (Edi) 38 [F1] (EDUARTH Ludvig [A])

416. LUDOVIC Emanuel 36 [B] Eugen Emanuel Manole [C] [D] Eugen Emanuel [E] Emanoil-Eugeniu (Manole) 35 [F1] (LUDVIG Emanuel [A])

417. LUPOVICI Bluma 26 [F] Blima [B] [C] [D] [E] Slima [A]

418. LUPOVICI Smil 27 [A] [B] [C] [D] [E] [F]

419. LUPU Bertina 22 [B] Berthina [C] [D] Bertina Strul [E] (STRUL Bertina [A] LUPU Bertina 21 & STRUL Bertina 21 [F1])

420. LUPU I. Strul 29 [E] [C] [D] (STRUL Lupu [A] LUPI Strul 29 [B] LUPU I. Strul 28 & STRUL Lupu 28 [F1])

421. MAGAZANIC Ofser 67 [B] Ofsei [C] [D] [E] Of(v)sei [F1] (MAGA-SOVICI Ofsia [A])

422. MAGDER Edmond 50 [B] [C] [D] [E] [F] (MAGDA Eduard [A])

423. MALLER Ladislau 22 [C] [D] [E] Lothar [F] (MAHLER Ladislau [A] MALER Ladislav 2 [B])

424. MANDEL Iacob 16 [A] [B] [C] [D] [E] [F]

425. MANOLE Lazar 22 [B] Lazar David Eliezer [E] Lazar-David [C] [F] (MACHE Lazar [A] MANOLE Lazar-David & LAZAR Manuela [D])

426. MARCOVICI Henry 20 **[A] [B] [C] [D] [E]** Heinrich **[F]**

427. MARCOVICI Moise **[A]** 28 **[B]** 26 **[C] [D] [E]** 29 **[F]**

428. MARCU Iacob **[D]**

429. MARCU Sorina 22 **[A] [F]** Sarina **[B] [D] [E]** Serine **[C]**

430. MARCU Suzeta 24 **[A]** Suzette **[B] [C] [D] [F1]** Susette **[E]**

431. MARCUS Ana **[A]** 32 **[B] [C] [D]** Anna-Nutza 26 **[E]** Anna 31 **[F1]**

432. MARCUS Aneta Lupu 41 **[C] [D] [E]** Aneta **[B]** Anetta **[F]** (HERSCU Lupu Aneta **[A]**)

433. MARCUS Avram 28 **[B] [C] [D]** Avram Aurel **[E] [F]** (MAROUS Avram **[A]**)

434. MARCUS Cila **[A]** Cijla 21 **[B]** Cila **[C] [D] [E]** Cila or Tila 23 **[F1]**

435. MARCUS Ivette 7 **[B]** Ivette Lupu **[C] [D] [E]** Ivette 6 **[F1]** (HERSCU Lupu Iveta **[A]**)

436. MARCUS Lupu Herscu 42 **[E] [F]** Herscu Lupu **[D]** Lupu H. **[B]** (HERSCU Lupu Marcu **[A]** MARCU Lupu Herscu **[C]**)

437. MARCUS Malvina 21 **[B] [D] [E]** Malvina (Gallia) **[F1]** (MARCU Malvina **[A] [C]**)

438. MARCUS Marga Lupu **[D]** 13 **[E]** Marga **[B]** 12 **[F]** Maria Lupu 13 **[C]** (HERSCU Lupu Marga **[A]**)

439. MARCUS Mendel 69 **[B] [C] [D] [E] [F]** (MAROUS Mendele **[A]**)

440. MARCUS Leon 29 **[A] [B] [C] [D] [E]** P. Leon **[F]**

441. MARCUS Rosa 52 **[A]** Roza **[B] [C] [D] [E] [F1]**

442. MARGULIUS Aurel 23 **[C] [D] [E]** Anrel **[B]** L. Aurel 22 **[F1]** (MARGULIS Aurel **[A]**)

443. MARGULIUS Efraim 35 **[C] [D] [E]** 36 **[F]** (MARGULIS I. Efraim **[A]** MARGUILIUS Efraim 35 **[B]**)

444. MARGULIUS Emil 25 **[E] [C] [D]** Evel 24 **[B] [F]** (MARGULIS Emil **[A]**)

445. MARGULIUS Harry 20 **[B] [C] [D] [E]** 19 **[F]** (MARGULIS Hary **[A]**)

446. MARGULIUS Margarita 18 **[B]** Margherite **[C] [D]** Margueritte **[E]** Margareta 17 **[F]** (MARGULI Margareta **[A]**)

447. MATTES Lazar **[D]** 29 **[E]** MATHES or MATTES Lazar 25 **[F]** (MATES Lazar **[A]** MATTERS Lazar 29 **[B]** MUTTERA Lazar **[C]**)

448. MAYER Artur 32 **[B] [D] [E] [F]** Arthur **[A]** (MAZER Artur **[C]**)

449. MAYER L. Avram 27 **[E]** 30 **[F]** Avram 30 **[C] [D]**

450. MAYER M. Avram 23 **[F]** (MAYER M. Avram **[A]** MAIER Avram M. 30 **[B]**)

451. MAYER N. Fany Felicia 24 **[E]** N. Fany **[C] [D]** N. Fanny 23 **[F]** M. Fani **[A]** (MAIER Fani M. 24 **[B]**)

452. MAYER Silvia 20 **[A] [B] [C] [D] [E] [F1]** & IONAS Silvia (Maier) **[F1]**
453. MAYERSOHN Ana 26 **[A] [C] [E]** Anna **[D]** (MAYERSIHU Ana **[B]** MARCUS Nuta (Maierson) **[F1]**)
454. MAYERSOHN Hana 40 **[B]** Anny **[D]** Ana Hanny **[E]** Anna 39 **[F1]** (MAIERSON Hana **[A]** MAZERSOHN Anny 40 **[C]**)
455. MAYERSOHN Henry 43 **[B]** Harry **[C] [D] [E] [F]** (MAIERSON Henry **[A]**)
456. MEIROVICI Simon **[D]**
457. MENDELOVICI Haia 45 **[A] [F]** Clara **[B] [C] [D] [E]**
458. MENDELSOHN Eduard 29 **[A] [B] [C] [D] [E] [F]**
459. MERLAUB I. Moritz 37 **[A]** Moritz Ing. **[C]** Moritz **[E]** Moritz Ignat **[D]** Ignat Moritz (Titi) **[F1]** (MECRLAUB Moritz **[B]**)
460. MIHALOVICI Alterescu 45 **[A] [B] [D] [F]** (MIHAILOVICI Alterescu **[C] [E]**)
461. MIHALOVICI Dorel 17 **[A] [C] [D] [F]** (MIHAILOVICI Dorel **[B] [E]**)
462. MIHALOVICI Prima 40**[A]** Frima **[B] [D]** Prima or Frima **[F1]** (MIHAILOVICI Frima **[C] [E]**)
463. MINDIRIGIU Aurica 35 **[B] [D]** 34 **[F]** (MOCHIEN Aurica **[A]** MINDIRGIU Aur. Nahima 35 **[C]** MANDRIGIU Aurica **[E]**)
464. MINDIRIGIU Nachim Naftuli 41 **[B]** Nahum Naftuli **[D]** Nahum-Naftuli (Tuli) 40 **[F]** (MOCHIEN Naftuli **[A]** MINDIRGIU Nahum Naftuli 41 **[C]** MANDRIGIU Nahum Naftali **[E]**)
465. MITRANI Ionel 24 **[B]** Ionel (Nelu) **[F]** (METRANI Ionel **[A]** MITRANY Ionel **[C] [D]** Ionel Ithac **[E]**)
466. MOISE Ciprut **[A]** I. Ciprut 29 **[B] [C] [E]** MOISE Ciprut or CIPRUT Moise 28 **[F1]**
467. MOISESCU Frusina 38 **[A] [B] [C] [D] [E] [F]**
468. MOISESCU Iosif 44 **[A] [B] [C] [D] [E] [F]**
469. MOISESCU Mircea 10 **[A] [B] [C] [D] [E]** Iosif **[F]**
470. MOISESCU Nelu 13 **[A]** Velu **[B]** Nelu **[C] [D] [E] [F]**
471. MULER Mintia **[A]** (MUELLER Mintea 29 **[D] [E]** MULLER Mintea 29 **[B] [C]** Muntea 30 **[F]**)
472. MUNBLAT Samuel 19 **[A] [F1]** (MONBLATT Samuel **[B]** MOHNBLSTT Samuel **[C]** MONBLAT Samuel **[E]** MOHNBLATT Samuel **[D]**)
473. MUNTEANU Victor 26 **[A] [B] [C] [D] [E] [F]**

474. NACHMAN Estera 35 **[A] [B] [C] [E] [F]** (NAHMAN Estera **[D]**)
475. NACHMAN Lupu 39 **[A] [B] [C] [E] [F]** (NAHMAN Lupu **[D]**)

476. NACHMAN Mauriciu 21 [A] [C] [E] [F] (NAHMAN Mauriciu [B] [D])
477. NACHT Oscar 34 [A] [C] [D] [E] [F1] Oskar [B]
478. NADLER Albert [A] 30 [B] [C] [D] [E] 29 [F]
479. NADLER Iosef [A] 26 [B] Iosif 26 [C] [D] [E] 25 [F]
480. NADLER Marcel 33 [A] A. Marcel [C] [D] [E] [F1] H. Marcel [B]
481. NADLER Marcela [A] 26 [F]
482. NADLER Rosa 19 [A] [C] [E] Roza [D] Roza & Roza [F1](NAVLU Roza [B])
483. NAGY Mauriciu [A] (NAGI Mauriciu 16 [B] NAGHI Mauriciu 18 [C] [D] [E] 16 [F])
484. NAHIM Ionel 41 [F1] (NAHUM Josub [A] Ionel Iosub 38 [C] [D] NACHIM Iosub [B] Ionel Iosub Iosef 42 [E])
485. NAHIM Clara 31 [F1] (NAHUM Clara [A] Marcus Coca 27 [C] Coca [D] NACHIM Clara [B] Marcus Coca Clara 31 [E])
486. NAHIM Bruna 12 [F1] (NAHUM Buna [A] Bruna 2 [C] [D] NACHIM B. Mina [B] V. Bruna 2 [E])
487. NAIMAN Solomon [A] 28 [C] [D] [E] 27 [F] (NARMAN Solomon 28 [B])
488. NATANSON Sami 29 [A] [F1] Samy [E] (NATHANSOHN Sami [B] NATANSOHN Sami [C] Samy [D])
489. NESTOITU Sara 54 [D] [E] (NESTOITER Sara [A] [B] NESTOIU Sara [C] NESTOITLER (NESTOITU) Sara [F1])
490. NEUBERGER Ghitea 34 [B] Ghitla [C] [D] [E] (NEUBERGHER Ghitea 33 [F] NENBERGHER Gitla [A])
491. NEUBERGER Louis 46 [B] [E] 45 [C] [D] (NEUBERGHER Louis 45 [F] NENBERGHER Sonia [A])
492. NEUBERGER Valentina 8 [C] [D] [E] Valentian [B] (NEUBERGHER Valentina 7 [F] NENBERGHER Valentina [A])
493. NULLMAN Heinrich 18 [C] [D] [E] Ghenrich 17 [F1] (NUHMAN Genvik [A] NULMAN Genric [B])
494. NULLMAN Isac 42 [C] [D] Ithaco [E] Isac 41 [F] (NUHMAN Isac [A] NULMAN Isac 42 [B])
495. NULLMAN Sara 37 [C] [D] [E] 36 [F] (NUHMAN Sara [A] NUL-MAN Sara 37 [B])
496. NURENBERG Mathilda 18 [A] Matiwa [B] Matilda [C] [E] Mathilda [F] (NUERENBEREG Matilda [D])
497. NUSSBAUM Andrei 19 [C] [D] [E] Andrei-Andronic [F] (NUSEL-MAN Andrei [A] NUSBAUM Andronic [B])
498. NUSSBAUM Berta 53 [B] 54 [C] [D] [E] 53 [F] (NUSELMAN Berta [A])

499. ORMEANU Goldenberg Otto 46 **[C] [E]** Otto **[B]** (ORNEANU Goldenberg Otto **[D]** ORINEANU (GOLDENBERG) Otto 45 **[F1]**)

500. OSFELD Isac 25 **[E]** (OSTFELD Isac **[B] [C] [D] [F]** OSWALD Isac **[A]**)

501. PAUCKER Jean Leonard 27 **[B]** Jean Leonardo **[C] [D] [E]** (PAUKER Jean-Leonard 26 **[F]**)

502. PAUKER Rebeca Rifca 29 **[E]** (PAUCKER Rebeca 29 **[B] [C] [D]** 26 **[F1]**)

503. PEISIS Iosef 28 **[A]** Iosif **[D] [E] [F]** (PEISSIS Iosef **[B]** PAISIS Iosif **[C]**)

504. PENCOVICI Leon 16 **[B] [C] [D] [E]** Abraham **[F1]** (DENCOVICI Leon Avram **[A]**)

505. PERITZ Aneta **[A]** Anuta 30 **[F1]** (PERETZ Anutza 31 **[B] [E]** Anuta **[C] [D]**)

506. PERITZ Avram **[A]** 35 **[F1]** (PERETZ Avram 34 **[B] [C] [D] [E]**)

507. PERLMUTER Sara 17 **[A]** (PERLMUTTER Sarah **[B]** Sara **[C] [D] [E] [F]**)

508. PESCARU Iancu **[A]** 41 **[B]** 21 **[C] [D]** 42 **[E] [F1]**

509. PESCARU Sura 39 **[A] [B] [C] [D]** Sura-Sira **[E] [F1]**

510. PESKARIU Isac (Iancu) 25 **[F1]**

511. PICHER Friderich 51 **[A]** Friederick **[F1]** (PICKER Friederichi **[B]** Fridrich **[C] [D]** Friedrich **[E]**)

512. PICHER Herbert Fani **[A]** Fani 26 **[F1]** (PICKER Fany 27 **[B] [C] [D]** Fani **[E]**)

513. PICHER Herbert Iulius **[A]** Herbert-Julius 27 **[F1]** (PICKER Herbert Iulius 28 **[B] [D]** Herb. Iulius **[C] [E]**)

514. PICHER Marcel **[A]** (PICKER Marcel 31 **[B] [D] [E]** 16 **[F1]**)

515. PICHER Marian-Silvia 17 **[A]** Nir-Silvia **[F1]** (PICKER Miriam Sylora **[B]** Mir. Silvia **[C] [E]** Miriam Silvia **[D]**)

516. PICHER Roza **[A]** 43 **[F1]** (PICKER Roza 45 **[B] [D]** Rosa **[C] [E]**)

517. PINCU Herscu 40 **[A] [C] [D] [E] [F]** Hersen **[B]**

518. PINCU Iosefina 39 **[A] [B] [C] [D] [E]** Josefina **[F]**

519. PINCU Liviu 9 **[A] [C] [D] [E] [F]** Livin **[B]**

520. PITARU Ghizela 39 **[A] [B] [C] [D] [E] [F]**

521. PITARU Sulem 41 **[A]** Solomon **[B] [C]** Sol. Sulem **[E]** Sulim **[F]** (PITARU Solomon & PESCARU Solomon **[D]**)

522. PLAIN Denise (Pusa) 5 **[F]** Denis 6 **[B]** (PLEIN Denise (Pusa) **[D]**)

523. PLAIN Jacob 32 **[B]** Iacob **[F]** (PLEIN Iacob **[D]**)

524. PLAIN Nehama (Anisoara) 31 **[F]** Nehana **[B]** (PLEIN Hana (Anisoara) **[D]**)

525. PLATZMAN Adrian 14 [B] [C] [D] [E] 13 [F] (DLATZMAN Adrian [A])
526. PLATZMAN Moritz 43 [B] [C] [D] [E] [F] (DLATZMAN Moritz [A])
527. PLATZMAN Sofia 39 [C] [D] [E] 29 [F1] Sophie 39 [B] (DLATZMAN Sofia [A])
528. POMERANTZ I. Carol [A] 28 [B] Carol [C] [D] [E] (POMETANT I. Carol 27 [F])
529. POPLINGHER Alfred 18 [D] [E] [F] (POPELINGHER Adolf [A] POPLINGER Alfred [B] POLINGHER Alfred [C])
530. PRIKFER Marcel [A] (GRIEFER Marcel 22 [B] PRIFER Marcel 31 [C] [D] 22 [E] [F1])

531. RABINOVICI Arnold [A] 28 [B] [E] 21 [C] [D] [F]
532. RABINOVICI Ida 21 [A] [B] [C] [D] [E] [F]
533. RACHTER Bella 19 [A] (ROTTER Bela [B] [C] [D] [E] RATLER Bela [F1])
534. RADER H. Iehil 43 [A] Ichil [B] [C] [D] Ihil Ilia [E] Ilia [F1]
535. RADULESCU Misu 20 [A] [B] [C] [D] [E] RADULESCU (ROSEN-BERG) Misu [F1]
536. RAZMILEN F. Avram [A] (RADZWILLER Avram 35 [B] [E] RADZI-WILLER Avram 35 [C] Avram & Benny [D] RADZIVILLER Avram 34 [F])
537. RAZMILEN Mina [A] (RADZWILLER Nina 27 [B] [E] RADZI-WILLER Nina 27 [C] [D] RADZIVILLER Nina (Back-Flax) 25 [F])
538. RECHTMAN Dela [A] Perla 39 [B] [D] [E] 35 [F1] (RACHTMAN Perla 39 [C])
539. RECHTMAN Iacob 38 [A] [D] [E] [F] Jacob [B] (RACHTMAN Iacob [C])
540. RECHTMAN Moni 8 [A] [B] Tony [D] Toni-Moni [E] [F] (RACHT-MAN Tony [C])
541. REICHMAN Clara [A] 31 [B] [C] [D] [E] 30 [F]
542. REICHMAN Henta 67 [A] [B] [C] [D] [E] (RECHTMAN Henta [F1])
543. REICHMAN Moritz 32 [A] [B] [C] [D] [E] (RECHTMAN Misu [F1])
544. REICHMAN Silvia 28 [A] [B] [C] [D] [E] (RECHTMAN Silvia [F1])
545. REINSTEIN Alfred 22 [A] [B] [C] [D] [E] [F]
546. RETER David 35 [A] (RETTER David [B] David Vicu [C] RITTER David [D] REITER David Icu [E] David (Vicu) [F])
547. RETTER Bruno 20 [A] (ROTTER Bruno [B] Bruno Alfred [C] [D] [E] [F])

548. RINTZLER Fany [A] Fani 38 [B] 42 [E] Fanny 38 [C] [D] [F]

549. RINTZLER M. Aviel 46 [A] Aron [B] Arnold [C] [D] Arnold Aron [E] M. Arnold (Ariel) [F]

550. ROMAN Francisc 20 [A] (RISMAN Francisc [B] ROSMAN Francisc [C] [D] [E] [F])

551. ROSEN Hugo 28 [A] Hugues [B] Hugo [C] [E] (ROSE Hughes-Hugo [F] ROSEN Hugo & ROSSEL Hugo [D])

552. ROSENBERG Dana [A] 21 [C] [D] Dana (Paulus) 21 [E] Diana 19 [F] (ROSEMBERG Palina 21 [B])

553. ROSENBERG Elisabetha [A] Elisabeta 50 [C] [D] [E] Elisabeta 49 [F] (ROSEMBERG Elizabeta 50 [B])

554. ROSENBERG Maria 12 [A] [C] [D] [E] [F] (ROSEMBERG Maria [B])

555. ROSENBERG Simon [A] Simion 54 [C] [D] [E] 53 [F1] (ROSEM-BERG Simion 54 [B])

556. ROSENFELD Marcel 15 [A] [B] [C] [D] [E] [F]

557. ROSENTZWEIG Aurica [A] (ROSENZWEIG Aurica 15 [B] [E] Aurica & Aurel [D] ROSENWEIG Aurica 15 [C] ROZENZWEIG Aurica 14 [F1])

558. ROSENTZWEIG Etty [A] (ROSENZWEIG Elly 15 [B] Etty [D] Etty [E] ROSENWEIG Etty 15 [C] ROZENZWEIG Etty 14 [F1])

559. ROSENTZWEIG Harry [A] (ROSENZWEIG Harry 17 [B] [D] Hary [E] ROSENWEIG Hary 17 [C] ROZENZWEIG Harry (Relu) 16 [F1])

560. ROSENTZWEIG Pincu [A] (ROSENZWEIG Pincu 47 [B] Pincu Pinhas [E] Pincu (Pinhas) & Polly [D] ROSENWEIT Pincu 47 [C] ROZEN-ZWEIG Pincu 46 [F1])

561. ROSENTZWEIG Solomon [A] (ROZENZWEIG Solomon 23 [B] ROSENWEIG Solomon 23 [C] ROSENZWEIG Solomon & Sidi [D] Solomon Bercu Dov [E] ROZENZWEIG S. Bercu (Dov) 31 [F1])

562. ROSENZWITT Solomon [A] 31 [D] [E] (ROSENZNITT Solomon [B] ROSENZWEIT Solomon [C] ROSENWITT Solomon 30 [F1])

563. ROTENBERG Saul [A] 23 [E] 21 [F] (ROTTENBERG Saul 21 [B] [C] [D])

564. ROTTMAN Iancu 21 [A] [C] [D] (ROTMAN Jancu [B] Iancu [E] [F])

565. ROTTMAN Sonia [A] 18 [C] [D] (ROITMAN Sonia [B] ROTMAN Sonia [E] 19 [F])

566. ROZEN Israel 25 [A] (ROSEN Israel [B] [C] [D] [E] Israel (Toto) [F])

567. ROZENTHAL Noel [A] (ROSENTHAL Noel 32 [B] [C] [D] [E] 31 [F])

568. ROZENTZWEIG Betty [A] (ROSENZWEIG Betty 39 [B] [C] [D] [E] ROZENZWEIG Betty [F1])

569. ROZNER Berl Bernard 52 [A] (ROSNER Bernard [B] [C] [D] [E] B. Bernard [F])

570. ROZNER Etty 51 [A] (ROSNER Ietti [E] Etty [B] [C] [D] [F])

571. RUBINSTEIN Figa 33 [A] Fanny [B] Fany [C] [D] Fani [E] Feigha (Fani) [F1]

572. RUBSEL Mihail 29 [B] [C] [D] [E] Mihai 28 [F1] (RUBSCH Michail [A])

573. SAFRAN Samuel [A] 19 [D] Samuel (Savian) Smil [E] Samuel-Savian (Smil) 20 [F1] (LAFRAN Samuel 19 [B] SEFRAN Samuel [C])

574. SAILOVSCHI Ella 25 [B] [C] [D] [F] (SAILOFSCHI Ella [A] SMILOVICI Ella [E])

575. SALAMOVICI Simon [A] (SALOMOVITZ (ZALMANOVICI) Simon 24 [E] SALAMOVITZ Saimon 24 [B] Simon [C] Simon & ZAL-MANOVICI Simon [D] SALMOVITZ Zaimon (Simon) 23 [F1])

576. SAMUEL Leopold 34 [A] [B] [C] [D] Leopold (Leibi) [F1] Leopold Lebi [E]

577. SAPIRO B. Mayer 21 [E] B. Meer [B] B. Maier [C] M. Maier [D] (SCHAPIROV or SAPIROV Meir (Michey) 20 [F1])

578. SCHACHTER Blima 42 [B] Bluma [C] [E] (SCHATRE Blima [A] SCHAECHTER Bluma [D] Blima [F1])

579. SCHACHTER Burah 44 [B] [E] Burach [C] (SCHATRE Burah [A] SCHAECHTER Burach [D] Burah [F1])

580. SCHACHTER Charlotte 35 [B] [C] (HERSU Charlotte [A] SCHECHTER Charlotte 35 [E] SCHAECHTER Charlotta [D] Charlotte (Tita) 39 [F1])

581. SCHACHTER Clara 11 [C] Claris [E] (SCHECHTER Claris [A] Cudris 11 [B] SCHAECHTER Claris [D] 10 [F1])

582. SCHACHTER Eugen 7 [B] Eug. Iancu [C] Eugen Iancu [E] (SCHA-TRE Eugen [A] SCHAECHTER Eugen Iancu [D] [F1])

583. SCHACHTER H. Calman H. 40 [B] Kalman Hahamu [C] Herscu (Hahamu Calman) [E] (HESCU Kalman [A] SCHAECHTER Hers Kalman Hahamu [D] Herscu-Hahamu Calman (Colman) 39 [F1])

584. SCHACHTER Iosef 16 [B] [C] Iosef Haham [E] (SCHAECHTER Iosef [D] Haham-Iosif 20 [F1])

585. SCHACHTER Leon 26 [A] (SAHTER Leon [B] Leca [C] SCHAECHTER Leon [D] Leon-Leo [F1] SCHATER Leon [E])

586. SCHACHTER Max [A] 20 [B] [C] Max Marcel [E] (SCHACHTER Max 20 & SCHAECHTER Max [D] SCHAECHTER Marcel 19 [F])

587. SCHACHTER Riven Paul 46 **[E]** (SCHECHTER Riven Paul **[A]** Rivan Paul **[C]** Pincu Paul 46 **[B]** SCHAECHTER Rubin Paul **[D]** Paul (Pinhas) 45 **[F1]**)

588. SCHACHTER Ruhla 40 **[C]** **[E]** (SCHECHTER Rivala **[A]** Ruchla 40 **[B]** SCHAECHTER Ruhla (Rahel) **[D]** Ruhla 39 **[F1]**)

589. SCHACHTER Sura 22 **[A]** (SAHTER Sara **[B]** SACHTER Sara **[C]** **[E]** SCHAECHTER Sara **[D]** Sura-Sara **[F1]**)

590. SCHACHTER Titi **[C]** Tili 24 **[E]** (SCHAECHTER Cili **[D]** Tili or Cili 18 **[F1]**)

591. SCHAECHTER A. Leia 33 **[F]** (SCHATNER A. Leia **[A]**)

592. SCHAECHTER Francisca 20 **[D]** **[F]** (SCHACHTER Francisco **[A]** Francisca **[B]** **[C]** SCHAERF Francisca **[E]**)

593. SCHALICK Gerson 41 **[D]** **[E]** Gersun **[C]** (SALIC Gherson **[A]** SCHALICK & SALIC Gherson **[F1]** SALIK Gherson **[B]**)

594. SCHALICK Sonia 35 **[C]** **[D]** **[E]** (SALIC Sonia **[A]** SALIK Sonia **[B]** SCHALICK & SALIC Sonia **[F1]**)

595. SCHAPIRA Max 50 **[A]** **[E]** **[F]** (SAPIRO Max **[B]** **[C]** **[D]**)

596. SCHARF Clara 19 **[B]** **[C]** **[D]** (SCHERF Clara **[A]** SCHAERF Clara **[E]** **[F1]**)

597. SCHARF Nessi-Ita 56 **[B]** Ita Nessi **[C]** **[D]** (SCHERF Nesi-Ita **[A]** SCHAERF Ita Nessy **[E]** Nesia-Ita **[F1]**)

598. SCHARF Smil 57 **[B]** **[D]** Samil **[C]** (SCHERF Smil **[A]** SCHAERF Smil **[E]** **[F1]**)

599. SCHATTNER Abraham Leo 33 **[B]** **[D]** Abr. Leo 53 **[C]** (SCHATNER Abr. Leon 53 **[E]** SCHACHTER Leon & SCHATTNER Abraham-Leon 53 **[F1]**)

600. SCHATTNER Beno 30 **[B]** **[D]** **[E]** Benno 29 **[F1]** (SCHECHTER Beno **[A]** SCATTNER Beno 30 **[C]**)

601. SCHEMNITZ Ernest 28 **[B]** **[D]** **[E]** Ernst 27 **[F]** (SCHEMRITZ Ernest **[A]** SCHEMITZ Ernest 28 **[C]**)

602. SCHEMNITZ Mina 26 **[B]** 25 **[C]** **[D]** **[E]** 24 **[F]** (SCHEMRITZ Mina **[A]**)

603. SCHENKER Zecu Zecrand **[A]** Z. Zegrund **[E]** Z. Zegrand **[C]** **[D]** Z. Zeegrand **[F1]**

604. SCHERTZER Nicolae **[D]** **[E]** (SCHECHTER Nicolae **[A]** SCHETZER Nicolae **[C]** SCHERTER Nicolae 16 **[F]**)

605. SCHIFF Alexandru 25 **[B]** **[C]** **[D]** Alex **[E]** Alexandru (Alex) **[F1]** (SCHEIFF Alexandru **[A]**)

606. SCHIFF Eva 23 **[B]** **[C]** Eva (Hava) **[D]** Eva Hana **[E]** Evelyna (Eva Hava) **[F1]** (SCHEIFF Eva **[A]**)

607. SCHMATNIK Leo 39 **[B]** **[E]** **[F1]** (SCHMATRIC Leon **[A]** SCHMATICK Leo **[C]** SCHMATNICK Leo **[D]**)

608. SCHMATNIK Trily 40 **[E]** Trili **[B]** Trilli or Tili **[F1]** (SCHMATRIC Tili **[A]** SCHATNIK Trili **[C]** SCHMATNICK Trili **[D]**)

609. SCHMETTERLING Ernest Emanuel 19 **[B]** **[D]** **[E]** Emanuel-Ernst **[F1]** (SCHWATERLING Edust Emanuel **[A]** SCHMATTERLING Ernest Em. **[C]**)

610. SCHMETTERLING Frieda 49 **[B]** **[D]** **[E]** 42 **[F1]** (SCHWATER- LING Frida **[A]** SCHMATTERLING Frida 49 **[C]**)

611. SCHMETTERLING Marcu 62 **[B]** **[D]** **[E]** Marcus (Marcu) **[F1]** (SCHWATERLING Marcus **[A]** SCHMATTERLING Marcu **[C]**)

612. SCHMETTERLING Victor 22 **[B]** **[D]** **[E]** **[F]** (SCHWATERLING Victor **[A]** SCHMATTERLING Victor **[C]**)

613. SCHNAPP Erich Heinz (Uri Zwi) 20 **[E]** Heinz Erich 22 **[B]** Erich Heinz **[D]** (SCHNAPI Hentz Erlich **[A]** SCHAPP Herich Heinz 22 **[C]** SCHNAP Hans-Erich 21 (Uri-Zwi) **[F1]**)

614. SCHONBERGER A. Ladislau 21 **[B]** Ladislau **[C]** Ladisl. **[E]** (SCHOINBERGER A. Ladislau **[A]** SCHOENBERGER Ladislau **[D]** SCHOENBERG (ER) Ladislau 20 **[F1]**)

615. SCHONBERGER Pavel 26 **[B]** Pav. Dorel **[C]** **[E]** (ASCHOEN- BERGHER A. Dorel **[A]** SCHOENBERGER Pavel Dorel **[D]** SCHOENBERG (ER) Al. Paul-Dorel **[F1]**)

616. SCHONFELD Hugo 18 **[B]** **[C]** **[E]** (SCHANFELD Hugo **[A]** SCHOENFELD Hugo **[D]** **[F]**)

617. SCHOR Julieta 21 **[A]** Julietta **[B]** SCHOR HERSCOVICI Juliata **[C]** SCHOR HERSCOVICI Julieta **[D]** **[E]** SCHOR-HERSCOVICI Juli- etta **[F1]**

618. SCHTERNBERG Moritz Brukenstein **[A]** (STERNBERG M. Brucken- stein **[C]** **[D]** M. Buckenstein 19 **[E]** STERNBERG M. Brukenstein 43 **[F1]** STEMBERG Monty 42 **[B]**)

619. SCHWARTZ Avram **[A]** 30 **[B]** **[C]** **[D]** **[E]** 29 **[F]**

620. SCHWARTZ Clara **[A]** 33 **[B]** Clara Ghinsberg **[C]** **[D]** Clara Ghinzberg **[E]** Clara 32 **[F]**

621. SCHWARTZ Frieda 27 **[C]** **[D]** **[E]** Freida **[B]** Frieda 26 **[F]** Trida **[A]**

622. SCHWARTZ Haia 36 **[A]** **[B]** **[C]** **[D]** **[E]** **[F]**

623. SCHWARTZ Iosef Iancu 43 **[E]** Iosef Iancu & Iancu **[D]** Iosub **[B]** Ios. Iancu **[C]** Iancl **[A]** (SCHWARTZ or SFART Iosub-Iancu **[F1]**)

624. SCHWARTZ Marcu Alter **[A]** 27 **[C]** **[D]** Marcu Alter Mordehai 28 **[E]** Marcu-Alter (Mordchai) 29 **[F1]** (SCHWARZ Marcu Alter 27 **[B]**)

625. SCHWARTZ Miriam 1 **[A]** **[C]** **[D]** **[E]** **[F]** Miryam **[B]**

626. SCHWARTZ N. Lupu 20 **[A]** M. Lupu **[B] [C] [D] [E]** (SCHWART M. Lupu **[F]**)

627. SCHWARTZ Rebeca **[A]** Rebeca 28 **[C] [D]** Rebeca Betty **[E]** Rebecca (Becca Farchi) 28 **[F1]** (SCHWARZ Rebacca 28 **[B]**)

628. SCHWARTZ Solomon 37 **[A] [B] [D] [E] [F]** (SCHORTZ Sol. **[C]**)

629. SCHWARTZ Sorin **[A]** 5 months **[B] [C] [D] [E]** 3 **[F1]**

630. SCHWARTZ Tamara 4 **[A] [B] [C] [D] [E] [F]**

631. SCHWARTZ Henriette 29 **[A] [B]** Titi Marcus **[C]** Henrietta Haia & Titi Marcus **[D]** Titi Marcus Herieta **[E]** (SCHWARTZ or SFART Henriette-Haia (Tili) **[F1]**)

632. SCHWARTZ Valentin 7 **[A] [B] [E]** Valentina **[C] [D]** (SCHWARTZ or SFART Valentin **[F1]**)

633. SCHWEIFEL Ana Sara 28 **[E]** Ana Sura **[B] [C] [D]** Hana-Sura **[F]** (SCHWEIFELD Hana-Sura **[A]**)

634. SCHWEIFEL Manase Manole 31 **[E]** Manole (Menasa) **[F1]** Manasse **[B]** Manase **[C]** Manasse Manole **[D]** (SCHWEIFELD Manase **[A]**)

635. SCHWEIFEL S. Mircea 3 **[C] [E]** Mircea-Serban 3 **[B] [D]** 13 **[F]** (SCHWEIFELD Mircea Serban **[A]**)

636. SEGAL Clotilda 29 **[C]** 28 **[F]** (SEGALL Clotilda 29 **[B] [D]** Clotilda Clara **[E]** SILEN Matilda **[A]**)

637. SEGAL Filip 20 **[A] [B] [F]** (SEGALL Filip **[C] [D] [E]**)

638. SEGAL Hermina 29 **[A] [F]** (SEGALL Hermine **[B]** Herman **[C]** Hermina **[D] [E]**)

639. SEGAL Jeanetta 29 **[A]** Jeanette **[B]** Jeanette **[F1]** (SEGALL Janette **[C] [D]** Jeanette **[E]**)

640. SEGAL Jules 29 **[A] [B] [F]** (SEGALL Jules **[C] [D] [E]**)

641. SEGAL Lupu Ghizela 20 **[A]** Ghizela **[B] [F]** (SEGALL Ghizela **[C] [D] [E]**)

642. SEGAL Lupu Leibu 53 **[A]** Lina **[B]** Leiba **[F]** (SEGALL Lupu Liba **[C] [E]** Liba (Lupu) **[D]**)

643. SEGAL Lupu Robert 25 **[A]** Robert **[B]** Lupu-Robert **[F]** (SEGALL Robert **[C] [D] [E]**)

644. SEGAL P. Haim **[A]** 31 **[F1]** (SEGALL Haim 30 **[B] [C] [D] [E]**)

645. SEGAL Saul 33 **[A] [B] [F1]** (SEGALL Saul **[C] [D] [E]**)

646. SEGAL W. Silen 29 **[F]** (SEGALL Silene 30 **[B]** Silens **[C]** Silena **[D] [E]** SILEN Wilhem Segal **[A]**)

647. SEGALESCU Henrietta 22 **[A]** Henriette **[B] [C] [D] [E] [F]**

648. SENATER Fredrich 22 **[B]** Friederich **[C]** Friedrich **[D]** Fridrich **[E]** Friedrich 22 or 53 **[F]** (SERATER Friederich **[A]**)

649. SIGMUND A. Iosef 21 **[B] [D] [E]** A. Josif 21 **[C]** 20 **[F]** Iozef **[A]**

650. SILBERBUSCH Gerhard 33 [D] [E] [F1] Gerh. [C] (SILBERBUS Gherhard [A] SILBERBUCH Gerhard [B])
651. SILBERMAN Eleonora 28 [B] [C] [D] [E] 27 [F] (LIBERMAN Eleonora [A])
652. SILBERMAN Rubin 32 [B] [C] [D] [E] 31 [F] (LIBERMAN Rubini [A])
653. SILBERSTEIN Gerson 36 [A] [E] Gherson [F1] Gherson [C] (SIEBER-STEIN Gherson [B] SILBERMAN Gherson [D])
654. SILVIAN D. Emil 28 [A] [B] [C] [D] [E] [F]
655. SILVIAN Maxim [A] 28 [B] [C] [D] [E] 27 [F]
656. SIMON B. Simon 42 [A] [B] [C] [D] [E] [F]
657. SIMON I. Carolina known as STILOVICI 30 [A] Carolina [B] SIMON (STRULOVICI) Carola [C] [E] [F] SIMON Carola STRULOVICI [D]
658. SIMON I. Iosef known as STILOVICI 30 [A] Iosef [B] SIMON STRULOVICI Ficu [C] SIMON (STRULOVICI) Ficu Iosef [E] Iosif (Ficu) STRULOVICI [D] Iosif-Ficu (STRULOVICI) [F]
659. SIMON Lucian 19 [A] [B] [C] [D] [E] [F1]
660. SIMON Moise [A] 26 [B] Misu [C] [D] Misu-Mose [E] Moise (Misu) 25 [F1]
661. SIMON Pesta 32 [A] Pesla [B] Pepi [C] [D] Pepi Pesia [E] Pesta [F]
662. SIN Smial Smaia 34 [B] Smaia Smil [C] [D] [E] (SIN SMAIA Smil 20 [F1] SNI Smaia Smil [A])
663. SLOIMOVICI Emanuel 19 [B] [E] Emanuel (Manole) [F1] Emanoil [C] [D] (SOLOMOVICI Emanuel [A])
664. SLOIMOVICI Peisah Iacob 30 [A] Peisich (Jacob) [B] Peis Iacob [C] [E] Pesah Iacob [D] Peisic-Iacob [F]
665. SLOMOVICI Maria [A] 39 [F] (SLOIMOVICI Maria 29 [B] [C] [D] [E])
666. SLOMOVICI Rosa 16 [A] Riza (Roza) [F] (SLOIMOVICI Roza [B] [D] Rosa [C] [E])
667. SLOMOVICI Smil 15 [A] Saul (Smil) [F] (SLOIMOVICI Smil [B] [C] [D] [E])
668. SMIL Israel [A] 28 [B] [C] [D] [E] [F1]
669. SMIL Rifca [A] 29 [B] [C] [D] [E] 27 [F]
670. SMILOVICI Ana 20 [A] [B] [D] [F] Anna [C] [E]
671. SMILOVICI Beno 26 [B] [D] [E] [F] Bano [C] Neno [A]
672. SMILOVICI Burah 37 [E] [F] Burach [C] [D]
673. SMILOVICI Ida [A] 39 [B] 45 [C] [D] [E] 38 [F]
674. SMILOVICI Leonard 44 [B] [C] [D] [E] [F1] Leobard [A]
675. SMILOVICI Nora 17 [A] [B] [C] [D] [E] [F]
676. SOLOMON David Lazar [A] 23 [B] David Lazar [C] [E] 22 [F] Dov Lazar [D]

677. SOLOMON Dorel 20 **[B] [C] [D]** Dorel C.**[E]** Doru **[F]** Docelu **[A]**
678. SOLOMON Efraim **[D]**
679. SOLOMON Virgiliu 17 **[A]** Virgil **[B] [C] [D] [E]** Virgiliu **[F1]**
680. SONNENREICH Abram 33 **[F]** Adolf (Abraham) **[D]** (ZONENRAICH Avram **[A]** SONENRAICH Avram **[B]** Adolf **[C] [E]**)
681. SONNENREICH Rasela 30 **[F]** Rahel Rica **[D]** (ZONENRAICH Rachela **[A]** SONENRAICH Rachela **[B]** Rica Rahel **[E]** Sica Rasela 40 **[C]**)
682. SONNENREICH Sami 3 **[F]** Samilica **[D]** (ZONENRAICH Samuel **[A]** SONENRAICH Sami **[B]** Samilica **[C]** Sami Lica **[E]**)
683. SPAHARIU Dvoira 18 **[A]** Dvora **[B] [C] [D]** Dvora (Ciobotaru) **[E]** (Ciobotaru) Dvoire **[F1]**
684. SPEISER L. Bernard 20 **[B] [C] [D] [E]** 18 **[F1]** (SPISER Bernard **[A]**)
685. SPIEGEL Avram 41 **[A] [B] [C] [D] [E] [F]**
686. SPIEGEL Clonde-Claudia 5 **[A] [F]** Claude **[B] [C] [D] [E]**
687. SPIEGEL Lena **[A]** Etty Enta 36 **[B]** Etty **[C]** Etti (Enta) **[D]** Ietti **[E]** Seine (Lena, Etty) 38 **[F1]**
688. SPIEGEL Mauriciu 7 **[B] [C] [D] [E] [F]** Marincu **[A]**
689. SPIEGEL Soliem **[A]** 11 **[F]** Solien **[C]** Solian **[D]** Solion **[E]** Solein 36 **[B]**
690. SPIRER Basil-Julian 16 **[F1]** Bus Iulian **[E]** Basil-Jubal **[A]** (SPIERER Basil Iulian **[B] [D]** Bas. Iulian **[C]**)
691. SPIRER Rudolfina **[A]** 49 **[E]** 48 **[F]** (SPIERER Rudolfina 49 **[B]** SPERER Rudolfina **[C] [D]**)
692. SPIRER Samuel 52 **[E]** Iosif-Samuel 51 **[F]** (SPIRED Iosef **[A]** SPIERER Samuel Iosif 52 **[B]** Samuel 32 **[C]** Samuel-Iosef **[D]**)
693. SPIVACK Avram 32 **[B]** Avram-Iancu **[D] [F]** Avr. Iancu 32 **[C]** 33 **[E]** (SOLUVAC Iancu **[A]**)
694. STAHL Desideriu 19 **[B] [D] [E] [F]** Dizideriu **[C]** (SAHL Dezideri **[A]**)
695. STAHL Jacques 32 **[B] [D] [F]** Jaques **[C] [E]** (SCHTHAL S. Jaques **[A]**)
696. STAROSTE Ester 44 **[E]** 47 **[C] [D]** (STAROSTA Ester **[B]** LUZER Estera **[A]** Ester-Leib 43 **[F]**)
697. STAROSTE Lazar (Eliezer) 60 **[E]** Luzer **[C]** Eliezer **[D]** (STAROSTA Luzer **[B]** LUZER Storesta **[A]** Starosta 61 **[F]**)
698. STEIN I. Moise **[A]** 35 **[E]** 34 **[F]** Moise 35 **[C] [D]** (STERN Moise **[B]**)
699. STEINBACH Reica 26 **[B] [D]** Raica **[E]** Ruca 28 **[F]** (STAINBACH Ruha **[A]** SZEINBACH Reica **[C]**)
700. STEINBACH Leo Henry 26 **[B] [E]** L. Henri **[C]** L. Henry **[D] [F]** (STAINBACH Leon Henry **[A]**)
701. STERNBERG Manole 17 **[A] [C] [D] [E]** Menelas **[F]** (STENBERG Menelas **[B]**)
702. STIER Anisoara 8 months **[B] [C] [D] [E] [F]** (STEIER Anisoara **[A]**)

703. STIER Etty 21 [B] [C] [D] Etti [E] Ietty [F1] (STEIER Ietty [A])
704. STIER Samuel 31 [B] [C] [D] [E] A. Samuel [F1] (STEIER Samuel [A])
705. STORFER Norbert 22 [A] [B] [C] [D] Norbert Bubi [E] [F]
706. STORFER Saul 31 [E] (STOFER Saul [A] STOFFER Saul [B] [D] Saul (Titel) [F1] STEFFER Saul [C])
707. STRAUSS Elisabeta [A] 32 [B] [D] [E] Elisabeth 31 [F1] (STARUSS Elisabeta 32 [C])
708. STRAUSS Israel Walter [A] Walter Israel [D] Israel-Walter 29 [F1] STRAUSS Walter Israel & WALTER Isr. Straus 31 [E] (WALTER Israel Strauss [B] Isr. Strauss [C])
709. SUCHARD William 30 [B] Iulia [C] Iulian [D] [E] Julian or William [F1] (SUHARA Iulian [A])
710. SUCHARD Sonia 27 [F] Loive 22 [B] Serna [C] [E] Cerna [D] (SUHARA Sonia [A])
711. SULIMOVICI N. Iosefleib 19 [A] Iosef [E] Iosef (Iosca) [D] Iosif (Iosca) [F] (SEILIMOVICI Iosif [B] SALOMOVICI Iosif [C])
712. SULIMOVICI Rebeca [A] Rebecca 32 [B] Rebeca [C] [D] Rebeca-Beca 33 [E] Rebecca (Becca) 32 [F1]
713. SULIMOVICI Sami [A] Samy 33 [B] Sami 32 [C] [D] 33 [E] 32 [F]
714. SULITEANU Moritz 25 [A] [D] S. Moritz [C] [E] Morit (Moise) [F1] (SULITZEANU Mortiz S. [B])
715. SUREI Moritz [C] [D] 18 [E] Morit [F] (SNEI Moritz [A] LUZEI Moritz [B])

716. TALISMAN David 17 [A] [B] [C] [D] [E] [F]
717. TAUBER Ana 38 [F] (TOMBLER Ana [A] TAMBER Ana 33 [B] [C] [D] TOMBER Ana [E])
718. TECUCEANU Isac 22 [B] [C] [D] [E] [F] Iosif [A]
719. TENENBAUM Leo 28 [A] [E] (TAVENBAUM Leo [B] TENNEN-BAUM Leo [C] [D] [F])
720. TERCATIN Itzhac (Puiu) 26 [E] Isac-Ithac (Puiu) [F] (TERKATINI Isac [A] TEREATIN Isac 25 [B] TREKASTIN Isac [C] TERKATIN Isac [D])
721. TERKEL Fania 24 [C] [D] [E] [F] (TERCHEL Fania [A] TERCKEL Lavria [B])
722. TERKEL Lazar 26 [C] [D] [E] [F] (TERCHEL Lazar [A] TERCKEL Lazar [B])
723. TETTELZWEIG Ana [D] 26 [E] [F] 25 [C] (TOTELZWIG Ana [A] TETELZWERG Ana 26 [B])

724. TETTELZWEIG Isac 30 **[C] [D] [E]** 29 **[F]** (TITELZWEIG Isac **[A]** TETELZWERG Isac **[B]**)
725. TZIMAND Jack **[A]** Jacques 25 **[B]** 24 **[E]** Jaques **[C]** Jacques **[D]** Jacques (Jili) **[F]**
726. TZIMAND Saul 23 **[F]**

727. UNGAR Albert 20 **[A] [B] [C] [D] [E]** (UGAR Albert **[F1]**)

728. VOGEL Carol 43 **[B] [D] [E] [F]** 41 **[C]** (WOGEL Carol **[A]**)

729. WACHTEL Jova 21 **[E]** Jojo **[C]** Zopa (Jojo) **[F]** M. Iosia **[A]** (WACHTELL Zozo **[B]** WACHTER Jojo **[D]**)
730. WAGNER Regina 49 **[E]** Reghina **[B] [D]** Rechina **[C]** (WEGNER Reghina **[F1]**)
731. WAGNER Walter 21 **[B]** Walt. Israel **[C]** Walter-Israel **[D]** Welt Israel **[E]** (WEGNER Walter-Israel **[F1]**)
732. WAGNER Wilhem Israel 49 **[A]** Wilhelm **[B]** Wilh. Israel **[C]** Wilhelm Israel **[D]** (WEGNER Wilhem-Israel **[F1]**)
733. WALTER Elisa 33 **[F]** Eliza **[B] [C] [D]** Elias **[E]** (MAURICIU Elisa **[A]**)
734. WALTER Mauriciu 33 **[B] [C] [D] [E] [F]** (MAURICIU Walter **[A]**)
735. WALTER Mignon 5 **[C] [D] [E]** 4 **[F]** Mingon 5 **[B]** (MAURICIU Mignon **[A]**)
736. WASSERMAN Toby **[A]** Tobi 22 **[C] [E]** Tobi-Tobias 19 **[D] [F]** (WASSERMANN Fobi 22 **[B]**)
737. WECHSLER Elias 30 **[C] [D]** 31 **[E]** 29 **[F]** (WEXLER Elias **[A]** WEC-SLER Elias 30 **[B]**)
738. WECHSLER Etty Iehudith 21 **[E]** Etty **[C] [D] [F]** (WEXLER Etty **[A]** WECSLER Etty **[B]**)
739. WEINBERG Avram **[C] [D] [E]**
740. WEINBERG Clara **[A]** 22 **[B] [C] [D]** Clara Beatrice Bety **[E]** Clara 29 **[F]**
741. WEINBERG Moise Aron **[D] [E]** 21 **[C]**
742. WEINBERG Natan 29 **[A] [B] [C] [D] [E] [F]**
743. WEINBERG Rubin Dudi 30 **[E]** Rubin **[B] [C] [D]** Rubin (Dudu) 29 **[F]** Rubini **[A]**

744. WEINGARTEN Avram-Ida [A] [D] Avr. Ida 22 [C] [E] Armide 26 [F1] (WENIGARTEN Aivamivec 22 [B])

745. WEINGARTEN Beniamin 18 [C] [D] [E] [F] Benjamin [B] Meir-Beniamin [A]

746. WEINGARTEN Meir [A] 53 [F] Meyer 52 [B] Aazer [C] Mayer [D] [E]

747. WEINGARTEN Tipora [D] 51 [E] Tifia [B] Tipra [C] Tipra 52 [F] Tipra [A]

748. WEINSTEIN A. Simon 25 [A] Simon [C] [D] [E] [F] (WANSTEIN Simon [B])

749. WEINSTEIN Iosef [A] Iosif 23 [B] Iosef [C] [D] [E] Iosif 29 [F1]

750. WEINSTEIN Moritz 25 [A] [C] [D] [E] [F] (WANSTEIN Mintz [B])

751. WEINTRAUB Julian 38 [E] Julius [B] Iul. Iuli [C] Iulius-Iulian [D] Julius-Julian [F] Iulian [A]

752. WEISS Avram 29 [A] [B] [D] [E] Abraham [F] (WEIS Avram [C])

753. WEISS Maria [A] 26 [B] [C] [D] [E] 21 [F1]

754. WEISS Paul 3 [A] [B] [C] [D] [E] [F]

755. WEISSBERG Hedwig 33 [E] 38 [F] Hedvig [D] (WEINBERG Herlich [A] VEISBERG Hedwig 33 [B] WEISBERG Hedvig [C])

756. WEISSBERG Rudolf [D] 39 [E] 38 [F] (WEINBERG Rudolf [A] VEIS-BERG Rudolf 39 [B] WEISBERG Rudolf [C])

757. WEISSLER Marcu 26 [B] [D] [E] [F] (WASHER Marcu [A] WEISLER Marcu [C])

758. WEITMAN Avram 23 [B] [C] [D] [E] Avram (Mielu) [F] (WEITZ-MAN Avram [A])

759. WEITRAUB Leon 19 [A] [E] Leon-Lulu [F] (WEINTRAUB Leo [B] [C] Leon-Lulu [D])

760. WITENBERG Simon 28 [A] (WITTENBERG Simon [B] [C] [D] WITTENBERG Simon [E])

761. WOLFSHAUT Hans 28 [C] [D] [E] 27 [F] (WOLFSCHANT Hans [A] WOLFSHANT Hanz 28 [B])

762. ZAHARIA Marcu 34 [B] [C] [D] [E] [F] (MAROUS Zaharia [A])

763. ZALMANOVICI Saul 28 [B] [C] [D] [E] [F] A. Smil [A]

764. ZEITS Bendit 44 [C] [D] [E] (BENDIT Zait [A] ZAITZ Bendit [B] [F1])

765. ZEITS Rebeca 17 [C] [D] [E] (BENDIT Reveca [A] ZAITZ Reveca 26 [B] Reveka [F1])

766. ZEITS Sara 45 [C] [D] [E] (BENDIT Sara [A] ZAITZ Sara [B] Sarah [F1])

767. ZELLERMAYER Carol 36 [C] [D] 29 [F1] (ZELERMAYER Carol [A] ZELLER Mayer Carol 38 [B] ZOLLERMAYER Carol [E])

768. ZELLERMAYER Gustav 36 [C] Gusta 28 [D] [F] (ZELERMAYER Gusta [A] ZELLER Mayer Gusta 36 [B] ZOLLERMAYER Gustav [E])

769. ZIGHELMAN Andrei-Puiu 6 [E] Andrei [D] (ZIGELMAN Andrei [F] SIEGELMAN Andrei [A] [B] ZIEGELMAN Andei [C])

770. ZIGHELMAN Solomon [D] I. Solomon 36 [E] (SIEGELMAN Solomon [A] Solomon E. [B] ZIGELMAN I. Solomon [F] ZIEGELMAN Solomon [C])

771. ZIGHELMAN Rasela 31 [C] [D] Rashela [E] (ZIGELMAN Rasela (Coca) 32 [F] SIEGELMAN Rachela [A] 31 [B])

772. ZILBERMAN Burah [A] Burach Arh. [C] Burah 37 [F1] Baruch Arh. [D] Baruch [E] (SILBERMAN Burah [B])

773. ZILBERMAN Frida [A] Frieda [C] [D] Frida Frederica 29 [E] Frieda [F] (SILBERMAN Freida [B])

774. ZILBERMAN Isac 18 [A] [F] (SILBERMAN Isac [B] [C] [D] [E])

775. ZILBERMAN Pinhas 24 [A] [D] Penchas [B] [C] Pinhas Alterica [E] Pinchas [F1]

776. ZILBERMAN Rebeca [A] [C] [D] 60 [F1] 70 [E]

777. ZILBERMAN Silvia [A] [C] [D] 29 [E] 24 [F] (SILBERMAN Silvia 24 [B])

778. ZISMAN Sura 58 [A] Sofia Sura [E] (ZISSMAN Sura [B] Sofia [C] Sofia-Sara [D] ZISSMAN or ZUSSMAN Sura (Sofia) [F])

779. ZISMAN Zisu Rebeca [A] Rebeca [E] (ZISSMAN Z. Rebeca [C] [D] ZISMAN or ZISU Rebeca 29 [F1])

780. ZISSU P. Avram [A] Avram 30 [B] Avram Codel [D] Avr. Godel [E] Avram-Godel [C] 29 [F]

781. ZOTKOVER Louis 21 [E] (ZOLKIVER Louis [B] [C] ZOLLKOVER Louis [D] JOLCOVER Louis [F1] ZALHIVED Lonis [A])

Table 2.

THE CREW OF THE STRUMA

1. DIKOF Lazar Ivanof, Chief Mate (Bulgarian) [C] [D] [E] 46 [F1]
2. EGER Golda (Jewish) [C] [D] [E] [F1]
3. GARABATENKO Grigor Tomofei, Captain (Bulgarian) [C] Grigor

Tomofef **[D]** (GARABETENKO Grigor Tomofef **[E]** GARBATENCO Grigor-Timofef 42 **[F1]**)
4. GARABEDOF Florsep (Bulgarian) **[C]** Florsed **[D]** (CARABADOF Florsop **[E]** GARABIDOF Horsrp 39 **[F1]**)
5. HILSENRAD Thea 22 (Jewish) **[C]** **[D]** **[E]** **[F1]**
6. KOMLOS Tiberiu (Hungarian) **[C]** **[D]** **[E]** (KOLOMOSH Tiberiu 25 **[F1]**)
7. MALTEF Blagoy Atanasov (Bulgarian) **[C]** Blagoy Atanasof **[D]** **[E]** (BLAGOY Atanasof-Maltef 46 **[F1]**)
8. MOLNAR Nadar (Jewish?) 22 **[A]** Nandor **[C]** **[D]** (MAHLER Nador or MALLER Lothar **[F1]**
9. SOLOMON Alfred (Jewish) 26 **[C]** **[D]** **[E]** **[F1]**
10. STATANOF Daminian (Bulgarian) **[C]** Damion **[D]** **[E]** Damian 31 **[F1]**

Table 3.

PASSENGERS ALLOWED TO LEAVE THE *STRUMA* IN ISTANBUL

1. BRETSCHNEIDER Benimin Fedor 21 **[A]** Theodor Benjamin **[B]** Benjamin Theodor 21 **[F1]** (BRETTSCHNEIDER Beniamin Teodor **[C]**)
2. FRENK David 19 **[B]** (FRENCK David **[C]** FRENC David **[A]** **[F1]**)
3. FRENK Israel 25 **[B]** (FRENCK Israel **[C]** FRENC Israel **[A]** **[F1]**)
4. FRENK Tivia 24 **[B]** (FRENCK Tevia **[C]** FRENC Tina **[A]** **[F1]**)
5. GEFFNER or GHEFNER Emanuel 27 **[B]** Emanoil 27 **[F1]** (GEFNER Emanuel **[A]** CHEFNER Emanoil **[C]**)
6. SALAMOWITZ Mede or SALAMOVITZ Medea 22 **[B]** (SALAMOVICI Maria **[A]** Medeea **[C]** SALAMOVITZ Medea **[F1]**)
7. SEGAL Alexandru-Victor **[A]** son **[B]** M. child **[C]** Al. Victor 14 **[F1]**)
8. SEGAL Elvira **[A]** wife **[B]** M. wife **[C]** Elvira 35 **[F1]**)
9. SEGAL Martin **[B]** Saul **[A]** M. husband **[C]** Martin 34 **[F1]**

The Sole Survivor

STOLIAR David 19

Sources

We have endeavored to provide an accurate reconstruction of the events surrounding the voyage of the *Struma* and the diving expedition in 2000. We have relied on interviews with survivors from the *Struma* and participants in the diving expedition, interviews with other people with knowledge of the events, archives in Britain, Israel, Turkey, and the United States, and web sites, books, monographs, documentary films, and articles from newspapers and magazines. There is also an extensive bibliography.

Interviews with the following people were invaluable:

Izak Abudaram	Tudor Chefner
Ahmet Akarsu	Esther David
Ishak Alaton	Misha David
Samuel Aroni	David Dinari
Ismail Aslan	Murat Draman
Ami Atir	Rosemary Feenan
Elda Atir	Yosef Govrin
Izmit Ay	Rabbi Efraim Guttman
Rifat Bali	Rabbi Elhanan Ia'acov Josef Guttman
Tami Barak	Radu Ioanid
Itzhac Guttman Ben-Zvi	Joel Ives
Ruth Ben-Zvi	Simcha Jacobovici
Ilana Blum	Elena Kindler
Marta Brod	Hayim Eliezer Kohen
Greg Buxton	Teddy Kollek
Michael Buxton	Jonathon Lewis
Rabbi Suzanne Carter	Ambassador David Logan
Fritzi Chefner	Rabbi Barry Marcus

Miyriam Rintzler	Marda Stoliar
Ogen Rintzler	Bernard Tercatin
Betty Rosenblatt	Ruth Vichansky
Alexander Scarlat	Joseph Wechsler
David Stoliar	Levent Yuksel

The list of sources that follows is not all inclusive. We provide primary sources for each chapter and highlight critical documents, books, and articles. We offer this as a map for those who might follow our research and to give credit to the writers and researchers who came before us.

Prologue

INTERVIEWS: David Stoliar.

DOCUMENTS: Statement of David Stoliar, May 3, 1942, to police in Jaffa, Palestine, Yad Vashem Archives (YVA), Jerusalem.

Chapter One

INTERVIEWS: Greg Buxton, Michael Buxton.

BOOKS: Wasserstein, Bernard. *Britain and the Jews of Europe 1939–1945.* Second Edition. London and New York: Leicester University Press, published in association with the Institute for Jewish Policy Research, 1999.

Chapter Two

INTERVIEWS: Radu Ioanid, D. Stoliar.

BOOKS: Aliav, Ruth and Peggy Mann. *The Last Escape.* London: Coronet Books, 1975. Bauer, Yehuda. *American Jewry and the Holocaust: The American Jewish Joint Distribution Committee, 1939–1945.* Detroit: Wayne State University Press, 1981. Ioanid, Radu. *The Holocaust in Romania: The Destruction of Jews and Gypsies Under the Antonescu Regime, 1940–1944.* Chicago: Ivan R. Dee, published in association with the United States Holocaust Memorial Museum, 2000. St. John, Robert. *Foreign Correspondent: How a Green American Reporter Suddenly Found Himself at Ringside in the Wildest Period in Balkan History.* New York: Doubleday & Company, Inc., 1957. Wasserstein.

DOCUMENTS: Ancel, Jean, "Documents Concerning the Fate of Romanian Jewry During the Holocaust," The Beate Klarsfeld Foundation, 12 volumes, Jerusalem, 1986.

Chapter Three

INTERVIEWS: Elhanan Guttman, Ioanid.

BOOKS: Aliav. Bauer. St. John.

Chapter Four

INTERVIEWS: Aroni, Atir, Ioanid.

BOOKS: Bauer. Gilbert, Martin. *The Holocaust: A History of the Jews of Europe During the Second World War.* New York: Holt, Rinehart and Winston, 1985. Ioanid. Wasserstein.

DOCUMENTS: United States Holocaust Memorial Museum, Washington, D.C. (USHMM), Romanian Ministry of Foreign Affairs and Romanian Intelligence Service, and United States State Department, 1940–1944; of particular significance is the August 19, 1941, report by the American legation in Bucharest.

INTERNET SOURCES: Aroni, Samuel. "Memories of the Holocaust: Kishinev 1941–44." International Studies and Overseas Programs at the University of California, Los Angeles. www.aud.ucla.edu/holocaust/people/bystand.htm.

Chapter Five

INTERVIEWS: Dinari.

BOOKS: Glasberg, Ruth. *Ruth's Journey: A Survivor's Memoir.* Gainesville, Florida: The University of Florida Press, 1996. Ioanid. Wasserstein.

DOCUMENTS: The Nightmare of Struma: Interview with David Dinari, Haganah Archives (HA), Tel Aviv.

ARTICLES: Interview of the Week, with Israel Dinari, by Rafael Bashan, *Ma'ariv*, May 14, 1965.

Chapter Six

INTERVIEWS: G. Buxton.

BOOKS: Barsky, Steven. *Adventures in Scuba Diving.* St. Louis: Mosby Lifeline, 1995.

INTERNET SOURCES: Duncan, George R. "Maritime Disasters of World War II." www.members.iinet.net.au/~gduncan/maritime.html.

Chapter Seven

BOOKS: Gilbert. Ofer, Dalia. *Escaping the Holocaust: Illegal Immigration to the Land of Israel, 1939–1944.* New York: Oxford University Press, 1990. (Ofer provides an authoritative account of the Holocaust at sea and important information about the *Struma*.) Wasserstein.

DOCUMENTS: Public Records Office (PRO), The National Archives, London. Files of the Foreign Office—General Correspondence (Political) FO 371. Colonial Office Files, CO 733, CO 443, CO 446/4, CO 537. Files of the Prime Minister from 1940 to 1942 on Illegal Entry into Palestine, PREM 4/51/1. Files of the Cabinet, CAB 65 and CAB 66.

Chapter Eight

Direct quotes between Simon Brod and Ruth Kluger and other details of the night the *Salvador* foundered come from *The Last Escape*. Kluger later changed her name to Ruth Aliav and wrote her memoirs with Peggy Mann.

INTERVIEWS: Marta Brod.

BOOKS: Aliav. Ofer. Wasserstein.

DOCUMENTS: PRO; of particular significance is a report by Richard T. E. Latham regarding illegal immigration at sea raising the prospect of sinking the ships carrying Jews.

Chapter Nine

INTERVIEWS: Dinari.

DOCUMENTS: Dinari, YVA.

ARTICLES: *Ma'ariv*.

Chapter Ten

INTERVIEWS: Aroni.

BOOKS: Bauer. Ioanid. Ofer.

DOCUMENTS: USHMM; of particular significance is the Report of Inquiry of the Commission Appointed by Order of Marshal Ion Antonescu, the Leader of the State, for the Investigation of Irregularities in the Ghetto of Chisinau, translated by Samuel Aroni.

INTERNET SOURCES: Aroni.

Chapter Eleven

INTERVIEWS: Ilana Blum.

BOOKS: Aliav. Bauer. Ofer.

DOCUMENTS: Struma fitness report and prospectus, Central Zionist Archives (CZA), Jerusalem, USHMM. "Struma Document, June 1945," YVA.

Chapter Twelve

INTERVIEWS: Aroni, G. Buxton, M. Buxton, Tudor Chefner, Dinari, Miyriam Rintzler, Ogen Rintzler, Bernard Tercatin.

BOOKS: Gilbert. Ioanid. Weissman.

DOCUMENTS: Ancel, Jean, "Plans for Deportation of the Romanian Jews and Their Discontinuation in Light of Documentary Evidence," Yad Vashem Studies, Jerusalem, 1984.

Chapter Thirteen

INTERVIEWS: Aroni, D. Stoliar.

DOCUMENTS: Interview of Stoliar by Duke Jennings, 1995. USHMM; of particular interest is the 1997 interview with Stoliar. Interview with Stoliar, 1963, translated by Joseph Wechsler.

INTERNET SOURCES: The Salamowitz story is recounted in Rubinstein, Shimon, "Comments on Several Personal Tragedies that were part of the General Tragedy Called *Struma*," www.alpas.net/uli/struma/PersonalTragedies.htm.

Chapter Fourteen

INTERVIEWS: Dinari, Alexander Scarlat.

BOOKS: Ofer. Perl, William R. *Operation Action: Rescue from the Holocaust.* New York: Frederick Ungar Publishing Co., 1983.

Chapter Fifteen

INTERVIEWS: Dinari, Scarlet, D. Stoliar.

BOOKS: Ofer.

DOCUMENTS: CZA, files of Aliyah Department, S6. HA, files of Aliyah Bet, personal files, ship files, oral testimonies.

Chapter Sixteen

INTERVIEWS: Alaton, G. Buxton, Ioanid, Barry Marcus, D. Stoliar.

Chapter Seventeen

BOOKS: Rubin, Barry. *Istanbul Intrigues: A True-Life Casablanca.* New York: McGraw-Hill Publishing Company, 1989. Shaw, Stanford J. *Turkey and the Holocaust: Turkey's Role in Rescuing Turkish and European Jewry from Nazi Persecution, 1933–1944.* New York: New York University Press, 1993. Sumner-Boyd, Hilary and John Freely. *Strolling Through Istanbul.* Istanbul: SEV Matbaacilik ve Yayincilik A.S., 1997.

DOCUMENTS: PRO.

Chapter Eighteen

INTERVIEWS: Brod, Dinari, D. Stoliar.

DOCUMENTS: USHMM; of particular significance from the State Department files is the December 26, 1941, report S.S. *Struma* of Panamanian Registry, Carrying Jewish Refugees and Other Enemy Subjects from Romania to Haifa, Palestine, Samuel W. Honaker, American Consulate General, Istanbul. PRO; of particular significance is the exchange of memos regarding the initial British and Turkish reactions to the arrival of the *Struma*, found in PRO CO 733/449 (P3/4/30), PRO PREM 4/51/1/40, and PRO CO 773/446.

Chapter Nineteen
INTERVIEWS: Izak Abudaram, Alaton, Bali.
BOOKS: Juhasz, Esther, editor. *Sephardi Jews in the Ottoman Empire: Aspects of Material Culture.* Jerusalem: The Jerusalem Publishing House, 1990. Shaw.

Chapter Twenty
INTERVIEWS: Alaton, Brod, Hayim Kohen, D. Stoliar.
ARTICLES: Ofer, Dalia. *Rescue Attempts During the Holocaust: Proceedings of the Second Yad Vashem International Historical Conference.* Jerusalem: Yad Vashem, 1977.

Chapter Twenty-one
INTERVIEWS: Dinari, Scarlat, D. Stoliar.
ARTICLES: Manning, Olivia, "The Tragedy of the Struma," *Observer*, London, March 1, 1970.
BOOKS: Carmely, Touvia. *The Real Story of* Struma *or Breaking Down a 60 Years Old Conspiracy of Silence*, self-published in English. Haifa: 2000. Ofer.
DOCUMENTS: CZA; of particular significance is Captain Gorbatenko's letter to the port captain in Istanbul. HA.

Chapter Twenty-two
INTERVIEWS: Yosef Govrin, Scarlat.
BOOKS: Koc, Vehbi. *My Life Story.* Istanbul: Koc Holding, 1983. Rubin.
Quotes from conversations regarding Turkey's agreement to allow the Segals off the boat come from Koc. Rubin provides an excellent history of Walker's overall actions in Istanbul.
The discovery of Stalin's order to sink neutral ships in the Black Sea was made in 2001 by Gennadi Kibardin, a historian in Kiev, Ukraine, and disclosed in the documentary film *The Struma,* by Simcha Jacobovici, Associated Producers, Toronto. The film's co-producer, Felix Golubev, initially uncovered evidence of Stalin's secret war against neutral shipping in Soviet naval archives in Moscow. Yosef Govrin also researched the *Struma*'s sinking in Soviet archives and provided the authors with substantial new information.

Chapter Twenty-three

INTERVIEWS: Brod, Scarlat.

BOOKS: Carmely. Ofer. Wasserstein.

DOCUMENTS: CZA; of particular interest are the Merlaub letters. HA; of particular interest is the testimony of Ze-ev Shind and an anonymous report about conditions on the *Struma*. PRO.

Chapter Twenty-four

INTERVIEWS: Dinari, O. Rintzler, Scarlat, D. Stoliar.

BOOKS: Ofer.

DOCUMENTS: Accounts of passengers who disembarked are at the CZA and HA.

ARTICLES: *Ma'ariv.*

INTERNET SOURCES: Rubinstein.

Chapter Twenty-five

INTERVIEWS: D. Stoliar.

BOOKS: Bauer. Ofer.

DOCUMENTS: CZA; of particular significance is Joseph Goldin's correspondence. Postcards written by Grigore Bucspan provided by Greg Buxton. PRO; of particular significance is the exchange of memos on the fate of the children on the *Struma,* found in PRO FO 371/32661. Turkish Government archives.

The Turkish government claimed *Struma*'s engine was repaired in Istanbul harbor. The assertion contradicts letters written by Moritz Ignat Merlaub (the passenger who supervised the attempted repairs), historians, and Stoliar. In January 1942, the captain complained in writing to authorities that the ship was not seaworthy. Merlaub described attempts by Turkish mechanics to repair the engine. Some letters were hopeful, but Merlaub's last one, written two days before the ship was towed, indicated that the engine had not been repaired.

The Turkish government has refused requests from the authors and other researchers for access to its *Struma* files. One government official permitted the authors to view five documents written in 1942 and selected by the ministry; copying was prohibited, but the contents were re-created from notes. The documents said the engine ran for two hours on February 10 and indicated that it may have gone on a test voyage. Yet after that date, Merlaub wrote that the engine was not working and did not mention a voyage. In a memo after the ship sank, Turkey's interior minister said the ship had been able to sail safely and he blamed its failure to leave the Black Sea on the refusal of the Bulgarian crew to proceed.

Stoliar recalled no test voyage and was adamant the engine was not working. Likewise, Dinari said the engine was not working when he left on February 5.

There are no reports of any voyage from the Jewish Agency and others who monitored the ship during its quarantine.

The Turks did try to repair the engine, but the Turkish government assertion that it was working when the *Struma* was towed from the harbor falls in the face of logic and all other evidence.

Chapter Twenty-six

INTERVIEWS: D. Stoliar.

BOOKS: Carmely. Offer. Wasserstein.

DOCUMENTS: CZA, Merlaub letters. PRO.

Chapter Twenty-seven

INTERVIEWS: D. Stoliar.

DOCUMENTS: Stoliar interview with Jennings. Stoliar interview, USHMM. Stoliar interview translated by Wechsler. Stoliar statement in Jaffa.

There are minor discrepancies in Stoliar's recollections, but he is consistent and clear on major elements. We resolved discrepancies through follow-up interviews with Stoliar. When conflicts remained, we relied on his earliest recollections.

Chapter Twenty-eight

INTERVIEWS: Ahmet Akarsu, Ismail Aslan, Izmit Ay.

Chapter Twenty-nine

INTERVIEWS: Brod, D. Stoliar.

DOCUMENTS: PRO.

Please see Chapter 25 for a full discussion of the research on the ship's engine.

Chapter Thirty

BOOKS: Carmely. Ofer. Wasserstein.

DOCUMENTS: PRO; of particular interest are Churchill's comments at PRO CO 733/446/11 and MacMichael's response to the sinking at PRO CO 733/446/1.

ARTICLES: Jewish Refugee Tragedy, *Manchester Guardian,* February 26, 1942. Loss of Refugee Ship in Black Sea, *Times of London,* February 27, 1942. New Approaches, *Manchester Guardian,* March 2, 1942. Struma: Diplomatik Pazarliklardan Trajik Sonra, Dr. Esra Danacioglu, *Toplumsal Tarih,* September 2000.

Chapter Thirty-one

INTERVIEWS: Bali.

BOOKS: Hirschmann, Ira. *Life Line to a Promised Land.* New York: The Jewish Book Guild of America, 1946.

DOCUMENTS: PRO; of particular interest are the exchanges between the Foreign Office and Lord Halifax and the memos about secret German pressure on the Turks to turn away the ship at PRO FO 371/32662.

Chapter Thirty-two
INTERVIEWS: Akarsu, Brod, D. Stoliar.

Chapter Thirty-three
INTERVIEWS: Blum, M. Buxton, E. David, Dinari, Ioanid, M. Rintzler, O. Rintzler.
BOOKS: Ioanid.

Chapter Thirty-four
INTERVIEWS: Alaton, M. Atir, Bali, R. Ben-Zvi, Brod, Marcus, D. Stoliar, M. Stoliar.
BOOKS: Bali, Rifat N. *Cumhuriyet Yillarinda Turkiye Yahudileri: Bir Turklestirme Seruveni 1923–1945.* Istanbul: Iletisim, 1999. Shaw.

Chapter Thirty-five
INTERVIEWS: G. Buxton, Murat Draman, Govrin, Levent Yuksel.
BOOKS: Rohwer, Jurgen. *Die Versenkung der judischen Fluchtlingstrangsporter Struma und Mefkure im Schwarzen Meer.* Frankfurt: Bernard & Graefe Verlag Fur Wehrwesen, 1965.

The sinking of the *Cankaya* on February 23 was revealed in memos in the files of the Foreign Office at PRO and described in various contemporary press accounts.

Kibardin's discovery was disclosed in *The Struma*, a documentary film released in 2001 by Simcha Jacobovici, Associated Producers, Toronto.

Chapter Thirty-six
INTERVIEWS: G. Buxton, Jonathon Lewis.

Chapter Thirty-seven
INTERVIEWS: G. Buxton, Simcha Jacobovici, Lewis.

Chapter Thirty-eight
INTERVIEWS: Tami Barak, Blum, Brod, G. Buxton, T. Chefner, Teddy Kollek, Lewis, M. Rintzler, O. Rintzler, Betty Rosenblatt, D. Stoliar.

Epilogue
INTERVIEWS: Aslan, D. Stoliar, M. Stoliar.

Bibliography

Books:

Aliav, Ruth, and Peggy Mann. *The Last Escape*. London: Coronet Books, 1975.

Ancel, Jean, ed. *Documents Concerning the Fate of Romanian Jewry During the Holocaust*. 12 vols. Jerusalem: The Beate Klarsfeld Foundation, 1986.

Arendt, Hannah. *Eichmann in Jerusalem: A Report on the Banality of Evil*. New York: Penguin Books, 1977.

Avriel, Ehud. *Open the Gates! The Dramatic Personal Story of "Illegal" Immigration to Israel*. New York: Atheneum, 1975.

Bali, Rifat N. *Cumhuriyet Yillarinda Turkiye Yahudileri: Bir Turklestirme. Seruveni 1923–1945*. Istanbul: Iletisim, 1999.

Bali, Rifat N. *Musa'nin Evlatlari Cumhuriet'in Yuttaslari*. Istanbul: Iletisim, 2001.

Bauer, Yehuda. *American Jewry and the Holocaust: The American Jewish Joint Distribution Committee, 1939–1945*. Detroit: Wayne State University Press, 1981.

Bethell, Nicholas. *The Palestine Triangle: The Struggle for the Holy Land, 1935–48*. New York: G.P. Putnam's Sons, 1979.

Carmely, Touvia. "The Real Story of *Struma* or Breaking Down a 60 Years Old Conspiracy of Silence, the English version entirely revised and updated by Touvia Carmely." Haifa, 2000.

Encyclopedia of the Holocaust. New York: Macmillan Publishing Co., 1990.

Gilbert, Martin. *Churchill: A Life*. New York: Henry Holt and Company, 1992.

Gilbert, Martin. *The Holocaust: A History of the Jews of Europe During the Second World War*. New York: Holt, Rinehart and Winston, 1985.

Gilbert, Martin. *The Macmillan Atlas of the Holocaust*. New York: Macmillan Publishing Co., 1982.

Gold, Ruth Glasberg. *Ruth's Journey: A Survivor's Memoir*. Gainesville, Fla: The University Press of Florida, 1996.

Hadari, Ze'ev Venia and Ze'ev Tsahor. *Voyage to Freedom: An Episode in the Illegal Immigration to Palestine*. London: Vallentine, Mitchell, 1985.

Hirsch, Ellen, ed. *Facts about Israel*. Jerusalem: Ahva Press, 1999.

Hirschmann, Ira. *Life Line to a Promised Land*. New York: The Jewish Book Guild of America, 1946.

Hirschmann, Ira. *Caution to the Winds*. New York: David McKay Co., 1962.

Ioanid, Radu. *The Holocaust in Romania: The Destruction of Jews and Gypsies Under the Antonescu Regime, 1940–1944*. Chicago: Ivan R. Dee, published in association with the United States Holocaust Memorial Museum, 2000.

Jagendorf, Siegfried, edited with commentary by Aron Hirt-Manheimer. *Jagendorf's Foundry: A Memoir of the Romanian Holocaust, 1941–1944*. New York: HarperCollins Publishers, 1991.

Juhasz, Esther, ed. *Sephardi Jews in the Ottoman Empire: Aspects of Material Culture*. Jerusalem: The Jerusalem Publishing House, 1990.

Kalderon, Albert. *Abraham Galante: A Biography*. New York: Sepher-Hermon Press, for Sephardic House at Congregation Shearith Israel, 1983.

Kimche, Jon, and David Kimche. *The Secret Roads: The "Illegal" Migration of a People, 1938–1948*. New York: Farrar, Straus and Cudahy, 1955.

Koc, Vehbi. *My Life Story*. Istanbul: Koc Holding, 1983.

Lookstein, Haskel. *Were We Our Brothers' Keepers? The Public Response of American Jews to the Holocaust, 1938–1944*. New York: Vintage Books, 1985.

Malaparte, Curzio. *Kaputt*. New York: E. P. Dutton & Co., 1946.

Ofer, Dalia. *Escaping the Holocaust: Illegal Immigration to the Land of Israel, 1939–1944*. New York: Oxford University Press, 1990.

Perl, William R. *Operation Action: Rescue from the Holocaust*. New York: Frederick Ungar Publishing Co., 1983.

Powell, Lawrence N. *Troubled Memory: Anne Levy, the Holocaust, and David Duke's Louisiana*. Chapel Hill: The University of North Carolina Press, 2000.

Rohwer, Jurgen. *Die Versenkung der Judischen Fluchtlingstransporter Struma und Mefkure im Schwarzen Meer (Februar 1942, August 1944)*. Frankfurt: Bernard & Graefe Verlag Fur Wehrwesen, 1965.

Rubin, Barry. *Istanbul Intrigues: A True-Life Casablanca*. New York: McGraw-Hill Publishing Co., 1989.

Safran, Alexandre. *Resisting the Storm: Romania, 1940–1947, Memoirs*. Jerusalem: Yad Vashem, 1987.

Saveanu, Simion. *Salvati Onoarea Cililizatiei or Save the Honor of Civilization*. Israel: Minimum, 1996.

Sebastian, Mihail. *Journal 1935–1944: The Fascist Years*. Chicago: Ivan R. Dee, published in association with the United States Holocaust Memorial Museum, 2000.

Shaw, Stanford J. *Turkey and the Holocaust: Turkey's Role in Rescuing Turkish and European Jewry from Nazi Persecution, 1933–1945*. New York: New York University Press, 1993.

Shaw, Stanford J. *The Jews of the Ottoman Empire and the Turkish Republic*. New York: New York University Press, 1991.

St. John, Robert. *Foreign Correspondent: How a Green American Reporter Suddenly Found Himself at Ringside in the Wildest Period in Balkan History*. New York: Doubleday & Co., 1957.

Sturdza, Prince Michel. *The Suicide of Europe: Memoirs of Prince Michel Sturdza, Former Foreign Minister of Rumania*. Boston: Western Islands Publishers, 1968.

Vaneyev, G. I. *Soviet Fleet in the Black Sea During the Great Patriotic War*. Moscow: Military Publishing House, Ministry of Defense, USSR, 1978.

Volkan, Vamik D., and Norman Itzkowitz. *The Immortal Ataturk: A Psychobiography*. Chicago: University of Chicago Press, 1984.

Wasserstein, Bernard. *Britain and the Jews of Europe 1939–1945*. 2nd ed. London and New York: Leicester University Press, published in association with the Institute for Jewish Policy Research, 1999.

Internet Sources:

Aroni, Samuel. "Memories of the Holocaust: Kishinev (Chisinau) 1941–1944." International Studies and Overseas Program (ISOP) at the University of California (UCLA), Los Angeles. http://www.aud.ucla.edu/~aroni/kishinev/

"Bystanders." A Teacher's Guide to the Holocaust. http://fcit.coedu.usf.edu/holocaust/people/bystand.htm

Duncan, George R. "Maritime Disasters of World War II." http://www.members.iinet.net.au/~gduncan/maritime.html

Friedberg, Uli. "The *Struma* Tragedy." http://www.alpas.net/uli/struma/struma_engl.htm

"History of Turkish Jews." Mersina. http://www.mersina.com/lib/turkish_news/history/foreword.htm

Ives, Joel. "About David Stoliar and the *Struma*: An Amazing Adventure in Washington." http://www.alpas.net/uli/struma/Ives.htm

Ives, Joel. "The Passengers on the *Strumah*." ROM-SIG News: The Journal of the Special Interest Group for Romanian Jewish Genealogy. http://www.jewishgen.org/romsig/newsletter/vol5/struma.html

Museum of Tolerance, Simon Wiesenthal Center Multimedia Learning Center Online. http://motc.wiesenthal.com

"Project *Struma*—Expedition Exodus 2000." Documentation of the *Struma* Shipwreck with Technical Diving Methods, an Independent Technical Diving

Project Financed and Realized by the Istanbul-based Underwater Research Society." http://www.sad-uwrs.org/bage/index.htm
"The *Struma* Project." http://www.struma.org

Articles and Reports:

Ancel, Jean, "Plans for Deportation of the Rumanian Jews and Their Discontinuation in Light of Documentary Evidence (July–October 1942)," *Yad Vashem Studies* 16 (1984).

Arnold, Michael S, "The 'Struma': The Outrage Resurfaces," *Jerusalem Post*, July 13, 2000.

Friedler, Ya'acov, "The Survivor's Story," *The Jerusalem Post Weekly*, February 27, 1967.

"Jewish Refugee Tragedy: Disastrous Voyage, Palestine Entry Barred," *Manchester Guardian*, February 26, 1942.

Lubell, Samuel, "War by Refugee," *Saturday Evening Post*, March 29, 1941.

Manning, Olivia, "The Tragedy of the Struma: How the World Stood By and Watched 760 Jews Sail to Their Deaths," *The Observer*, March, 1, 1970.

Melzig, Herbert, "Memorandum Concerning the Tragedy of the Jewish Refugee Ship Struma, sunk in the Black Sea on February 12, 1942, Probably in the Territorial Waters of Turkey," *Yad Vashem Studies* 6:182–89 (1983).

"New Approaches," *Manchester Guardian*, March 2, 1942.

Ofer, Dalia. "The Activities of the Jewish Agency Delegation in Istanbul in 1943," *Rescue Attempts During the Holocaust: Proceedings of the Second Yad Vashem International Conference.* Jerusalem: Yad Vashem, 1977, 435–450.

Reinhold, Yaron, "The *Struma* Tragedy." American Israel Numismatic Association. March-April, 1992.

Sources for Official Documents:

A.C.M.E.O.R. World Cultural Association of Jews from Romania, Tel Aviv.

Central Zionist Archives, Jerusalem (CZA), Files of Aliyah Department, S6, Files of the Political Department S-25, Files of the Office of the Zionist Organization in London Z-4, Files of the Personal Representatives in Istanbul L-15, Personal Files of Simon Brod A203.

Haganah Archives, Tel Aviv, (HA) Files of Aliyah Bet, Personal Files, Ships Files, Oral Testimonies.

Public Records Office (PRO), The National Archives, London. Files of the Foreign Office—General Correspondence (Political) FO 371. Colonial Office Files, CO 733, CO 443, CO 446/4, CO 446/10, CO 537. Files of the Prime Minister from 1940 to 1942 on Illegal Entry into Palestine, PREM 4/51/1. Files of the Cabinet, CAB 65 and CAB 66.

United States Holocaust Memorial Museum Archives has thousands of Romanian documents. The documents used for this book came primarily from the Romanian Intelligence Service (SRI) and Romanian Ministry of Foreign Affairs (RMFA). Yad Vashem Archives, Jerusalem (YVA), mainly the "*Struma*" files.

Published Oral Testimonies:

David Dinari, undated interview from Haganah Archives, Tel Aviv.

David Stoliar, "The Struma Catastrophe," an interview given in the C.I.D. Office in Jaffa, Israel, May 3, 1942, Yad Vashem Archives, 011–66.

David Stoliar, produced by Duke Jennings, February 18, 1995.

David Stoliar, United States Holocaust Memorial Museum, August 20, 1997.

Acknowledgments

The story of the *Struma* is not our own. We have no personal connection with the unfortunate ship. We, like our readers, can only stand back and wonder at this tale, which simultaneously portrays the darkness of mankind's failings and the enduring panorama of human courage.

"So, why the book?" we were asked repeatedly while gathering the threads that compose the fabric of this account of nearly 800 Jewish refugees—men, women, and children—who set sail for a new life and met instead with an untimely death at dawn on February 24, 1942.

The answer is simple: We wanted our children to know this story.

We wanted our children to know a man like David Stoliar, whose will to survive not only kept him alive for twenty-four hours on the freezing Black Sea, but gave him the courage to relive those memories for us decades later. Greg Buxton, who went looking for his grandparents' grave site almost sixty years after their demise, and embodied the spirit of a true adventurer, someone willing to stake everything on the pursuit of a dream.

We concentrated on just a few people in the telling of this story, allowing their lives to stand for numerous others. Many more also contributed to our knowledge and understanding. From among the *Struma* family—those who lost relatives and friends—we would like to thank Ami and Elda Atir; Ilana Blum; Michael Buxton; Rabbi Susan Carter; Tudor and Fritzi Chefner, and their daughter, Tami Barak; Esthi and Micha David; David Dinari; Elena Kindler; Dan and Mihal Radar; Ogen and Miyriam Rintzler and their daughter, Ruth Vichansky; Betty Rosenblatt; Alexander Scarlat; and Baruch Tercatin.

Rabbi Hersh Guttman, the man who gave David Stoliar his blessing before he departed on the *Struma*, founded a synagogue in Tel Aviv following the war. We would like to thank the people of this synagogue who welcomed us to the services in commemoration of the *Struma* and shared their memories. We offer special thanks to the rabbi's son, Rabbi Efraim Guttman, who runs this remarkable institution, dedicated to the Romanian Holocaust, his son, Rabbi Elhan Ia'acov Josef Guttman, and his brother, Itzhac Guttman Ben-Zvi. We are indebted to Ruth Ben-Zvi for a quiet morning in her apartment when she made it possible to imagine that we too had seen Romania during the war.

One of the most heroic figures in our research was the chain-smoking, irascible Istanbul textile merchant, Simon Brod. It is our hope that when our children turn the pages of this book, they will learn to discern the difference between the Simon Brods of the world, who do what is right even when it hurts, and the Harold MacMichaels of the world, who do not. We wish Simon Brod were alive today so that we could thank him personally, but instead we thank his daughter, Marta, for the memories of her remarkable father. Thank you also, Ben Sperer.

Miraculously, some people in the Black Sea village of Sile remember the *Struma* and we thank them for their time and memories. Ismail Aslan told his story with courage and Izmit Ay recounted his memories vividly. The men of the Sile watchtower continue to do the same job that their brave predecessors did decades ago when they brought Stoliar in to shore.

Many people whose families never touched the decks of the *Struma* have been enormously generous. Sam Aroni, who survived the sinking of the *Struma* only because he was arrested before he could get on the ship, has devoted years to the exploration of the Romanian Holocaust. From the dozen disparate passenger lists available, he produced for us the first compilation, a complicated chore that he executed with clarity and simplicity. He also kept us on what we hope was the right path when it came to Romanian history.

Joseph Wechsler, an author himself, was invaluable with his ability to translate documents, from all the languages involved in these events, into English for us. He was quick and accurate and his judgment regarding the importance of each of these documents proved invaluable.

Thank you also to Joel Ives and Dr. Duke Jennings for keeping these memories alive and sharing them so generously.

It was through Ishak Alaton's eyes that we visited Istanbul of the 1940s. Rifat Bali, however, opened the doors to Istanbul's Jewish community today through his own books and recollections.

Thank you to Hayim Eliezer Kohen and Isak Abudaram for talking to us about their wartime experiences in Istanbul.

Also among the Turkish diving community we would like to thank Levent Yuksel and Murat Draman.

Among the British diving team, we would like especially to extend our thanks to Jonathon Lewis for his blow-by-blow account of the dive and his observations of his close friend Greg Buxton. We must also thank Mark Brill for sharing his excellent photographs.

In Israel, we met the former mayor of Jerusalem, Teddy Kollek, who shared the memories of his year in Istanbul during the war. Ambassador Dr. Yosef Govrin opened our eyes to international political maneuverings—past and present. Thank you Slomo Leibovici-Laish at the World Cultural Association of Jews from Romania for your generosity in opening your files.

In London, we would like to thank Rabbi Barry Marcus of the Central London Synagogue.

Many staff members at archives around the world contributed their time and expertise, and perhaps some would even prefer to be left off this list, but they know who they are. Special thanks to the Haganah Archives, Central Zionist Archives and Yad Vashem Archives in Israel, the Public Records Office in London, and the United States Holocaust Memorial Museum in Washington, D.C.

Radu Ioanid, associate director of the international program at USHMM, encouraged us to begin this project and was unfailingly helpful throughout. His book, *The Holocaust in Romania,* is the definitive book on that tragedy in English and it was invaluable to us.

Thank you to Elise Meyers and Sebnem Arsu for the assistance in research and with interviews. Thanks also to Carol Boas and Cath Conneely for your willingness to be sounding boards. Thanks, Sener Yavaser, for the rides.

Julia Serebrinsky, our editor, understood early on, even before we did, how the story should unfold and we thank her for her insight, patience, and ability to make it all happen. It is a much better book for her involvement and for the careful copyediting of Cecilia Hunt.

As always, thank you to our agent, Dominick Abel, for his great shepherding skill.

Marda Stoliar, as much as her amazing husband, helped to make this book possible. She is a careful observer and has stored up insights into both the man and the times.

And finally, we thank our children. Elizabeth, our oldest, helped enormously with the research and put her excellent Arabic to good use. Nicholas and Rebecca listened carefully to our stories, indulged our obsessions, and, along with Elizabeth, inspired us to keep going to the end so that they could understand this sad story and its relevance today.